"According to Thompson, the crisis facing the Western church is not its survival but rediscovering its purpose. Probing the theological depths of Paul, this book offers a model for the contemporary church that is deeply challenging to the 'emerging' and 'missional' church and to those who see the church as a political action group, for example. Rather, chosen to participate in the destiny of the crucified Lord, the church lives for others. For Paul, the church, as Thompson argues, is characterized by holiness and as an outpost of the world to come—by bringing together different cultures in one community that is both local and ecumenically engaged. This is essential reading for those seeking a model for the contemporary church that is scripturally informed."

—**Graham H. Twelftree**, School of Divinity, Regent University

"James Thompson applies his exegetical skill, literary sensitivity, and theological acumen to the topic of Paul and the church. He corrects those who emphasize Paul's soteriology but neglect his ecclesiology. Thompson sets that ecclesiology in the context of Paul's theology. Ecclesiology and Christology are thus inseparable.'"

—**Everett Ferguson**, Abilene Christian University

"From the seasoned hand of James Thompson, who has already authored excellent books on pastoral ministry and moral formation in the Pauline letters, comes this lucid, timely, and insightful study, *The Church according to Paul*. Thompson deftly engages the Pauline witness and offers challenging reflections, in light of Paul's writings, about the contemporary ecclesiological context in Europe and North America. For Western Christians attempting to embody a biblically informed vision of the church in a post-Christian culture, there is perhaps no better resource available to stimulate fruitful reflection on Paul's ecclesiology than this gem of a book."

—**David Downs**, Fuller Theological Seminary

THE CHURCH
ACCORDING TO PAUL

❖

REDISCOVERING THE COMMUNITY
CONFORMED TO CHRIST

JAMES W. THOMPSON

Baker Academic

a division of Baker Publishing Group
Grand Rapids, Michigan

© 2014 by James W. Thompson

Published by Baker Academic
a division of Baker Publishing Group
P.O. Box 6287, Grand Rapids, MI 49516-6287
www.bakeracademic.com

Printed in the United States of America

Library of Congress Cataloging-in-Publication Data
Thompson, James, 1942–
    The church according to Paul : rediscovering the community conformed to Christ / James W. Thompson.
        pages cm
    Includes bibliographical references and index.
    ISBN 978-0-8010-4882-1 (pbk.)
    1. Bible. Epistles of Paul—Theology. 2. Bible. Epistles of Paul—Criticism, interpretation, etc. 3. Church—Biblical teaching. I. Title.
    BS2655.C5T46 2014
    262—dc23   2014009995

14 15 16 17 18 19 20   7 6 5 4 3 2 1

Dedicated to the memory of my friend and colleague

Charles A. Siburt Jr.

a devoted servant of the church

❖

CONTENTS

PREFACE

This study is both a continuation of themes I have developed in earlier books on Paul and a response to recent literature by practitioners who have proposed a new understanding of the church. In *Pastoral Ministry according to Paul*, I maintained that Paul's pastoral ambition was the moral formation of his churches. I elaborated on this theme in *Moral Formation according to Paul*, demonstrating the ecclesial character of Paul's ethic. Issues raised in the first two books have led me to offer this comprehensive examination of Paul's ecclesiology, continuing my dialogue between Pauline scholarship and the issues in the life of the contemporary church.

Because Paul's voice is largely missing in the recent attempts to redefine the church, I write in the hope that his voice will be heard. I am convinced that Paul's task of forming churches in the pre-Christian culture can inform our attempts to shape churches in a post-Christian culture.

I am grateful both to my dialogue partners and to readers who helped in the preparation of the book. My wife, Carolyn, has devoted many hours both as copy editor and as compiler of the bibliography. Wesley Dingman and Mason Lee read earlier drafts and made suggestions. Dr. Carson Reed, professor of practical theology at the Graduate School of Theology at Abilene Christian University, offered helpful comments on parts of the book. I am also grateful to Mrs. Kay Onstead and the late Robert Onstead, who established the Onstead Chair in Biblical Studies, which provided the funding for travel and research.

I dedicate this book to the memory of Dr. Charles A. Siburt Jr., my conversation partner, colleague, and friend over four decades. Dr. Siburt, who was professor of practical theology at Abilene Christian University until his death in 2012, devoted his life to churches throughout the United States, and left a lasting impression on congregations, students, colleagues, and many others, including me. Countless congregations, especially in Churches of Christ, are indebted to him for his wise counsel.

ABBREVIATIONS

OLD TESTAMENT

Gen.	Genesis	Eccles.	Ecclesiastes
Exod.	Exodus	Songs (Song)	Song of Songs
Lev.	Leviticus	Isa.	Isaiah
Num.	Numbers	Jer.	Jeremiah
Deut.	Deuteronomy	Lam.	Lamentations
Josh.	Joshua	Ezek.	Ezekiel
Judg.	Judges	Dan.	Daniel
Ruth	Ruth	Hosea	Hosea
1 Sam.	1 Samuel	Joel	Joel
2 Sam.	2 Samuel	Amos	Amos
1 Kings	1 Kings	Obad.	Obadiah
2 Kings	2 Kings	Jon.	Jonah
1 Chron.	1 Chronicles	Mic.	Micah
2 Chron.	2 Chronicles	Nahum	Nahum
Ezra	Ezra	Hab.	Habakkuk
Neh.	Nehemiah	Zeph.	Zephaniah
Esther	Esther	Hag.	Haggai
Job	Job	Zech.	Zechariah
Ps(s).	Psalms	Mal.	Malachi
Prov.	Proverbs		

NEW TESTAMENT

Matt.	Matthew	Acts	Acts of the Apostles
Mark	Mark	Rom.	Romans
Luke	Luke	1 Cor.	1 Corinthians
John	John	2 Cor.	2 Corinthians

Gal.	Galatians	Heb.	Hebrews
Eph.	Ephesians	James	James
Phil.	Philippians	1 Pet.	1 Peter
Col.	Colossians	2 Pet.	2 Peter
1 Thess.	1 Thessalonians	1 John	1 John
2 Thess.	2 Thessalonians	2 John	2 John
1 Tim.	1 Timothy	3 John	3 John
2 Tim.	2 Timothy	Jude	Jude
Titus	Titus	Rev.	Revelation
Philem.	Philemon		

ANCIENT TEXTS, TEXT TYPES, AND VERSIONS

LXX   Septuagint

APOCRYPHA AND SEPTUAGINT

Jdt.	Judith	Sir.	Sirach
1–4 Macc.	1–4 Maccabees	Wis.	Wisdom

OLD TESTAMENT PSEUDEPIGRAPHA

2 Bar.	2 Baruch	Sib. Or.	Sibylline Oracles
1 En.	1 Enoch	T. Dan	Testament of Dan
Jub.	Jubilees	T. Levi	Testament of Levi
Pss. Sol.	Psalms of Solomon	T. Mos.	Testament of Moses

DEAD SEA SCROLLS AND RELATED TEXTS

1 QH	Thanksgiving Hymns	1 QS	Rule of the Community
1 QM	War Scroll	1 QSa	Messianic Rule

GREEK AND LATIN AUTHORS

Aristotle		*Dionysius of Halicarnassus*	
Pol.	Politica (Politics)	Ant. rom.	Antiquitates romanae

Cicero		*Diogenes Laertius*	
Flac.	Pro Flacco	Vit.	Vitae philosophorum
Leg.	De legibus		(Lives of Eminent
Off.	De officiis		Philosophers)

Epictetus

Diatr.   Diatribai (Dissertationes)

Josephus

Ant.   Jewish Antiquities
J.W.   Jewish War

Philo

Abraham   On the Life of
             Abraham
Alleg. Interp. Allegorical
             Interpretation
Decalogue   On the Decalogue
Embassy   On the Embassy to
             Gaius
Heir   Who Is the Heir?
Moses   On the Life of Moses
Names   On the Change of
             Names
Prelim. Studies On the Preliminary
             Studies

QE   Questions and Ans-
             wers on Exodus
Rewards   On Rewards and
             Punishments
Spec. Laws   On the Special Laws

Plato

Resp.   Respublica (Republic)
Tim.   Timaeus

Plutarch

Quaest. conv. Quaestionum convivi-
             alum libri IX

Seneca

Ira   De ira

Tacitus

Ann.   Annales

SECONDARY SOURCES

BDAG   Bauer, Walter, F. W. Danker, W. F. Arndt, and F. W. Gringrich. *Greek-English Lexicon of the New Testament and Other Early Christian Literature.* 3rd ed. Chicago: University of Chicago Press, 2000.

EDNT   *Exegetical Dictionary of the New Testament.* Edited by Horst Balz and Gerhard Schneider. 3 vols. Grand Rapids: Eerdmans, 1990–93.

JSNTSup   Journal for the Study of the New Testament: Supplement Series

LCL   Loeb Classical Library

NovT   *Novum Testamentum*

OTP   *Old Testament Pseudepigrapha.* Edited by James H. Charlesworth. 2 vols. New York: Doubleday, 1983.

TDNT   *Theological Dictionary of the New Testament.* Edited by Gerhard Kittel and Gerhard Friedrich. Translated by G. W. Bromiley. 10 vols. Grand Rapids: Eerdmans, 1964–76.

TLNT   Spicq, Ceslas. *Theological Lexicon of the New Testament.* Translated and edited by James D. Ernest. 3 vols. Peabody, MA: Hendrickson, 1994.

WUNT   Wissenschaftliche Untersuchungen zum Neuen Testament

INTRODUCTION

Reimagining the Church

Shortly after the fall of the Berlin Wall, my wife and I visited a village church in East Germany. Like the churches throughout other towns and villages of Germany, it stood at the center of town, with a spire that was visible from a distance. We entered a beautiful building that seated at least three hundred, but only twelve were in attendance on this Sunday morning—including the preacher, the organist, and us. If this village church was like others throughout Europe, it once would have been the center of community life, and the seats would have been filled. Now, however, it appeared to be a relic of the past.

Similar scenes are occurring throughout Europe and North America. In a society that is increasingly post-Christian, churches everywhere are losing their place in the public square. Even if not to the extent of that German village church, we watch as attendance at traditional churches declines and the average age increases. Indeed, the fastest growing category in the religious census is that of the "nones"—those who have no religious affiliation.[1] This group is especially prominent among those under thirty, a third of whom are unaffiliated with a church.[2] While the majority in North America and Europe still describe themselves as Christians, an increasing number are not associated with a church.

1. Pew Forum, "'Nones' on the Rise," The Pew Forum on Religion and Public Life, October 9, 2012, http://www.pewforum.org/2012/10/09/nones-on-the-rise/.
2. Amy O'Leary, "Building Congregations around Art Galleries and Cafes as Spirituality Wanes," *New York Times*, December 29, 2012, http://www.nytimes.com/2012/12/30/us/new -churches-focus-on-building-a-community-life.html.

In response to this trend, established churches are reinventing themselves, and new experimental forms of church are emerging in an attempt to maintain contact with the increasing number of unaffiliated people. Strategies for addressing this problem are abundant in contemporary literature. Some reinvent the church according to consumer tastes or perceived popular demand, hoping to regain market share. Many recognize the negative associations of the word *church* and avoid the term, identifying their groups as "spiritual communities" and meeting in buildings designed not to look like a church. Many have chosen to plant new churches rather than work with established ones in order to be free to experiment with new forms of church. While the prescriptions for an ailing church vary, they concur that the church must address this changing situation if it is to survive.

I am not writing to offer an additional suggestion for reinventing the church or restoring its place of prominence in the public square. Nor am I convinced that the church should have the place in society that it once had. Indeed, I am convinced that the aging congregation with a declining membership is no less a faithful witness than the growing church. Having observed the numerous attempts at reimagining the church, I am convinced that the most basic questions are not being asked. In the various strategies for reinventing the church, the theological identity of the church is assumed but not examined. The crisis of the church pertains not only to the loss of numbers but also to the fundamental question, what kind of church should survive? That is, what is the purpose of the church?

The modern church, like its ancient counterpart, exists alongside numerous other communities. People enter the church with expectations that have been shaped by a variety of experiences. Thus the church inevitably faces the challenge of defining itself and its mission among people who have been shaped by other experiences of community. Assuming that revitalization begins with knowing who we are, our challenge is to delineate the distinguishing marks of the church.

CHALLENGES TO ECCLESIOLOGY

Although growing secularism plays a role in the decline of the church, other factors also contribute to the current situation. Protestantism originated as a protest against the established church, and a basic uneasiness about the church has continued in Europe and North America. If we were to ask which item in the Nicene Creed resonates least in popular American culture, the answer would probably be "We believe in one holy catholic and apostolic church."

One can observe this fact in the gap that exists between the number of people who believe in God, pray regularly, and consider themselves "spiritual" and those who participate in a believing community. Indeed, the word *unchurched*, commonly used for self-identified Christians who are unaffiliated with a congregation, suggests the popular separation between Christian practice and church membership.

One contributing factor in this decline is the popular conviction that the church distorted the pure religion of Jesus from the beginning. Nineteenth-century liberals attempted to return to the religion of Jesus instead of following the church's religion about Jesus. The numerous lives of Jesus written during that period were attempts to recover the real Jesus that had been obscured by the church. At the beginning of the twentieth century, Adolf Harnack gave a classic expression of this, arguing that "individual religious life was what [Jesus] wanted to kindle and what he did kindle."[3] He maintained that the two primary tenets of the message of Jesus were "God the Father, and the human soul so ennobled that it can and does unite with him."[4] He describes the kingdom of God in individualistic terms.

> If anyone wants to know what the kingdom of God and the coming of it meant to Jesus's message, he must read and study his parables. He will then see what it is that is meant. The kingdom of God comes by coming to the individual, by entering into his soul and laying hold of it. True, the kingdom of God is the rule of God; but it is the rule of the holy God in the hearts of individuals; *it is God himself in his power.* From this point of view everything that is dramatic in the external and historical sense has vanished; and gone, too, are all the external hopes for the future. Take whatever parable you will—the parable of the sower, of the pearl of great price, of the treasure buried in the field—the word of God, God himself, is the kingdom. It is not a question of angels and devils, thrones and principalities, but of God and the soul, the soul and its God.[5]

Although Harnack recognized the communal aspect of Christianity, his focus was on the individual. This emphasis on the religion of Jesus reflected the common view that the church distorted the authentic religion of its founder.

While Jesus continues to rate favorably in the modern mind, the church has received a continuing barrage of bad press. Consequently, a steady stream of books—both popular and scholarly—has offered proposals for returning

---

3. Adolf Harnack, *What Is Christianity?*, ed. T. Bailey Saunders (New York: Harper & Row, 1957), 12.

4. Ibid., 68.

5. Ibid., 56. I owe this citation to Gerhard Lohfink, *Jesus and Community: The Social Dimension of Christian Faith* (Philadelphia: Fortress, 1984), 1–2.

to Jesus, peeling away the church and the religion about Jesus. Evangelicals, capitalists, socialists, feminists, the socially liberal, and the socially conservative have all expressed either loyalty to or admiration of Jesus while criticizing the church. In 1928 Bruce Barton presented a capitalist Jesus in *The Man Nobody Knows*, challenging readers to go behind the creeds and find in the Gospels a Jesus who had all the qualities of leadership required for the free enterprise system.[6] Others have discovered in Jesus one whose care for the poor and advocacy of the redistribution of wealth were subverted by the church.[7] Feminists have discovered a Jesus whose work of liberating women was rejected by the church.[8] A common theme in contemporary literature is that Jesus's acceptance of sinners was soon abandoned by the church.[9] According to Robert Funk, Jesus was a "party animal"[10] and the subverter of everything around him but whose vision was subverted by the church.[11] The attempts of the Jesus Seminar to peel away the distortions by the church and discover the enlightened and iconoclastic Jesus who speaks in aphorisms and parables are also attempts to rescue Jesus from the church and present a version of Jesus that is compatible with the social ideals of the authors.[12] What

6. Bruce Barton, *The Man Nobody Knows: A Discovery of Jesus* (Indianapolis: Bobbs-Merrill, 1925). Barton discovered in Jesus personal magnetism, executive ability, and the capacity to recognize potential in others. Jesus was a sociable man and an outdoorsman who taught about "a happy God, wanting his sons and daughters to be happy" (28).

7. See John Dominic Crossan, *Historical Jesus: The Life of a Mediterranean Jewish Peasant* (San Francisco: HarperSanFrancisco, 1991), 421–22. Richard A. Horsley, *Jesus and the Powers: Conflict, Covenant, and the Hope of the Poor* (Minneapolis: Fortress, 2011), 100–104.

8. Cf. Elisabeth Schüssler Fiorenza, *In Memory of Her: A Feminist Theological Reconstruction of Christian Origins*, (New York: Crossroads, 1984); Leonard J. Swidler, *Jesus Was a Feminist: What the Gospels Reveal about His Revolutionary Perspective* (Lanham, MD: Sheed and Ward, 2007). According to both Schüssler-Fiorenza and Swidler, Paul maintained the egalitarianism of the Jesus movement, but the suppression of women began with the Pauline tradition (e.g., Eph. 5:22; Col. 3:18; 1 Tim. 2:8–15). They regard 1 Cor. 14:33b–36 as a post-Pauline addition. For a critique of the egalitarian interpretation of Jesus, see John H. Elliott, "Jesus Was Not an Egalitarian," *Biblical Theology Bulletin* 32 (2002): 75–91.

9. See Marcus Borg, *Jesus, a New Vision: Spirit, Culture, and the Life of Discipleship* (San Francisco: HarperSanFrancisco, 1991), 91–93.

10. Robert W. Funk, *Honest to Jesus: Jesus for a New Millennium* (San Francisco: HarperSanFrancisco, 1997), 208.

11. Ibid., 302–4.

12. Robert W. Funk and Roy W. Hoover (*The Five Gospels: The Search for the Authentic Words of Jesus; New Translation and Commentary* [New York: Macmillan, 1993], 32–33) insist that the work of the Jesus Seminar is outside church control. N. T. Wright suggests that Burton Mack's *A Myth of Innocence* (Philadelphia: Fortress, 1988) presents a Jesus who was compatible with the anti-Reaganism of many academics in that period (*Jesus and the Victory of God* [Minneapolis: Fortress, 1996], 39). See also James D. G. Dunn, *Jesus Remembered*, vol. 1 of *Christianity in the Making* (Grand Rapids: Eerdmans, 2003), 62: The Jesus rediscovered by the Jesus Seminar "is a Jesus who could well be imagined in many a twentieth-century faculty staff

Albert Schweitzer said at the beginning of the twentieth century about lives of Jesus written in the previous century has continued into the twentieth and twenty-first centuries.[13] The portrayals of Jesus become a reflection of the authors' own ideologies. Thus Jesus stands for the values of the interpreter. These values became lost with the emergence of the church that abandoned the liberating message of Jesus by introducing creeds, doctrines, and a church that Jesus never intended.

Recent popular literature continues to communicate the separation between Jesus and the church, maintaining that following Jesus is an individual pursuit. The lead article in a recent issue of *Newsweek* bore the title "Forget the Church. Follow Jesus."[14] The focus on the individual is also evident in contemporary popular evangelical literature. George Barna speaks of a revolutionary Christianity in which believers are "devout followers of Jesus Christ who are serious about their faith, who are constantly worshiping and interacting with God, and whose lives are centered on their belief in Christ. Some of them are aligned with a congregational church, but many are not."[15] Barna probably speaks for a large number of Americans, going to great lengths to commend these "millions of deeply devout Christians" who "live independently of a local church."[16]

The sharp contrast between Jesus and the church is easy to make. We know Jesus only through the portraits from his followers, and we can reconstruct his teaching by giving preference to the sayings that are most compatible with our own cultural setting. In keeping with the twenty-first-century interest in being nonjudgmental, Jesus is remembered as the one who said to the adulterous woman, "Neither do I condemn you" (John 8:11), but not as the one who made demanding claims about radical obedience and the indissolubility of marriage (cf. Mark 10:1–11). Thus Jesus becomes protean in our culture. On the other hand, we know the church from two thousand years of history, and its sins over this period are notorious. It has frequently stood on the side of the rich, abandoned the poor, and pursued its own power.[17] When Dostoyevsky's

---

room or as an independent 'loose cannon' academic, with his unsettling anecdotes, disturbing aphorisms, and provocative rhetoric."

13. Albert Schweitzer, *The Quest of the Historical Jesus: A Critical Study of Its Progress from Reimarus to Wrede* (New York: Macmillan, 1964), 4. "Each successive epoch of theology found its own thoughts in Jesus; that was, indeed, the only way in which it could make Him live." He adds, "There is no historical task which so reveals a man's true self as the writing of a Life of Jesus."

14. Andrew Sullivan, "Forget the Church. Follow Jesus." *Newsweek*, April 10, 2012.

15. George Barna, *Revolution* (Wheaton: Tyndale House, 2005), 8.

16. Ibid., 112; see Keith D. Stanglin, "Barna's Revolution and the Devolution of Ecclesiology," *Stone-Campbell Journal* 11, no. 1 (2008): 63.

17. Cf. Hans Küng, *The Church* (New York: Sheed and Ward, 1967), 24–29.

Grand Inquisitor says to Jesus, "Go and come no more," he is undoubtedly speaking for the church in many eras. As Gerhard Lohfink has shown in his excellent book *Jesus and Community*, the church has not been the community that Jesus intended.[18] Lohfink demonstrates that the church abandoned some of the major commitments of Jesus's ministry and calls on believers to recover Jesus's original intention.

An additional factor is the legacy of the focus on the individual's relationship to God apart from the church, which is deeply rooted in Protestant Christianity. Martin Luther's desire to find a gracious God was an individual quest. He found the answer in the doctrine of justification by faith. Although he remained a man of the church, he brought a concept of individual salvation that affected his understanding of the church. Indeed, the Protestant Reformation, with its reaction to the perceived triumphalism of the church, left unclear the relationship between the church and individual salvation. According to the Augsburg Confession, "The Church is a congregation of saints, in which the gospel is rightly taught and the sacraments are rightly administered." This understanding of the marks of the true church became standard among the Protestant Reformers.[19] It leaves unclear, however, the relationship between Christology, soteriology, and ecclesiology. Oliver O'Donovan describes the weakness of the Thirty-Nine Articles of Religion, the Anglican confession of faith. The first article on the church (article 19) echoes the Augsburg Confession, defining the church as "a congregation of faithful [people], in which the pure Word of God is preached, and the Sacraments duly ministered according to Christ's ordinance in all those things that of necessity are requisite to the same." Prior to that statement is a series of articles on salvation. But the relationship between the church and salvation is unclear. O'Donovan concludes, "The ecclesiastical theory of the Reformation was tacked on as a large and overgrown appendix to an evangelical theology which had no real place for the church."[20] This results in a doctrinal breach between salvation and the

---

18. The title of the German original asks this question forthrightly: *Wie hat Jesus die Gemeinde gewollt?* (*What Did Jesus Intend for the Church to Be?*)

19. Cf. John Calvin, "Wherever we see the Word of God purely preached and heard, and the sacraments administered according to Christ's institution, there, it is not to be doubted, a Church of God exists." *Institutes of the Christian Religion* 4.1.9, trans. Henry Beveridge (Grand Rapids: Eerdmans, 1962), 2:289. Cf. the Thirty-Nine Articles of the Anglican Church: "The visible Church of Christ is a congregation of faithful men, in which the pure Word of God is preached, and the sacraments duly ministered according to Christ's ordinance, in all those things that of necessity are requisite to the same."

20. Oliver O'Donovan, *On the Thirty-Nine Articles: A Conversation with Tudor Christianity* (Exeter, UK: Paternoster, 1986), 92. I am indebted to Jeremy S. Begbie, "The Shape of Things to Come? Wright amidst Emerging Ecclesiologies," in *Jesus, Paul and the People of God* (Downers Grove, IL: IVP Academic, 2011), 187.

church and an individualistic understanding of salvation.[21] Nicholas Perrin maintains that "at its worst, Western Protestantism has functionally defaulted to a notion that views the church as little more than a loose association of Jesus's Facebook friends."[22]

Rudolf Bultmann combines Luther's legacy of individual salvation with the existential encounter of the individual with God. He organizes his *Theology of the New Testament* around "man prior to the revelation of faith" and "man under faith." This division reflects the most important feature of Bultmann's treatment of human identity: the *generic* individual.[23] While Bultmann recognizes the communal nature of faith, he places his focus on the individual's decision to receive salvation.

The Protestant focus on the individual has a long history in evangelistic movements and revivalism. This emphasis has been especially dominant in North America, as leading thinkers have focused on individual freedom. Revivalists have presented the individual as alone before God and in need of salvation. They have called on individuals to make a decision for Christ but have said little about incorporation into the church.[24] Parachurch organizations commonly conduct their ministries independently from the church. Thus evangelicalism, according to Stanley Grenz, is a movement that "has never developed or worked from a thoroughgoing ecclesiology."[25]

The emphasis on the individual is the legacy not only of Protestantism but also of the Enlightenment, which provided an individualist impulse and promoted such values as personal freedom and self-interest.[26] This individualism has deep roots in the American tradition. It is present, for example, in Jefferson's claim that the individuals are endowed by their Creator with certain inalienable rights. Tocqueville saw individualism as the distinguishing feature of American life and maintained that it led people to extreme selfishness.[27]

21. Begbie, "Shape of Things to Come?," 187.

22. Nicholas Perrin, "Jesus's Eschatology and Kingdom Ethics: Ever the Twain Shall Meet," in *Jesus, Paul and the People of God*, 102.

23. Ben C. Dunson, "The Individual and Community in Twentieth- and Twenty-First-Century Pauline Scholarship," *Currents in Biblical Research* 9 (2010): 65.

24. Gerry C. Heard, *Basic Values and Ethical Decisions: An Examination of Individualism and Community in American Society* (Malabar, FL: Krieger, 1990), 6. An example of the individualistic focus, according to Heard, is the preaching of the Great Awakening of the 1730s and 1740s. In these meetings preachers such as George Whitefield and Jonathan Edwards called upon people to repent in order to avoid punishment and to be united with God.

25. Stanley J. Grenz, *Renewing the Center: Evangelical Theology in a Post-Theological Era* (Grand Rapids: Baker, 2000), 288.

26. Ibid., 322.

27. Alexis de Tocqueville, *Democracy in America* (New York: New American Library, 1956), 193–94.

The individualist tradition claims the primacy of the individual over all other forms of social life, which it regards as the result of contracts between individuals.[28] The idea of the "social contract," composed of free persons who enter into a contract to live under common laws in order to support the interests of the individual, has been an important feature of Western thought.[29] This contractualism has an ecclesiological counterpart in modern views of the church as a voluntary association of individual believers.[30] As Gary Badcock maintains, "The individualism of late capitalism is perfectly matched by the notion that the church is a 'voluntary association,' so that the important thing in its realization is that each person makes his or her own decisions to belong."[31] According to this view, individuals find their identity as Christians prior to and apart from membership in the church.[32] They experience a personal relationship with Christ and then join a church that exists to promote the spiritual well-being of the individual. The church is the aggregate of the individual Christians who "contract" with each other to form the community.[33] Thus relationships within the church become instrumental to the goals of individual self-interest.[34]

The result of the primacy of the individual self-interest is that the church now competes for members in a marketplace for consumers. In *The Churching of America, 1776–1990*, Roger Finke and Rodney Stark argue that the choice made by the Founding Fathers of not having an established church resulted in an economic understanding of religious life. They maintain that, where religious affiliation is a matter of choice, religious organizations must compete for members. Consequently, the "invisible hand" of the marketplace is at work in the church in the same way as in the marketplace.[35]

Another contributing factor to the decline of the church is the general loss of what Robert Putnam calls "social capital"—the general decline of associational life. Putnam observes that individual bowlers increased by 10 percent from 1980 to 1983, while league bowling dropped by 40 percent. Similarly, people

28. John R. Franke, *Character of Theology: An Introduction to Its Nature, Task, and Purpose* (Grand Rapids: Baker Academic, 2005), 167.
29. Gary D. Badcock, *The House Where God Lives: Renewing the Doctrine of the Church for Today* (Grand Rapids: Eerdmans, 2009), 167.
30. Ibid., 168.
31. Ibid.
32. Stanley J. Grenz, "Ecclesiology," in *The Cambridge Companion to Postmodern Theology*, ed. Kevin J. Vanhoozer (Cambridge: Cambridge University Press, 2003), 257. See also Heard, *Basic Values and Ethical Decisions*, 3.
33. Grenz, "Ecclesiology," 257.
34. Begbie, "Shape of Things to Come?," 187.
35. Roger Finke and Rodney Stark, *The Churching of America, 1776–2005: Winners and Losers in Our Religious Economy* (New Brunswick, NJ: Rutgers University Press, 2005), 9.

no longer participate in the PTA, labor unions, or political groups that rely on face-to-face interaction as they did in the past.[36] The internet has replaced these institutions as vehicles for bringing people together for a common purpose. These forces join together to create a loss of communal relationships in general.

THE RENEWAL OF THE CHURCH IN RECENT THOUGHT

In the past generation Protestants from various traditions have indicated their dissatisfaction with the traditional understanding of the church as the place where the word is preached and the sacraments are administered. The recognition that the institutional church has lost its privileged place in Western society and the decline of church membership have provided the occasion for new proposals for the church in a changing culture. We now confront competing claims for the nature and purpose of the church.

Political Action Committee

James Davison Hunter describes the "relevance to" paradigm of the church, according to which the task of the Christian community is to speak to the pressing issues of the day and shape public policy.[37] While liberals and conservatives choose different issues, they agree that the task of the church is to mobilize and influence public opinion in a democracy. Liberals have addressed the most contentious issues of the day: wars in Vietnam and Iraq, the rights of the marginalized, and the evils of corporate capitalism.[38] Conservatives have mobilized to shape public policy on sexual mores, abortion, and the maintenance of a "Christian America." Despite their differing priorities, both hope to inject Christian values into the larger society, and both exist in continuity with the Constantinian relationship between church and society.[39]

The Church as Corporation

In response to the decline of church membership, others have focused on church growth. In 1989 Donald McGavran articulated a vision of church

---

36. Robert D. Putnam, *Bowling Alone: The Collapse and Revival of American Community* (New York: Simon and Schuster, 2001), 111–13. See also Robert N. Bellah et al., "Individualism and the Crisis of Civic Membership," *Christian Century* 113, no. 16 (May 1986): 510–12.

37. James Davison Hunter, *To Change the World: The Irony, Tragedy, and Possibility of Christianity in the Late Modern World* (New York: Oxford University Press, 2010), 215.

38. Ibid., 215–16.

39. This view fits with H. Richard Niebuhr's typology of "Christ the Transformer of Culture." See H. Richard Niebuhr, *Christ and Culture* (New York: Harper & Row, 1951), 190–229.

growth based on social science models.[40] According to McGavran, "The chief and irreplaceable purpose of mission is church growth."[41] Assuming an ecclesiology that places numerical growth at the center, McGavran proposes a basic strategy based on the building of homogeneous churches. The literature consistently maintains that, because people do not like to cross socioeconomic lines, the church can grow only when potential converts can associate with people like themselves. Thus the homogeneous church has the greatest prospects for growth. With a heavy reliance on marketing practices, advocates argue that one can predict the results by applying principles that work in the marketplace. With its focus on growth as the primary aim of the church and its use of market analysis, the movement represents an ecclesiology heavily influenced by the principles of free market capitalism.[42] The inevitable result of this market-driven approach to the church is the competition among the churches. In subsequent chapters I will address the conflict between this reductionistic view of the church and the witness of the New Testament of a community where there is "no longer Jew or Greek" (Gal. 3:28).

The Church as Theater

Growth is the focus of the megachurch, which also reflects dissatisfaction with the traditional ecclesiastical forms.[43] While the megachurch is not a formal ecclesiology, it assumes an ecclesiological vision based on the increase in numbers. The church is primarily evangelistic, encouraging individuals to increase the size of the church. Consequently, the worship and ministries of the church are designed to attract new members and be sensitive to the perceived needs of the audience. The seeker-sensitive church seeks continuity between the church at worship and its attractiveness to the seeker; thus it focuses on entertainment.[44] Megachurches require a more theatrical style than the tradi-

40. Donald McGavran, *Church Growth: Strategies That Work* (Nashville: Abingdon, 1980).
41. Donald McGavran, *Understanding Church Growth*, rev. ed. (Grand Rapids: Eerdmans, 1980), 90. Charles Van Engen criticizes the church growth movement: "The true church exists apparently to grow the church which exists to grow more church." *Growth of the True Church: An Analysis of Church Growth Theory* (Amsterdam: Rodopi, 1981), 479.
42. See Jeanne Halgren Kilde, *When Church Became Theatre: The Transformation of Evangelical Architecture and Worship in Nineteenth-Century America* (Oxford: Oxford University Press, 2002), 216. "The oft-told story of Willow Creek Community Church founder Bill Hybels going door to door to ascertain just what would appeal to suburban Chicago residents in a church is emblematic of the utilitarian bent of the megachurch movement: identify the needs and desires of the target group and fulfill them."
43. See Laceye Warner, "Mega-Churches: A New Ecclesiology or an Ecclesial Evangelism?" *Review and Expositor* 107 (Winter 2010): 22.
44. Ibid., 25. See also Kilde, *When Church Became Theatre*, 215–17, 19. Kilde (220) speaks of the audience-centered nature of evangelical worship demonstrated by architectural trends.

tional church, with an emphasis on the performance of professionals rather than the participation of the congregation. Traditional Christian symbols, including the pulpit and the table, no longer have the central place they once had. Sound systems and lighting are of paramount concern, in keeping with the emphasis on the church as theater.[45] The shape of the worship service is determined less by theological reflection than by the preferences of consumers who are engaged in comparison shopping among churches. Practitioners emphasize the methods for attracting others but assume the ecclesiology of growth without establishing theological foundations. While they assume an ecclesiology of growth, their assumptions grow out of the experience of the marketplace.[46] They ignore the fact that, with the exception of Acts, the New Testament writings indicate little interest in numerical growth.[47] This emphasis is an expression of modern individualism, and the effect will be a church incapable of challenging the values of this world.[48]

The Church as Association

A wide variety of clubs and associations bring together people who enjoy the company of those who pursue common interests. Members pay fees to join and participate, and they receive benefits in return. They enjoy the social interaction with each other and the activities that the group provides. One may, in fact, hold membership in multiple associations to pursue one's interests. The mission of the association is to meet the needs of its members in order to grow.[49] As in Paul's day (see below, under the heading "Paul and the Renewal of the Church"), the church may find a model in associations and clubs as it meets the needs of its members, providing social contacts and a variety of programs. Unlike many other associations, the church can offer benefits for every age group.

Because the association is bound together by individuals who share a common interest, people join and leave the group based on its capacity to meet their needs.[50] It belongs to the members and is responsible to them. The association

---

45. Kilde, *When Church Became Theatre*, 217.

46. Lesslie Newbigin, *The Open Secret: An Introduction to the Theology of Mission*, rev. ed. (Grand Rapids: Eerdmans, 1978), 125. "When numerical growth is taken as the criterion of judgment on the church, we are transported with alarming ease into the world of the military campaign or the commercial sales drive."

47. Ibid.

48. Hunter, *To Change the World*, 283.

49. Ellen T. Charry, "Sacramental Ecclesiology," in *The Community of the Word: Toward an Evangelical Ecclesiology*, ed. Mark Husbands and Daniel J. Treier (Downers Grove, IL: IVP Academic, 2005), 201.

50. Gerhard Lohfink, *Gegen die Verharmlosung Jesu: Reden über Jesus und die Kirche* (Freiburg: Herder, 2013), 257–58.

belongs to one segment of the member's life but does not make claims on the member's marriage, vocation, or leisure time. The group is the sum of the individual parts. As I will argue in this book, the church is more than the sum of its parts. It belongs not to the members but to God. We do not join it, as we might join the health club, because the church is composed of the people who are called by God. While it, like the association, provides a place to belong, it is not an association of individuals but the people of God united in Christ.

The Missional Church

The missional church movement rejects the marketing approaches that preceded it and focuses not on the benefits of church membership to consumers but on the mission of the church. Advocates trace the roots of the missional church movement to Lesslie Newbigin's observations about the Western world as a mission field.[51] Newbigin recognized the diminishing role of the institutional church in a post-Christian world and articulated a call for a church that is faithful in the new situation after Christendom. Advocates of the missional church have observed that the traditional understanding of the church as the place where the word is preached and the sacraments are administered fits within the context of Christendom but is inadequate in a post-Christian era, for its focus on the church as "the place where" offers no understanding of its mission.[52] George Hunsberger writes of the need for "reinventing or rediscovering the church" in the modern world.[53] Advocates of the missional church speak with a keen awareness that the church no longer has a privileged place in society and can no longer serve as "chaplain to the culture and society,"[54] and they reject the attractional model of church in favor of a focus on the mission of the church. This is a call for recovery of the essence of the church in the purpose of God.

Although the word *missional* has been widely used and co-opted by many,[55] one can delineate the most prominent features of the missional church move-

51. See David J. Bosch, *Transforming Mission: Paradigm Shifts in Theology of Mission* (Maryknoll, NY: Orbis, 1999), 389–90, for the influence of Karl Barth in formulating the idea of the *missio Dei* as the foundation for mission.

52. George Hunsberger, "Missional Vocation: Called and Sent to Represent the Reign of God," in *Missional Church: A Vision for the Sending of the Church in North America*, ed. Darrell L. Guder (Grand Rapids: Eerdmans, 1998), 79.

53. Ibid., 77.

54. Ibid., 78.

55. Cf. Allan J. Roxburgh's comment, "The word 'missional' seems to have traveled the remarkable path of going from obscurity to banality in one decade." Quoted in Craig Van Gelder and Dwight J. Zscheile, *The Missional Church in Perspective: Mapping Trends and Shaping the Conversation* (Grand Rapids: Baker Academic, 2011), 1.

ment. As the term suggests, the missional church's central concern is ecclesiology. According to Darrell Guder, "Mission is not just a program of the church. It defines the church as God's sent people."[56]

The central foci of the missional church movement include the following:

1. The Mission of God (*missio Dei*). The missional church is a turn from an ecclesiocentric view to a theocentric view of the church and its mission. God is a missionary God who sends the church into the world. This understanding shifts the agency of mission from the church to God. It is God's mission that has a church rather than the church that has a mission. According to Guder,

> "Mission" means "sending," and it is the central biblical theme describing the purpose of God's act in human history. God's mission began with the call of Israel to receive God's blessings in order to be a blessing to the nations. God's mission unfolded in the history of God's people across the centuries recorded in Scripture, and it reached its revelatory climax in the incarnation of God's work of salvation in Jesus ministering, crucified, and resurrected. God's mission continued then in the sending of the Spirit to call forth and empower the church as the witness to God's good news in Jesus Christ.[57]

This view focuses on the mission of God the Father, who sends the Son into the world, and who, with the Son, sends the Holy Spirit into the world. The church is not the vendor of religious goods and services but the people called and sent. Its task is to discern what God is doing in the world and to participate in this mission.[58]

2. The Reign of God. The mission of God finds expression in the gospel of the reign of God as announced by Jesus. Although conceding that the gospel of the early church was *about* Jesus, Hunsberger devotes his primary attention to the gospel that Jesus preached. Because the central message of Jesus was the reign of God, the faithful church will continue to proclaim this message. Hunsberger summarizes the message of the kingdom as a "world characterized by peace, justice, and celebration."[59] This understanding makes the work of God in the world larger than the mission of the church, although the church is directly involved in the kingdom.

3. The Church of God. The church, which is rooted in the message of the reign of God, is an alternative community. Lois Barrett says that, living in anticipation of the ultimate reign of God, "the church as an alternative

56. Darrell L. Guder, "From Sending to Being Sent," in Guder, *Missional Church*, 6.
57. Ibid., 4.
58. For a critique of the trinitarian missiology, see Van Gelder and Zscheile, *Missional Church in Perspective*, 52.
59. Hunsberger, "Missional Vocation," 90–91.

community can make a powerful witness when it chooses to live differently from the dominant society even at just a few key points."[60] It rejects the dominant values of the world in order to represent the reign of God. Writers define what this means in a variety of ways.

Advocates of the missional church have offered a welcome alternative to the entertainment and marketing model and have attempted to offer a theological foundation for ecclesiology. They correctly call for the church to recognize its diminished role in Western culture and to accept its countercultural status as the harbinger of a new world. This approach, however, leaves unanswered questions. The claim that mission originates in the mission of God may be ultimately true, but it is reductionistic. While a major theme of Scripture is God's role of calling and sending, God cannot so easily be confined to that category. Nor is the self-understanding of the church limited to being sent, as I will argue in this book. It is not clear that the whole character of God or of the church can be defined by mission.

The claim that the mission of the church is founded on Jesus's proclamation of the reign of God is also problematic, for it places the synoptic portrayal of Jesus at the center and marginalizes the early church's self-understanding after Easter. Indeed, Hunsberger asks when the church lost as its defining quality the gospel of the reign of God that Jesus preached. The answer is that the church made the transition with the christological claims about Jesus. For example, Paul mentions the kingdom only rarely. In most cases he employs the language with reference to the realm that one enters after death. In his epistles, he replaces Jesus's proclamation of the kingdom with the announcement of the revelation of God's righteousness. The focus on Jesus's message rather than the religion about Jesus is remarkably similar to that of the nineteenth century liberals' advocacy of the religion *of* Jesus rather than the religion *about* Jesus.

One is left with uncertainty about what is meant either by the *missio Dei* or by the kingdom. Should the *missio Dei* be understood primarily as God's work in redemption, and thus the church is the primary way that God works in the world? Or should the *missio Dei* be understood as God's work in all creation? The latter view marginalizes the church and envisions God at work outside the religious sphere. The task of the church, according to this understanding, is to discover what God is doing and then seek to participate in it.[61]

A similar question emerges in the focus on the reign of God. Hunsberger offers the theological foundation in the ministry of Jesus and the sending of the

60. Lois Barrett, "The Church as Apostle to the World," in Darrell L. Guder, ed., *Missional Church: A Vision for the Sending of the Church in North America* (Grand Rapids: Eerdmans, 1998), 127.
61. Van Gelder and Zscheile, *Missional Church in Perspective*, 31.

disciples. In the Gospels' portrayal, Jesus inaugurated the kingdom, which was present in his words and deeds. He also gathered a community of those who repented and conformed their lives to the reality of the kingdom. Therefore the kingdom could not be separated from Christology. Jesus did not invite his listeners to discover what God was already doing, but announced that the long-awaited kingdom was present in his ministry. While others healed and did acts of compassion, only Jesus inaugurated the kingdom. Thus one is left to wonder what the missional church advocates mean by their references to the kingdom.

If the proposals for the missional church leave uncertainty about the mission of God in the world, they also leave questions about the identity and message of the church. What is the role of the sacraments? What polity is most appropriate for the Christian community? The church's identity, as I will argue in this book, cannot be understood apart from its Christology and soteriology. What about the edification of the community? The missional church reiterates the low ecclesiology that is common in Protestantism. If the church's role is to discover what God is doing and then join in that, the kingdom of God could function without the church.

The Emerging Church

Dissatisfaction with the traditional church and with evangelicalism has evoked an alternative vision that advocates call the emerging church. The term is so diffuse that one has difficulty defining it or knowing who speaks for it.[62] Nevertheless, some common themes characterize the movement, which is based on the premise that the church must respond to postmodern culture. As the designation "emerging church" indicates, it is an attempt to fashion a new ecclesiology. The common themes include (a) the necessity for change, (b) an emphasis on orthopraxy rather than orthodoxy, (c) submersion into the postmodern culture, (d) a highly communal existence, (e) a refusal to be pinned down to a single ecclesiology and an openness to all ecclesiologies, (f) a reluctance to place boundaries describing who is in and who is out, (g) participation in spiritual activities, and (h) identification with the life of Jesus.[63]

Advocates of the emerging church also draw a wedge between Jesus and the church, proposing an ecclesiology based on a return to the way of Jesus of the Gospels. Brian McLaren says in *A Generous Orthodoxy*, "Often I don't think Jesus would be caught dead as a Christian, were he physically here today. . . .

62. See Paul Doerksen, "The Air Is Not Quite Fresh: Emerging Church Ecclesiology," *Direction* 39, no. 1 (2010): 4.

63. See Scot McKnight, "Five Streams of the Emerging Church," *Christianity Today* 51, no. 2 (2007): 35–39.

Generally, I don't think Christians would like Jesus if he showed up today as he did 2,000 years ago."[64] McLaren maintains that a church is a "community that forms disciples who work for the liberation and healing of the world, based on Jesus and the good news of the gospel."[65]

These basic tenets raise questions about the viability of this alternative ecclesiology. While its focus on worship, community, and mission are appropriate, weaknesses in its outlook prevent it from being a viable alternative today. While its central premise of the need for change has some value, the total submersion of the movement in postmodern culture prevents it from being an effective counterculture. Because all institutions need boundaries that establish identity, the reluctance of this movement to draw boundaries will ultimately undermine its identity. Moreover, the openness to all ecclesiologies and the preference for praxis over theology leaves the movement without an adequate doctrinal foundation as a basis for praxis.

PAUL AND THE RENEWAL OF THE CHURCH

Attempts to reimagine the church have focused on strategies and often assume an ecclesiology without offering a critical analysis of the identity of the church. A special irony can be seen in the near absence from the discussion of Paul, the one who shaped communities more than anyone else we know. Paul offers the first written reflection on the nature of the church. Neither the attractional models of the church growth movement nor the missional or emerging church models incorporate Pauline theology at a substantive level into their understanding of the church. The rare appeals to the Pauline literature do not engage the larger theological context of Paul's thought.[66] Thus when George Hunsberger says, "It is hotly debated when and how the church lost its sense of this gospel of the reign of God,"[67] he need look no further than Paul, who proclaimed Christ crucified (1 Cor. 2:2) rather than the message of the reign of God. As Alfred Loisy famously said, "Jesus foretold the kingdom, and it was the church that came."[68]

64. Brian McLaren, *Generous Orthodoxy: Why I Am a Missional, Evangelical, Post/Protestant, Liberal/Conservative, Mystical/Poetic, Biblical, Charismatic/Contemplative, Fundamentalist/ Calvinist, Anabaptist/Anglican, Methodist, Catholic, Green, Incarnational, Depressed-Yet-Hopeful, Emergent, Unfinished Christian* (Grand Rapids: Zondervan, 2004), 87.

65. McLaren, *Everything Must Change: Jesus, Global Crises, and a Revolution of Hope* (Nashville: Thomas Nelson, 2007), 292.

66. Charry, "Sacramental Ecclesiology," 204.

67. Hunsberger, "Missional Vocation," 91.

68. Alfred Loisy, *The Gospel and the Church*, trans. Christopher Home (Philadelphia: Fortress, 1976), 166. Responding to Adolf Harnack's criticism of the Roman Catholic Church, Loisy

Although Jesus's message of the kingdom implies a community committed to God's reign,[69] the church was not a topic of his discourses. It was Paul who established churches. Wherever he preached Christ, new communities emerged, united by their reception of the basic christological confession. Although the word *ekklēsia*, which appears only three times in the Gospels, probably originated in the earliest Jerusalem church as a self-designation of Christ believers, Paul developed this usage. He nurtured his communities through his personal catechesis, letters, and visits. In his letters, he rarely speaks to individuals but establishes corporate consciousness by speaking to the whole church. English translations obscure the fact that, with rare exceptions (cf. Rom. 2:1–16; 8:2), he speaks only in the second-person plural.[70] He has "anxiety for all the churches" (2 Cor. 11:28) because his ultimate ambition is to present communities to Christ at the end (cf. 2 Cor. 1:14; 11:1–4). As an apostle who preaches where Christ has not been named, he does not speak of individual conversions but speaks of the establishment of churches. Thus he knows of no believer who is not affiliated with a community.

Paul's ecclesiology may be overlooked because he gives no extended treatment of the major themes commonly associated with the church. He does not speak at length about church polity, and his references to baptism and the Lord's Supper are scattered among the letters. Moreover, the individualistic reading of Paul has led interpreters to overlook his ecclesiology. Nevertheless, Paul is the first to offer sustained reflection on the identity of the church.[71]

Because we know more about Paul's churches than we know about any other community in the New Testament, the apostle is the indispensable guide for anyone who looks for scriptural resources for reimagining the church. We can observe not only his practices of community formation but also his reflections on the nature of the church. His letters record both his initial work of establishing a church and his responses to challenges to communal identity.

Although Paul gives no separate treatment of ecclesiology, it is central to his thought and woven into all the major issues that he faced. Indeed, the major controversies are actually ecclesiological matters indicating how the churches define themselves. Paul's converts brought with them views of community that undoubtedly shaped their own understanding of the church. Parallels to

---

insisted on the continuity between Jesus and the church. On Loisy's meaning, see Badcock, *The House Where God Lives*, 69–74.

69. Lohfink, *Jesus and Community*, 26–29.
70. Paul's second-person singular is always used as a literary device known as "apostrophe."
71. Charry, "Sacramental Ecclesiology," 204.

existing practices, including initiatory rituals,[72] communal meals,[73] and religious instruction,[74] would have evoked associations with ancient communal practices. Because of similarities between other communities and the church in which they were now members, converts undoubtedly understood the church in ways that corresponded to their previous experiences. Paul's task was to offer an alternative vision of community.

The earliest Jewish converts saw the parallels with the synagogue and interpreted the church accordingly. The fact that in many instances the church emerged from the synagogue indicates the abiding influence of synagogue life and worship. The reading of sacred texts in the assembly, the call for holy living, and the nature of the leadership would have led the Jewish converts to interpret their own experiences in these ways.[75] The use of the term *ekklēsia* and the sense of belonging to a worldwide movement would have been analogous to the self-understanding of the synagogue.[76] Indeed, the ethnic associations of the synagogue would have shaped the Jewish converts' understanding of membership in the church, thus creating one of the major issues for Paul's task of community formation. Paul's challenge, particularly in Galatians and Romans, is to offer an alternative understanding of community.

The term *ekklēsia*, which Paul inherited from the earliest Palestinian community, could have resonated with non-Jewish listeners, who would have understood the church as a new kind of civic gathering. E. A. Judge and others have argued that the observer would have identified Christian groups as philosophical schools.[77] The Christian apologist Justin and the pagan physician

72. For the literature on the initiatory rituals of the mysteries, see Richard S. Ascough, *What Are They Saying about the Formation of Pauline Churches?* (New York: Paulist Press, 1998), 50–70.

73. See Wendell L. Willis, *Idol Meat at Corinth: The Pauline Argument in 1 Corinthians 8 and 10*, Society of Bibilical Literature Dissertation Series 68 (Atlanta: Scholars Press, 1985; repr., Eugene, OR: Wipf and Stock, 2004), 7–64.

74. Loveday Alexander, "Paul and the Hellenistic Schools," in *Paul in His Hellenistic Context*, ed. Troels Engberg-Pedersen (Minneapolis: Fortress, 1995), 67; Clarence E. Glad, *Paul and Philodemus: Adaptability in Epicurean and Early Christian Psychagogy*, Novum Testamentum Supplement Series 81 (Leiden: Brill, 1995), 335.

75. See John G. Gager, *Kingdom and Community: The Social World of Early Christianity* (Englewood Cliffs, NJ: Prentice-Hall, 1975), 126–40; James Tunstead Burchaell, *From Synagogue to Church: Public Services and Offices in the Earliest Christian Communities* (Cambridge: Cambridge University Press, 1992), 277–87; Richard Ascough, "Translocal Relationships among Voluntary Associations and Early Christianity," *Journal of Early Christian Studies* 5 (1997): 234.

76. Wayne Meeks, *The First Urban Christians: The Social World of the Apostle Paul* (New Haven: Yale University Press, 1983), 80.

77. Cf. E. A. Judge, "The Early Christians as a Scholastic Community," in *The First Christians in the Roman World*, WUNT 2/229 (Tübingen: Mohr Siebeck, 2008): 4–15; Robert Wilken, "Collegia, Philosophical Schools, and Theology," in *The Catacombs and the Colosseum: The*

Galen both referred to the Christian movement as a school.[78] Several have observed the parallels to the Epicurean communities. Clarence E. Glad suggests that Paul's "psychagogic" practice, his style of caring for the community, has affinities with that of the Epicureans.[79] In both communities, the Pauline and the Epicurean, there is a pattern of "mutual participation by community members in exhortation, edification and correction."[80] Epicurus, like Paul, attempted to maintain unity among his scattered followers by writing letters to his friends in distant places.

Numerous types of voluntary associations provide the background for the converts' understanding of community. Some of the voluntary associations incorporated persons who shared the same craft or trade. Rituals and communal meals were common among their activities. These voluntary associations frequently functioned as burial societies.[81] Pythagorean communities were characterized by a community of goods, a required daily regimen, and strict taboos on diet and clothing.[82]

Although *thiasos* (Latin *collegium*) was the most common designation for these voluntary associations, a few inscriptions indicate that some designated themselves as *ekklēsia*.[83] In some instances the leadership structure involved overseers (*episkopoi*) and servants (*diakonoi*).[84] Some voluntary associations, like Paul's churches, imposed strict regulations for moral purity.[85]

Paul's task was to define the community of believers in ways that did not conform to ancient concepts of community. When he converted people from different social classes and ethnic groups, he formed a community that was unparalleled in the ancient world. Thus his task was to build lasting communities, and his letters are attempts at ecclesial self-definition that challenged the common views of community.

Contemporary attempts at reimagining the church have provided the stimulus for this study, in which I bring Paul into dialogue with the current conversation. My task is to offer the theological foundation for the rediscovery of

---

Roman Empire as the Setting of Primitive Christianity, ed. S. Benko and J. J. O'Rourke (Valley Forge, PA: Judson, 1971), 268–91.

78. See Wilken, "Collegia, Philosophical Schools, and Theology," 274.

79. Glad, *Paul and Philodemus*, 8.

80. Ascough, *What Are They Saying?*, 45.

81. Meeks, *First Urban Christians*, 74.

82. Diogenes Laertius, *Vit.* 21.95–100. Cited in Meeks, *First Urban Christians*, 83.

83. Richard S. Ascough, "Voluntary Associations and the Formation of Pauline Christian Communities: Overcoming the Objections," in *Vereine, Synagogen und Gemeinden im kaiserzeitlichen Kleinasien*, ed. Andreas Gutsfeld and Dietrich-Alex Koch, Studien und Texte zu Antike und Christentum 25 (Tübingen: Mohr Siebeck, 2006), 159.

84. Ibid., 165–69.

85. Ibid., 179.

the church by examining Pauline ecclesiology within the larger framework of the apostle's theology. Thus my study will not be limited to the traditional ecclesiological categories—polity, sacraments, ministry, and worship. Nor do I limit Paul's view of the church to the numerous images for the community (e.g., body, temple, bride),[86] for his ecclesiology is not limited to these traditional categories. Because Paul does not treat ecclesiology as a separate category, but integrates ecclesiological reflection into the major themes of his theology, this study will examine the significance of the major theological themes for Paul's understanding of the church. Indeed, all the letters struggle with the question of the identity of the community, which Paul cannot discuss without demonstrating the interdependence of the major themes.

In this book I explore Pauline ecclesiology in the conviction that Paul's ecclesiology, expressed to communities in a pre-Christian world, offers insights for ecclesiology in the post-Christian world. I am convinced that the voice of Paul needs to be heard in the contemporary conversation about the identity and mission of the church. While we cannot reproduce the Pauline churches in the twenty-first century, we can learn from Paul's articulation of communal identity.

In chapter 1 I will explore Paul's task of community formation in an analysis of the church of the Thessalonians, the first of Paul's churches about which we have information. In this catechetical letter, Paul shapes a corporate identity for readers who have experienced diverse types of community. He identifies gentile readers with Israel, providing a communal narrative and ethos for new converts and boundaries that will distinguish them from others in that city. He also introduces the imagery of siblings, which will become a constant feature in all his letters.

In chapter 2 I will demonstrate the role of Christology in defining Paul's communities. They are not collections of individuals who have joined together for a common cause but rather the people "in Christ" and in the body of Christ. Their identity comes not from their social contract but from their incorporation into the risen Christ. Their unity with Christ is the basis for their unity with each other. A community incorporated in Christ will share a common destiny with Christ and abolish the common distinctions between ethnic and socioeconomic groups.

Although Paul says little about baptism and the Eucharist, the scattered references indicate that his churches, like other communities of believers, practice baptism as the rite of entry into the community and observe the

---

86. Cf. Paul S. Minear, *Images of the Church in the New Testament* (Philadelphia: Westminster, 1960).

Eucharist regularly. Because analogies to these practices existed among other groups, Paul's converts probably interpreted both practices in ways that were consistent with pagan rituals. In chapter 3 I will argue that Paul interprets both baptism and the Eucharist as manifestations of the believers' identity in Christ and their share in the destiny of Christ. Both practices express the solidarity of the community with Christ and with each other. Unity within the community creates boundaries from the larger society.

In chapter 4 I will argue that Paul establishes a community of memory and hope. As the community of the new creation, it looks back to its entrance into God's new world and forward to its ultimate destination. In the present, it is the community that is being transformed into the image of Christ and sanctified in anticipation of final salvation. Because Paul envisions the church in the present as the foretaste of the ultimate redemption, he challenges the church to be a counterculture wherever it exists.

In chapter 5 I will describe the communal dimension of Paul's doctrine of justification. As the scholarship of the last generation has shown, the doctrine of justification was not primarily an individual concern but a corporate matter that would redefine the nature of the community. Justification by faith was a foundation for Paul's view of the church as the community in which ethnic and social barriers are erased. His vision of a united church composed of Jews and gentiles was based on the doctrine of justification.

In chapter 6 I will explore the mission of the churches that Paul founded, recognizing the distinction between Paul's apostolic mission and the task of his churches. Paul does not commission his churches to imitate his work as missionary but to be lights in the world by demonstrating the reconciling power of the gospel. While Paul offers little social ethic or missionary mandate for his churches, he calls on them to be the community that shares in the death and resurrection of Jesus.

Having demonstrated in earlier chapters that Paul's churches are full manifestations of the people of God, in chapter 7 I will explore whether the concept of the universal church is present in the undisputed letters of Paul, maintaining that, while the church is local, churches are united into the nascent universal church. Although Paul establishes local communities that are not organically connected to each other, he insists that the scattered churches encourage each other and give financial support to each other. He acknowledges the differences among churches in different locations, but he envisions mutual recognition among all of them. The collection for the saints in Jerusalem is the primary example of Paul's desire for a united church.

In chapter 8 I will focus on the legacy of Paul in the disputed letters of the Pauline corpus, observing the points of continuity and discontinuity between the earlier and later letters. Colossians, Ephesians, and the Pastoral Epistles reflect a later stage in ecclesiological reflection. In Colossians and Ephesians the universality of the church, a theme that is largely implicit in the undisputed Pauline letters, becomes explicit as a result of the changing situation. These letters offer the vision of a cosmic church, the true "megachurch." The Pastoral Epistles play an important role in maintaining the Pauline legacy. Contrary to a popular view, the primary focus of the Pastoral Epistles is not the establishment of a church order but the preservation of the apostolic faith in Paul's absence. Within each house church, leaders emerge to pass on the tradition to the next generation.

The distinctive feature of Paul's communities is the absence of positions of power and the active participation of the whole church in building the community. In chapter 9 I will examine the leadership structures that grow out of the Christian message. Paul prepares the church to act in his absence and to continue his work in the dialectical relationship between the leaders who employ their gifts for the community and the involvement of everyone in the same tasks.

In the conclusion I will synthesize the major aspects of Pauline ecclesiology and bring them into dialogue with contemporary conversations about the nature of the church and its mission. The Pauline model does not guarantee numerical growth; however, it offers the means for the church not to mirror other communities but to challenge our understanding of the community.

1

A COMMUNITY LIKE NO OTHER

The Key Themes—from Paul's First Letter

Most studies of Pauline ecclesiology do not begin with 1 Thessalonians, for the epistle says little or nothing about the major themes commonly associated with the topic. It does not mention the body of Christ or the sacraments, and it does not give explicit instructions about church polity.[1] Indeed, the term *ekklēsia* is used only twice (1:1; 2:14). Nevertheless, because 1 Thessalonians is probably the first record of Paul's attempt at community formation, it provides a valuable resource for understanding Paul's ecclesiology and the corporate identity he intended for his readers. As both a record of Paul's original catechetical instruction and an anticipation of future correspondence, the letter introduces the basic themes of ecclesiology that Paul will develop as he encounters new questions.

THE ORIGIN OF THE CHURCH OF THE THESSALONIANS

Paul addressed his first letter to the "church of the Thessalonians in God the father and the Lord Jesus Christ" (1 Thess. 1:1) only months after the establishment

---

1. Raymond Collins, "Church of the Thessalonians," in *Studies on the First Letter to the Thessalonians*, Bibliotheca ephemeridum theologicarum lovaniensium 66 (Leuven: University Press/Peeters, 1984), 285. Abraham J. Malherbe, "God's New Family at Thessalonica," in *The Social World of the First Christians: Studies in Honor of Wayne A. Meeks*, ed. L. Michael White and L. O. Yarbrough (Minneapolis: Fortress, 1995), 116.

of this community. According to the narrative in Acts, the community began when "some of them were persuaded" by Paul's preaching in the synagogue (Acts 17:4) and joined him and Silas, while others reacted with hostility. Among the converts, Luke mentions only devout Greeks and a few leading women (Acts 17:12). Although Luke says little about the collective identity of Paul's converts and does not describe the founding of an *ekklēsia*, he suggests their corporate identity when he recalls that "brothers" (*adelphoi*, NRSV "believers")—presumably the new converts—helped Paul and Silas escape to Berea (Acts 17:10). Luke's narrative suggests that the "brothers" had come from the synagogue but now were separated from it. Paul's address to the "church of the Thessalonians" reflects his assumption that the converts understand their identity as an *ekklēsia* separate from the synagogue and other communities.

Although 1 Thessalonians depicts the converts in Thessalonica as gentiles who "turned to God from idols" (1 Thess. 1:9), not as former members of the synagogue (cf. Acts 17:1–4), the epistle agrees with the narrative of Acts in one important respect: the preaching of the gospel resulted in the formation of a community composed of those who responded to Paul's preaching of Christ. They "were persuaded" by Paul's preaching, "received the word" (1 Thess. 1:6; 2:13), and "turned to God," separating themselves from the synagogue and from the surrounding society. Paul indicates that his gospel (*euangelion*) remains the foundation of the church's existence (1 Thess. 1:5; 2:2, 4, 8–9; 3:2), reaffirming that "we believe that Jesus died and rose again" (1 Thess. 4:14) and "died for us" (1 Thess. 5:10). His original preaching was also an appeal to the listeners to "[turn] to God from idols, to serve a living and true God, and to wait for his Son from heaven, whom he raised from the dead" (1:9–10), an adaptation of synagogue missionary preaching.[2] Both 1 Thessalonians and the narrative of Acts indicate the divisive character of Paul's preaching. While some received his message, hostility emerged from the populace (cf. Acts 17:5–6; 1 Thess. 1:6; 2:14; 3:2–4). Conflict between church and society existed from the beginning and also existed in the other communities that Paul planted (cf. Phil. 1:28; 1 Cor. 6:4; 2 Cor. 1:3–7).

Paul's other letters demonstrate a similar interest in the preaching that called the community into existence. According to 1 Corinthians, Paul had preached "Jesus Christ, and him crucified" (2:2), "planted" a vineyard (3:6), laid a foundation (3:10), and "fathered" (*egennēsa*, NRSV "became your father") the community through the gospel (4:15). He offers a different image in

2. Malherbe, "God's New Family at Thessalonica," 116; Franz Laub, "Paulus als Gemeindegründer (1 Thess)," in Josef Hainz, ed. *Kirche im Werden: Studien zum Thema Amt und Gemeinde im Neuen Testament—in Zusammenarbeit mit dem Collegium Biblicum München*. (Wien: Schöningh, 1976), 25.

2 Corinthians 3:2, indicating that the church is the letter that he had delivered (*diakonētheisa*, literally "ministered"). In Galatians he declares that there is no other gospel than the one that he had preached (1:6–9) and that he had originally "publicly exhibited" Christ as the crucified one (3:1). Similarly, he recalls that in the Philippians' conversion, God "began a good work" among them (Phil. 1:6). The existence of churches, therefore, was the manifestation of God's power in Paul's preaching (cf. 1 Cor. 1:18; Phil. 2:13; 1 Thess. 1:5). Thus Paul does not speak of the conversion of individuals but speaks of the corporate response to the gospel and the beginning of the community. For Paul, to be a believer is to be in a church.[3]

The Holy Spirit played a decisive role in the founding of the church. It first empowered Paul's preaching (1 Thess. 1:5; cf. 1 Cor. 1:18; 2:1–4), demonstrating that Paul did not come as an orator with words alone, but with power. As a result of the Thessalonians' reception of that word "with the joy of the Holy Spirit" (1:6 NASB), they became a model of changed lives throughout the wider region (1:6–10). The Spirit is a continuing reality empowering the community for ethical living (4:7). Paul probably does not distinguish it from "God's word, which is also at work [*energeitai*]" among them (1 Thess. 2:13 NRSV).[4] Thus the church is united not only by a common possession but also by the power at work in its midst.

The presence of the Spirit is a constant theme in Paul's other letters. Believers receive the Spirit at conversion (cf. 1 Cor. 12:12–13; 2 Cor. 3:1–3; Gal. 3:1–6; Rom. 5:5), and they continue to "live by the Spirit" (Gal. 5:16–18; cf. Rom. 8:4), which empowers them to live the ethical life (cf. Rom. 8:1–11; Gal. 5:22–29), work miracles (1 Cor. 12:10; Gal. 3:5), speak in tongues (1 Cor. 12:10, 28), and prophesy (1 Cor. 12:10; 14:1–5). The church is thus the community that lives by the power of the Spirit.

Although 1 Thessalonians says little about the demographics of the converts, it indicates that they were gentiles brought together in a community defined only by its allegiance to Christ. One may also assume that gentiles were incorporated into the community without circumcision and lived alongside Jewish converts from the synagogue. The Thessalonian church, like other Pauline churches,[5] probably included people of means as well as those who engaged in

3. Udo Schnelle, *Apostle Paul: His Life and Theology*, trans. M. Eugene Boring (Grand Rapids: Baker Academic, 2005), 559.

4. Cf. Phil. 2:13, "It is God who works [*ho energōn*] among you"; cf. also 1 Cor. 12:6, "It is the same God who activates [*ho energōn*] the gifts of the Spirit'"; 12:11, "One and the same Spirit activates [*energei*] all of [the gifts]" (my translations).

5. Studies of the demographics of Pauline churches have been based primarily on the analysis of 1 Corinthians. Cf. Gerd Theissen, *The Social Setting of Pauline Christianity: Essays on Corinth* (Philadelphia: Fortress, 1982), 69–119; Abraham J. Malherbe, *Social Aspects of Early*

manual labor.[6] The exhortation to "work with the hands," which is unique to the Thessalonian letters (1 Thess. 4:11; cf. 2 Thess. 3:12), suggests that at least some depended on manual labor for their existence.[7] Although Paul does not mention the presence of women and children, one may assume their presence in the Thessalonian community.[8] Indeed, the household baptisms reported in both Acts (10:2; 11:14; 16:15; 18:8) and the Pauline letters (1 Cor. 1:16) suggest the presence of entire family units, including slaves (cf. 1 Cor. 7:17–24; Gal. 3:28), in Paul's churches.[9] Such diversity was unprecedented among ancient associations.[10] It presented a potential for conflict, as Paul's subsequent correspondence indicates. Thus communities defined only by their acceptance of Paul's preaching included Jews and gentiles, various ethnic groups, the rich and the poor, free people and slaves, and men and women in the close proximity of the house church (cf. 1 Cor. 1:26–28; 7:17–24).[11]

Christianity (Baton Rouge: Louisiana State University Press, 1977), 29–59; Meeks, *First Urban Christians*, 51–71. Georg Schöllgen ("Was wissen wir über die Sozialstruktur der paulinischen Gemeinden?" *New Testament Studies* 34 [1988]: 71–82) has shown that one cannot generalize about the demographics of all of Paul's churches. See also Roger W. Gehring, *House Church and Mission: The Importance of Household Structures in Early Christianity* (Peabody, MA: Hendrickson, 2004), 168–69.

6. Robert Jewett, *The Thessalonian Correspondence: Pauline Rhetoric and Millenarian Piety* (Philadelphia: Fortress, 1986), 103; Gehring, *House Church and Mission*, 133, 151. See also Richard Ascough, *Paul's Macedonian Associations: The Social Context of Philippians and 1 Thessalonians*, WUNT 2/161 (Tübingen: Mohr Siebeck, 2003), 162–90. Ascough's argument that the Thessalonian church was composed of manual laborers (174) rests exclusively on the advice in 4:11, which is probably traditional paraenetic instruction, as the context in 4:9–10 suggests.

7. See the discussion in Ascough, *Paul's Macedonian Associations*, 165–76. Ascough argues that the Thessalonians were composed only of manual laborers who shared the same trade as Paul. The fact that Paul sent aid from Philippi to Macedonia (Phil. 4:16) suggests that the Thessalonians were poor. Ascough's evidence that the entire church is poor is not conclusive.

8. Ascough ("The Thessalonian Christian Community as a Professional Voluntary Association," *Journal of Biblical Literature* 119 [2000]: 187) argues that "there are some indications in 1 Thessalonians that the community was composed primarily of men." This conclusion is drawn from the fact that Paul (a) addresses the community as *adelphoi*, (b) does not mention women or children, and (c) addresses only men in 1 Thess. 4:4. See also Lone Fatum, "'Brotherhood in Christ': A Gender Hermeneutical Reading of 1 Thessalonians," in *Constructing Early Christian Families: Family as Social Reality and Metaphor*, ed. Halvor Moxnes (London: Routledge, 1997), 183–97. This conclusion is unwarranted, however. Paul rarely mentions women and children specifically in the letters, although their presence is assumed.

9. Peter Pilhofer ("Περὶ δὲ τῆς φιλαδελφίας . . . [1 Thess 4:9]: Ekklesiologische Überlegungen zu einem Proprium früher christlicher Gemeinden," in *Die frühen Christen und ihre Welt: Greifswalder Aufsätze 1996–2001*, WUNT 2/145 [Tübingen: Mohr Siebeck, 2002], 216) observes that it would have been inconceivable to join ancient associations with one's slaves.

10. Ibid.

11. John M. G. Barclay ("Thessalonica and Corinth: Social Contrasts in Pauline Christianity," *Journal for the Study of the New Testament* 47 [1992]: 49–74) has shown the limitations of assuming that the numerous churches established by Paul were identical in composition or in the issues that emerged among them. However, his attempt to distinguish between the Thessalonian

Establishing Corporate Identity: The People of God

Paul's task is unprecedented in antiquity. The creation of a corporate identity for converts whose only common interest was the conviction that Jesus suffered, died, and was raised from the dead (cf. 1 Thess. 4:14) separated the believers from the communities from which they had come—the family, the clan, the tribe, the civic assembly (*ekklēsia*)—and brought them together with those whom they did not choose. This new community came together in a house church, which played a major role in shaping its identity as a household.[12] In his catechetical instruction to new converts, Paul established the corporate identity of his converts. The consistent use of the second-person plural indicates that Paul speaks not to individuals but to the entire community.

> Our message of the gospel came to you . . . and you became imitators of us and of the Lord, . . . so that you became an example. . . . For the word of the Lord has sounded forth from you. (1:5–8)

> We also constantly give thanks to God for this, that when you received the word of God that you heard from us, you accepted it not as a human word but as what it really is, God's word, which is also at work in you believers. (2:13)

> As for us, brothers and sisters, when, for a short time, we were made orphans by being separated from you . . . we longed with great eagerness to see you face to face. (2:17)

As his use of the "you" plural indicates, Paul writes to communities, creating a collective identity. In the present they suffer together (3:2–3) and encourage one another (4:13; 5:11) in the context of various trials. Because Paul is anxious about their endurance, he sends Timothy to encourage their faithfulness (3:2, 6). He prays that the community will be sanctified at the parousia (3:13). They are his "joy" and "crown" (2:19). Thus he envisions a community that

---

and Corinthian congregations rests on the limited evidence of 1 Corinthians and 1 Thessalonians, both of which were written to answer specific questions. For example, Barclay's argument that the two communities experienced different relations with outsiders (hostility from outsiders in 1 Thessalonians, peaceful relations in 1 Corinthians) cannot be determined from the text. As 2 Cor. 1:3–7 indicates, Paul assumes that the community in Corinth shares with others in suffering.

12. See below on the church as family. On the relationship between the household setting and Paul's ecclesiology, see Meeks, *First Urban Christians*, 75–77. See also Malherbe, "God's New Family at Thessalonica," 116; Karl Olav Sandnes, *A New Family: Conversion and Ecclesiology in the Early Church with Cross-Cultural Comparisons*, Studies in the Intercultural History of Christianity (Berlin: Peter Lang, 1994), 93–111; Gehring, *House Church and Mission*, 153; Robert Banks, *Paul's Idea of Community: The Early House Churches in Their Historical Setting* (Grand Rapids: Eerdmans, 1980), 33–42.

is on a corporate journey that began with conversion and will end at the parousia. From the beginning, allegiance to Christ involved participation in the community.

The formation of the community involves the resocializing of the converts by providing them with a new self-designation, a demarcation between insiders and outsiders,[13] a social dialect that would distinguish them from other groups, and a new way of life.[14] The frequency of the meetings of the community undoubtedly played a role in the resocialization process. Paul's instruction that the letter be read to the whole community (1 Thess. 5:27) is probably his expectation for all his letters. The meetings provided the members an opportunity to "encourage one another and build one another up" (4:18; cf. 5:11) and to admonish others (5:14). This identity is a major dimension in Paul's ecclesiology. His designation for the community is a window into his ecclesiology.

The new social dialect of the Thessalonians expressed the continuity of this gentile community with Israel as the people of God. Indeed, they stand in solidarity with Jewish believers in Judea who have suffered at the hands of "the Jews, who killed both the Lord Jesus and the prophets" (1 Thess. 2:14–15). Thus Paul affirms that his converts belong to Israel. Indeed, the foundational image for the church in 1 Thessalonians is that of the people of God, as Paul's distinctive vocabulary indicates.

Ekklēsia

Paul addresses the community as the "church (*ekklēsia*) of the Thessalonians in God the Father and the Lord Jesus Christ," using a variant of his address to the other communities he had founded. Indeed, he writes also to the *ekklēsia* in Corinth (1 Cor. 1:1; 2 Cor. 1:1), to the *ekklēsiai* of Galatia (Gal. 1:2), and to the *ekklēsia* in Philemon's house (Philem. 2). These designations reflect the

13. Paul contrasts the believers with "outsiders" (1 Thess. 4:12; cf. 1 Cor. 5:12–13), "others" (1 Thess. 4:13; 5:6), and the "children of darkness" (1 Thess. 5:5; cf. Phil. 2:15). In 1 Corinthians he contrasts believers with unbelievers (cf. 1 Cor. 7:12; 10:27; 14:22–23), and "us who are being saved" with "those who are perishing" (1 Cor. 1:18). See James W. Thompson, *Moral Formation according to Paul: The Context and Coherence of Pauline Ethics* (Grand Rapids: Baker Academic, 2011), 46.

14. Paul Trebilco, *Self-Designations and Group Identity in the New Testament* (Cambridge: Cambridge University Press, 2012), 11–12. The insider vocabulary that Paul mentions in 1 Thessalonians includes Greek terms that take on new meanings within the community. These include *euangelion* ("good news," 1:5; 2:2, 9), *logos* ("word," 1:6, 8; 2:13), *eklogē* ("election," 1:5), and *pistis* ("faith," 3:2, 6). Elsewhere he refers to his *kērygma* ("proclamation," 1 Cor. 1:21; 2:4). This new dialect is central to their self-understanding as a community. See also Thompson, *Moral Formation*, 59–62.

collective identity of his converts, which Paul inculcated while he was present with them. The fact that Paul writes to churches rather than to individuals also indicates the communal nature of his pastoral work.

Any Greek-speaking audience would have been familiar with the term *ekklēsia*, which could be used for any assembly (cf. Acts 19:32) and was widely used for the assembly of the free men entitled to vote (cf. Acts 19:39).[15] The popular assembly (*ekklēsia tou dēmou*) was an essential part of the Greek system of governance.[16] Having at least some features in common with the Pauline *ekklēsia*, it was a place for instruction and reasoned discourse as well as the location where factions developed.[17] Indeed, the "church of the Thessalonians" would have been one of numerous communities in the city. The other communities included various voluntary associations, mystery cults, and philosophical or rhetorical schools as well as the Jewish synagogue.[18] None of these groups, however, identified themselves as an *ekklēsia* of God or as "holy ones."[19]

The designation of the community as "the church of the Thessalonians in God the Father and the Lord Jesus Christ" distinguishes the readers from the political assembly and the other assemblies and associations in Thessalonica, including the local synagogue.[20] The unusual partitive genitive ("of the Thessalonians") also distinguishes the community from the surrounding populace, signifying that they are a gathering "from among the Thessalonians."[21] In contrast to his customary practice, Paul focuses on the community rather than the location.[22] This designation is parallel to Paul's

15. J. Roloff, "ἐκκλήσια," *EDNT* 2:411. See also Küng, *The Church*, 81.

16. Raymond F. Collins, *The Many Faces of the Church: A Study in New Testament Ecclesiology* (New York: Crossroad, 2004), 1. On the view that Paul's use of *ekklēsia* is derived from Greek political discourse, see George H. Van Kooten, "'Εκκλησία τοῦ θεοῦ: The 'Church of God' and the Civic Assemblies (ἐκκλησίαι) of the Greek Cities in the Roman Empire: A Response to Paul Trebilco and Richard A. Horsley," *New Testament Studies* 58 (2012): 522–48. Van Kooten maintains that Paul deliberately uses *ekklēsia* to contrast the communities of Christ believers with political assemblies and to claim that his converts formed an alternative society (532). For an extensive analysis of the Greek *ekklēsia*, see Klaus Berger, "Volksversammlung und Gemeinde Gottes: Zu den Anfängen der christlichen Verwendung von 'Ekklesia,'" *Zeitschrift für Theologie und Kirche* 73 (1976): 167–207.

17. Van Kooten, "'Εκκλησία τοῦ θεοῦ," 540–46.

18. See Meeks, *First Urban Christians*, 71–84.

19. Ibid., 79.

20. Collins, *Many Faces of the Church*, 2. For the view that Paul is contrasting the "church of the Thessalonians in God the Father" from a community gathered in the name of Roman leaders, see Karl P. Donfried, "The Assembly of the Thessalonians: Reflections on the Ecclesiology of the Earliest Christian Letter," in *Ekklesiologie des Neuen Testaments, für Karl Kertelge*, ed. Rainer Kampling and Thomas Söding (Freiburg: Herder, 1996), 393.

21. Collins, *Many Faces of the Church*, 2. See also "churches of the Gentiles" (Rom. 16:4).

22. Malherbe, "God's New Family at Thessalonica," 119.

more customary usage, "the churches of God . . . in Judea" (2:14), which also have an identity separate from the synagogue. Unlike the other groups in Thessalonica, they are "in God the Father and the Lord Jesus Christ." Thus, among other communities, only they have been established and exist in God.[23] They express their collective identity in their rituals and their distinctive pattern of life (cf. 4:1–5:10).

Pauline usage maintained the connotation of an assembly, for he assumes that the readers will hear his words as they are gathered for worship (cf. 1 Thess. 5:27). Indeed, he employs *ekklēsia* elsewhere to describe the occasion when the whole community gathers together (1 Cor. 11:18; 14:19, 28, 34–35).[24] However, in most instances Paul employs the word for the community itself, assuming that the assembly is a distinguishing characteristic of its existence.[25] His use of the plural "churches" (Rom. 16:4, 16; 1 Cor. 11:16; 14:33; 16:1; 2 Cor. 8:1, 18; 1 Thess. 2:14) and the numerous references to the church in someone's house (Rom. 16:5; 1 Cor. 16:19; Philem. 2; cf. Col. 4:15) indicate that the self-designation of each of the local communities was an *ekklēsia*, a local manifestation of the one *ekklēsia* (cf. 1 Cor. 15:9). As both Acts and the letters agree, "the church of the Thessalonians" is one of numerous *ekklēsiai* founded by Paul, who maintains the designation *ekklēsia* consistently throughout his correspondence.[26]

Paul's consistent use of the terminology of "the church(es) of God" (*ekklēsia[i] theou*) further distinguishes the local communities from other *ekklēsiai*.[27] Paul employs a phrase that is an appropriate translation of the Hebrew *qahal 'el* (cf. Deut. 23:2, 4; 1 Chron. 28:8; Neh. 13:1), a term used for Israel in the Old Testament. *Qahal* can refer either to an assembly that

---

23. Ibid.

24. Everett Ferguson, *The Church of Christ: A Biblical Ecclesiology for Today* (Grand Rapids: Eerdmans, 1996), 131.

25. Udo Schnelle, *Theology of the New Testament* (Grand Rapids: Baker Academic, 2009), 329. Traugott Holtz (*Der erste Brief an die Thessalonicher*, Evangelisch-Katholischer Kommentar zum Neuen Testament 13, 3rd ed. [Neukirchen: Neukirchener Verlag, 1998], 38) suggests that *ekklēsia* portrays the community as a public assembly in contrast to the mysteries. Peter Pilhofer ("Die Ökonomische Attraktivität christlicher Gemeinden der Frühzeit," in *Die frühen Christen und ihre Welt*, WUNT 2/145 [Tübingen: Mohr Siebeck, 2002], 207) indicates that the frequency of the meetings distinguished Paul's converts from religious cults and other associations. Lohfink (*Gegen die Verharmlosung Jesu*, 266) indicates that the word *ekklēsia* indicates the public character of the community: "The church is not an esoteric circle, nor a group of friends."

26. Only Titus and 2 Timothy do not contain the word.

27. The full form *ekklēsia theou* appears also in 1 Cor. 1:2; 10:32; 11:16, 22; 15:9; 2 Cor. 1:1; Gal. 1:13. It appears in abbreviated form in twenty-five instances in the singular. The plural abbreviated form appears in 1 Cor. 7:17; 14:33–34; 16:1, 19; 2 Cor. 11:28. See Wolfgang Kraus, *Das Volk Gottes: Zur Grundlegung der Ekklesiologie bei Paulus*, WUNT 2/85 (Tübingen: Mohr Siebeck, 1996), 112.

has been called together for a special purpose[28] or to the congregation as an organized body.[29] The LXX translators rendered *qahal* into the Greek *ekklēsia* 73 times out of 123 occurrences of the term, while the remaining passages employ *synagōge*.[30] *Qahal 'el*, however, is rendered only once as *ekklēsia theou* (Neh. 13:1); it is most frequently rendered in the LXX as *ekklēsia kyriou* or as *synagōgē kyriou*. Indeed, *synagōgē* is used more frequently than *ekklēsia* in the LXX for the people of God.[31] Consequently, several scholars have argued that *ekklēsia theou* is not taken from the LXX but is a translation of *qahal 'el*, which is frequently in apocalyptic literature for the "assembly of God."[32] This phrase was frequently used in the Dead Sea Scrolls and other apocalyptic literature for the eschatological people of God.[33] Indeed, the reference to the *ekklēsia kyriou* in Deuteronomy 23:2–4 plays an important role in Second Temple Judaism as a *terminus technicus* for the true Israel as the *qahal 'el*.[34] According to 1 QSa 2:4, for example, "No man smitten with any human uncleanness shall enter the assembly of God; no man smitten with any of them shall be confirmed in his office in the congregation."[35] Thus *qahal 'el* became a term in the Second Temple period for the true Israel.[36] This designation indicates that Paul taught the Thessalonians that they were the eschatological people of God, the renewed community anticipated by the prophets.[37]

Although *ekklēsia theou* is unique to Paul in the New Testament, his designation of the community as *ekklēsia* is shared by some other New Testament writers. The word is the common designation for the community in

28. It is used for evil counsel (Gen. 49:6), civil affairs (1 Kings 12:3; Prov. 5:14; 26:28; Job 30:28), war or invasion (Num. 22:4; Judg. 20:2; 21:8; 1 Sam. 17:47; Ezek. 16:49; 38:7), and the company of returning exiles (Jer. 31:8).

29. It is used of Israel as a congregation or organized body (Lev. 16:17, 33; Num. 16:3; 20:4; Deut. 2–4, 9; Neh. 13:1), for the restored Israel (Ezra 10:12, 14; Neh. 8:17), for a company of angels (Ps. 89:6), and for an assembled multitude (Gen. 28:3; 35:11; 48:4; Num. 22:4). F. Blass, A. Debrunner, and R. W. Funk, *A Greek Grammar of the New Testament and Other Early Christian Literature* (Chicago: University of Chicago Press, 1961), 874.

30. Paul Trebilco, "Why Did the Early Christians Call Themselves ἡ ἐκκλησία?," *New Testament Studies* 57 (2011): 446.

31. Roloff, "ἐκκλησία," 2.411.

32. Donfried, "Assembly of the Thessalonians," 404. Cf. Peter Stuhlmacher, *Gerechtigkeit Gottes*, 211n2.

33. Roloff, "ἐκκλησία," 2.411.

34. See Andrie Du Toit, "Paulus Oecumenicus: Interculturality in the Shaping of Paul's Theology," *New Testament Studies* 55 (2009): 135.

35. Translation in Geza Vermes, *The Complete Dead Sea Scrolls in English* (London: Penguin, 2004), 161. Cited in Donfried, "Assembly of the Thessalonians," 404.

36. Walter Klaiber, *Rechtfertigung und Gemeinde: Eine Untersuchung zum paulinischen Kirchenverständnis* (Göttingen: Vandenhoeck & Ruprecht, 1982), 17; Kraus, *Das Volk Gottes*, 126–27.

37. Lohfink, *Gegen die Verharmlosung Jesu*, 269.

Acts,[38] 3 John (6, 9–10), and Revelation (1:4, 20; 2:1, 7–8, 11–12, 18; 3:1, 7, 14). Among the Gospels, only Matthew employs the term as the designation for the community formed by Jesus (16:18). This evidence suggests that, while Jesus formed a community to live under God's reign, *ekklēsia* is the term first used by the post-Easter church to designate the followers of Jesus. Paul probably inherited the term from his Greek-speaking predecessors in Jerusalem who used it to distinguish themselves from other Jewish groups and to claim that they were the eschatological people of God.[39] Thus the church's exclusive use of *ekklēsia* is noteworthy, for it differentiated the community from the empirical synagogue and expressed its conviction that it was the eschatological people of God.[40] Although *synagōgē* is frequently used synonymously for *ekklēsia* in the LXX, those who believed in Christ avoided the former term because it already designated Jewish communities.[41] Indeed, what distinguishes this community from the synagogue is that it exists "in God the Father and the Lord Jesus Christ." As the people who will be saved from God's wrath (1 Thess. 1:10), the *ekklēsia* of God does not share the destiny of those among the *Ioudaioi* who forbid the gentile mission, for the wrath of God has come upon the latter (2:16).

The twofold reference to "God the Father and the Lord Jesus Christ" anticipates the inseparability of the Father and Son throughout 1 Thessalonians. The community has "turned to God from idols" and awaits the return of the "Son from heaven" (1:9–10). The word about Christ is nothing less than the "gospel of God" (2:2, 9). Paul prays that God will reunite him with the Thessalonians and that the Lord will multiply their love for one another (3:11–13). The "churches of God . . . in Judea" are "in Christ" (2:14). Thus the eschatological people of God are those who are "in Christ," believing that Jesus died and arose (4:14), and they await his return (1:10; 4:13–18).

"In God" (*en theō*) is unusual for Paul and may be analogous to "in Christ" (*en christō*, cf. 4:16; cf. 2:14; 5:18) and "in the Holy Spirit" (*en pneumati hagiō*, 1:5; cf. Rom. 8:9).[42] Malherbe suggests that *en* is used in an instrumental sense to mean "the assembly of the Thessalonians brought into being by God the Father and the Lord Jesus Christ."[43] However, the instrumental and incorporative uses of *en* are not always distinguishable.[44] Parallel phrases in 1 Thes-

---

38. Acts 5:11; 8:1, 3; 9:31; 11:22, 26; 12:1, 5; 13:1; 14:23, 27; 15:3–4, 22, 41; 16:5; 18:22; 19:32; 20:17, 28.

39. Lohfink, *Gegen die Verharmlosung Jesu*, 268.

40. Schnelle, *Theology of the New Testament*, 328.

41. Trebilco, "Why Did the Early Christians?," 451–58.

42. Abraham J. Malherbe, *The Letters to the Thessalonians*, Anchor Bible 32B (New York: Doubleday, 2000), 99.

43. Ibid.

44. Donfried, "Assembly of the Thessalonians," 400.

salonians indicate that the familiar "in Christ" has more than an instrumental significance. Paul's goal is that they "stand firm in the Lord" (3:8) in the midst of persecution. To stand "in the Lord" is also to be "imitators . . . of the Lord" in affliction, like Paul (1:6) and the believers in Judea (2:14). Paul also speaks of "the dead in Christ" (4:16), who will be gathered with those who are alive at his return and join them in the air (4:17). "In Christ," therefore, suggests a relationship with Christ that began with conversion (1:5) and extends to the eschaton (4:13–18).[45] In the present the community joins Paul and others in imitating the afflictions of Christ (cf. 1:6; 2:1–2, 14–16), but it anticipates the time when it will be with Christ at the parousia. Both the faithful ones who have died and those who remain will be "with the Lord forever" (4:17; cf. "with him," 4:14). Thus Paul anticipates the idea of the communion of the saints, which will be later articulated in the Apostles' Creed.

Believers remain "in Christ" under all circumstances because the word that was preached is at work (*energeitai*) among them (2:13). This divine energy is the equivalent of the power (*dynamis*) that was present in the first preaching of the gospel (1:5). One may compare Paul's use of *energein* elsewhere to describe the divine work among the believers. God works among believers (Phil. 2:13, literally "among you") through the Spirit (1 Cor. 12:6; Gal. 3:5). Thus the community is unlike all other communities, for it exists "in God" and "in Christ," just as God lives in the community through the Holy Spirit (cf. 1 Thess. 4:8).

The designation of the community as *ekklēsia* suggests that Paul affirms the continuity of the church with Israel. Along with his predecessors in Jerusalem, he found in the term an appropriate designation for the community because the main alternative term, *synagogē*, was the common term for the remaining Jewish community.[46] Those who believed in Christ could employ the term without suggesting that they no longer belonged to the synagogue.[47] Gentile converts were no longer among the *ethnē* but were now incorporated into Israel.[48] What distinguished this *ekklēsia* from others was its incorporation into Jesus Christ.

The Believers

Paul employs other terms to differentiate the *ekklēsia* of the Thessalonians from other communities. Those who responded to the preaching of the good

45. Ibid. For further discussion of "in Christ," see chap. 2 below.
46. Trebilco, *Self-Designations and Group Identity*, 206.
47. Ibid.
48. Kraus, *Das Volk Gottes*, 154.

news are the "believers" (*pisteuontes*, 1:7; 2:10), a term that Paul uses frequently in his letters. While the noun *pistis* and the verb *pisteuō* would have been known to a Greek audience, Paul employs the words with a significance that would have been unusual in the larger culture. He speaks the language of the Septuagint, which employs *pist-* with an object for those who place their trust in God (Gen. 15:6; Prov. 30:1; Isa. 28:16) or the law (Sir. 32:24). In a few instances, *pist-* is used without an object for "the faithful" (cf. Ps. 100:6; Wis. 3:9; *1 En.* 108:13). Thus, like *ekklēsia*, the designation of "believers" was a part of the vocabulary of Judaism. In using the language without elaboration in 1 Thessalonians, Paul assumes that the term is the shorthand expression of the readers' collective identity.[49]

Although Paul speaks of the believers without specifying the object, his usage of *pistis* in the letter indicates the wider scope of this shorthand expression. Like the Israelites, the Thessalonians believe in God (1:8) but also "believe that Jesus died and rose again" (4:14), a conviction that separates them from the synagogue. This word anticipates Paul's later use of the term for those who share in the christological confession: those who "believe in [their] heart that God raised [Jesus] from the dead . . . will be saved" (Rom. 10:9). As Paul indicates elsewhere, believing is the appropriate response to the proclamation of Christ, and it is the continuing response of the community (cf. 1 Thess. 3:2, 6). Thus the present participle *pisteuontes* suggests that ongoing faith is a distinguishing feature of Pauline communities.[50]

Just as "the believers" is a badge of identity for the Thessalonians, it also signifies the boundary separating the community from the rest of society. At the beginning the believers "received the word" in spite of persecution (1:6), which has continued (3:2–3) as a result of their conversion. Paul distinguishes the believers from "the Gentiles who do not know God" (4:5), "the others" (4:13), and from "outsiders" (4:12).

In subsequent letters, the designation of believer serves as a means both of establishing boundaries from the world and of indicating the social inclusion within the community. In 1 Corinthians Paul distinguishes regularly between the believers and the unbelievers, indicating that the world is divided between those who believe and those who do not (cf. 1 Cor. 1:21; 14:22; cf. 2 Cor. 6:15). However, the saving events are for "everyone who has faith/all who believe" (Rom. 1:16; 3:22; cf. Gal. 3:26). The community is thus defined by faithfulness rather than ethnic identity (cf. Rom. 10:4; 10:9, 14).

---

49. See Collins, "Church of the Thessalonians," 295: "It is not the believing individuals as such who are cited as examples for the believers of the Grecian provinces, rather it is the belief of the church as such which is exemplary."

50. Trebilco, *Self-Designations and Group Identity*, 74.

As the other New Testament witnesses indicate, the designation of the community as "the believers" did not begin with Paul. Its prominence in all four Gospels, Acts, the Pauline letters, Hebrews, and 1 Peter indicates that the terminology was a self-designation in the earliest church. While forms of *pist-* appear in the LXX, the word group has a prominence in the New Testament that is unmatched in Jewish literature. Trebilco makes the plausible suggestion that the special place of this word in the new vocabulary goes back to Jesus.[51]

The Elect

Just as *ekklēsia* is a term that places this gentile community within the story of Israel, other words that Paul employs identify the community with Israel. When he describes their conversion as their election (*eklogē*, NRSV "[God] has chosen you," 1 Thess. 1:4),[52] he employs a term that was fundamental to Israel's identity.[53] The election tradition is one of the great symbols of Israelite faith, as the use of *eklegein* and *eklektos* indicates. The Deuteronomist repeatedly recalls that God chose Israel, "the fewest of all peoples" (Deut. 7:7). God demonstrates the selection of Israel in the saving events that called it into existence (4:37) and in the covenant with succeeding generations (7:7–11). Indeed, the refrain throughout Deuteronomy is the description of Israel as the people whom God chose (12:5, 11, 18, 21; 16:6, 7, 11, 15, 16; 17:8, 10, 15) in separating Israel "out of all the peoples" (14:2).

Election is especially important in the exilic literature. The prophet promises the exiles that God "will again choose Israel" (Isa. 14:1). Second Isaiah repeatedly addresses the exiles as the people whom God has chosen, using forms of *eklegein* (Isa. 41:8–9; 43:10; 44:1–2; 49:7). Despite the humiliation that the exiles have suffered, they remain God's elect (*eklektos*, NRSV "chosen," Isa. 42:1; 43:20; 45:4; 65:9). In the apocalyptic literature the term refers to the eschatological people of God (*1 En.* 62:2; *T. Mos.* 10:10).[54]

The echo of Israel's election tradition is also evident in the identification of the community as "beloved by God" (1 Thess. 1:4), a phrase that is unusual in the New Testament but is characteristic of the election tradition. According to Deuteronomy, Moses tells the Israelites, "Because [God] loved your ancestors, he chose their descendants after them" (Deut. 4:37). God chose Israel, not because they were more numerous than the other nations, but because he

---

51. Ibid., 119–20.

52. *Eklogē*, used also in Acts 9:15; Rom. 9:11; 11:5, 7, 28, does not appear in the LXX, which expresses the concept of election with *eklegein* and *eklektos*.

53. N. T. Wright, *The New Testament and the People of God* (Minneapolis: Fortress, 1992), 259–68. Ferguson, *Church of Christ*, 78.

54. J. Eckert, "ἐκλεκτός," *EDNT* 1:417.

loved them (Deut. 7:7–8). God "set his heart in love on your ancestors alone and chose you, their descendants after them, out of all the peoples" (Deut. 10:15). Second Chronicles 20:7 indicates the importance of the designation of Israel as God's beloved. Jehoshaphat stands in the assembly (*ekklēsia*) and recalls that God gave the land to the descendants of Abraham, "God's beloved" (NRSV "friend").[55] Thus, in addressing the Thessalonians as "beloved by God," Paul equates them with the people of Israel.[56]

The Calling

In 1 Thessalonians, as in the Old Testament and later Jewish literature, the theme of God's election is inseparable from God's calling. The community has come into existence not by its own choice but because of God's call, which determines the lives of the people both in the present and in the future. Paul speaks once in the aorist tense to remind the readers that they were called (4:7) and twice in the present tense to describe God as the one who calls (2:12; 5:24). The two tenses reflect the dynamics of Paul's ecclesiology of God's calling. He reminds his readers of "God, who calls you into his own kingdom and glory" (2:12). God called them to a life of holiness (4:7). God is "the one who calls you" (5:24).

The twofold use of the present participle, "the one who calls you" (*ho kalōn hymas*, 2:12; 5:24), is both an epithet for God and a description of the origin of the church's existence. Paul employs this epithet in eschatological contexts to reaffirm the ultimate destiny of the community. According to 2:12, God calls the community "into his own kingdom and glory." That is, the church that is saved from the coming wrath (1:10) looks forward to God's "kingdom and glory." The kingdom, the dominant theme in the synoptic accounts of the message of Jesus, is employed only rarely by Paul, for whom the word applies to the final triumph of God (cf. 1 Cor. 15:24–25) at the parousia.[57] It forms a hendiadys with "glory" (*doxa*), which Paul also employs for the final triumph of God (cf. Rom. 5:2; 8:18). The coming of Christ at the parousia will usher in the kingdom of God (cf. 1 Thess. 2:19; 3:13; 4:15; 5:21–24). God's kingdom and glory are the ultimate destiny for believers who are found "blameless" (3:13; 5:23) at the parousia of Christ (cf. 3:13; 4:15; 4:23). As Paul says in later epistles, only those who avoid the vices listed in his catechetical instructions will "inherit the kingdom of God" (1 Cor. 6:9; Gal. 5:21; cf. Eph. 5:5). Consequently, Paul distinguishes sharply between those who are called into

55. Kraus, *Das Volk Gottes*, 127.
56. Ibid.
57. Collins, "Church of the Thessalonians," 290.

God's kingdom and "others" (*loipoi*) who have no hope (4:13; cf. 5:6). Thus the final destiny of Israel in God's kingdom (cf. Dan. 2:44) is the destiny of the gentile church.

While God's kingdom and glory are the church's future destiny, the community has experienced only persecution (*thlipsis*) since its founding (1:6; 3:3–4, 7). Undoubtedly, conversion to Paul's gospel resulted in the hostility from family members and neighbors in Thessalonica. Consequently, the believers have imitated Paul in his own suffering (1:6; 2:2). Recognizing the challenge that persecution presents to the faith of his converts, Paul sent Timothy to encourage the Thessalonians not to be "shaken by these persecutions" (3:3). He adds, "You yourselves know that this is what we are destined for" (3:3). In fact, during his initial visit he had "kept on telling" (cf. *proelegomen*) them that they would suffer.[58] Thus persecution is the prelude to the community's entrance into God's kingdom and glory.

The persecutions suffered by the church belong to the believers' ecclesiological identity, as Paul will explain in subsequent letters (see chaps. 3–5). His statement that "we are destined [*keimetha*] for this" suggests that he envisions the community's suffering within the context of their incorporation into Israel's story. *Keimai* suggests a destiny determined by God (cf. Luke 2:34; Phil. 1:16). In apocalyptic literature, *thlipsis* is the prelude to the final eschatological victory (Dan. 12:1; Hab. 3:16; Zeph. 1:15).[59] This apocalyptic understanding is reflected in the encouragement offered to new churches in Acts, according to which "it is through many persecutions (*thlipseōn*) that we must enter into the kingdom of God" (Acts 14:22). As an eschatological community, the Thessalonian church shares the destiny of Israel as it endures sufferings in anticipation of the kingdom of God.

As Paul indicates elsewhere, the kingdom becomes a reality in the final triumph of God (cf. 1 Cor. 15:24, 50), the place that the righteous enter (1 Cor. 6:19; Gal. 5:21; cf. Eph. 5:5) at the end. Paul uses the term rarely but speaks more frequently of the return of Christ. The election of the community in 1 Thessalonians is a call into the kingdom (2:12). Unlike the rest of society, the church waits for the Lord (4:13). Paul repeatedly describes the church as the waiting community (cf. 1:9–10; 3:18; 4:13–18; 5:23). God has destined the community not only to experience persecution (3:2–3) but also "for obtaining salvation" (5:9). The eschatological future is the motivation for the church's ethical conduct in the present (3:13; 5:1–11) and the source of their mutual

58. For the translation, see Abraham J. Malherbe, *The Letters to the Thessalonians: A New Translation with Introduction and Commentary* (New York: Doubleday, 2000), 194.
59. J. Kremer, "*Thlipsis*," *EDNT* 2:152.

encouragement (4:18; 5:11).[60] Unlike others, the Thessalonians were able to comfort other believers because they believed in God's eschatological purpose for them.[61]

Paul speaks of the kingdom primarily in paraenetic texts, indicating that entrance into the future kingdom requires appropriate moral conduct in the present. Thus the reference to the kingdom in 2:13 appears in a passage that recalls Paul's original catechetical instruction for communal moral norms. He had encouraged and urged and appealed to the Thessalonians to "lead a life worthy of God, who calls [the community] into his own kingdom and glory" (2:12). To "walk" (*peripatein*) recalls the term for ethical behavior in ancient Israel. To walk "worthily" is to live in such a way that the future kingdom impinges on the present.[62] Paul prays that the church will be sanctified at the coming of Christ (3:13) and reminds the Thessalonians that their conversion was the occasion when God called them (4:7) to holiness. Similarly, the gnomic statement that "the kingdom of God is not food and drink, but righteousness and peace and joy in the Holy Spirit" (Rom. 14:17) suggests that the future kingdom determines conduct in the present.

The Holy Ones

Election is a call to holiness (4:3, 7). Although Paul does not address the community as saints (*hagioi*),[63] as in the other letters (cf. Rom. 1:7; 1 Cor. 1:2; 2 Cor. 1:1; Phil. 1:1; Col. 1:2), holiness is a major theme. The repeated use of *hag-* indicates that holiness (*hagiasmos*) is a central focus of the letter. Indeed, the entire ethical section is framed by a reference to the community's holiness (4:3; 5:23).[64] Paul introduces the ethical section with the prayer that God will strengthen the hearts of the community "in holiness" (*hagiōsynē*) so that they may be blameless at the return of Christ (3:13) and concludes it with the benediction, "May the God of peace himself sanctify [*hagiasai*] you entirely; and may your spirit and soul and body be kept sound and blameless at the coming of our Lord Jesus Christ" (5:23). The ethical section of

60. See Collins, "Church of the Thessalonians," 291.
61. Malherbe, "God's New Family at Thessalonica," 123.
62. Holtz, *Der erste Brief an die Thessalonicher*, 92.
63. In the only reference to the *hagioi* in 1 Thessalonians, Paul refers to heavenly beings. On angels as heavenly beings, cf. Ps. 89:6, 8; Job 15:15; Dan. 4:10=4:17 LXX; cf. also *1 En.* 1:9; 12:2; 14:23; 20:1–7; 1 QH 3:22; 10:35; 1 QM 10:11. *Hagios* is used elsewhere as an adjective in reference to the Holy Spirit (1:5–6; 4:8) and holy kiss (5:26).
64. Maren Bohlen, *Sanctorum Communio: Die Christen als "Heilige" bei Paulus*, Beihefte zur Zeitschrift für die neutestamentliche Wissenschaft und die Kunde der älteren Kirche 183 (Berlin: de Gruyter, 2011), 115.

the letter (4:1–5:23) is a description of the holiness (cf. *hagiasmos* in 4:3, 7) to which God has called the community. Paul's prayer for the holiness of the community at the end time indicates the corporate nature of holiness. Paul envisions a final status for the corporate community and anticipates ultimate redemption only for the elect and holy (4:13; cf. 3:13); others "have no hope" (4:13). Holiness involves drawing sharp boundaries between the community and the surrounding society.

Paul uses the root word *hag-* in more than one dimension in 1 Thessalonians. In the prayers in 3:13 and 5:23, the word stands for the final status of believers, who have not yet reached that goal.[65] Paul uses the word in a similar way near the end of Romans, declaring that his ambition is to do priestly service to God in presenting the gentiles "sanctified by the Holy Spirit" (Rom. 15:16). In the meantime, holiness defines the practice of believers in the present, presenting sharp alternatives between modes of existence. The Thessalonians have been called to sanctification (*hagiasmos*) rather than uncleanness (*akatharsia*, 4:7). Sanctification becomes a reality in their avoidance of fornication and the sexual practices of the gentiles (4:3–5).

As with the other designations for the community in 1 Thessalonians, the focus on holiness identifies the church with Israel, whom God called to be holy (Lev. 19:2).[66] Indeed, the sexual ethics of 1 Thessalonians 4:3–8 and the call for brotherly love (4:9–12) are indebted to the holiness code (Lev. 17–26). This description of the members of the community as the saints is derived not only from the holiness code but also from apocalyptic literature, in which the eschatological people of God are the "holy ones."[67]

Paul instructs the community to have shared moral norms that are consistent with holiness (cf. 4:3–7) and not to behave "like the Gentiles" (4:5). While he divides the world between insiders and outsiders, the community does not live in total isolation; nor is its moral conduct totally countercultural, for he advises the believers to behave "respectably" (*euschēmonōs*) toward outsiders.

The designations for the church in 1 Thessalonians are indebted to the Old Testament and Jewish apocalyptic literature. Thus, although Paul does not describe the church as the new Israel, he addresses the church with terms that

---

65. Eckart David Schmidt, *Heilig ins Eschaton: Heiligung und Heiligkeit als eschatologische Konzeption im 1. Thessalonicherbrief*, Beihefte zur Zeitschrift für die neutestamentliche Wissenschaft 167 (Berlin: de Gruyter, 2010), 337, suggests that in 1 Thessalonians Paul avoids referring to the believers as saints (*hagioi*) because he consistently indicates that sanctification remains incomplete until the end.

66. See Andy Johnson, "The Sanctification of the Imagination in 1 Thessalonians," in *Holiness and Ecclesiology in the New Testament*, ed. Kent E. Brower and Andy Johnson (Grand Rapids: Eerdmans, 2007), 276–78.

67. Klaiber, *Rechtfertigung und Gemeinde*, 22–23.

would have been largely unintelligible to the gentile audience but were familiar designations for Israel. He resocializes the converts by identifying them with the eschatological people of God.

The Church as the People of God in the Other Letters

The identification of the *ekklēsia* as the chosen and the called characterizes Paul's view of the church in the other letters. Paul regularly describes the conversion of his readers as their calling. Just as Paul is an apostle only by God's calling (cf. *klētos*, Rom. 1:1; Gal. 1:15), the community owes its existence not to its own choice but to the calling of God (Rom. 1:6; 8:28; 1 Cor. 1:9, 26; 7:15; Gal. 1:6; 5:13), who has chosen the foolish things of the world to shame the wise (1 Cor. 1:27). Paul applies the ancient theme of God's election of Israel, an insignificant people by the world's standards (Deut. 7:7–11), to the gentile converts. As a consequence of God's choice, he describes the gentile communities of Galatia as "the Israel of God" (Gal. 6:16). Those who believe in Christ are the legitimate descendants of Abraham (3:7–29).

Paul develops the theme of election in Romans, as he addresses gentile converts whom he includes as the descendants of Abraham (Rom. 4:1–25; cf. Gal. 3:6–29). These gentile converts are "called" (Rom. 8:28, 30) and "elect" (8:33). This claim raises the questions that Paul seeks to answer in Romans 9–11: If the gentile churches are God's elect, what is the status of the physical descendants of Abraham? Has God's original election been nullified (9:6, 14)? Paul appeals to the election tradition to answer the question, maintaining that the presence of gentiles is evidence not of divine injustice (9:14) but of God's consistency in working out the divine purpose through election (9:11). The children of the promise rather than the physical descendants are the heirs of Abraham (9:8). The claim of Scripture that through Isaac their descendants will be named (literally "called," 9:7) applies to the gentiles. One is not saved by works but by the divine call (9:12). Indeed, Paul appeals to a classic election text (Hosea 2:23) to claim that God has called not only Jews but gentiles also: "Those who were not my people I will call 'my people,' and her who was not beloved I will call 'beloved'" (Rom. 9:25).

Although God has called both Jews and gentiles, a remnant of the Jews remains, and they are called by election (Rom. 11:7). The remainder of Romans 11 is an affirmation that the situation that now prevails is not permanent, for ultimately Israel will be saved (11:26), and God will be merciful on them as he has been on the gentiles. Indeed, according to Romans 9–11, God works out the divine plan through election and has now called gentiles in the same way that he once called the Jews. These same themes persist in the disputed letters (cf. Eph. 1:4; Col. 3:12; 2 Tim. 2:10; Titus 1:1) and among other New Testament writers.[68]

Holiness is also a consistent theme throughout Paul's letters. Paul describes holiness as a condition that has been attained at conversion. The perfect participle in 1 Corinthians 1:2 (*hēgiasmenos*) indicates a status that the Corinthians have already attained. Similarly, Paul urges the Corinthians to abstain from the sexual vices of Corinthian society because they have been sanctified (1 Cor. 6:11). In Romans Paul urges those who are "called to be saints" (1:7) to choose between two alternatives. Whereas they once presented their members as slaves of uncleanness to lawlessness, their task is now to present their members as slaves of righteousness for sanctification (6:19). Indeed, Paul suggests that they have already been freed from sin; they now bear fruit for sanctification (6:22). In each instance, sanctification is the term for the new status of believers and their radical separation from their past. This separation also implies separation from the surrounding culture.

As the alternative to sanctification, the image of uncleanness (Rom. 1:24; 6:19; 1 Thess. 4:7) provides further insight into the nature of holiness. Paul employs the imagery to indicate the radical separation of insiders and outsiders.[69] He describes the community as the temple of God, Israel's holiest place (1 Cor. 3:16; 2 Cor. 6:16). According to 2 Corinthians 6:14–7:1, the presence of God in the temple is the basis for the community to "come out from them" and touch nothing unclean (6:17). As a result, Paul urges the readers, "Let us cleanse ourselves [*katharisōmen heautous*] from every defilement of body and of spirit" (7:1).

Just as God called Israel to be a holy people (Lev. 19:2; Deut. 7:6), God also calls the church to holiness. Thus the use of forms of *hag-* are also rooted in Israel's self-understanding and are closely related to the concept of election. According to Deuteronomy 7:6, Israel is "holy to the Lord," for God has chosen Israel from all the nations of the earth. At the gathering at Sinai, God declares, "You shall be for me a priestly kingdom and a holy nation" (Exod. 19:6). In the holiness code (Lev. 17–26), the laws articulate all that is involved in being a holy people (Lev. 19:2). Elsewhere, the *hagioi* is used as a substantive to describe either the angels (cf. Job 15:15; Dan. 4:14; 7:27; Zech. 14:5) or the faithful people of God (Ps. 73:3 LXX; 82:4–5 LXX). The word is used with special frequency in *1 Enoch* and in the Dead Sea Scrolls for the eschatological people of God.[70]

---

68. See James 2:5; 1 Pet. 1:1; 2:4, 9; 2 Pet. 1:10; 2 John 1; Rev. 17:14.
69. Bohlen, *Sanctorum Communio*, 129.
70. Cf. *1 En.* 43:4; 51:2; 100:5; 1 QM 10:9–11. See Trebilco, *Self-Designations and Group Identity*, 122–28.

Hagioi, like the other designations for the community, identifies the gentile community with Israel. Paul's consistent use of the plural *hagioi* indicates that he includes all believers rather than a select few.[71] In some instances he addresses his letters to the "saints" (*hagioi*) rather than to the *ekklēsia* (cf. Rom. 1:7; Phil. 1:1; Col. 1:1), while in other instances he employs forms of both words (cf. 1 Cor. 1:2; 2 Cor. 1:1). "Holy ones" (*hagioi*) is apparently a synonym for *ekklēsia* and a significant aspect of the election tradition. Paul describes the gentile readers in Romans and 1 Corinthians as "called to be saints" (Rom. 1:7; 1 Cor. 1:2). The holy ones have been called (Rom. 8:30; 9:12, 24; 1 Cor. 1:9; 7:15, 17, 21; Gal. 1:6) and chosen (Rom. 8:33; 11:5, 7, 28; 1 Cor. 1:27).

The remarkable feature of Paul's doctrine of election is that he regularly employs the categories of election and holiness to describe gentile communities, using the same categories that functioned to separate Israel from the nations. In order to protect Israel's identity, writers of the Second Temple period appealed to the election traditions to ensure Israel's separation from the peoples. According to Nehemiah, the returned exiles reconstituted the community, appealing to Deuteronomy 23:1–2: "It was found written that no Ammonite or Moabite should ever enter the assembly of God" (Neh. 13:1). Paul engages in a remarkable tour de force when he employs the language of election to gentile churches to distinguish them from others—including the "Judeans" (NRSV "Jews") who persecute the followers of Christ among them (1 Thess. 2:14–15). For Paul, however, the foreigners constituted the renewed people of God.

This vocabulary would have been scarcely intelligible to the gentile audience. The churches founded by Paul lived in continuity with ancient Israel. Community formation thus involved the establishment of a new identity. Paul's gentile converts have been incorporated into Israel's identity. By resocializing the community with categories drawn from Scripture, Paul indicates that the church is nothing new but has deep roots in Israel's story. To be God's *ekklēsia* is to be called and loved by God and separated from the peoples.

Children of Light

Paul's description of the Thessalonian community as "children of light and children of the day" (1 Thess. 5:5) also echoes the election traditions of Israel. In Jewish literature the designation of Israel as "sons" or "children" is common. In the Dead Sea Scrolls, the image of sonship is used to describe

71. Trebilco, *Self-Designations and Group Identity*, 128.

both the "sons of light" (1 QS 1:9; 2:16; 3:13, 24–25; 1 QM 1:3, 9, 11, 13) and the "sons of darkness" (1 QS 1:10; 1 QM 1:17, 10, 16; 17:8; 1 QH 6:29).[72] As in Jewish literature, Paul uses the term to establish boundaries between the community and the rest of the world, who live in darkness (1 Thess. 5:4–6).

The Family of God

Paul develops the imagery of the family in distinctive ways. The description of believers as "children [literally "sons"] of light" and "children of the day" suggests that they are God's children.[73] Paul develops the image of the family in a variety of ways, although he never speaks of the church as a family. God is the Father (1:1) and Jesus is his Son (1:10). Paul uses the language of the family to describe his relationship to them. When he was with them, he was gentle, "like a nurse tenderly caring for her own children" (2:7).[74] In this role he shared not only the gospel but his very self, because the Thessalonians were "beloved" (2:8–9; *agapētoi*, NRSV "very dear"). He was also like a father instructing the children about proper behavior (2:11–12). When he was absent from them, he was "orphaned" (*aporphanisthentes*), longing to see their face (2:17). As a parent he regards them as his glory and joy (2:20).

The *ekklēsia* in Christ, unlike the synagogue, is not an *ethnos*,[75] a nation in the conventional sense, but an assembly of people from diverse backgrounds. The persecution (*thlipsis*, 1:6; 3:3) that accompanied their conversion undoubtedly involved the loss of family relationships.[76] Consequently, Paul discovers in family life the most appropriate image to describe a community composed of those who were alienated from their closest relatives. While this image is known in Greek and Jewish communities for those who are not physical relatives,[77] its

72. Eduard Schweizer, "υἱός," *TDNT* 8:359.
73. Reidar Aasgaard, *"My Beloved Brothers and Sisters!" Christian Siblingship in Paul*, JSNTSup 265 (London: T&T Clark, 2004), 121.
74. On the rendering of *trophos* as "wet nurse," see Malherbe, "God's New Family at Thessalonica," 121.
75. See my *Moral Formation according to Paul*, 56.
76. See Sandnes, *New Family*, 21–31. The story *Joseph and Aseneth* describes the alienation from families that new converts to Judaism faced. Aseneth cries out, "All people have come to hate me, and on top of those my father and mother, because I, too, have come to hate their gods and have destroyed them. . . . Therefore my father and mother and my whole family have come to hate me and said, 'Aseneth is not our daughter'" (11:4; translation by C. Burchard in *OTP*). See also Abraham J. Malherbe, *Paul and the Thessalonians: The Philosophic Tradition of Pastoral Care* (Philadelphia: Fortress, 1987), 34–52; Kraus, *Das Volk Gottes*, 82–83.
77. See Trebilco, *Self-Designations and Group Identity*, 16–18, for the use of "brother" at Qumran and in other ancient religious communities. Cf. 1 QS 6:10, 22. For *adelphos* as a designation for fellow Israelites, see Ps. 22:23, where "your brothers" is identical with *qahal*,

frequency is remarkable in the Pauline letters.[78] It has an especially significant place in 1 Thessalonians.

The most common use of the image is the identification of believers as siblings to Paul and to each other. Indeed, Paul addresses the readers as *adelphoi* thirteen times—the highest frequency of the word in all his letters.[79] He describes various believers as brothers (cf. 3:2; 4:6), and he extends that term to include believers in Macedonia (4:10). As a comprehensive term for the members of the community, *adelphoi* includes not only the men but also the women and children.[80] The family image for a community composed of people from different ethnic groups and social strata was unparalleled in antiquity.

The image of the family shapes the behavior of the community and determines their relationships with each other. Paul's instructions are largely about the treatment of siblings, the avoidance of familiar sibling quarrels, and the appropriation of family responsibilities. Indeed, Paul's frequent use of "one another" reflects the family relationship and the solidarity of the community.[81] Paul prays that the Thessalonians "will abound in love for one another and for all," just as he abounds in love for them (3:12); he has taught them the value of "love of the brothers and sisters" (*philadelphia*, literally "brotherly love")—that they should "love one another" (4:9) as well as the siblings in Macedonia. He challenges the readers to "encourage one another" (4:18; 5:11), to "build up each other" (5:11), and to seek the good of one another (5:15). The reciprocal pronoun "one another" (*allēlous*) suggests two dimensions of communal identity that shape the moral conduct of the readers. In the first place, it suggests that believers care for "one another" without regard for social position. In the second place, the term indicates the equal status of all members within the group.[82] The term indicates the community's primary

the cultic community. The frequency of *adelphos* in early Christian communities distinguishes it from the ancient associations, in which the word was rare. See Eva Ebel, *Die Attraktivität früher christlicher Gemeinden: Die Gemeinde von Korinth im Spiegel griechisch-römischer Vereine*, WUNT 2/178 (Tübingen: Mohr Siebeck, 2004), 211; Klaiber, *Rechtfertigung und Gemeinde*, 25.

78. Reidar Aasgaard, "'Role Ethics' in Paul: The Significance of the Sibling Role for Paul's Ethical Thinking," *New Testament Studies* 48 (2002): 516.

79. Malherbe, "God's Family at Thessalonica," 122.

80. Pilhofer, "Περὶ δὲ τῆς φιλαδελφίας," 149. In letters where Paul specifically mentions women of the congregation, he also addresses the whole church as *adelphoi* (cf. 1 Cor. 1:10–11, 26; 5:11; 7:12–14; Phil. 4:1–2).

81. Thompson, *Moral Formation*, 57.

82. Michael Wolter, "Die ethische Identität christlicher Gemeinden in neutestamentlicher Zeit," in *Woran orientiert sich Ethik*, ed. Wilfried Härle and Reiner Preul, Marburger Jahrbuch Theologie 13 (Marburg: Elwert, 2001), 86.

focus on the care for siblings in the new family rather than the care for others outside the group.[83]

Like the terminology of election and holiness, the sibling image distinguishes members of the family from "outsiders" (4:9–12) and "others" (4:13). While Paul does not limit loving action to insiders (cf. 3:12), his primary concern is the care for the siblings. Within the intimacy of the community, he instructs men not to wrong a brother by making advances toward his wife (4:6). The Thessalonians' task is to honor those who lead (5:12–13), be at peace within the community (5:13), encourage the fainthearted (5:14), and help the weak. All of these were the responsibilities of family members toward each other in antiquity. Those who had formerly been strangers to each other have now transcended the barriers of class and ethnicity to take on a common identity as family.[84]

As in ancient Israel, the community's identity also determines its ethical norms. Its sexual conduct reflects both its call to be a holy people (4:3, 7; cf. Lev. 18–19) and the sibling relationship of the members, as Paul indicates in the instruction not to defraud a brother in sexual matters (4:6). Throughout the epistle, moral conduct is an expression of the relationship among siblings. "What they are (i.e., siblings) has consequences for how they are (their ethical praxis)."[85] The task of the siblings was to maintain the family honor, to "behave properly toward outsiders" (4:12).[86] Indeed, Paul's frequent use of "one another" reflects the family relationship and the solidarity of the community.[87] As siblings, they practice "brotherly love" (*philadelphia*), a word that was used in antiquity for love within a natural family, because they have been taught to "love one another" (4:9).

The image of family also shapes the emergence of leadership and polity in the Thessalonian church. The epistle never refers to priests, elders, pastors, or any other title to designate recognized leaders.[88] The community does not come together in a hierarchical relationship, for the familial relationship creates the members' reciprocal care for each other.

While Paul employs a variety of images for the church, the image of the family is predominant throughout his correspondence. He addresses the readers

---

83. Cf. Lucian, *The Passing of Peregrinus*, 13. "Their first lawgiver persuaded them that they are all brothers of one another after they have transgressed once for all by denying the Greek gods and by worshipping that crucified sophist himself and living under his laws" (trans. A. M. Harmon, LCL).

84. Thompson, *Moral Formation*, 56; Aasgaard, *"Beloved Brothers and Sisters,"* 307.

85. Klaus Schäfer, *Gemeinde als "Bruderschaft": Ein Beitrag zum Kirchenverständnis des Paulus*, Europaische Hochschulschriften (New York: Peter Lang, 1989), 25.

86. Thompson, *Moral Formation*, 57.

87. Schäfer, *Gemeinde als "Bruderschaft,"* 27.

88. See chap. 8.

as *adelphoi* in all the letters, refers to individuals as *adelphos* (cf. 2 Cor. 1:1; 2:13; 8:18, 22; Phil. 2:25), and assumes that his readers will regard each other as *adelphoi*. Thus his instructions commonly presuppose the family relationship. A brother should not stand in judgment against a brother (Rom. 14:10), despise him (14:11), or place a stumbling block in his path (15:13, 15; cf. 1 Cor. 8:11–13). Because family relationships establish boundaries from others, siblings should not take members of the family to court before unbelievers (1 Cor. 6:1–11). Nor should siblings be guilty of jealousy, strife, or quarreling (cf. Gal. 5:19–21).[89]

The image of the family is not only Paul's predominant designation for the church; it is also the predominant image for the church in the New Testament. In Acts, the image is sometimes used as a designation for the people of Israel (2:29, 37; 3:17, 22; 7:2, 13, 23, 25–26, 37; 13:15, 26, 38; 15:7), but it is also used to distinguish those Christ believers from the "unbelieving Jews" (14:2; 16:2, 40; 17:6, 10, 14; 18:18, 27; 21:7, 17, 20; 28:14–15). The author of Hebrews addresses his readers as "holy brothers and sisters" (3:1) and describes Jesus as one who was "like his brothers and sisters in every respect" (2:17). He addresses the social alienation of his people, recalling previous acts of compassion for each other (6:9–10; 10:32–34) that were normally the tasks of the family. James uses *adelphos* nineteen times to describe both his relationship to his readers[90] and his readers' relationships as siblings who care for each other in times of need (cf. 2:14–26) and do not speak evil of each other (5:7–9). Although 1 Peter uses *adelphos* only once (5:12), the family imagery is pervasive, for the community belongs to a "family of believers" (*adelphotēs*, 2:17; 5:9; cf. 4:17), and they assume the family responsibility of caring for one another in the context of hostility from outside (1:22–25). The image is also common in the Johannine letters (cf. 1 John 2:9–11; 3:10–16; 4:20; 3 John 3, 5, 10) and in Revelation (12:10; 19:10).

While the household setting of early Christianity influenced the community's self-understanding as family, this image precedes the Christian movement. The address to Jewish listeners in Acts as *adelphoi* (cf. Acts 2:29, 37; 7:2) probably reflects common usage. Jesus's use of kinship language to describe the disciples (cf. Mark 3:31–35; 10:29–30) refines the term by suggesting kinship based on loyalty to him and the kingdom. This family relationship did not include all Israel but included only those who followed Jesus.[91]

---

89. On these vices as common hindrances to family life, see Philip Francis Esler, "Family Imagery and Christian Identity in Galatians 5:13 to 6:10," in *Constructing Early Christian Families: Family as Social Reality and Metaphor*, ed. Halvor Moxnes (London: Routledge, 1997), 134–38.
90. He uses the vocative *adelphoi* fifteen times.
91. Lohfink, *Jesus and Community*, 39–44.

First Thessalonians as a Window
to Paul's Ecclesiology

As Paul's first letter to a community that he founded, 1 Thessalonians offers an important window into his ecclesiology. Inasmuch as this letter repeats the catechesis that Paul offered to these new converts, it reflects the self-understanding that he gave to converts who had abandoned the previous sources of identity. Paul offers a coherent vision of the church that will distinguish it from all other *ekklēsiai* in Thessalonica. These gentile converts do not comprise a new community but now belong to the people of God whose roots lie in ancient Israel. Inasmuch as Paul maintains this image throughout his correspondence, it is his most foundational metaphor for the church. As I shall demonstrate in the next chapter, Paul transforms the image with his Christology. Indeed, his correspondence consistently demonstrates the significance of Christ for the church's identity as the people of God. Gentile converts are the children of Abraham (Rom. 4:3–22; Gal. 3:7–9, 26) and the descendants of Isaac (Rom. 9:6–13; Gal. 4:21–31) and of the ancestors in the wilderness (1 Cor. 10:1–11). They are the children of the promise to ancient Israel and the people in whom the new covenant promised by Jeremiah (31:31–34) has become a reality (2 Cor. 3:6). This gentile community is the "Israel of God" (Gal. 6:16), in contrast to the "Israel according to the flesh" (1 Cor. 10:18; NRSV "people of Israel").

As the *ekklēsia* of the Thessalonians, the believers are not only a local community. They also belong to a larger movement that includes "the churches of God . . . in Judea" (1 Thess. 2:14) as well as *ekklēsiai* of God in many other cities. Their roots in Israel are so deep that they now regard outsiders as gentiles (4:5). Paul has taught them to identify themselves as the elect, the holy, the believers, and as brothers and sisters—terms that are borrowed from Israel's Scripture and Jewish tradition.

God has chosen (1:6) a people rather than isolated individuals. Consequently, the church that exists because of God's sovereign choice is neither the result of a social contract between persons nor the result of consumer choice. It is composed of those who have responded to the divine initiative, receiving the word (1:6) and being incorporated into the community through faith. Because God is the one who chooses a people, the church is composed not of those whom we have chosen but of all who believe.

While they designate themselves with the categories from Scripture, the converts are not, like Israel, an *ethnos* but a community united only by their reception of the gospel that Paul preached. Faith that Jesus died and arose (4:14) unites them and separates them from the synagogue and from the rest of society, drawing hostility from family and friends. In place of the alienation from their own families, Paul brings them together as a family. As a diverse community united only by the reception of the message and a common conviction, they are unparalleled in antiquity.

Paul's attempt at community formation leaves numerous unanswered questions that will emerge in future correspondence. If gentiles have been incorporated into Israel, what is the status of what Paul will later call Israel "according to the flesh" (*kata sarka*, Rom. 9:3)? Can gentile converts who have not been circumcised and do not observe the food laws actually sit at the table with Jewish Christ believers? Who are the children of Abraham? In Galatians, Paul will develop the family imagery further, arguing that those who believe in Jesus Christ are the real children of Abraham and God's heirs (Gal. 3:7–4:6) and that the truth of the gospel requires Jewish and gentile believers to sit down at the same table. In 1 Corinthians, Paul will confront the issue of whether the rich and the poor can come together at the same table with mutual respect. The major task of Paul's letters is to define the nature of the community of believers in response to those who attempt to maintain old models of community. Paul has only introduced a sketch in 1 Thessalonians that he will fill out as he encounters new questions.

CONCLUSION: COMMUNITY FORMATION THEN AND NOW

Paul's attempt at community formation in a pagan culture provides insights for the church in a post-Christian culture. Paul knows nothing of the individual Christian, for people respond to the gospel by living in communities. As people united by the confession of the death and resurrection of Christ (1 Thess. 4:14), the church is unlike other communities, which are defined by ethnicity, gender, social status, and the personal choice of the members. If the church lives by its confession, it will discover, with the Thessalonians, that the majority culture is likely to reject it and to respond with disdain or hostility. If we are disturbed that the Christian faith has lost its privileged place in Western society, the Thessalonian church is a reminder that the first communities had no expectation of public acceptance. From the beginning, the church has lived in tension with its culture because it was brought together by beliefs that most people do not accept. The task of the Christian community is to be faithful under difficult circumstances and to define itself by its basic confession rather than by the standards common to other communities.

Like all communities, the church is united by a shared narrative.[92] A faithful

---

92. See Grenz, "Ecclesiology," 255: "The role of a group as a community of reference is connected to its ability to forge a link to both the past and the future." He adds, "A community has

community acknowledges that its confession of Jesus Christ is part of a long narrative of Israel's story and recognizes its indebtedness to Israel. It retells Israel's story, speaks the dialect that it has learned from Israel's Scripture, and makes moral choices based on that narrative. Indeed, the end of the narrative (1 Thess. 4:13–5:11) determines the common life of the community in the present. The community does not exist by consumer choice; rather, it has been chosen by God and lives among others who were also chosen to live out that narrative. Thus this shared narrative establishes the solidarity of the members with each other. As participants in Israel's story, the church is destined for both suffering (3:2–3) and ultimate vindication (4:13–5:11). Its ultimate goal is to be sanctified in Christ (3:13; 5:23).

A church that participates in the ancient narrative of Israel will resist becoming a consumer commodity that exists to meet popular demand. As a participant in Israel's story, the church experiences exile and restoration, disappointment and hope. Its task is to be faithful under all circumstances, even when it appears not to be successful. Adoption into ancient Israel brings believers together from all cultures into a common inheritance.[93] With its roots in ancient Israel, the church does not identify itself with popular ideology, the national interest, or political causes, for the confession that brought it into existence transcends other loyalties.

Commitment to the Christian confession creates boundaries between the church and the dominant culture. A community defined by its belief that Jesus rose from the dead and will return (1 Thess. 4:13–18) is a community of hope, in contrast to the majority culture (cf. 4:13). The hope for God's coming kingdom provides the basis for ethical seriousness (cf. 5:1–11) to live "worthy of God, who calls [the community] into his own kingdom and glory" (2:12). Thus the community's cohesion is evident in its moral behavior. It rejects the majority culture's view of sexuality and lives in holiness. It practices self-giving on behalf of both believers and nonbelievers. The members participate in building up the community.

We know nothing about Paul's expectations for the growth of these communities. Paul's catechesis is aimed at ensuring that the members live "worthily of God" by accepting the behavioral norms that define this community. Indeed, Paul's praise of their "work of faith and labor of love and steadfastness of hope" (1 Thess. 1:3) reflects his goal for the church. Paul

---

a history; in fact, it is, in an important sense, constituted by that history, a history that begins in the past and extends into the future." On the role of memory in establishing community, see Stanley Hauerwas, *A Community of Character: Toward a Constructive Christian Social Ethic* (Notre Dame, IN: University of Notre Dame Press, 1981), 53–71.

93. N. T. Wright, *Paul and the Faithfulness of God* (Minneapolis: Fortress, 2013), 1023–24.

assumes that their transformed lives will make an impression on the rest of society (cf. 4:12).

The faithfulness of the community requires the cohesion and solidarity of members who did not choose each other. The church is not only the place where the word is preached and the sacraments are administered, but it is also a holy people who live in continuity with ancient Israel. It is also a family in which the members encourage one another, support the weakest among them, and continue to recall the confession that brought them into existence. Life in this community requires the intimacy of brotherhood and mutual support among people who were formerly isolated from each other by the barriers of social class and ethnicity. Thus both the "church of the Thessalonians" and the church at any other location is God's creation, a community unlike other communities.

❖ 2 ❖

NOT JUST ANY BODY

The Church and Paul's Corporate Christology

Paul's basic catechesis, as 1 Thessalonians indicates, aims to create a common identity and ethos for the disparate individuals who have received his message. As I argued in chapter 1, the dominant image for this gentile church is that of Israel, the people of God. Although Paul rarely uses the term "people of God" or "Israel" (cf. Gal. 6:16), he maintains throughout his correspondence the images drawn from Israel's self-understanding, as the pervasiveness of the designations *ekklēsia* and "saints" indicates (cf. Rom. 1:7; 1 Cor. 1:2; 2 Cor. 1:1; Phil. 1:1; Philem. 7; cf. Eph. 1:1; Col. 1:2).[1] However, the image of the people of God is not sufficient for defining a community that is not constituted by circumcision as an entrance requirement.[2] The communities live not only in continuity with Israel but also in a discontinuity that resulted in separation from the synagogue. The discontinuity is rooted in the christological dimension that is expressed in the prepositions that link Christ and the church. Believers have been baptized "into Christ" (*eis christon*, Rom. 6:3; Gal. 3:27; cf. 1 Cor. 10:2; 12:13) and died "with Christ" (*syn christō*, Rom. 6:8; cf. 6:6; 8:17; Gal.

---

1. Wolfgang Kraus concludes that the theme of the people of God is the basic foundation of Paul's ecclesiology. Both the designations for the people (saints, elect, children of God, seed of Abraham) and the themes of the outpouring of the Holy Spirit and of ethics as sanctification are derived from the concept of the people of God. *Das Volk Gottes*, 352.

2. Udo Schnelle, *Apostle Paul: His Life and Theology* (Grand Rapids: Baker Academic, 2003), 564.

51

2:19; 2 Tim. 2:11). As a result, they now exist "in Christ" (*en christō*), "in him" (cf. 2 Cor. 5:21; Phil. 3:9) and "in the body of Christ" (Rom. 12:1–8; 1 Cor. 12:12–27). They are also "of Christ" (*christou*, 1 Cor. 3:23; Gal. 3:29). In addition, Paul affirms that Christ (or the Spirit) dwells (*oikei*) "in" believers (Rom. 8:9–10; 1 Cor. 3:16; 2 Cor. 6:16; cf. Gal. 4:19). Thus, as Wolfgang Kraus maintains, two major strands intersect in Pauline ecclesiology: one is the church as the people of God; the other is the church as the body of Christ.[3] Interpreters debate which of the two strands has priority.[4] Jürgen Roloff employs the geometric image of an ellipse to describe the relationship between the two focal points, maintaining that the interpreter must observe the relationship between them.[5]

Because the image of the body of Christ appears in only two of the undisputed letters of Paul, it is scarcely the central feature of Paul's ecclesiology. However, the image belongs to a larger complex of Pauline themes. As I will argue in this chapter, the body of Christ is an extension of "in Christ," which reflects the corporate Christology that is evident in the prepositional and syntactical phrases that link Christ and the church. This usage is an essential aspect of Paul's ecclesiology.[6]

IN CHRIST

The phrase "in Christ" has many dimensions for Paul. While the phrase is probably not Paul's creation,[7] its frequency indicates its central place in his theology.[8] The phrase appears eighty-three times in the Pauline corpus (including the disputed letters). Outside the Pauline corpus it appears only in 1 Peter (5:14).[9] Paul also employs the equivalent phrase "in the Lord" (*en kyriō*) forty-seven times and "in him" six times.[10]

3. Kraus, *Das Volk Gottes*, 6–7.
4. See Jürgen Roloff (*Die Kirche im Neuen Testament*, Grundrisse zum Neuen Testament, Das Neue Testament Deutsch Ergänzungsreihe 10 [Göttingen: Vandenhoeck & Ruprecht, 1993], 90) for a summary of the debate.
5. Ibid.
6. See Stephen Anthony Cummins, "Divine Life and Corporate Christology: God, Messiah Jesus, and the Covenant Community in Paul," in *Messiah in the Old and New Testaments*, ed. Stanley E. Porter (Grand Rapids: Eerdmans, 2007), 201.
7. Schnelle, *Apostle Paul*, 481, points to pre-Pauline formulae (1 Cor. 1:30; Gal. 3:26–27) as evidence that the phrase originated before Paul.
8. Ibid.
9. James D. G. Dunn, *The Theology of Paul the Apostle* (Grand Rapids: Eerdmans, 1998), 396.
10. See Lars Klehn, "Die Verwendung von ἐν Χριστῷ bei Paulus: Erwägungen zu den Wandlungen in der paulinischen Theologie," *Biblische Notizen* 74 (1994): 68.

En christō and *en kyriō* do not have a single technical meaning. In some instances the phrases are used instrumentally under the influence of the Hebrew preposition *b* (cf. Rom. 1:2, 17; 5:2, 15, 21; 10:6, 9; 12:13; 15:30; 1 Cor. 11:25).[11] The instrumental, or causal, use is clearly evident in the statement that "in Christ God was reconciling the world to himself" (2 Cor. 5:19),[12] where "in Christ" is indistinguishable from "through Christ."[13] Indeed, "in Christ" (*en christō*) is often used with the parallel construction "through Christ" (*dia christou*).[14] In other instances it describes the manner in which an action takes place, as when Paul says, "I am speaking the truth in Christ" (Rom. 9:1). In numerous instances Paul uses the phrase as a formula to mean "Christian" (Rom. 16:3, 7, 9, 10; 2 Cor. 12:2; Gal. 1:22; Phil. 1:1; 4:21; Philem. 23).[15] The dominant and original sense, however, is local, and in this sense it refers to a sphere of being (cf. 1 Cor. 1:30; 15:18, 22; 2 Cor. 5:17; Gal. 3:26–29).[16] This local usage becomes a central feature of Paul's ecclesiology, for it suggests the relationship between the believers and Christ and their relationship to each other. Communion with Christ is inseparable from communion with fellow believers.[17] Paul clarifies the expression in situations that call for him to expand on the meaning.

11. A. J. M. Wedderburn, "Some Observations on Paul's Use of the Phrases 'in Christ' and 'with Christ,'" *Journal for the Study of the New Testament* 25 (1985): 86. For the range of meanings of *en*, see Murray J. Harris, *Prepositions and Theology in the Greek New Testament: An Essential Reference Resource for Exegesis* (Grand Rapids: Zondervan, 2012), 123–25.

12. Mark A. Seifrid, "In Christ," in *Dictionary of Paul and His Letters*, ed. Gerald F. Hawthorne, Ralph P. Martin, and Daniel G. Reid (Downers Grove, IL: InterVarsity, 1993), 433.

13. Wedderburn, "Some Observations," 89, lists the following passages: Rom. 8:2, "The law of the Spirit of life has freed you in/through Christ Jesus"; Rom. 12:5, "So in/through Christ we the many are one body"; 1 Cor. 1:2, "Those consecrated in/through Christ Jesus"; 1 Cor. 1:4, "God's grace given to you in/through Christ Jesus"; 1 Cor. 1:5, "In every place enriched in/through him"; 1 Cor. 15:22, "In/through Christ will all be made alive"; Gal. 2:4, "The freedom which we have in/through Christ Jesus"; Gal. 3:28, "You are all one in/through Christ Jesus"; Phil. 3:14, "God's upward call in/through Christ Jesus"; Phil. 4:7, "God's peace . . . will guard your hearts and thoughts in/through Christ Jesus"; Phil. 4:13, "I can do everything in/through him who strengthens me"; Phil. 4:19, "My God will fulfill your every need . . . in/through Christ Jesus."

14. Cf. Rom. 5:21/6:23; 7:25/8:39; 1 Cor. 15:21/22; 2 Cor. 5:18/19; 1 Thess. 4:14/16. Cited in Klaiber, *Rechtfertigung und Gemeinde*, 86.

15. Ibid., 86n70.

16. Schnelle, *Apostle Paul*, 481. For the complexity of usages of *en*, see Constantine R. Campbell, *Paul and Union with Christ: An Exegetical and Theological Study* (Grand Rapids: Zondervan, 2012), 68: "Without question, the preposition *en* is the most significant and, at the same time, the most perplexing of the relevant prepositions." See also BDAG 326 for the variety of usages of *en*. Campbell notes that only the context determines the precise meaning of *en*. In numerous other instances the meaning of *en christō* is debated. Schnelle (*Apostle Paul*, 481) includes "in Christ" in Phil. 2:1, 5 as denoting a location, while Campbell (104–6) maintains that the phrase is to be rendered "because of Christ" in 2:1 and the mind that Christ has "within himself" in 2:5.

17. Schnelle, *Apostle Paul*, 481. See also David G. Horrell, "'No Longer Jew or Greek': Paul's Corporate Christology and the Construction of Christian Community," in *Christology,*

"In Christ" and "with Christ" in 1 Thessalonians

While the church of the Thessalonians shared Israel's identity as the elect and the holy, its identity as "the church of the Thessalonians in God the Father and the Lord Jesus Christ" inevitably separated it from the synagogue. Thus the intersection of the concepts of the people of God and the people in Christ appears in Pauline thought from the beginning. Indeed, the christological dimension also separated the Thessalonians from the larger society, evoking hostility (1:6; 2:14; 3:2–4) from their fellow countrymen (2:14) and creating a sharp demarcation between the congregation and the "others" (4:13; 5:6). As a repetition of Paul's earlier catechesis (cf. 4:1–2, 9; 5:1), 1 Thessalonians offers a window into the christological foundations of the community's identity. The people are the *ekklēsia* "in God the Father and the Lord Jesus Christ" (1:1), and they have become imitators of the "churches of God in Christ Jesus in Judea" (2:14).

Although "in Christ" appears elsewhere in 1 Thessalonians in a modal (3:8) or instrumental (4:1; cf. 5:12) sense,[18] it has a local meaning in 1:1 and 2:14, indicating that both the Thessalonian community and the churches of Judea have been incorporated into Christ, the sphere in which they live. Both communities suffer for their faith (1:6; 2:14; 3:2–3), joining in a community of suffering with Christ.[19]

Paul develops this theme further in 4:13–5:11 in response to the events in Thessalonica. The frame of the passage—"so that you may not grieve" (4:13) and "encourage one another" (5:11)—suggests that the believers are disoriented because some have died. The exhortations "encourage one another" (4:18) and "encourage one another and build up each other" (5:11) indicate the communal identity of the readers. The central focus of Paul's response is his appeal to the community's creed, which he cites in variant forms near the beginning of this section (4:14) and at the end (5:10):

since [*ei*] we believe that Jesus died and rose again (4:14)

our Lord Jesus Christ, who died for us (5:9–10)

The claim that Christ "died for us" is the earliest reference in the New Testament to the interpretation of the death of Jesus "for us" (cf. "for our sins" in

---

Controversy, and Community: New Testament Essays in Honour of David R. Catchpole, ed. David G. Horrell and Christopher M. Tuckett (Leiden: Brill, 2000), 325.

18. Udo Schnelle, *Gerechtigkeit und Christusgegenwart: Vorpaulinische und paulinische Tauftheologie* (Göttingen: Vandenhoeck & Ruprecht, 1982), 112–13.

19. Ibid.

1 Cor. 15:3).[20] Paul does not elaborate on the meaning of "for us." The purpose clause in 5:10 ("so that whether we are awake or asleep we may live with him") indicates only that the death of Jesus is the presupposition for future life with him. The solidarity of Jesus in dying "for us," together with Jesus's resurrection, is the basis of the claim that believers will share in his resurrection. This solidarity is the basis for the conclusion that Paul draws from the creed:

> even so, through Jesus, God will bring with him those who have died (4:14)

> so that whether we are awake or asleep we may be with him (5:10)

Paul's use of prepositions indicates the deep solidarity of believers with Christ. "Through [*dia*] Jesus" God has acted to save (5:9), and "through [*dia*] Jesus" God will bring the people to be "with [Jesus]" (4:14). Indeed, the threefold "with him" (or "with the Lord," 4:14, 17; 5:10) speaks of the future hope in which both those who have died and those who are alive will be with Jesus. In the present Paul challenges his readers to "stand firm in the Lord" (3:8; cf. Phil. 4:1). The phrase suggests that Christ is the sphere or location in which they live.[21]

The foundation for the comfort that Paul offers to grieving people is the solidarity of believers with Christ, which is inseparable from the solidarity of believers with each other. Those who will be "with him" in the future are "in him" (1 Thess. 1:1) in the present. The first-person plural indicates the collective identity of the people as members of a community. Indeed, Paul anticipates the later idea of the *sanctorum communio* by affirming that both "we who are alive" (4:17; i.e., those who are in Christ, 1:1) and those who are "dead in Christ" (4:16) will be "with him" in the future.[22] The church came into being "through him" in the past, lives "in him" in the present, and will be "with him" in the future.

Because they are a community of hope in Christ, the believers "encourage one another and build up each other" (5:11; cf. 4:18). The ethical advice that

20. Daniel G. Powers, *Salvation through Participation: An Examination of the Notion of the Believers' Corporate Unity with Christ in Early Christian Soteriology*, Contributions to Biblical Exegesis and Theology 29 (Leuven: Peeters, 2001), 38.

21. Campbell, *Paul and Union with Christ*, 161–62.

22. See Schnelle, *Gerechtigkeit und Christusgegenwart*, 114: "When Paul designates the deceased church members as *hoi nekroi en christō*, he emphasizes that for them death cannot be the end of the fellowship with Christ that began in baptism" (my translation). Here, as in 1:1, "in Christ" is to be understood in a local sense as the sphere of being in which the believer is incorporated. Thus Paul indicates the continuity of existence from the time that the believers were incorporated in Christ until the time when they will be "with Christ."

Paul offers in 5:12–22 rests on their common hope for the return of Christ. They recognize their leaders (5:12–13), admonish the disorderly, live together in peace (5:14), and bear with the weak (5:14) because they all share a common destiny in the kingdom of God (cf. 2:12). Existence "in Christ" is a life in the company of others who share in the destiny of Christ (2:14). Ecclesiology and Christology are thus inseparable. The church is unlike all other communities, because the people died "with Christ" and now live "in Christ." Thus the individual believer apart from the community is inconceivable to Paul.

The Mind of Christ: Incorporation in Christ in Philippians

In Philippians, Paul writes "to all the saints in Christ Jesus" (1:1), identifying them with the people of God. Their group identity is evident in the opening thanksgiving (1:3–11), in which Paul expresses gratitude for the community. His repeated use of the plural "you" (ten times) in this section indicates his close relationship with the entire church. Paul is confident that the God who began a good work among them ("among you") at their conversion will bring it to completion (1:6). Thus as a community they are the new humanity in whom God is at work. Paul longs to see the community (1:8, "all of you") and prays for their ethical formation (1:9–11). Because the community is not yet complete (1:9–11), Paul offers in this paraenetic letter guidance toward their ultimate goal. As people who have not reached the goal, they are citizens of heaven (3:20), living out their citizenship (1:27, *politeuesthe*) in a strange land by standing together in one spirit and one mind.

The Philippians live in Christ (1:1) because they have been incorporated into him.[23] The "peace of God, which surpasses all understanding, will guard [their] hearts and [their] minds in Christ Jesus" (4:7). Paul is a model for the Philippians in his desire that his "boasting in Christ Jesus" (1:26) will abound at the return of Christ and in his intention to be "found in him" (3:9), not having a righteousness of his own. In reaching this goal only through sharing the sufferings of Jesus and being conformed to his death (3:10), he demonstrates that being "in Christ" involves sharing the destiny of Christ. Those who are incorporated into Christ now live in the power of the resurrection (3:10).

The Philippians' existence in Christ is the basis for the exhortations, as Paul indicates in 2:1–11. Inasmuch as the successive "if" clauses in 2:1 can be translated "since," Paul indicates that his appeal in 2:3, 5 is based on the people's new existence. Because they are "in Christ" and experience joint participation (*koinōnia*) in the Spirit (2:1), Paul challenges them to "be of the

23. Peter Thomas O'Brien, *The Epistle to the Philippians: A Commentary on the Greek Text* (Grand Rapids: Eerdmans, 1991), 46.

same mind" (*to auto phronein*, 2:2; cf. 4:2). As Paul indicates in 2:5, believers can have the "same mind" when they have the mind of Christ. The RSV translates this verse appropriately: "Have this mind among yourselves [*en hymin*], which is yours in Christ Jesus [*en christō Iēsou*]."[24] That is, existence in Christ Jesus gives a new corporate mind-set that is shaped by the narrative of the Christ who "emptied himself" (2:7). Paul reinforces this exhortation when he encourages Euodia and Syntyche to "be of the same mind in the Lord" (4:2). Thus existence "in the Lord" creates a new kind of community, a church united by a common mind-set (*phronēsis*). A community united by the mind of Christ lives in harmony, rejecting the normal self-seeking that undermines community life.

The People in Christ and Christ among the People: Galatians

New ecclesiological issues in Galatia require further reflections on Christ and the people of God. Paul now faces the basic ecclesiological question, what are the conditions of membership in the people of God?[25] This question shapes the argument of Galatians. After being initiated by Paul into the community, the Galatian converts confront two alternate visions of the nature of the people of God. Paul has offered an unprecedented understanding by admitting gentile converts without circumcision, insisting that both Jews and gentiles are justified by faith in Jesus Christ (cf. Gal. 2:16; 3:26). The two alternative understandings of the people of God become evident in Antioch over questions of table fellowship. Although the pillars in Jerusalem have agreed on the legitimacy of Paul's mission to the gentiles (Gal. 2:1–10), they have apparently not worked out the full implications of their agreement, for the "men from James" (2:12 NASB) insist that uncircumcised gentiles may not sit at the same table with Jewish Christians. The latter continue to separate the law-observant believers from the new gentile converts (2:11–14).[26] Although the opponents agree with Paul that Jesus is Israel's Messiah, they insist that the covenant with Abraham remains inviolable. Indeed, they probably follow the common interpretation that Abraham was the first proselyte,[27] insisting that circumcision was the sign of the covenant for Abraham and all his seed. Paul's introduction of Abraham into the story (Gal. 3:6–29) suggests that the opponents have already

24. The NRSV renders this, "Let the same mind be in you that was in Christ Jesus."

25. See Kraus, *Das Volk Gottes*, 203–6, who correctly identifies ecclesiology as the central question of Galatians.

26. Although Paul uses the phrase "faith of Christ" (*pistis christou*, 2:16), he also speaks of believing "in Christ" (2:16; 3:26). On Abraham's obedience to the law, see Sir. 44:20; 1 Macc. 2:52; Jub. 6:19.

27. Cf. Philo, *Names* 16. See Joachim Jeremias, "*Abraam*," *TDNT* 1:8.

argued that the "children of Abraham" are those who maintain the covenant of Abraham.[28] The absence of "children of Abraham" elsewhere in the Pauline literature suggests that the opponents introduced that term in insisting on the continuity of the church with Israel.[29] This understanding has implications for all aspects of community life, including table fellowship (cf. Gal. 2:14–21).[30] While Paul regularly insists on the continuity of his gentile communities with Israel, his insistence that Jews and gentiles come to the table together reflects an ecclesiology of discontinuity with the traditional understanding.

In Galatians 3:6–29 Paul offers a theological justification for his alternative ecclesiology. In response to the opponents' claim that only the circumcised are the children of Abraham, Paul answers with the midrash based on the primary text, "Abraham 'believed God, and it was reckoned to him as righteousness'" (Gal. 3:6; cf. Gen. 15:6). The opponents probably followed common Jewish tradition, maintaining that Abraham demonstrated his faith(fulness) by keeping the law (cf. 1 Macc. 2:52; Sir. 44:20). Paul concludes (*ara*, 3:8) that the reference to Abraham also defines his children (*huioi*, literally "sons"), who are also righteous "by faith" (*ek pisteōs*);[31] that is, one may assume solidarity between the one progenitor and the many descendants.[32] This theme becomes the central assumption in the argument. Inasmuch as Paul introduces no chris-

---

28. The opponents probably hold to the traditional Jewish view of the seed of Abraham as the designation for the people of God. See 2 Chron. 20:7; Ps. 105:6; Isa. 41:8; Sir. 44:19; *Ps. Sol.* 9:9; 18:3; *T. Levi* 18:5; 3 Macc. 6:3; 4 Macc. 18:1.

29. Paul describes himself as the descendant of Abraham (2 Cor. 11:22) and argues that not all descendants of Abraham are "Abraham's children" (Rom. 9:7–8; cf. 11:1).

30. See chap. 7 for the ecclesiological significance of the incident at Antioch (Gal. 2:11–14).

31. J. Louis Martyn, *Galatians: A New Translation with Introduction and Commentary*, Anchor Bible 33A (New York: Doubleday, 1997), 299, observes that Paul nowhere else refers to believers as "children of Abraham."

32. A common theme in the Old Testament is that the one represents the many. Israelites saw their destiny bound up with that of their king. See Cummins, "Divine Life and Corporate Christology," 200. Cf. Powers, *Salvation through Participation*, 17: "An important element in the Jewish experience was the solidarity of the many with the one and the one with the many." While the older idea of corporate personality, introduced by H. Wheeler Robinson (*Corporate Personality in Ancient Israel* [Philadelphia: Fortress, 1967]) has largely been rejected, the fact remains true that God relates not only to individuals but also to Israel as a whole. See Joel S. Kaminsky, *Corporate Responsibility in the Hebrew Bible*, Journal for the Study of the Old Testament: Supplement Series (Sheffield: Sheffield Academic, 1995), 11. See also Stanley K. Stowers, "What Is 'Pauline Participation in Christ'?," in *Redefining First-Century Jewish and Christian Identities: Essays in Honor of Ed Parish Sanders*, ed. Fabian E. Udoh, with Susanna Heschel, Mark Chancey, and Gregory Tatum, Christianity and Judaism in Antiquity 16 (Notre Dame, IN: University of Notre Dame Press, 2008), 359: "Paul may have been just as literal as Hebrews 7, which argues that although he was not yet born, Levi paid [tithes] to Melchizedek because he was in the loins of Abraham as seed when Abraham paid tithes to Melchizedek." See also N. T. Wright (*Paul and the Faithfulness of God* [Minneapolis: Fortress, 2013], 2.827–30) for further development of this theme. Wright observes the significance of the story of David and Goliath

tological referent here, his conclusion would have been widely acceptable to the opponents, who would have agreed that the children of Abraham share his faithfulness, which they would define as the keeping of Torah.

As a supporting text to Genesis 15:6, Paul cites a promise to Abraham, "All the Gentiles shall be blessed in you" (Gal. 3:8), a combination of citations from Genesis (12:3; 18:18). In anticipation of the developing argument that will describe those who are "in Christ" (cf. Gal. 3:14, 28), Paul quotes the phrase "in Abraham," introducing a passage that uses "in" (*en soi*) with a proper name (Abraham). The *en* is a rendering of the Hebrew *b*; thus it is used in an instrumental sense in the LXX.[33] The citation also introduces gentiles into the argument, promising that "all the Gentiles shall be blessed in [i.e., 'by'] Abraham." Paul draws a second inference in 3:9 (cf. *hōste*), indicating that "those who have faith" receive the blessing mentioned in the citation (Gen. 12:3; 18:18). The combination of passages results in a syllogism:

Abraham's children are those who have faith (*pistis*).

The *ethnē* have faith.

Those who have faith (including gentiles) are the children of Abraham.

Thus Paul works from the common assumption that the destiny of the one shapes the identity of the many.

Since Paul has given no christological referent in his interpretation of the two passages, his conclusions appear on the surface to offer common ground with the opponents and Jewish tradition. The fact that Paul speaks in the third person suggests that he is stating general principles derived from his interpretation of Scripture. In the argument that follows, Paul defines *pistis* in a new way, making it the antithesis of works of the law (cf. 3:10) and introducing the christological referent. With this redefinition of *pistis*, he also redefines the traditional understanding of the blessing to include the *ethnē*, arguing that they are included among those who have faith without works of the law (cf. 3:26–29).

Paul's interpretation of the Genesis texts becomes explicit in Galatians 3:26–29, which forms an inclusio with 3:7–9. He changes from the third-person plural (3:7–9) to the second-person plural (3:26–29) as he applies general principles from the passage to his gentile readers. What was implicit in 3:7–9

---

as an indication that the one person represents the people, adding that "western individualism finds it hard immediately to grasp" this incorporative language (830).

33. Wedderburn, "Some Observations," 89.

becomes explicit in 3:26–29. "Those who have faith" (3:7) are now "all" (*pantes*, 3:26, 28) and "as many of you as" (*hosoi*, 3:27) are baptized into Christ. The "faith" (or the "faith of Abraham") is now "faith in Christ" (3:26 NASB). In making explicit in 3:26–29 what was implicit in 3:7–9, Paul departs from the common ground that he shares with the Jewish tradition. The seed of Abraham is no longer physical Israel (3:29) but a new humanity that includes all who believe in Christ.

Inasmuch as 3:26–29 forms an inclusio with 3:7–9, we may analyze the argument as a self-contained rhetorical unit. The initial inferences in 3:7–9 function as the *propositio* of the argument, which Paul develops in a methodical way in the midrash. As a restatement of the propositio, 3:26–29 functions as the *peroratio* of the argument. Indeed, this conclusion ends with a rhetorical flourish that is appropriate for a peroratio.

Paul's explicit claims in 3:26–29 are not comprehensible apart from the argument in 3:10–25, which builds the case for Paul's concluding claims. This section functions as the argument (*probatio*) for Paul's redefinition of the people of God. Paul's first step in the argument is to redefine faith as the antithesis of works of the law (3:10). Insofar as the "works of the law" under consideration are the boundary markers of circumcision and ritual purity in table fellowship,[34] Paul has severed faith from the common understanding as faithfulness in keeping the law, removing ethnic privilege. He becomes more explicit about the loss of ethnic privilege when he describes those who depend on works of the law as under a curse (3:10–11), as he introduces Christ into the argument for the first time. "Christ redeemed us from the curse of the law by becoming a curse for us" (3:13). Here Paul employs the first-person plural for the first time, suggesting that Christ is the representative of all people. The purpose clause in 3:14 indicates how gentiles receive the blessing: "in order that in Christ Jesus the blessing of Abraham might come to the Gentiles, so that we might receive the promise of the Spirit through faith." The gentile readers are included in the blessing to Abraham (cf. 3:8) through Christ, because Christ is the representative of all humanity. The implication is that Christ took the curse for all, opening the blessing of Abraham to the gentiles.

The conclusions stated in 3:26–29 require an additional step in the argument. Paul must still indicate how gentiles are incorporated. Having stated that "we might receive the promise" (3:14), he now indicates that the promise to Abraham was to his seed (Gen. 17:8) and that the seed was singular (Gal. 3:16). Whereas *sperma* in Jewish tradition (and for the opponents) referred to

---

34. See James D. G. Dunn, *The Theology of Paul's Letter to the Galatians*, New Testament Theology (Cambridge: Cambridge University Press, 1993), 76–78.

physical descendants of Abraham and those who were incorporated through circumcision, Paul argues that it refers to one person, that is, to Christ. In 3:22 he repeats the promise, indicating that "so what was promised through faith in Jesus Christ [*pistis Iēsou christou*] might be given to those who believe." Here the most likely reading of *pistis Iēsou christou* is "faith of Jesus Christ," who is the seed. The promise to the one seed thus becomes the promise to others, "those who believe." The one thus becomes the source of salvation for the many.

Christ is the inclusive person who represents the gentile readers ("us") and rescues all who believe. This argument allows Paul to move from the general statements in 3:7–9 to the explicit claims in 3:26–29. The plural offspring of Abraham come into existence only when human beings are incorporated into Abraham's singular seed.[35] This argument becomes the foundation for the exclamation in 3:26–28, which may be a variant form of a baptismal confession commonly known in the early church (cf. 1 Cor. 12:13; Col. 3:11).

As the climax of the argument over the identity of the children of God, Galatians 3:26–28 is a carefully structured declaration of the reality of the new aeon in six lines.[36] The first and sixth lines form an inclusio:

For in Christ Jesus you are all children of God through faith. (3:26)

For all of you are one in Christ Jesus. (3:28)

The shift from the aorist to the present tense (3:23–29) marks the climax of the argument, describing the reality of the new aeon.[37] With the emphasis on "all" (*pantes*), Paul redefines the people of God, contrasting "all" to ethnic Israel. The second-person plural (*este*) in 3:26 personalizes this reality for the readers, and the present tense contrasts the new situation with the old aeon. Those who live in the new aeon no longer need to observe the boundary markers to become members of the children of Israel (cf. 3:7–9). The parallel between lines one and six indicates that "all" (*pantes*) are children of God (3:26) and all are one in Christ (3:28), the inclusive person (cf. 3:16). Thus the converts did not choose each other but came together because they are "in Christ."

Gar in line two introduces the basis for the claim that Paul makes in lines one and six. "As many as" (*hosoi*) in 3:27 is parallel to "all" (*pantes*) in 3:26, 28 and elaborates on the new definition of the people of God. The parallel

35. Martyn, *Galatians*, 340.
36. See Hans Dieter Betz, *Galatians: A Commentary on Paul's Letter to the Churches of Galatia*, Hermeneia (Philadelphia: Fortress, 1979), 181–82.
37. A critical part of the argument is the distinction between "before faith came" (3:23) and "now that faith has come" (3:25). Cf. also 3:19, "until the offspring would come."

"you are all" (3:26) and "as many as" (3:27) indicates the inclusion of the gentiles (3:8). In the statement "As many of you as were baptized into Christ have clothed yourselves with Christ" (3:27), Paul links faith (3:26) and baptism, indicating that the past event ("have been baptized") determines the readers' present (*este*, "you are," in 3:26, 28) status. Believers are "in Christ" (3:28) because they have been baptized "into Christ" (*eis christon*). Christ is the "place" into which the baptized person is now incorporated.[38] Faith and baptism are inseparable as the response to God's saving act. They are not boundary markers but the signs of inclusion. Believers have "put on" Christ as a new garment and are enclosed by Christ.[39] This imagery elaborates on "in Christ" and signifies the spatial aspect of being incorporated into Christ, the inclusive person in whom all baptized people live.

Lines three through five further define "all" and "as many as" with the threefold "there is no longer" (*ouk heni*, 3:28; literally "there is not").[40] The similarity of the three pairs to other formulations (1 Cor. 12:13; Col. 3:11) suggests that Paul is citing a familiar slogan. Line three is the focal point of the argument. In the new aeon the distinction between ethnic groups—Jew and Greek—no longer exists. Line four announces the end of social status—slave or free. Line five even claims that there is no longer "male and female"—an echo of Genesis 1:27. Thus the ethnic, social, and gender distinctions of the old aeon are now removed, for the church is the community that has been rescued "from the present evil age" (Gal. 1:4) and is the people of the new creation (6:15). The church is thus the new humanity, from which the realities of the old humanity have been removed.[41]

As the parallel statements in 3:28 indicate, incorporation into Christ creates a new community where the seed of Abraham is not limited to a privileged group but applies to all who believe. Incorporation into Christ creates a community that knows no distinctions between Jew and gentile, slave and free, male and female. This new kind of community is unprecedented and can only become a reality among those who have been rescued from the current age (1:4). A church composed of both Jew and Greek comprises the "children of

38. Martyn, *Galatians*, 376.
39. Helmut Umbauch, *In Christus getauft, von der Sünde Befreit: Die Gemeinde als Sündenfreier Raum bei Paulus*, Forschungen zur Religion und Literatur des Alten und Neuen Testaments 181 (Göttingen: Vandenhoeck & Ruprecht, 1999), 220.
40. BDAG 336. The NRSV "no longer" fits the argument well, contrasting the old aeon with the new.
41. See Horrell, "'No Longer Jew or Greek,'" 327. Paul does not argue that the old distinctions have no meaning at all. In other instances (Rom. 14:1–15:13; 1 Cor. 11:2–16; cf. Col. 3:13–4:1; Eph. 5:21–6:9), he argues that one must continue to live within the old structures. See also Wright, *Paul and the Faithfulness of God*, 2.875.

Abraham" or "seed of Abraham." Paul makes the transition from "people of God" to "in Christ," offering a new understanding of the people of God. The new humanity is "in Christ" and "of Christ" (3:29). Paul speaks not of individuals in Christ but of the church in Christ.

The argument in 3:6–29 began as an answer to the question, who are the children of Abraham? It ends by affirming that those who believe in Christ are both "Abraham's offspring" (3:29) and "children of God" (3:26). The image of the law as "disciplinarian" (*paidagōgos*) provides the transition from "children of Abraham" to the designation "children of God." Both were common metaphors for Israel in the Old Testament and Judaism.[42] Thus Paul has redefined the people of God, describing Christ as the representative one whom believers "put on" in baptism (3:27). While Paul assumes the presence of a diversity of people within the church, he does not envision a balkanized community of separate identities; he envisions one community where old identities are subordinated to the new identity among those who are in Christ.

Paul summarizes the argument, proceeding from the negative "there is no longer" to the positive "you are one in Christ" (3:28) and you "belong to Christ" (3:29). The plural "you are" (*este*) includes all who have been baptized into Christ (3:27)—both Jews and Greeks. To be "one in Christ" is to overcome the divisions mentioned in 3:28. Just as there is one seed, the Christ (3:16), there is only one new humanity in which ethnic, social, and gender identities are left behind. Paul does not address the numerous questions that emerge in the modern context, and he does not indicate how the reality of the new aeon is implemented in practice. His focus is on the overcoming of separation between groups that has taken place in Christ. Paul does not employ the Greek and modern category of equality but envisions a unity among those who are in Christ.

Paul develops the metaphor of the children of God in 4:1–6, restating the argument of 3:23–29 and speaking once more in the first-person plural (cf. 3:13). The two purpose clauses in 4:5 ("in order to redeem those who were under the law" and "so that we might receive adoption as children") recall the purpose clauses of 3:13–14 ("Christ redeemed us from the curse of the law . . . in order that in Christ Jesus the blessing of Abraham might come to the Gentiles, so that we might receive the promise of the Spirit through faith"). Paul describes the saving work of Christ once more in terms of redemption (4:5;

---

42. "Children of God" (literally "sons of God"; LXX *huioi theou*) is a designation for Israel in the Old Testament (Deut. 14:1; 32:19; Isa. 43:6; 45:11; Hosea 2:1; cf. 14:1). In Jewish literature, Israel's status as God's children is often used in contrasts between Israel and the nations (Jdt. 9:13; Ps. Sol. 17:26–27; *Jub.* 1:23–28; 2:20; 19:27–29). See Kraus, *Das Volk Gottes*, 224.

cf. 3:13) but now speaks of the adoption (4:5) by which the gentiles become children and heirs of God (4:6).[43] Because God sent his Son (4:4), believers now become God's children (*huioi*, literally "sons"). As in ancient Israel, the children of Abraham are also the children of God. This relationship comes only through the Son.

This is an ecclesiological argument, a redefinition of the people of God. Christ is the representative. The identity of Christ and believers is inseparable. Paul has moved from the instrumental use of *en* to the inclusive, locative meaning, defining the church as the people of God who are in Christ, the person who incorporates all who believe. Paul presupposes the concept of the inclusive person, according to which the descendants of the ancestor share the fate and identity of their progenitor. According to Romans 5:12–21, Christ is the second Adam who reverses the effects of the sin of the first man. Just as the sin of one man determined the destiny of the many, the righteousness of one man made many righteous (cf. Rom. 5:18–21). As in Galatians, the new humanity shares the destiny of Christ (Rom. 6:1–11). In 1 Corinthians 15:20–28, Paul contrasts those who are "in Adam" with those who are "in Christ," concluding that the one determines the destiny of the many: "As in Adam all die, so also in Christ shall all be made alive" (1 Cor. 15:22 RSV). Christ is thus the one founder of the new humanity that is "in him" (Gal. 3:28), having clothed itself with him in baptism.[44]

Paul moves easily between the claim that believers are in Christ and the affirmation that Christ is among believers. In Galatians he declares that believers are "one in Christ" (3:28) because they have been baptized "into Christ" (3:27). When he describes their relapse, he refers to them as "my little children, for whom I am again in the pain of childbirth until Christ is formed in you" (4:19). Because English translations do not distinguish between the singular and plural of the second person, they obscure Paul's statement. J. Louis Martyn has appropriately translated this "until Christ is formed among your congregations."[45] The translation is not "in you" (singular) but "among you." Paul envisions corporate formation, which becomes evident as members take on the qualities described in Galatians 5 and 6. The church is a unity only because it is in Christ (3:29), and now the goal is that Christ be formed in the congregations. Indeed, Paul has already presented himself as a representative of Christian experience when he says, "It is no longer I who live, but it is Christ who lives in me" (2:20).

43. Paul uses the image of adoption (*huiothesia*) also in Rom. 8:15, 23; 9:4; cf. Eph. 1:5.
44. See Roloff, *Die Kirche im Neuen Testament*, 93.
45. Martyn, *Galatians*, 425.

As the argument of Galatians indicates, this ecclesiology is not an abstraction, for it manifests itself in the table fellowship between Jews and Greeks. Indeed, Paul's vision of the church would become a challenge to the church in all ages, for it would extend to the separation between ethnic and socioeconomic groups that live in isolation from each other. While the immediate concern is the unity of Jews and gentiles in Christ, Paul points with the phrases "there is no longer slave or free" and "there is no longer male and female" (3:28) to the greater significance of the new definition of the people of God. All are one because they are incorporated into the founder of the new humanity.

THE TEMPLE OF THE HOLY SPIRIT AND THE BODY OF CHRIST IN 1 CORINTHIANS

Paul responds to new issues in Corinth that threaten the ecclesial identity of the community. Partisan rivalries (1 Cor. 1:10–17; 3:1–5), expressed in the slogans "I belong to Paul" and "I belong to Apollos," echo ancient political discourse, suggesting that some Corinthians envision a church modeled on a political community.[46] Extreme individualism, expressed in the slogan "all things are lawful" (6:12; 10:23), also undermines community life. Corinthian interaction with outsiders and their immoral practices removes the boundary between saints (6:1–2) and the world. Anticommunal forces rooted in the ancient division between the rich and the poor destroy the unity of the Lord's Supper (11:17–34). Corinthian competition in corporate worship also destroys Paul's ideal of communal solidarity. Consequently, Paul's task is to rebuild the ecclesial identity of the Corinthians, offering a vision of a community unlike that of their past experience. Like the Galatians, this community erases the divisions between "Jews or Greeks, slaves or free" (1 Cor. 12:13; cf. Gal. 3:28).

As in the other letters, Paul associates the ecclesial identity of the Corinthians with the people of God. He addresses them as "saints" and "those who are sanctified" (1 Cor. 1:2) and divides the world into the "saints" and the "unrighteous" (6:1), describing their conversion as the occasion when they were "washed," "sanctified," and "justified" (6:11). Like Israel, they have been called (1:2, 26; 7:17), and they look to the ancient Israelites as their ancestors (10:1). Paul insists that they maintain the boundaries between insiders and

46. See Margaret M. Mitchell, *Paul and the Rhetoric of Reconciliation: An Exegetical Investigation of the Language and Composition of 1 Corinthians*, Hermeneutische Untersuchungen zur Theologie 28 (Tübingen: Mohr Siebeck, 1991), 68–111. See also chap. 8.

outsiders (5:1–11:1) in accordance with their collective identity as holy people.[47] However, their identity as heirs of ancient Israel is only one dimension
of ecclesial identity. They are the ones who "are sanctified in Christ" and "call
on the name of our Lord Jesus Christ" (1:2). As in the other epistles, Paul's
Christology in 1 Corinthians reshapes the concept of the people of God.

God's Building and Temple

Paul employs two dominant and intersecting images—the building and
the body—alongside the additional image of the cultivated field to express
the solidarity of the members in Christ. In parallel statements he declares,
"You are God's field, God's building" (3:9), "you are God's temple" (3:16),
and "you are the body of Christ and individually members of it" (12:27). In
each instance he responds to anticommunal forces to remind the rival groups
of their collective identity. These images intersect, as we shall notice, in Paul's
discussion of sexual immorality, when he asks, "Do you not know that your
bodies are members of Christ?" (6:15), anticipating the later reflection on
the body of Christ (12:12–27). Paul raises the additional question, "Do you
not know that your body is a temple of the Holy Spirit within you?" (6:19).

Paul introduces the images of the field and the building in response to
the partisan strife in Corinth as a reminder that the rivalry over individual
leaders is inconsistent with their identity as a community. In response to the
Corinthians' understanding of community as a place for partisan politics,
he insists that individual leaders—whether himself or Apollos—are of no
consequence (3:6–7). Using the metaphor of the field, he states that neither
the one who plants nor the one who waters is anything (3:7). He adds, "We
are God's servants, working together; you are God's field [geōrgion], God's
building [oikodomē]" (3:9), indicating the corporate identity of the church
and the common task of leaders. The word order (theou geōrgion, theou
oikodomē) emphasizes that the church is God's possession, and those who
destroy it with partisan politics will also be destroyed (3:17). The images of
both the field and the building are derived from Israel's self-understanding.[48]
The metaphor of the dwelling (oikodomē) is a dominant image for the church

47. See Thompson, *Moral Formation*, 47–48.

48. See Kraus, *Das Volk Gottes*, 172–74. On the imagery of planting, see Ps. 80:9; Isa. 5:2,
7; 60:21; 61:13; Jer. 1:10; 2:21; 18:9; 24:6; 1 QS 8:5; 11:8; 1 QH 6:15; 8:6; 4 Ezra 5:23–30. On
God's building, see Jer. 1:10, 31. The combination of the two images appears in Jer. 1:9–11;
24:6; 31:27–28; 42:10; 45:4; Ezek. 36:26; 1 QS 8:4–10. See also Christoph Gregor Müller, *Gottes
Pflanzung—Gottes Bau—Gottes Tempel: Die metaphorische Dimension paulinischer Gemeinde-
theologie in 1. Kor 3,5–17*, Fuldaer Studien 5 (Frankfurt am Main: Knecht, 1995), 67–72, 80–91;
Klaiber, *Rechtfertigung und Gemeinde*, 36.

in 1 Corinthians,[49] as it is in the other letters.[50] Paul elaborates on the image of the building in 3:10–15, indicating that Christ is the foundation (3:10), which others build on. The image of the foundation is a reminder to those who compete for leadership roles that there is no other basis for the existence of the church than Jesus Christ himself. Just as the foundation (*themelios*) of the ancient building provided the support and determined its shape,[51] Christ determines the nature of the church. With the image of the foundation, Paul indicates the christological dimension of the people of God.

Paul alters the building imagery with a reminder of his previous catechetical instruction (3:16): "Do you not know that you are God's temple and that God's Spirit dwells in you?" The building has now become the temple. The statement that "you [plural] are God's temple" (3:16) is parallel to "you [plural] are God's building" (3:9). Once more the plural "you" reflects the corporate identity of the people. The appropriate translation of the second clause is "the Spirit which dwells among you." While the Corinthians probably considered the church a community of Spirit-filled individuals, Paul challenges the individualism of some of the leaders, insisting that the Spirit dwells in the whole church. He argues that the Corinthians are an organic whole and that the presence of the Spirit unifies the community and negates the tendency toward factionalism.[52]

Paul draws on the Old Testament images of the temple as the dwelling place of God.[53] God instructs, "Make me a sanctuary, so that I may dwell among them" (Exod. 25:8), and promises, "I will place my dwelling in your midst" (Lev. 26:11).[54] This theme continues among other writers. Tobit recalls the temple as "the dwelling of God" (1:4), and 1 Maccabees 14:35 speaks of "the temple of [God's] habitation." This theme is the background for Paul's affirmation that the Holy Spirit dwells in the church, the temple of God.

The focus of the image in 1 Corinthians 3:16 is on the holiness of the temple. Thus partisan rivalries are of great consequence, for one either builds on to the foundation laid by Paul (3:10) or destroys the building (3:17), which is nothing less than the place where the Holy Spirit dwells. To undermine the

---

49. See the verb *oikodomein* in 8:1, 10; 10:23; 14:4, 17. The noun *oikodomē* is used in 3:9; 14:3, 5, 26.

50. Cf. Rom. 14:19; 15:2; 15:20; 2 Cor. 12:19; 1 Thess. 5:11. See chap. 8.

51. See Thomas Söding, *Jesus und die Kirche: Was sagt das Neue Testament?* (Freiburg: Herder, 2007), 49, for the significance of the foundation in ancient construction.

52. John R. Levison, "The Spirit and the Temple in Paul's Letters to the Corinthians," in *Paul and His Theology*, ed. Stanley Porter (Leiden: Brill, 2006), 195.

53. Michel, "*oikos*," *TDNT* 5.120, indicates that *oikos theou* is a fixed term for the sanctuary in the Old Testament.

54. Albert L. A. Hogeterp, *Paul and God's Temple: A Historical Interpretation of Cultic Imagery in the Corinthian Correspondence*, Biblical Tools and Studies 2 (Leuven: Peeters, 2006), 264.

unity of the church is to destroy the holy temple, "and you are that temple" (3:17). The repeated "you [plural] are" (3:9, 17) indicates the corporate identity of God's holy people.

Paul echoes the same concept in 2 Corinthians in his appeal to the Corinthians to separate from everything unclean. He reaffirms, "We are the temple of the living God," citing God's promise from the holiness code, "I will live [*enoikēsō*] in them and walk among them" (2 Cor. 6:16; cf. Lev. 26:11).[55] As the remaining citations indicate, Paul's focus is on the communal holiness of the renewed people of God as they return from exile. Whereas he had spoken in 1 Corinthians 3:16 of the dwelling of the Holy Spirit among the people, here it is God who dwells among the people. In each instance, God dwells "among" the people rather than "within" individuals.

Paul returns to the theme of the temple in 1 Corinthians 6:19, once more recalling earlier catechetical instruction ("do you not know," cf. 3:16) and echoing the earlier claim that the church is the temple in which the Holy Spirit dwells. In this instance, however, he says, "Do you not know that your body is a temple of the Holy Spirit within you, which you have from God . . . ?" The introduction of the body as the temple of the Holy Spirit reflects a change of focus that is consistent with the topic of sexuality in the immediate context (6:12–20). According to the traditional reading, Paul has shifted the emphasis from the corporate community as God's temple to the individual's own body as a temple of the Holy Spirit. Thus scholars have been puzzled about the compatibility between Paul's two statements about the temple as the dwelling place of the Spirit, since "you are the temple of God" (3:16) is undoubtedly an expression of corporate identity.

To what extent has Paul shifted the focus from the group to the individual? English translations obscure the collective consciousness that is present in Paul's use of "among you" ("in you" RSV, 3:16; 6:19). Paul responds to reports of sexual immorality (*porneia*) at Corinth with a concern for the integrity and holiness of the entire community: "It is actually reported that there is sexual immorality [*porneia*] among you" (5:1). He compares this offender to leaven that pollutes the whole lump, adding, "as you [plural] really are unleavened" (5:7), and insisting that they "drive out the wicked person from among you" (5:13). He introduces reflections on the evils of *porneia* with an additional appeal to their collective consciousness: "You were washed, you were sanctified, you were justified" (6:11). The plural "you" indicates the solidarity of the community.

---

55. The LXX does not have "I will live [*enoikēsō*] in them." It has instead "my soul will not abhor you."

The appeal to the collective consciousness of the church is the context for the elaboration on sexual immorality in 6:12–20. In response to the individualism expressed in the slogan "all things are lawful" (6:12), which some Corinthians had apparently applied to the desires of the human body, Paul offers an alternative view of bodily existence. "Food is meant for the stomach and the stomach for food" (6:13) is probably a Corinthian slogan, to which Paul responds that (a) the body is for the Lord and (b) the body is destined for resurrection (6:13–14). Referring once more to previous instruction, Paul says "do you not know" three times (6:15, 16, 19). In 6:15 he says, "Do you not know that your bodies [sōmata] are members of Christ?" The question anticipates the discussion of the church as a body with many members (cf. 12:14–27). Thus not only are individuals members of the body of Christ; bodily existence is experienced as membership in the one Christ. Not only "you" are members, Paul explains, but your bodies are members. Paul speaks of the individual when he says, "Do you not know that whoever is united to a prostitute becomes one with her?" (6:16), and then, "But anyone united to the Lord becomes one spirit with him" (6:17).

In the third appeal to previous catechetical instruction ("do you not know" in 6:19), Paul continues the discussion of bodily existence. We may appropriately translate the rhetorical question as "Do you not know that the body of all of you [hymōn] is a temple of the Holy Spirit, which is among you?" Paul does not say "your bodies (sōmata) are temples of the Holy Spirit" but says "your body [sōma, literally 'the body of you (plural)'] is the temple of the Holy Spirit." Here we see the critical relationship between the individual and the community. The individual element is undeniable. However, the corporate dimension is also evident. These individuals in their bodily existence are together the members of Christ. The Holy Spirit "is among you." Thus the individual and the corporate dimensions come together here. Individual existence is inseparable from corporate existence. God calls for a holy community. Individuals act as members of communities.

The Body and the Building

The images of the body of Christ and the building continue to intersect in chapters 11–14, as Paul addresses the rivalries over spiritual gifts within the context of corporate worship. As an attempt to overcome competition in Corinth, he describes the local church as a unity with a diversity of gifts (12:4–11) and then illustrates this principle with the elaboration on the church as a body (12:12–27). This image has no direct antecedent in the Old Testament but was widely used in the ancient world, especially in political contexts.

Michelle Lee has shown that the particles *kathaper . . . houtōs* ("just as . . . so it is") frequently signaled the comparison between the political entity and a body, as in 1 Corinthians 12:12.[56] The best known example of this image is the story by Menenius Agrippa, in which the members of the body politic conspire to withhold food from the stomach because they are tired of the stomach's taking without giving anything in return (Livy 2.32; Epictetus, *Diatr.* 2.10.4–5).[57] Paul first challenges Corinthian individualism with the argument that the body is one with many members, illustrating the claim by reminding the listeners that the eyes and the head cannot exist without the body (12:14–21). This argument was common in antiquity. Paul's claim that the "weaker" (*asthenestera*), "less honorable" (*atimotera*), and "less respectable" (*ta aschēmata*) parts of the body are indispensable (12:22–24) also echoes ancient sources.[58] Describing the body as one with many parts (cf. 1 Cor. 12:14), exercising different functions, was commonplace (cf. Dionysius of Halicarnassus, *Ant. rom.* 6.86.1). The vital role played by each part (cf. 1 Cor. 12:14–19) is a major issue in Menenius Agrippa's fable. That all parts suffer together when one part suffers (cf. 1 Cor. 12:26) was also a common theme.[59] Ancient writers employed the image to urge listeners to behave in such a way as to maintain the unity of the body.

Like other ancient writers, Paul employs the image of the body to challenge the anticommunal behavior of his readers. The image of the body provides the vehicle for reinforcing the unity of the group with its diversity of gifts. Paul has probably adapted an ancient metaphor for his own purposes. However, while the comparison of the church to a body parallels ancient reflection on the unity of the group, the frame of Paul's extended metaphor sets his image apart from ancient usage. Indeed, ancient writers would have agreed with the claim "Just as the body is one and has many members, and all the members of the body, though many, are one body . . ." The inclusio that frames the imagery of the body indicates Paul's transformation of this image. While the

56. Michelle V. Lee, *Paul, the Stoics, and the Body of Christ*, Society for New Testament Studies Monograph Series 137 (Cambridge: Cambridge University Press, 2006), 30.

57. Timothy L. Carter, "Looking at the Metaphor of Christ's Body in 1 Corinthians 12," in *Paul: Jew, Greek, and Roman*, Pauline Studies 5, ed. Stanley E. Porter (Leiden: Brill, 2008). See the image also in Dionysus of Halicarnassus, *Ant. rom.* 6.82.2; Seneca, *Ira* 2.31.7; Cicero, *Off.* 3.5.22–23; Plato, *Resp.* 5.462d; Aristotle, *Pol.* 5.1302b 33–40. See the discussion in Andreas Lindemann, "Die Kirche als Leib: Beobachtungen zur 'demokratischen' Ekklesiologie bei Paulus," in *Zeitschrift für Theologie und Kirche* 92 (1995): 144–45.

58. Carter, "Looking at the Metaphor," 104–14, observes numerous parallels in ancient discussions of the necessary parts of the body. He does not, however, offer parallels for the metaphorical use of these terms for people within the body politic.

59. Lee, *Paul, the Stoics, and the Body of Christ*, 40–41.

readers expect Paul to say, "so it is with the church," he says instead, "so it is with Christ" (12:12). The new dimension is the claim in the main clause—that is, Christ is one and has many members. The reality of the crucified and risen Christ is the basis for the unity of the congregation.[60] This claim forms an inclusio with the concluding statement of this unit, "Now you are the body of Christ and individually members of it" (12:27). Individual identity is derived from being a member of the body of Christ. The local church is not merely compared to a body; it is the body of Christ. The whole is greater than the sum of its parts. Paul's claim that incorporation into the body of Christ (12:13) in baptism unites Jews and Greeks, slaves and free into one body is parallel to the affirmation in Galatians that all who have been baptized into Christ have put on Christ and now exist in a community where there are no distinctions between Jew and Greek, slave and free, male and female (Gal. 3:27–28). Thus while "in Christ" is not identical to "in the body of Christ," the latter phrase probably develops the former.[61] Paul has combined the theme of the inclusive person, which is common in the Old Testament, with the Greek image of the corporate body. Just as Christ is the foundation for the building (1 Cor. 3:9), he is the inclusive person who incorporates individuals into his body.

Paul anticipates this description of the church as the body of Christ throughout the letter. In response to Corinthian partisanship, he asks, "Is Christ divided?" (1 Cor. 1:13 KJV). Speaking to the whole community, he rebukes the focus on specific leaders, saying, "You belong to Christ, and Christ belongs to God" (3:23). Individual bodies are "members [*melē*] of Christ" (6:15). Here we see the implications of being incorporated into the risen Christ. Christ and the Spirit live among all the believers, creating a new kind of community.

Paul also anticipates this image in his interpretation of the eucharistic words (10:16–17). These reflections appear within the larger context of concerns about the boundaries between believers and unbelievers (8:1–11:1), which have become an issue in questions about the eating of meat sacrificed to idols. Some of the Corinthians have approached the subject as a matter of individual freedom, claiming that "all things are lawful" (10:23–24). Paul responds to the Corinthians with the reminder that concern for the weak transcends personal freedom, for the one who could be destroyed by this exercise of freedom is one "for whom Christ died" (8:11). The memory of the cross, therefore, places the concern for the whole community above individual freedom. Similarly, Paul appeals to the memory of the cross in the eucharistic words of 10:16–17. He does not develop his eucharistic theology here but anticipates the discussion

60. Klaiber, *Rechtfertigung und Gemeinde*, 43.
61. See Lindemann, "Die Kirche als Leib," 141.

in 11:17–34, when he corrects the Corinthians' abuse of the Lord's Supper. Paul's first use of the image of the body probably comes from his reflection on the sharing of the cup and the bread (10:16). In sharing the blood and body of Christ, the community becomes one body (10:17). That is, believers become one body when they share in the destiny of Christ. Paul anticipates the later discussion of both the Lord's Supper (11:17–34) and the body of Christ (12:12–31). Both the Eucharist and baptism bring the community together as one body (cf. 12:13), as I will argue in the following chapter.

As a development of the eucharistic interpretation (10:16–17), the words indicate the close relationship between Christ and the church. The church is not identical to Christ but has no existence apart from Christ. The church is not a collection of individuals but a community that is one in Christ.[62]

Just as the community is brought together in one body at the Eucharist, "we were all baptized into one body" (12:13). The body of believers is not constituted by joint participation in baptism; rather, believers are baptized into the body that precedes them. "It does not come into being by human decisions and mergers but is a pre-given reality."[63] The statement is parallel to the claim that believers were "baptized into Christ" and have "put on Christ" (Gal. 3:27 KJV). In both instances, baptism into Christ brings one into a body that is distinguished not only by its diversity of gifts but also by the diversity of people. The body of Christ includes "Jews or Greeks, slaves or free" (12:13).

Paul develops the image of the body of Christ in only one other place in the undisputed letters. In Romans 12:3–8 he appeals to this image to illustrate the unity of the church with its diversity of gifts. This comes at the beginning of Paul's paraenetic conclusion to the argument of Romans to illustrate that members should not think more highly of themselves than they ought to think (12:3). As the preceding argument indicates, God's new humanity includes both Jews and gentiles (cf. 1:14–17; chaps. 9–11). Life in the new aeon that is not conformed to this world (12:1–2) is experienced in the multiethnic community in which all "are members one of another" (12:5).

The image of the body of Christ is an extension of "in Christ," which is a dominant feature of Paul's ecclesiology used primarily in paraenetic contexts. The eucharistic origins of the image indicate that Paul goes beyond the popular metaphor of the body politic to describe the church specifically as the body of Christ. Thus Paul knows no Christian existence apart from the body. The

---

62. Roloff, *Die Kirche im Neuen Testament*, 108. See chap. 3 for additional aspects of baptism and Eucharist.

63. Schnelle, *Apostle Paul*, 220.

church that participates in the destiny of Jesus is the body of Christ, a community in Christ composed of all who believe.

Sharing the Destiny of Christ in 2 Corinthians

As Paul's conversation with the Corinthians continues, the topic shifts from the partisan rivalries in Corinth to Paul's qualification as a minister of Christ (2 Cor. 11:23; cf. 10:7). Although apparent breaks in the argument of 2 Corinthians raise questions about the integrity of the letter, the major issue throughout the letter is Paul's defense of his ministry. As 2:14–7:4 demonstrates, any discussion of Paul's ministry has major ecclesiological implications. In contrast to the opening section (1:12–2:13), Paul speaks here of himself in the first-person plural, sometimes distinguishing between himself ("we") and the church (the plural "you," 3:2–3; 4:12, 14–15) and elsewhere speaking of "we all" (cf. 3:18; 5:10), indicating his unity with the church. These pronouns offer an important insight into his ecclesiology. Paul is the minister of the new covenant promised by Jeremiah, while the community, metaphorically, is the letter delivered by him (cf. 3:1–6).[64]

In 1 Corinthians and Romans, the body of Christ is the local congregation. Local communities are not gatherings of like-minded people who have chosen each other but the people who are incorporated into the risen Christ and unified only by their existence in him. Incorporation into Christ is inclusion in the people of God, which in the new covenant includes all who participate in Christ.

"If Anyone Is in Christ": Incorporation in 2 Corinthians

Paul indicates the ecclesiological dimension of his defense most clearly as he alternates between "we" and the plural "you" in 2 Corinthians 5:11–6:2, the theological center of his argument and a summary of his defense.[65] He initiates the summary by declaring, "If we are beside ourselves, it is for God; if we are in our right mind, it is for you" (5:13). "For you" is the defining feature of Paul's ministry, as the repeated reminders of his sacrificial work on behalf of the Corinthians indicates (cf. 1:6–7 [twice]; 2:4; 4:15). In 5:14–19 Paul gives the theological basis for his conduct. He is not his own master, for "the love of Christ urges us on" (*synechei hēmas*, 5:14a).[66] Paul explains the

---

64. See chap. 4.

65. See Steven J. Kraftchik, "Death in Us, Life in You: The Apostolic Medium," in *Pauline Theology*, vol. 2, *1 and 2 Corinthians*, ed. David M. Hay (Minneapolis: Fortress, 1993), 167–68.

66. The language of compulsion recalls Paul's description of himself as God's captive in a victory processional (2 Cor. 2:14) and the recipient of a prophetic call (1 Cor. 9:15–18; Gal. 1:15).

love of Christ in 5:14 by appealing to the creedal statement "one has died for all," which is an abbreviated form of the confession "Christ died for our sins" (1 Cor. 15:3)—the supreme manifestation of Jesus's sacrificial love for others (cf. Rom. 5:8).[67] Paul engages in a ministry for others in accordance with the creed that shapes his entire existence, demonstrating his love for the Corinthians (cf. 2 Cor. 2:1–4; 7:2–4).

He offers an interpretation of the creed in 5:14b: "therefore all have died." Inasmuch as he is justifying his ministry, "all have died" indicates his role in sharing in the death of Jesus. However, "all" includes more than Paul alone (cf. "we all" in 3:18; 5:10). Indeed, the contrast between "one" and "all" recalls his argument elsewhere that the fate of the one affects the many (cf. Rom. 5:12–21; 1 Cor. 15:21–23; 1 Thess. 4:13–18). That "all" is a reference to the believing community becomes apparent in 5:15, when Paul repeats the creed ("he died for all") and adds the additional interpretation "so that those who live might live no longer for themselves, but for him who died and was raised for them." Because the church also shares in the death of Christ, the people no longer live for themselves. Paul appeals to the same principle in Romans 14:7: "We do not live to ourselves, and we do not die to ourselves." The event of the cross not only occurred in the past but is the event that defines the church in the present. Thus as in earlier letters (cf. 1 Cor. 10:16–17; 1 Thess. 4:13–18), the community is united by its joint participation in the cross.

As the parallel *hōste* clauses (NRSV "therefore" in 5:16; "so" in 5:17) in 5:16–17 indicate, Paul elaborates here on the relationship between himself and the church. The contrast between "once" and "no longer/from now on" in 5:16 indicates the radical change that took place in Paul's epistemology when he was compelled by the love of Christ. "We" refers to Paul, who once knew Christ "from a human point of view" but no longer does. In the explanatory statement in 5:17, Paul moves from the change in his own way of seeing to that of the church. With the phrase "if anyone is in Christ," he moves beyond his own experience to that of the community. "If anyone" recalls the earlier "all" (5:14) and "those who no longer live for themselves" (5:15). The community composed of those who died with Christ has been incorporated "in Christ," and for them "there is a new creation" (5:17). Just as Paul's life proceeded with the decisive break from "once" to "no longer," for them "the old has passed away" and "the new has come" (5:17 ESV). The church is the people of the new creation. As it shares in the destiny of Christ, it also lives as people of the new age who do not see the world and ministry from "a human point of view."

67. Paul uses the *hyper* formula for the sacrificial death of Christ in Rom. 5:8; 8:3; 15:15; 1 Cor. 8:10; Gal. 1:4; 2:20; 3:13; 1 Thess. 5:10.

"In Christ" and "with Christ" in Romans

In Romans Paul develops themes that he introduced in 1 Corinthians, reflecting further on the church's identity in Christ, the founder of a new humanity. After announcing the revelation of God's righteousness for those who believe (Rom. 1:16–17), he lays the foundation for a redefinition of the people of God in 1:1–4:22, indicating that there is no partiality with God (2:11) and declaring that circumcision is not a guarantee of belonging to the people of God (2:25–29). Indeed, the argument that Abraham is the father not only of the circumcised but of all who have faith (4:1–22) is also a redefinition of the people of God.

Paul first addresses his readers with the first-person plural in 4:23 and continues to include his readers throughout chapters 5–8. "We" in these chapters includes those "who believe in him who raised Jesus our Lord from the dead" (4:24). As his anguished discussion of Israel in chapters 9–11 indicates, Paul speaks primarily to gentile readers (cf. 1:13) in chapters 5–8. As the inclusio in 5:1, 11 indicates, the community ("we") has peace with God "through our Lord Jesus Christ." He elaborates in the comparison between the "one man" (5:12), the founder of the old humanity, and the "one man" who is the founder of the new humanity (5:12–21). Just as the many "were made" (*katestathēsan*) sinners by the one, the many "will be made righteous" (*katastathēsontai*) by one man's obedience. Here, as in Paul's previous letters (cf. 1 Cor. 15:21–23; 1 Thess. 4:13–18), the one determines the destiny of the many.

The reflection on the founders of the old and the new humanity (5:12–21) provides the context for Paul's appeal to the readers' memory of their baptism. The new humanity that has been made righteous by Christ is composed of those who were baptized "into Christ" (*eis christon*). Verses 6:1–11 elaborate on the relationship between the one and the many. The compounds with *syn-* indicate the christological dimension of the community's existence. We were "buried with [*synetaphēmen*] him" (6:4), "united [*symphytoi*, literally "planted together"] with him" (6:5), and "crucified with [*synestaurōthē*] him" (6:6); we have "died with [*apethanomen*] Christ" and will "live with [*syzōsomen*] him" (6:8). We share in his death and will share in his resurrection (6:5, 8), and we are now "alive to God in Christ Jesus" (6:11). Having shown that believers have shared the destiny of the death of Christ, Paul declares that we are "joint heirs" (*synklēronomoi*) with Christ, provided that "we suffer with [*sympaschomen*] him so that we may also be glorified with [*syndoxasthōmen*] him" (8:17). We who shared in his death will ultimately be "conformed to" (*symmorphous*) the image of the exalted Christ (8:29).[68]

---

68. See Walter Grundmann, "σύν, κτλ," *TDNT* 7:766–67.

Paul employs the *syn-* compounds to describe the experience of believers in the past and future. In the present there is "no condemnation for those who are in Christ Jesus" (8:1). Paul proceeds from the general statement in the third person in 8:1 to the first-person plural that dominates the remainder of the chapter (second-person plural is used in 8:9–11), describing the new humanity that lives by the Spirit and fulfills the just requirement of the law (8:4). Offering the alternative to the wretched man in whom sin dwells (*oikei*, 7:20), Paul continues the image of the dwelling.

> You are in the Spirit, since [literally "if"] the Spirit of God dwells [*oikei*] in you. (8:9)

> But if Christ is in you . . . (8:10)

> If the Spirit of him who raised Jesus from the dead dwells in you . . . (8:11)

In each instance Paul employs the conditional "if" (*ei*), which can be rendered "since," to describe the experience of the new humanity. He uses Christ and the Spirit interchangeably, indicating that believers are "in Christ" (8:1) just as Christ is "in you" (8:10), and the Spirit is "in you" just as you are "in the Spirit" (8:9). As in Galatians 4:19, "in you" is more appropriately rendered "among you," as the second-person plural indicates. Believers who share the destiny of Christ are "in Christ," and Christ is "among believers." Paul does not think of this experience in individualistic terms but speaks to a community in the plural. The church is the new humanity that is destined to be conformed to the image of the Son.[69]

CONCLUSION: THE PEOPLE OF GOD AND THE NEW HUMANITY IN CHRIST

As I have argued in this chapter, Paul's gentile converts find their identity as members of the people of God with their roots in Israel's story. Paul transforms the concept of the people of God with his claim that the converts share the destiny of Christ and are now in him. This redefinition of the people of God shaped the church's practice and has continuing implications. The church lives "in Christ" and "with Christ," just as Christ is "in" the community (cf. Rom. 8:9–11). These prepositions reflect the sharp distinction between the church and other communities.

69. See chap. 4 for further development of this theme.

Life in Christ is no private matter. Paul does not speak of a "personal relationship to Jesus Christ" but speaks of the community in Christ. Individuals do not come together in a social contract or to have their needs met. To be "in Christ" is to be in the company of others who come together not only for worship but also to share a common life in congregations that live and proclaim the story of Christ. The church is the community of those who have been baptized into one body and "live no longer for themselves" (2 Cor. 5:15).

The body was a familiar image in antiquity for communities, and it is commonly used today to describe the group. For Paul, however, the community of believers is not merely a body but the body of Christ. When Paul says that "you were baptized into one body" (1 Cor. 12:13), he indicates that the body preceded the individuals. Thus the church is not merely a gathering of individuals, for the whole is greater than the sum of the parts. To be a member is not to be a "card carrier," in which one pays dues in exchange for the benefits. Those who are "in Christ" share in the destiny of the one who sacrificed himself for others, and they live in harmony with others.

Existence in Christ is both inclusive and exclusive. A consistent theme in Paul's transformation of the election tradition is that in Christ the ethnic and social distinctions have been removed. The church is not a homogeneous group but a community composed of people whom we did not choose. Paul consistently reiterates this theme in the letters. At the same time, existence in Christ has sharp boundaries, for the church is the community that shares the destiny of Christ. Its unity with him in suffering and death is the prelude to union with him in resurrection and new life.

3

THE CHURCH MADE VISIBLE

Baptism and the Lord's Supper in 1 Corinthians,
Galatians, and Romans

According to Peter Lampe, "It may be disappointing to say so, but the sacraments are of no special theological interest to Paul's thought."[1] Although baptism and the Lord's Supper are the common practices of almost all Christian traditions, neither Paul nor the other New Testament writers speak at length about these topics. Paul discusses the Lord's Supper only in 1 Corinthians, and only in response to abuses by the community. The undisputed letters of Paul refer to baptism explicitly in only three places (Rom. 6:2–4; 1 Cor. 12:13; Gal. 3:27), and in each case baptism is the illustration rather than the main topic of discussion. Nevertheless, the passing references in the letters indicate that all of Paul's churches practice baptism as a rite of initiation. The care with which Paul reminds the Corinthians of the Lord's Supper tradition that he passed on to them (1 Cor. 11:23–26) suggests that this tradition was part of his basic catechesis to all the churches, which observed this meal regularly.

The universality of baptism and the Lord's Supper indicates that Paul probably inherited these practices from the Jerusalem church. The statement "I received from the Lord what I also handed on to you" (1 Cor. 11:23) suggests

---

1. Peter Lampe, "The Eucharist: Identifying with Christ on the Cross," *Interpretation* 48 (1994): 36.

that Paul learned the Lord's Supper from his predecessors, the church he had once persecuted.[2] His assumption that the Roman believers, whom he had not visited previously, had been baptized (Rom. 6:3–4) indicates that the practice of baptism came from Paul's predecessors. While we do not know how Paul's predecessors and his contemporaries interpreted these practices, we can assume that these were the badges of identity for the new movement from its inception.

Although Paul does not speak at length about baptism and the Lord's Supper, he appeals to these practices in the midst of critical theological reflection on the believers' identity in Christ. Indeed, as I argued in chapter 2, the prepositional phrases "in Christ," "with Christ," "into Christ," and "through Christ" reflect Paul's corporate Christology, indicating the inseparability of Christ and the church. Paul's appeal to baptism and the Lord's Supper in these contexts raises the question of the role of these practices in his corporate Christology. Believers have been "buried with him through baptism" (Rom. 6:4 NIV) and "baptized into" the one body of Christ (1 Cor. 12:13) and have "put on Christ" (Gal. 3:27 KJV). In the Lord's Supper they share in the body and blood of Christ (1 Cor. 10:16). In this chapter I will investigate the place of baptism and the Lord's Supper in Paul's ecclesiology in 1 Corinthians, Galatians, and Romans, showing how baptism and the Lord's Supper offer important visible manifestations of Paul's major theological themes.

BAPTISM AND THE LORD'S SUPPER IN 1 CORINTHIANS

Paul offers his most extensive teaching on baptism and the Lord's Supper in 1 Corinthians in response to the Corinthians' practice. While he does not designate the two rituals as "sacraments," as the church did later, his response to the Corinthians suggests that his readers had already placed them in a single category. His recollection that "[our ancestors] were baptized into Moses" (10:2), ate "spiritual food" (10:3), and drank "spiritual drink" (10:4) implicitly compares baptism and the Lord's Supper to the passing through the water at the Exodus and the manna in the wilderness.[3] The description of Israel's di-

2. See W. R. Farmer, "Peter and Paul, and the Tradition concerning the 'Lord's Supper' in 1 Corinthians 11:23–26," in *One Loaf, One Cup: Ecumenical Studies of 1 Corinthians 11 and Other Eucharistic Texts*, The Cambridge Conference on the Eucharist, August 1988, ed. Otto Knoch and Ben F. Meyer (Macon, GA: Mercer University Press, 1988), 36.

3. "Baptized into Moses" is patterned after the baptismal formula "baptized into Christ" (cf. Rom. 6:3; Gal. 3:27). The references to "spiritual food" and "spiritual drink" are drawn from several Old Testament passages. "Spiritual food" refers to the manna tradition (Exod. 16:4–31); "spiritual drink" is drawn from the miracle of the water coming from the rock (Exod. 17:1–7).

sastrous fate (10:6–11) is evidently a warning to those who have misunderstood baptism and the Lord's Supper. Since both practices had analogous rites in the Greco-Roman world, the possibility of misunderstanding was considerable.[4] Paul's response suggests that the Corinthians interpret these rites against the background of Greco-Roman meals. This misunderstanding is probably the reason that Paul returns to these themes repeatedly throughout the letter.

Baptism probably played a role in the factionalism at Corinth. The unexpected introduction of the topic in the context of the claims of partisan loyalty to individual leaders (1:13–17) suggests that the Corinthians expressed loyalty to the leaders who baptized them, thus making baptism a source of division. Paul responds initially with three rhetorical questions (1:13), all of which anticipate a negative answer (1:13). Paul first asks, "Has Christ been divided [*memeristai*]?" The perfect tense refers to a past reality that still remains in effect. The question anticipates the later reflection on individuals as "members" of Christ (6:15) and the church as the one body of Christ (12:12–13).[5] Because Christ cannot be divided among the factions, the division of the community is nothing less than the division of Christ. The undivided Christ is the foundation for a united church, and believers are nothing less than members of Christ.

In the next two questions, Paul turns from the perfect tense to the aorist to describe two decisive moments. That is, present reality is the result of two events. The second question, "Was Paul crucified for you?" also requires a negative response, for Paul has taught the Corinthians already that "Christ died for our sins" (1 Cor. 15:3). The phrase "was crucified for you" (*estaurōthē hyper hymōn*) introduces a topic that Paul develops (1:18–2:17) in response to the Corinthians, whose Christology was not determined by the cross.[6] This question is not randomly selected but follows naturally from the first question. Because the death of Christ for others creates solidarity in the community (cf. 1 Cor. 8:11), Christ cannot be divided. His death should have created solidarity in the Corinthian community.

See Hans-Josef Klauck, *Herrenmahl und Hellenistischer Kult: Eine religionsgeschichtliche Untersuchung zum ersten Korintherbrief*, Neutestamentliche Abhandlungen, Second Series 15 (Münster: Aschendorff, 1982), 235.

4. For the cultic meals in the Greco-Roman world, see Klauck, *Herrenmahl und Hellenistischer Kult*, 31–33. See also John Fotopoulos, *Food Offered to Idols in Roman Corinth: A Social Rhetorical Reconsideration of 1 Corinthians 8:1–11:1*, WUNT 2/151 (Tübingen: Mohr Siebeck, 2003), 49–178.

5. Paul's use of the definite article (literally "the Christ") is rare in his writings. The usage may be an abbreviation for "the body of Christ." Christ and his body cannot be torn apart. See Wolfgang Schrage, *Der erste Brief an die Korinther*, Evangelisch-Katholischer Kommentar zum Neuen Testament 7.1, ed. Norbert Brox et al. (Neukirchener-Vluyn: Neukirchener Verlag, 1991–2001), *1 Korintherbrief*, 1:152.

6. Ibid., 1:153.

In the final question, also in the aorist tense, Paul asks, "Were you baptized in the name of Paul?" Paul assumes that the readers have been baptized into the name of Christ in a decisive turning point in their lives (cf. 6:11). The juxtaposition of the questions about the crucifixion of Christ and baptism suggests the close connection between the two. Baptism was the response to the preaching of the cross. Paul assumes that the readers know the tradition that believers are baptized "in the name of Jesus" (cf. Acts 10:48; 19:5; cf. 1 Cor. 6:11). He anticipates the later claims that believers were "baptized into his death" (Rom. 6:3) and that believers were "baptized into one body" (1 Cor. 12:12–13).

The three questions indicate the close connection between Christology, soteriology, and baptism. Paul appeals to the past experiences to recall Christian identity, knowing that it was Christ who was crucified for them and that their response in baptism brought them together in Christ. The united church exists because of these founding events.

Baptism into Christ precludes any focus on the baptizer. Thus Paul does not remember whom he baptized (1:14–17).[7] The unity of the church is no mere ideal or compromise between various parties; it is a reality in Christ. Anyone who divides it divides Christ himself and ignores the exclusive relationship to Christ.[8]

Boundaries, Baptism, and the Lord's Supper (1 Corinthians 5:1–11:1)

BAPTISM

Paul returns to the subject of baptism in 1 Corinthians 6:11 within the larger context of establishing boundaries between the community and the outsiders (5:1–11:1). The holiness of the church requires the purging of the evil from its midst (5:1–13) and the drawing of sharp boundaries between the saints (6:1–2) and the unrighteous (adikoi, 6:1, 9) and the unbeliever (apistoi, 6:6; 7:12; 10:27; cf. 14:22–23). After establishing the strict boundaries between the "saints" and the adikoi/apistoi, Paul describes the decisive break in the lives of community members. After listing the vices that exclude people from the kingdom of God, he adds, "This is what some of you used to be" (6:11). "Some" in the community used to belong to the world of the unbelievers, and now the entire community has made the radical break from the world. The transition from the imperfect tense ("this is what some of you used to be") to the three parallel aorist passive verbs indicates the decisive break in their

7. Ibid., 1:161.
8. Ibid.

lives. The parallel verbs point to a singular event in their lives that united the Corinthians in a common narrative and separated them from the world of the immoral people described in 6:9. "You were washed, you were sanctified, you were justified in the name of the Lord Jesus Christ" (6:11). "Washed" (*apelousasthe*) is probably a reference to baptism (cf. Acts 22:16; Eph. 5:26; cf. Titus 3:5), the ritual of entry when believers were cleansed of the vices described in 6:9–10 (cf. 5:10) and entered the community (cf. 12:13) of the new age (cf. Rom. 6:1–11). The image implies the cleansing from sin or moral defilement (cf. Acts 22:16).[9]

The parallel aorist passive verbs indicate that baptism was also the moment when the entire community was "sanctified" and "justified in the name of the Lord Jesus Christ." Anticipating a major issue in the letter, Paul had opened the letter by addressing the Corinthians as those who are "sanctified in Christ Jesus, called to be saints" (1:2). Paul's most characteristic designation for believers is "saints" (cf. 1 Cor. 14:33), which he employs to demarcate them from the world around them. Paul appeals to their identity as saints to encourage their total separation from the vices of the surrounding world (6:1–2; 7:14). Although sanctification is a process that continues until the end (cf. Rom. 15:16; 1 Thess. 5:23), it is also a past event that began with the community's entry into the people of God. As the perfect participle indicates in 1:2, believers stand in holiness because of a decisive moment in the past.

Believers were also "justified" at baptism, as Paul will later argue in Romans 6:1–11. Elsewhere Paul uses the aorist passive of *dikaioun* to tell of the decisive saving event that brought a radical break in the lives of the believers (cf. Rom. 5:1; 6:7; 8:30). Like sanctification, justification is an event both of the past and of the future. One decisive event in the past has established the boundaries between the community and the world. Paul insists that believers look back to that moment as a foundation for the boundaries that they maintain.

The Lord's Supper

The issue of boundaries is also the occasion for Paul's brief reference to the Lord's Supper in 10:16–17, which comes near the conclusion of the larger unit (8:1–11:1) on believers' participation in sacrificial meals. The availability of meat in the market that has been sacrificed to idols (1 Cor. 10:25) and invitations from unbelievers (10:27) to sacrificial meals poses a dilemma for believers who know that the gods do not exist (8:4–6). Moreover, some believers claim that "all things are lawful" (10:23) and insist on individual rights (8:9) to

9. BDAG 117. Cf. Philo, *Names* 49: "Infinite indeed are the defilements that soil the soul, which it is impossible to wash and scour away altogether."

ignore the boundaries with unbelievers. Paul's argument in 10:1–13 suggests that some of the Corinthians insist on the power of baptism and the Lord's Supper to ensure their salvation. In the inclusio of 8:1–6 and 10:23–11:1 Paul discusses the believers' participation in sacrificial meals as part of the larger issue of boundaries between believers and unbelievers. He develops the case in 8:7–10:22.

Paul first demonstrates that these meals undermine community cohesion, for not all recognize that the idols do not exist (8:7). As a result, a "brother for whom Christ died" is destroyed (8:11 RSV). The exercise of individual freedom, therefore, can be destructive to the community established by the cross of Christ. In 9:1–27 Paul presents himself as the model of one who does not use his freedom (9:1, 4–6, 12, 18) but who becomes a slave to all (9:19) in conformity with the message of the cross. In 10:1–13 he offers Israel as an example of those who were "baptized into Moses" (10:2) and ate "spiritual food" (10:3), implicitly comparing Israel to the believers who participate in baptism and the Lord's Supper. The fact that the Israelites were "struck down in the wilderness" (10:5) is a warning to the church that baptism and the Lord's Supper do not guarantee salvation.

The consequence of Israel's idolatry (10:1–13) is the background for the command to "flee from idolatry" (10:14 KJV), which reinforces the requirement of communal boundaries. Paul supports this demand by comparing the Lord's Supper to pagan meals (10:14–22). Appealing to the readers' own judgment (10:15), Paul's rhetorical questions in 10:16 suggest that he is citing a formula that was known to the Corinthians. The twofold "is it not" (*ouchi . . . estin*) anticipates a positive answer.[10] The wording ("cup of blessing" and "bread that we break"), which is unusual for Paul, employs Jewish terminology and indicates a pre-Pauline tradition and regular Christian practice. Paul assumes that the readers will agree that the cup is *koinōnia* in the blood of Christ and that the bread is *koinōnia* in the body of Christ. The parallel with the words of institution (cf. 11:23–26) suggests that *koinōnia* here is an interpretation of "is" (*estin*) in the words of institution (i.e., "this is my body . . . this cup is . . .").

Paul uses *koinōnia* to develop the sharp alternative between the Lord's Supper and other meals, contrasting the *koinōnia* in the blood and body of Christ with the *koinōnia* in other cultic meals. In establishing the unity of the believer with Christ, Paul also establishes Christ's exclusive claim. *Koinōnia* with Christ precludes *koinōnia* with idolatry (10:21–22), for one cannot share (*metechei*) the table of the Lord and the table of demons (10:17, 21). Unity with Christ creates boundaries from pagan cults. Thus participation in the

10. Powers, *Salvation through Participation*, 170.

Lord's Supper is not a guarantee of salvation, for the eating of spiritual food and the drinking of spiritual drink requires believers' total participation in the destiny of Jesus.

Paul's demand for separation at meals is reminiscent of the story of Joseph and Aseneth. In this novella, when Joseph first meets the Egyptian woman Aseneth, he refuses to kiss her, exclaiming, "It is not fitting for a man who worships God, who will bless with his mouth the living God and eat blessed bread of life and drink a blessed cup of immortality . . . to kiss a strange woman who will bless with her mouth dead and dumb idols and eat from their table bread of strangulation and drink from their libation a cup of insidiousness" (8:6). Later, when Aseneth prays to the God of Israel, she requests that God may "let her eat [the] bread of life, and drink your cup of blessing" (8:11).[11]

The sacred meal not only creates boundaries from others but also unites participants as partners (*koinōnoi*). Inasmuch as ancient people commonly associated meals with *koinōnia*, Paul can assume widespread agreement that meals establish community. Although the statement that the people of Israel are "partners [*koinōnoi*] in the altar" (10:18) has no basis in the Old Testament, the idea appears in Philo.[12] Paul says that those who participate in eating food offered to idols are "partners [*koinōnoi*] with demons" (10:20). He probably uses *koinōnia* because the word signifies a common feature in ancient meals.[13]

Hans-Josef Klauck has suggested that Paul derives the term *koinōnia* from pagan understandings of the meal,[14] according to which participants at the meal establish fellowship with the deity.[15] However, while Paul may be using the terminology known to the Corinthians, he is not simply following their understanding, for he speaks not only of the *koinōnia* among the participants but also of the *koinōnia* in the body and blood of Christ. Paul's use elsewhere of

---

11. Translation by C. Burchard in *OTP* 2.

12. See Philo, *Spec. Laws* 1.221: "The sacrificial meals should not be hoarded, but be free and open to all who have need, for they are now the property not of him by whom but of him to Whom the victim has been sacrificed, He the benefactor, the bountiful, Who has made the convivial company of those who carry out the sacrifices partners of the altar (*koinōnon . . . bōmou*) whose board they share." F. H. Colson and G. H. Whitaker, *Philo, with an English Translation*, Loeb Classical Library (Cambridge, MA: Harvard University Press, 1962). Cited in Harm W. Hollander, "The Idea of Fellowship in 1 Corinthians 10.14–22," *New Testament Studies* 55 (2009): 460.

13. See Sir. 6:10; Philo, *Spec. laws* 4.119; Plutarch, *Quaest. conv.* 707C.

14. Klauck, *Herrenmahl und Hellenistischer Kult*, 260–61. See also Jens Schröter, "Die Funktion des Herrenmahlsüberlieferung im 1. Korintherbrief: Zugleich ein Beitrag zur Rolle der 'Einsetzungsworte' im frühchristlichen Mahltexten," *Zeitschrift für die neutestamentliche Wissenschaft und die Kunde der älteren Kirche* 100 (2009): 84; Ebel, *Die Attraktivität früher christlicher Gemeinden*, 66–72.

15. See Powers, *Salvation through Participation*, 172, for texts.

koinōn- with the genitive indicates the nature of this participation. The readers "were called into the fellowship [*koinōnia*] of [God's] Son" (1 Cor. 1:9). As a model of Christian practice, Paul desires to know the "fellowship [*koinōnia*] of his sufferings" (Phil. 3:10 KJV). Believers are "partners" (*koinōnoi*) in the sufferings of Christ (2 Cor. 1:7). As Paul reminds the Corinthians, "One has died for all; therefore all have died" (2 Cor. 5:14). Thus believers participate in the destiny of Christ. Paul envisions the Lord's Supper as the expression of the unity of the believer with Christ in his death. Indeed, the Lord's Supper is an expression of the participation in the suffering of the cross. To share (*metechein*, 10:17) the cup is to become a participant in the death of Jesus. The *koinōnia* among believers occurs as all share in the death of Christ and the resulting eschatological salvation.[16] Thus while his use of *koinōnia* appears to be analogous to the ancient view that participants were partners with the deity, Paul makes a sharp distinction from ancient meals. Participation in the Lord's Supper is not only a *koinōnia* with Christ but also a *koinōnia* in Christ's death. Believers share in the destiny of the crucified Lord.

Paul has probably reversed the sequence of bread and cup in 10:16 in order to draw the inference from the breaking of bread in 10:17 and make explicit that *koinōnia* in the death of Jesus creates unity among the participants.[17] His contemporaries undoubtedly agreed that sharing a loaf creates *koinōnia* among those who share it. According to Diogenes Laertius, a precept of Pythagoras was "not to break bread," as friends once did. They "used to meet over one loaf" (*epi hena [arton] hoi palai tōn philōn ephoitōn*). He adds, "You should not divide bread which brings them together."[18] Thus Paul's comment that "because there is one loaf, we, who are many, are one body" (10:17a NIV) would resonate with the ancient audience, which both associated meals with unity and spoke of the group as a body. However, Paul subverts the ancient understanding with his interpretation in 10:17b (NIV): "for [*gar*] we all share [*metechomen*] the one loaf." Not only is the church a body in the common political sense but it is also the body of the Christ who suffered and is now exalted. *Gar* in 17b indicates the basis for the church's existence as the body. The sharing of the one loaf is the physical expression of the unity of the church. The inclusion of "all" in 10:17b also indicates the unifying nature of the Lord's Supper. As Paul indicates later in the letter, "all" who are baptized into

16. Schrage, *Der erste Brief an die Korinther*, 2:439.
17. Interpreters have observed that 10:17 interrupts the flow of the argument, which focuses on the boundary between insiders and outsiders. A. Andrew Das notes that Paul is "getting ahead of himself," anticipating the discussion of the Lord's Supper in 11:17–34. Das, "1 Corinthians 11:17–34 Revisited," *Concordia Theological Quarterly* 62 (1998): 204.
18. Diogenes Laertius, *Vit.* 35. Hollander, "Idea of Fellowship," 465.

Christ constitute his body (1 Cor. 12:13). Despite the divisive elements within the congregation, "all" who have been baptized share in the Lord's Supper.[19]

Whenever Paul speaks of the church as the body of Christ, he employs the imagery of the one body with many members. According to Romans 12:5, "we, who are many, are one body in Christ." According to 1 Corinthians 12:12, "the body is one and has many members." While in the latter passage baptism into the one body is the basis for the unity of the church, in 1 Corinthians 10:17 the sharing of the bread in the Lord's Supper is an expression of the unity of the church.

Baptism, the Lord's Supper, and Corporate Worship (1 Corinthians 11:2–14:40)

THE LORD'S SUPPER

Paul returns to the subjects of baptism and the Lord's Supper in 11:2–14:40, where he turns from relationships with outsiders to the community's internal relationships, especially when they "come together" as a church (11:17–18, 20, 33; 14:23, 26). Because the divisions (*schismata*) among the members (1:13) are present also in the assembly (11:18), Paul gives an extended description of corporate worship, which includes the Lord's Supper (11:17–34), prophecy (11:2–16; 12:10; 14:1, 3–5, 22, 24, 31), glossolalia (12:10, 28; 13:1; 14:2–6, 13–14, 18, 22–23, 26–27, 39), and other gifts (cf. 12:4–11). While Paul does not give a detailed description of the order of worship, he offers our most complete portrayal of an early Christian assembly as he responds to the problems that were evident when the community came together.

Before Paul confronts the readers for their abuses, he begins this unit in good rhetorical style by commending the readers for keeping the traditions (11:2) before offering guidance for proper attire for men and women who pray and prophesy (11:2–16).[20] In sharp contrast to his commendation, he introduces the topic of the Lord's Supper in 11:17–34, saying, "I do not commend you," which forms an inclusio with 11:22, "Should I commend you? In this matter I do not commend you!" In 11:18–22a, he describes the abuses that have provoked this response, and in 11:23–34 he attempts to correct the Corinthians' understanding and practice of the Lord's Supper.

19. Otfried Hofius, "Gemeinschaft am Tisch des Herrn: Das Zeugnis des Neuen Testaments," in *Einheit der Kirche im Neuen Testament*, Dritte europäische orthodox-westliche Exegetenkonferenz in Sankt Petersburg, 24.–31. August 2005, ed. Anatoly A. Alexeev, Christos Karakolis, and Ulrich Luz unter Mitarbeit von Karl-Wilhelm Niebuhr, WUNT 2/218 (Tübingen: Mohr Siebeck, 2008), 176.

20. Paul offers no indication that the section on attire (11:2–16) is intended to correct abuses at Corinth.

Although interpreters debate the precise nature of the abuses, some aspects are evident. The Corinthians come together regularly for an evening meal (*deipnon*),[21] which they probably call the Lord's Supper (*kyriakon deipnon*). Paul insists, however, that it is not the Lord's Supper (*kyriakon deipnon*) but their "own supper" (*to idion deipnon*, 11:21) that they eat, for the divisions (*schismata*) described in 1:13 are evident in the factions (*haireseis*, 11:19) present in the Lord's Supper. Not all are equally guilty in creating the factions, however, for the factions clarify who within the church is "genuine" (*dokimos*, 11:19).[22]

Paul's description in 11:20–22 clarifies why the *deipnon* is not a *kyriakon deipnon*, (literally "a meal belonging to the Lord"). The divisions are not theological but socioeconomic, and the wealthier members are the offenders. Scholars dispute what the offense was. Numerous translators render *prolambanei* (11:21) as "goes ahead" with the meal (cf. NRSV; NIV), suggesting that the wealthier members eat before the poor arrive. Correspondingly, they render the final exhortation in 11:33 as "wait for one another" (*allēlous echdechesthe*). Thus interpreters have traditionally argued that the problem involved wealthy Corinthians who arrived earlier and ate before the poor members could arrive.[23] Others, however, render *prolambanei* as "take" or "devour" and *echdechesthe* as "receive,"[24] suggesting that the wealthy and the poor ate unequal portions while at the same meal; the former ate "their own meal" composed of what they had brought without sharing with the poor, leaving them to go hungry.[25] According to this scenario, Paul's instruction is to "receive each other" by

21. The *deipnon* is the evening meal, in contrast to the *ariston*, a meal taken earlier in the day. The word *deipnon* also refers to a cultic meal, such as the Passover or meals in honor of a deity. BDAG 215; Lampe, "The Eucharist," 36–38.

22. The statement that "there have to be factions among you, for only so will it become clear who among you are genuine" (11:19) interrupts the description of the problem at Corinth with an apocalyptic maxim. *Dei* ("there have to be") is used in both 1 Cor. 15:25 and 15:53 for an eschatological necessity. Cf. *dei* in Mark 8:31; 13:10; Rev. 1:1 for what must take place. *Dokimos* is also commonly used for those who prove to be genuine because they pass the test. See the image of the testing by fire in 1 Cor. 3:13. See also Paul's desire not to be disqualified (*adokimos*, 1 Cor. 9:27). Paul's use of *dokimoi* anticipates the later instruction to "examine" (*dokimazetō*, literally "let a person examine himself [or herself]"). See also the controversy in 2 Corinthians over who is *dokimos* and *adokimos* (2 Cor. 13:1–10). See David Horrell, in *The Social Ethos of the Corinthian Correspondence: Interests and Ideology from 1 Corinthians to 1 Clement* (Edinburgh: T&T Clark, 1996), 150–51.

23. Lampe ("The Eucharist," 37–38) maintains that the wealthy Corinthians ate before other guests arrived in an evening meal, comparable to the "first tables" at ancient banquets. It was common for early guests to have a preliminary meal before other guests arrived.

24. For this interpretation, see Bruce W. Winter, *After Paul Left Corinth: The Influence of Secular Ethics and Social Change* (Grand Rapids: Eerdmans, 2001), 142–52.

25. Otfried Hofius, "The Lord's Supper and the Lord's Supper Tradition: Reflections on 1 Corinthians 11:23b–25," in Knoch and Meyer, *One Loaf, One Cup*, 91–93.

sharing in a common meal. While both alternatives are possible and attested in ancient practice, the latter is the more likely. If the eucharistic tradition recited in 11:23–26 reflects Corinthian practice, the meal began with the breaking of bread and concluded with the words over the cup "after supper." During the meal, the rich ate and drank to excess. Paul's questions in 11:22, "Do you not have homes to eat and drink in? Or do you show contempt for the church of God and humiliate those who have nothing?," indicate that it is "not the Lord's Supper" when the solidarity of the community is destroyed by social division. He addresses this issue in the concluding instructions: "If you are hungry, eat at home" (11:34). In this distinction between private and communal activity, Paul insists that the worship service is not the place to satisfy the hunger of individuals.[26] The primary issue, therefore, was the inequality in the portions of food.

As chapter 10 indicates, the Corinthians are familiar with cultic meals in honor of a deity (cf. 10:14–11:1), and they probably equate the Lord's Supper with the "spiritual food" and "spiritual drink" (10:2–4), assuming that participation guarantees their salvation. Because of the similarities between the Lord's Supper and Greek cultic meals, the Corinthians interpret the Lord's Supper against the background of the Greek symposium, which began with the offering of food to the divinity and concluded with libations and the singing of hymns.[27] Both the division between rich and poor and the unequal portions were commonplace, especially in a competitive and status-conscious society.[28] Jerome Murphy-O'Connor has described the architecture of the ancient house, demonstrating that the host and his friends probably met in the triclinium, the small room that could accommodate a limited number of people, while the rest met in the atrium.[29] Both the difference in portions and the placement of the guests were occasions for affirming one's status and humiliating others. Inasmuch as the Corinthians had been following their customary practice in cultic meals, they would have been surprised by Paul's reaction.[30]

Unlike the Corinthian church, however, the ancient associations were largely homogeneous groups.[31] While the competition for status in ancient groups

26. Ibid., 95.
27. Stephen M. Pogoloff, *Logos and Sophia: The Rhetorical Situation of 1 Corinthians*, Society of Biblical Literature Dissertation Series 134 (Atlanta: Scholars Press, 1992), 238.
28. Ibid., 240.
29. Jerome Murphy-O'Connor, *St. Paul's Corinth: Texts and Archaeology* (Collegeville, MN: Liturgical Press, 1990), 161–78.
30. Schröter, "Die Funktion der Herrenmahlsüberlieferung im 1. Korintherbrief," 85.
31. Gerd Theissen, "Social Integration and Sacramental Activity: An Analysis of 1 Corinthians 11:17–34," in *The Social Setting of Pauline Christianity: Essays on Corinth* (Philadelphia: Fortress, 1982), 146.

reflected some differences in rank, the groups had far less social stratification than the Pauline churches. The common membership in the community of ethnic and socioeconomic groups provided a special challenge for those who were accustomed to homogeneous groups.[32] The Corinthians would probably have been surprised to hear that, as a result of the social division, their meal was not the Lord's Supper, for they assumed that the distinctions of class and status would be present in meals.[33]

Paul responds to this situation in two parts. In 11:23–26 he reiterates the tradition that he had originally delivered to the Corinthians, which largely agrees with the Lukan version. This tradition provides the foundation for the specific instructions that he gives in the second part, 11:27–34. Paul assumes that the Corinthians know the tradition and recognize that the community's own practice should conform to the tradition. He does not call the Lord's Supper a repetition of the Passover meal, even though echoes from the Passover meal are evident in the breaking of bread and the explanation of the bread and cup. He indicates the authority of this tradition in the introductory words "I received from the Lord [kyrios]," who alone determines what the Lord's Supper (kyriakon deipnon) is. The same kyrios who gave the instructions is the kyrios who will return (cf. 11:26). Thus the form of the meal must correspond to the will of the Lord who instituted it. A kyriakon deipnon is not like the meals that are known to the Corinthians.[34]

In agreement with Luke's version, Paul cites the words "This is my body that is for you" (hyper hymōn, 11:24), rearranging the order of the words in synoptic accounts to provide a special emphasis. Whereas the synoptic accounts all have touto estin to soma mou ("this is my body"), Paul has touto mou estin to sōma ("this is my body").[35] In its regular practice, the community follows the command of Jesus, "Do this in remembrance of me" (11:24–25), by which the Lord's Supper is a way of bringing the past into the present. Like Luke, Paul indicates that the body of Christ taken in the bread is "for you." These words are similar to the interpretive words over the cup in Matthew and Mark, "for many" (hyper pollōn, Mark 14:24; cf. Matt. 26:28, peri pollōn), and the earliest interpretation of Jesus's death (cf. Mark 10:45). Paul recalls the creed,

---

32. Compare Plutarch's description of the ancient meal: "To have the company of others forced upon one" is unpleasant. "A dinner party is a sharing of earnest and jest, of words and deeds; so the diners must not be left to chance, but must be such as are friends and intimates of one another who will enjoy being together." He adds, "You could not get good and agreeable company at dinner by throwing together men who are different in their associations and sympathies" (Quaest. conv. 7.6). Cited in Pogoloff, Logos and Sophia, 257.
33. Das, "1 Corinthians 11:17–34 Revisited," 193.
34. Schröter, "Die Funktion der Herrenmahlsüberlieferung im 1. Korintherbrief," 99.
35. Winter, After Paul Left Corinth, 154; emphasis mine.

"Christ died for [*hyper*] our sins" (1 Cor. 15:3) and "one died for all" (2 Cor. 5:14). Paul has established earlier that the death of Christ for all has ethical implications, for the weaker brother is one "for whom Christ died" (1 Cor. 8:11). In the Lord's Supper tradition, Paul envisions the significance of the "bread which is for you," for the second-person plural is inclusive, indicating that Christ died for the entire assembled community. While the Corinthians probably know the formula, they do not understand its significance. The *deipnon* is no ordinary symposium, for it is an actualization of the death of Jesus as the foundation for individual self-denial, which is the basis for community cohesion.[36] The example of Jesus teaches the community to act on behalf of others rather than indulge themselves in the supper. "For you" includes both rich and poor.

Paul assumes that Jesus spoke the words interpreting the cup after the meal. He never speaks of the wine, only of the cup (cf. 1 Cor. 10:16), and quotes Jesus's words, "This cup is the new covenant in my blood" (11:25; cf. Luke 22:20). Paul elsewhere describes himself as the minister of the new covenant (2 Cor. 3:6). Here, combining Jeremiah 31 with Exodus 24:8, he speaks of the blood as the foundation. As in Romans 3:24 and 5:10, the blood is the reference to the self-sacrifice of Christ.

Both the body and the blood of Christ are expressions for the self-sacrifice of Christ, as Paul indicates in 11:26 when he says, "As often as you eat this bread and drink this cup, you proclaim the Lord's death until he comes." Paul assumes the regular repetition of the meal in response to the twofold command, "Do this in remembrance of me" (11:24–25).[37] *Kataggelein*, the word for Christian proclamation (1 Cor. 2:1; 9:14; Phil. 1:17–18; Col. 1:28), does not refer to the ministry of the word alongside the Lord's Supper, but to the impact of Christian practice on others. The selfless participation in the Lord's Supper is a witness to others.

After reciting the tradition in 11:23–26, Paul draws the consequences in two *hōste* clauses. Verses 27–32 describe the judgment that follows those who participate in the bread and cup "in an unworthy manner" (*anaxiōs*). Having established the alternatives between the cup of the Lord and the cup of demons (10:21), Paul indicates that those who participate unworthily will be "answerable" (*enochos*) for the body and blood of the Lord. To participate unworthily, therefore, is to fail to recognize the significance of the death of

36. Hofius, "Gemeinschaft am Tisch des Herrn," 182.
37. See Hofius, "The Lord's Supper," 104, who points out that remembering (Hebrew *zikkārón*) is used in the Old Testament for events in the past that remain foundational for the worshiper, who is included in them. Remembering is especially important in Passover traditions (cf. Exod. 12:14; 13:3, 9; Deut. 16:3; *Jub.* 49:7–23).

Jesus for the participants. This failure results in the social divisions at the meal and the abuse directed toward those who go hungry. That is, unworthy participation involves the behavior at meals that had been customary for the Corinthians. Sharing in the bread and the cup should shape the behavior of the participants. Those who share in Jesus's supreme self-sacrifice should also share his sacrifice by caring for others for whom Christ died (cf. 1 Cor. 8:11). Paul knows no middle ground: one either shares in the sacrifice of Christ for others or goes over to the side of those who crucified Jesus.

Individuals should "examine" themselves to ensure that they live in light of the cross (11:28; cf. 2 Cor. 13:5). This event will demonstrate who is *dokimos* ("genuine," 1 Cor. 11:19; cf. 1 Cor. 3:15). Those who eat and drink will eat and drink judgment in not discerning the body. The inevitable result of being answerable for the death of Jesus (11:27) is judgment. "Not discerning the body" is the equivalent to unworthy participation. Discerning the body is actually shorthand for discerning the body and blood of Christ, that is, recognizing the death of Christ as the act of self-sacrifice. Paul indicates that this judgment has already begun, for "many of you are weak and ill, and some have died" (11:30). Just as ancient Israelites died in the wilderness despite their eating of spiritual food and drinking spiritual drink, believers already experience judgment. Their participation in the blood of Jesus does not guarantee their salvation. Self-examination results in the church's not being condemned with the world.

In the second *hoste* clause, Paul calls for the opposite behavior from what he condemns in 11:17–22. Instead of being self-absorbed with one's own meal, one should regard "one another" in order not to fall into judgment (11:33). The Lord's Supper thus conforms to the nature of the sacrifice of the Christ, who gave himself for others (8:11).

Baptism

Divisions in the corporate worship at Corinth existed not only at the Lord's Supper but also in the exercise of the *pneumatika*, the subject of chapters 12–14. Having earlier appealed to baptism (1 Cor. 1:13–17; 6:11) and the Lord's Supper (10:16–17; 11:17–34) to address the issues at Corinth, Paul recalls their baptism in 12:13 to guide them in the use of the gifts. Within the larger context, he has already emphasized that the power of the Spirit was present in his preaching (2:1–4) and proclamation (2:5–17). He has also reminded the community that the Spirit is a continuing reality in the community (3:16; cf. 6:19). In response to an inquiry from the Corinthians over disorder in the assembly (cf. 12:1), Paul now addresses the place of *pneumatika* when they "come together" (14:26), attempting to overcome the apparent rivalries in the exercise of the gifts among the members. In 1 Corinthians 12 he lays the foundation for the specific instructions that he offers in chapter 14, focusing on the unity created by the Spirit. In 12:4–11 he affirms that "one and the same Spirit" has distributed a gift to each member (12:11). In 12:12–26 he illustrates the unity of the church with the image of the body and its members.

Paul had anticipated the image of the church as the body of Christ earlier in the letter, having asked "Has Christ been divided?" in response to Corinthian partisanship (1:13). His earlier reference to individuals as "members of Christ" also anticipated the extended image in 12:12–26. In 12:12 he introduces the extended image with the commonplace protasis, "Just as the body is one and has many members," adding, "so it is with Christ." That is, while other communities may conceive of themselves as a body, the church is the body of Christ. Thus it discovers its unity by being incorporated in Christ.

Paul supports this view of present reality (12:12) with a twofold reference to a past event: "In the one Spirit we were all baptized into one body" and "we were all made to drink of one Spirit" (12:13). The aorist passive *ebaptisemen* recalls the earlier question, "Were you baptized in the name of Paul?" (1:13). It also recalls the statement that our ancestors were "baptized into Moses" (10:2). Paul responds to the partisanship with the reminder that "we were *all* baptized." Each has received the Spirit (12:7, 11) and all were baptized. This aorist passive also recalls the earlier reminder of a singular event: "You were washed, you were sanctified, you were justified" (6:11). The current reality goes back to the decisive turning point in their existence. Baptism is not the beginning of an allegiance to a leader but incorporation into Christ.

The use of *pantes* recalls the emphasis on "each" and focuses on the unity established in baptism. As the entry for all, baptism erases the distinction between slave and free as well as the other divisions in Corinth. As with the Lord's Supper, baptism is into the body of Christ, the participation in his body. The community is not a collection of individuals but the people who have been incorporated into the Christ who preceded them.

Paul has spoken in the present tense to describe the Spirit as a continuing reality (12:4–11). In 12:13 he speaks of the decisive moment when the community received the Spirit. The parallelism between "we were all baptized" and "we were all made to drink of one Spirit" indicates that baptism was both incorporation into the body and the moment of reception of the Holy Spirit. The Spirit was active both in Paul's preaching and in the baptism of the believers.[38] The present possession of the one Spirit originated at a singular

---

38. Although "in the one Spirit" (*en heni pneumati*) can express either location or agency, here the Holy Spirit is the agent of the baptism. Thus one could render the phrase "by one

moment when the Corinthians were baptized. This moment shapes the ongoing existence of the church. The point is that all have a common beginning
and that the shared beginning is the reason for the community's common life.

BAPTISM IN GALATIANS

In Galatians 3:27 Paul mentions baptism in the middle of the argument with
this community that had deserted the God who called them, "turning to a
different gospel" (1:6; cf. 4:8–9) by accepting circumcision, the traditional
Jewish requirement for membership in the community (5:2–3; 6:12). Paul's
appeal to the story of Abraham in Galatians 3 is probably a response to the
opponents' insistence that the covenant of circumcision is the requirement for
all the children of Abraham. Consequently, the opponents argue, the Galatians'
conversion was incomplete, and the Galatians were not yet the children of
Abraham. Paul's task is to ensure the readers that they are already the children
of Abraham and that their conversion is complete; they need to meet no additional requirements to be children of Abraham (see chap. 2, "The People in
Christ and Christ among the People: Galatians").

Paul reaches that present-tense declaration only after he has described a
sequence of events that have brought the Galatians to that point. In the opening words, he anticipates the argument of the letter, declaring that the Lord
Jesus "gave himself for our sins to set us free from the present evil age" (1:4).
As the reference to the "present evil age" suggests, Paul understands the saving
event as the beginning of the new age anticipated by the prophets. This new
age is the equivalent of the "new creation" (6:15) mentioned at the end of the
letter. Paul speaks of this saving event repeatedly in the letter, dividing salvation history into "before faith came" (3:23) and "now that faith has come"
(3:25) and speaking of "the fullness of time" (4:4) when God sent his Son.

Paul also describes the past event when he preached that message (1:8) and
the Galatians became both children of Abraham (3:7–9, 29) and children of
God (4:5–7), having been justified by faith (2:16–17; 3:8, 11, 24). Indeed, Paul
describes a decisive break between their past and present existence. They are
"no longer" (*ouketi*, 3:25; 4:7) slaves but are children. They were once "enslaved to beings that by nature are not gods" (4:8), but they are no longer.
Their conversion was a new beginning, for they received the Spirit (3:2) and

---

Spirit." See Matthew Brook O'Donnell, "Two Opposing Views on Baptism with/by the Holy
Spirit and of 1 Corinthians 12:13: Can Grammatical Investigation Bring Clarity?" in *Baptism,
the New Testament and the Church*, ed. Matthew Brook O'Donnell (Sheffield: Sheffield Academic Press, 1999), 326–36.

"started with the Spirit" (3:3, 14; cf. 4:6), the gift of the new age, which is a continuing reality (3:5; cf. 5:16–6:10). Thus their present status as children of God began in a decisive break with the past. This break was the deliverance "from the present evil age" and the entry into the new age.

Paul refers to baptism at the climax of his appeal to the story of Abraham. After his description of the past events in 3:23–25a, he shifts to the present reality in 3:25b, indicating the Galatians' new status: "We are no longer subject to a disciplinarian." Having argued the principle of justification by faith in 3:7–25, he speaks directly to the readers in the parallel statements in 3:26–29, which may be drawn from a baptismal liturgy declaring the new status of believers before God, as the chiastic structure suggests.[39]

A "You are all children of God" (3:26).
   B "As many of you as were baptized into Christ have clothed your-selves with Christ" (3:27).
   B′ "There is no longer Jew or Greek, there is no longer slave or free, there is no longer male and female" (3:28).
A′ "You are Abraham's offspring [*sperma*], heirs according to the prom-ise" (3:29).

The present "you are" (3:26, 29) indicates the new status of the gentile con-verts—their decisive break from life under the disciplinarian (3:24) and slavery to "beings that are by nature not gods" (4:8). This present status is a result of an event of the past in which all shared, as 3:27 indicates. Paul employs the aorist passive tense to point to a moment when the readers were baptized. This radical break marks the transition from the old existence to the new beginning, the deliverance from the present evil age. The once-for-all event of baptism is a graphic image for this transition, indicating the importance of this ritual for the converts' new identity.[40]

The statements in 3:26–27 indicate the close relationship between faith and baptism in the Galatians' break with the past. As *gar* in 3:27 indicates, the new status of the Galatians through faith (3:26) is a result of their baptism (3:27). While faith and baptism are not identical, they are inseparable. Paul has not merely replaced one ritual (circumcision) with another (baptism), for baptism is not a supplement to faith.[41] Believers are justified by the saving act of Christ and respond in faith. Udo Schnelle has correctly observed, "The act of God postulated in Paul's doctrine of the justification of the sinner through

39. Betz, *Galatians*, 184.
40. Schnelle, *Apostle Paul*, 301.
41. Richard N. Longenecker, *Galatians*, Word Biblical Commentary (Dallas: Word, 1990), 156.

faith alone had to be placed in some particular relation to the reality of human existence. This is what the baptismal traditions do, in that they designate baptism as the place where God lets himself be encountered and experienced."[42]

Whereas in 1 Corinthians Paul says that we were baptized "into one body," here he says that we were baptized "into Christ." Baptism "into Christ" is not an abbreviation for "into the name of Christ" but is the occasion for incorporation into Christ, the inclusive seed of Abraham.[43] As a result, believers clothe themselves with Christ as a new garment and become transformed into a new being.

Paul points to the inclusive community that results from his gospel. Through faith "all" are children. In 3:27 Paul expands the statement, indicating that "as many of you as have been baptized into Christ have clothed yourselves with Christ." "As many of you" in 3:27 is parallel to "all" in 3:26. The parallel indicates that baptism is inseparable from faith. This moment is the new beginning when the readers received the Holy Spirit (cf. 3:2–5). This is also the case in 1 Corinthians 12.

Paul reinforces the emphasis on inclusiveness in 3:28, expanding on "all" (3:26) and "as many of you as" (3:27) with the declaration that the old divisions between Jew and Greek, slave and free, male and female have been removed. Although the issue in Galatians is the relationship between Jews and gentiles, Paul elaborates by adding the other common divisions in humanity. The similarity to the claim in 1 Corinthians that Jews or Greeks, slaves or free are all one body (12:13) suggests that forms of this saying were commonly associated with baptism (cf. Col. 3:11). Paul probably adds to the saying "for all of you are one in Christ Jesus" (Gal. 3:28) to indicate that baptism is an inclusive and unifying event. This claim corresponds to the community's incorporation into the new age. Baptism is not a boundary marker, but a marker of unity.

BAPTISM IN ROMANS

Writing to a church that he did not establish, Paul assumes that the Roman readers have been baptized. As in 1 Corinthians and Galatians, he mentions the occasion when the readers "were baptized" (Rom. 6:3; cf. 1 Cor. 12:13; Gal. 3:27), but he recalls this event only in response to the specific situation. He does not offer a comprehensive theology of baptism but turns to the subject as a critical part of the argument.

42. Schnelle, *Apostle Paul*, 301.
43. Hans Dieter Betz, "Transferring a Ritual: Paul's Interpretation of Baptism in Romans 6," in *Paul in His Hellenistic Context*, ed. Troels Engberg-Pedersen (Minneapolis: Fortress, 1995), 108.

The issue in Romans is the defense of Paul's ministry to the nations (cf. Rom. 15:14–15) and his vision of a united humanity that will ultimately be "conformed to the image of [God's] Son" (8:29) and "sanctified by the Holy Spirit" (15:16). In his ministry to the nations, Paul envisions a church that includes both Jews and Greeks who glorify God "with one voice" (15:6) in anticipation of ultimate salvation. He lays the foundation for his argument in Romans 1–4, declaring that his preaching is nothing less than the good news (cf. Isa. 52:7) announced by the prophets (Rom. 1:2; 3:21). Paul's thesis statement announces that the "righteousness of God is revealed" (*apokalyptetai*, 1:17). He reiterates and expands on this statement in 3:21, announcing that "the righteousness of God has been disclosed" (*pephanerōtai*). The focus of the first four chapters is on the turn of the ages that has already occurred; the good news announced by Deutero-Isaiah (Isa. 52:7) has become a reality. This apocalyptic moment is indicated by the verb *apokalyptetai* and "now" (*nyn*) in 3:21. "Now" is critical for Paul's thought. We live in the "now age" (3:26) of the fulfillment of God's promises. Paul returns later in Romans to this important word, saying, "*now* that we have been justified by his blood" (5:9) and "have *now* received reconciliation" (5:11). Paul announces that what Jewish believers had hoped for at the end of time has already happened in the coming of Jesus.[44] In this new situation God's righteousness is not limited to those who keep Torah but extends to "all who believe" (3:22; cf. 4:11, 16, 18, 24). The death of Jesus has effected the redemption from sin (3:21–24).

Paul speaks in the third person as he lays out his basic argument in 1:16–4:22, but he turns to the first-person plural in 4:23–24, indicating that the readers are among those who "believe in him who raised Jesus our Lord from the dead" (4:24). This statement anticipates chapters 5–8, which are dominated by the first-person plural. As Paul's grief over Israel in chapters 9–11 indicates (cf. 9:1–5), "we" refers to gentile believers who have received Paul's message.

Paul turns not only from the third-person singular to the first-person plural in chapters 5–8 but also from the past event to the future. The inclusio of 5:1–11 and 8:18–39 indicates that God's saving deed in the past is only the anticipation of the ultimate salvation in the future. "Since we are justified by faith" (5:1) summarizes the argument of the first four chapters and recalls the past event that has become a reality for the readers. Paul adds, "We have peace with God" (5:1) in the present and live in the hope that we will be saved (5:10–11). In the meantime, he confronts the challenge of claiming that the turn of the ages has come when the church still

44. N. T. Wright, *What Saint Paul Really Said: Was Paul of Tarsus the Real Founder of Christianity?* (Grand Rapids: Eerdmans, 1997), 36.

faces both suffering (5:2–4; 8:18–26) and the power of sin (5:12–8:17). Paul answers objections to his message, employing the diatribe in chapters 6–8. The discussion of baptism in 6:1–11 is a response to one of the potential objections to his message of grace: "Should we continue in sin in order that grace may abound?" (6:1).

Paul's appeal to baptism in 6:1–11 is a continuation of the section that began in 5:12–21. Having argued earlier that humanity is under the power of sin (3:23; cf. 1:18–3:20), Paul now indicates that sin entered into the world "through one man" (5:12), whose disobedience involved all humanity (5:12–14) in sin and death. Just as one man determined the destiny of humanity through disobedience, one man's act of obedience made the many righteous (5:18–21). Thus the first man is the founder of the old humanity, and Christ is the founder of the new humanity. The old and new humanity corresponds to the earlier distinction between the "now" (3:21) of the saving event and the previous age. Paul presents these eras as two dominions. "Death exercised dominion" (*ebasileusen*) in the old humanity (5:14), while "those who receive the abundance of grace and the free gift of righteousness exercise dominion [*ebasileusen*] in life through the one man, Jesus Christ" (5:17). Similarly, "sin exercised dominion" (*ebasileusen*) in the past, but grace exercised dominion through righteousness (5:21). The two powers are not of equal strength, however, for "where sin increased, grace abounded all the more" (5:20). Although Paul speaks in the third person in 5:12–21, he undoubtedly placed believers in the new domain where sin has been overcome.

Paul's argument in 5:12–21 raises inevitable objections that he must address. Why is sin a continuing reality? How does one enter the new aeon? The question, "Should we continue in sin in order that grace may abound?" continues the image of sin as a domain that remains a possibility for believers. This possibility is evident in the exhortations in 6:12–23, in which Paul changes the image from the domain to the institution of slavery and urges the readers to choose the proper ruler. Paul answers the question with the memory of the decisive event in their lives: "How can we who died to sin go on living in it?" (6:2). Having spoken of two domains, Paul continues to speak of opposites; sin and grace, death and life are mutually exclusive. The believers' death is an irrevocable moment, the occasion when the community was justified (cf. 5:1). He illustrates this moment with a memory of baptism, probably reciting a well-known baptismal tradition. The phrase "all of us who have been baptized into Christ Jesus were baptized into his death" (6:3) recalls the earlier claims that "we were baptized into one body" (1 Cor. 12:13) and "we have been baptized into Christ" (Rom. 6:3). The transition from faith (Rom. 5:1) to baptism indicates the inseparable relationship between the two (6:3).

To be baptized "into Christ" (*eis christon*) implies that Christ is a location and that believers are incorporated into him. Paul elaborates on the phrase "baptized into his death" in 6:4. Believers participated in the death of Jesus, entering into the new humanity described in 5:1–11. Paul continues this motif in 6:5–11. "We have been united with him [literally 'planted together'] in a death like his" (6:5), and the "old self was crucified" (6:6). Like the death of Jesus, this death is "once for all" (6:10). The image of being baptized into Christ's death indicates the irrevocability of the event in believers' lives when they left the domain of sin.

Paul knows the tradition that "Christ died for our sins . . . was buried, and . . . was raised " (1 Cor. 15:3) and applies this to the experience of the believers. Thus, according to 6:4, believers were not only baptized into his death but also were "buried with him by baptism into death," sharing in the destiny of the crucified one. The burial not only recalls the immersion in water but signifies the reality of death.

Interpreters have noted that, while Paul declares that "we died" and "were buried," he does not say that "we were raised with him," for the focus of the remainder of the chapter is on ethical living. Paul says instead, "So we too might walk in newness of life" (6:4). Baptism is thus the beginning of the new existence and entry into the new humanity, the church. Baptism "into Christ" is also baptism into the new aeon. Thus Paul moves easily from the discussion of faith as a response to God's saving event to baptism, for baptism is the objective reality of faith, the decisive point of entry into the new age. Paul insists that believers await the time when they will "live with him" (6:8) but make the irrevocable death to sin a reality in their lives in the present. "Cross, resurrection, and baptism are related to each other not only as cause and effect, for the original event is constantly present in its effects."[45]

This decisive break with the past is the recurring theme of chapters 6–8. After challenging the readers to choose the new domain of righteousness, Paul divides their existence into two eras separated by "now" (*nyn*), urging them to maintain their existence in the new aeon.

> For just as you once presented your members as slaves to impurity and to greater and greater iniquity, so now present your members as slaves to righteousness for sanctification. (6:19)

> When you were slaves of sin, you were free in regard to righteousness. . . . But now that you have been freed from sin and enslaved to God, the advantage you get is sanctification. (6:20, 22).

45. Schnelle, *Apostle Paul*, 328.

While we were living in the flesh, our sinful passions, aroused by the law, were at work in our members to bear fruit for death. But now we are discharged from the law, dead to that which held us captive. (7:5–6)

"Now" encompasses both the saving event at the cross (3:21–26; 5:9) and the entry into the new aeon when faith was actualized in baptism.

In Romans 8, Paul develops the significance of "now" further, declaring that "there is therefore now no condemnation for those who are in Christ Jesus" (8:1). Inasmuch as "condemnation" (*katakrima*) is the opposite of "justification" (*dikaiōma*), according to 5:16, this negative declaration is parallel to the earlier statements that we have now been "justified" (cf. 5:1, 9; 6:7). The third person "those who are in Christ," the equivalent to the first-person plural that appears throughout chapters 5–8,[46] includes those who have shared the destiny of Christ and entered the new aeon at baptism. As a result of the saving event, in which God sent "his own Son" (8:3), "the just requirement of the law might be fulfilled in us, who walk not according to the flesh but according to the Spirit" (8:4). The ethical demands that Paul urges on the Corinthians in 6:12–23 have become a possibility through the Spirit, the power of the new age. Echoing Jeremiah's promise of a new era when God's people will keep the commandments, Paul envisions a community empowered by the Spirit to keep "the just requirement of the law." As in 1 Corinthians and Galatians, Paul associates the gift of the Spirit with baptism, which marks the transition from the old to the new aeon. The Spirit empowers the community for the ethical life (Rom. 8:4–17; cf. Gal. 3:26–29; 5:13–6:10).

Baptism is the beginning of a lifelong process,[47] the entry point of incorporation into Christ. This process involves separation from the old existence and environment, the actualization of the new existence, and entry into the people of God.[48]

CONCLUSION: BAPTISM AND THE LORD'S SUPPER IN PAUL

Because Paul discusses baptism and the Lord's Supper primarily in response to controversy, one can ascertain neither a comprehensive theology of the sacraments nor a clear sense that his views developed over a period of time.[49]

46. Paul employs the third person in 5:12–21 and the first person in 7:7–25.
47. Betz, "Transferring a Ritual," 108.
48. Ibid.
49. Betz, *Galatians*, 187, argues that one can observe the development from a pre-Pauline theology of baptism to the varied portrayals in the letters. He concludes that one cannot harmonize Paul's statements about baptism. See also Betz, "Transferring a Ritual," 85, for the

The paucity of references to baptism and the Lord's Supper does not suggest, however, that these practices played an insignificant role in Paul's theology. The brief references in 1 Corinthians, Galatians, and Romans are embedded within major theological arguments in response to different issues and thus offer different perspectives. Despite these differences, a coherent understanding is evident. Unlike some of his converts, Paul never attributes automatic saving power to baptism and the Lord's Supper; thus he warns against an overemphasis on both practices.

Both baptism and the Lord's Supper offer important visible manifestations of Paul's major theological themes. While he can speak of participation in the death of Christ without reference to either ritual (cf. 2 Cor. 5:14), he appeals to both to describe the actualization of the death of Jesus in concrete ways. The Lord's Supper is a visible manifestation that the community becomes unified as it participates together in the death of Jesus. In baptism the community is united as the members actualize the death and resurrection of Christ. Both are practices that must be accompanied by appropriate conduct and actualized in community life. Both baptism and the Lord's Supper constitute the community as one body (1 Cor. 10:16–17; 12:12–13), communicating the believers' incorporation in Christ (cf. Gal. 3:27). Baptism is consistently "into Christ" (*eis christon*, Gal. 3:27; Rom. 6:3) or "into one body" (1 Cor. 12:13), while the Lord's Supper is the continuing practice of those who are in Christ.

---

view that Rom. 6 presents a later development in Paul's view of baptism. See chap. 4 for the importance of transformation in Paul.

❖ 4 ❖

SPIRITUAL FORMATION
IS CORPORATE FORMATION

The Transformative Church in Romans
and 2 Corinthians

After centuries in which the term "spiritual formation" was used in association with the preparation of priests, it has become a popular subject in contemporary literature, seminary curricula, and programs of the church. It is no longer a Roman Catholic topic but is a common concern among Greek Orthodox, mainline Protestant, and evangelical Protestant believers. Although these traditions interpret the concept in a variety of ways, they share common themes in their understanding of spiritual formation. These themes include an emphasis on spiritual disciplines, such as prayer, Sabbath keeping, fasting, and hospitality.

Although Paul never uses the term "spiritual formation," he is the ultimate source of this phrase. "Spiritual" (*pneumatikos*) is the term that Paul applies to believers (Gal. 6:1; cf. 1 Cor. 2:13–15), who have received the Spirit.[1] In addition, "formation" is a uniquely Pauline word. The apostle looks forward to the last day, when Christ will "transform the body of our humiliation that it may be conformed [*symmorphon*] to the body of his glory" (Phil. 3:21).

1. See James W. Thompson, "Paul and Spiritual Formation," *Christian Studies* 24 (2010): 7–8.

God's ultimate purpose is that believers be "conformed [*symmorphous*] to the image of his Son" (Rom. 8:29). Paul describes himself as the expectant mother in the midst of birth pangs "until Christ is formed" (*morphōthē*) among his readers (Gal. 4:19). He speaks twice of the "metamorphosis" among believers, both assuring them that we "are being transformed" (*metamorphoumetha*, 2 Cor. 3:18) and urging them not to "be conformed to this world" but to "be transformed" (*metamorphousthe*, Rom. 12:2) by the renewing of their minds.

The presence of forms of *morph-* in four of the undisputed letters indicates the importance of transformation in the theology of Paul. This concept is not limited, however, to one word, for Paul employs similar expressions to describe the change that takes place among believers. The goal of Paul's ministry, as he consistently declares, is a community that will be his boast at the day of Christ (2 Cor. 1:14; Phil. 2:16; 1 Thess. 2:19; cf. 2 Cor. 11:3). Although he has been called by God to preach where Christ has not been named (Rom. 15:20; cf. 1 Cor. 1:17; 9:16; Gal. 1:16), his ultimate task is to ensure that his converts are "unblamable in holiness" (RSV) at the return of Christ (1 Thess. 3:13; cf. Rom. 15:16; Phil. 2:15). This same theme resonates in his introductory thanksgiving prayers, as he expresses the hope that God will make the converts "blameless" (1 Cor. 1:8) at the end and will complete the work that began at conversion (Phil. 1:6, 10). Paul's images of himself as father (1 Thess. 2:11–12), mother (Gal. 4:19), and father of the bride (2 Cor. 11:2) all focus on the completion of his converts, who are his "joy and crown" (Phil. 4:1; cf. 1 Thess. 2:19). Thus, the frequent references to the completion of his task indicate the importance of formation for Paul.

In contrast to the popular understanding, Paul does not envision spiritual formation as a private matter. When he declares his pastoral ambition, he does not describe a ministry of saving individuals but speaks of communities that he will present to Christ (2 Cor. 11:2; cf. Rom. 15:16). He describes his "anxiety for all the churches" (2 Cor. 11:28) and the pain of childbirth (Gal. 4:19) associated with the outcome of his work among the churches. Thus he speaks of the corporate narrative of a community that has a shared beginning (cf. 1 Cor. 1:18–2:5; 2 Cor. 3:1–6; Gal. 3:1–6; Phil. 1:6; 1 Thess. 1:6–10) and a common hope.[2] In the meantime, the community awaits (*apechdechesthai*, Rom. 8:19, 23, 25; 1 Cor. 1:7; Gal. 5:5; Phil. 3:20) the end, when it will be conformed to the image of the Son. The present is thus the time of transformation. As the letters indicate, this goal is often in doubt, for Paul fears that his work will be in vain (Gal. 2:2; 4:11; cf. Phil. 2:16).

---

2. See James W. Thompson, *Pastoral Ministry according to Paul: A Biblical Vision* (Grand Rapids: Baker Academic, 2006), 20–21.

In the preceding chapters, I argued that the foundation of Paul's understanding of the church is the concept of the people of God as it has been redefined in Christ. Paul's focus on corporate formation is consistent with his understanding of the church as the people of God, for he has inherited from Scripture a focus on the collective identity of a community that lives between memory and hope.[3] Gentile converts have entered into the turning point of Israel's story and now live in the middle of the drama, awaiting its conclusion. Thus a focal point of Paul's ecclesial vision is the church as the community that is being transformed.

Inasmuch as Romans elaborates on the major themes from Paul's earlier letters,[4] it offers a window into Paul's understanding of the church as the community that is being transformed. With its extended treatment of the community's narrative of past, present, and future, it develops and clarifies a feature that is consistently present in his letters. In this chapter, I will argue that Paul develops in Romans a central theme from the earlier letters: the transformation of the community.[5] This theme is also present in the other letters, especially 2 Corinthians, as I will demonstrate in this chapter.

THE COMMUNITY OF MEMORY

Paul assumes that his converts began their journey in darkness. A common feature in his letters is the appeal to the community's memory of its radical break with its past and its new beginning. Paul often recalls his original preaching (1 Cor. 2:1–5; 2 Cor. 3:3; 11:2; Gal. 1:8; 4:13; 1 Thess. 1:5) and the community's response (cf. Gal. 3:1–5; 4:14; 1 Thess. 1:6–10). His consistent use of the aorist tense and the sharp distinction between "once" and "now" suggests a sudden transference or change of status. This contrast between the past and the present—once and now—is a common feature in both the undisputed and disputed letters of Paul and is a significant factor in Paul's view of transformation.

> You turned to God from idols, to serve the living and true God. (1 Thess. 1:9)

> You were enslaved to beings that by nature are not gods. Now, however, that you have come to know God . . . (Gal. 4:8–9)

3. See Richard Beaton, "Reimagining the Church: Evangelical Ecclesiology," in *Evangelical Ecclesiology: Reality or Illusion?* ed. John Stackhouse (Grand Rapids: Baker Academic, 2003), 221.

4. See Thomas H. Tobin, *Paul's Rhetoric in Its Contexts: The Argument of Romans* (Peabody, MA: Hendrickson, 2004), 47–76; Frances M. Young, "Understanding Romans in the Light of 2 Corinthians," *Scottish Journal of Theology* 43 (1990): 433–46.

5. See Morna Hooker, "Interchange in Christ and Ethics," *Journal for the Study of the New Testament* 25 (1985): 3–17. See also my *Pastoral Ministry according to Paul.*

And this is what some of you used to be. But you were washed, you were sanctified, you were justified in the name of our Lord Jesus Christ. (1 Cor. 6:11)

For once you were in darkness, but now in the Lord you are light. (Eph. 5:8)

These are the ways you also once followed, when you were living that life. But now you must get rid of all such things. (Col. 3:7–8)

Writing to gentile converts in Rome, Paul assumes a radical change in both the beliefs and behavior of the converts. This change is especially evident in Romans.[6]

You, having *once* been slaves of sin, have become obedient to the heart. (6:17)

You, having been set free from sin, have become slaves of righteousness. (6:18)

Just as you *once* presented your members as slaves to impurity and to greater and greater iniquity, so *now* present your members as slaves to righteousness for sanctification. (6:19)

When you were slaves to sin, you were free in regard to righteousness. . . . But *now* that you have been freed from sin, the advantage you get is sanctification. (6:20, 22)

While we were living in the flesh, our sinful passions . . . were at work. . . . But *now* we are discharged from the law, dead to that which held us captive. (7:5–6).

The plural pronouns "you" (Rom. 6:17–19, 22) and "we" (Rom. 5:1–11; 7:5–6; 8:1–39) reflect the ecclesial identity of the listeners and their common narrative as people who have been rescued from enslavement to sin and now enter into a new existence.

Paul anticipated the contrast between "once" and "now" in Romans 1:18–4:22, the first major unit of the letter, declaring, "But now [*nyni de*] the righteousness of God has been manifested" (3:21 RSV). This is a restatement of the letter's *propositio* (1:16–17), which declares that "the righteousness of God is revealed" (*apokalyptetai*). The good news promised earlier by the prophets (1:2) has become a reality in the death and resurrection of Christ (cf. 3:21–26; 4:23–25). As the verb *apokalyptetai* indicates (1:17–18),[7] the revelation that

6. See Michael J. Gorman, "Romans: The First Christian Treatise on Theosis," *Journal of Theological Interpretation* 5 (Spring 2011): 21.

7. For *apokalyptein* and *apokalypsis* as the revelation at the end, see Rom. 2:5; 8:18–19; 1 Cor. 3:13; Gal. 3:23; Phil. 3:15; 2 Thess. 2:3; 1 Pet. 1:5, 7, 12; 4:13; 5:1; Rev 1:1. For the eschatological revelation as a present reality, see 1 Cor. 2:10.

Israel expected for the end of the ages has become a reality, a demonstration "of [God's] righteousness at the present time" (3:26 NASB, *en tō nyn kairō*, literally "in the now age").

As the pervasive use of "all/every" (*pas*, 1:5, 16, 18; 3:4, 9, 12, 19–20, 22–23; 4:11, 16) in this section indicates, God's ultimate vindication is not limited to Israel but extends to "all [*pas*] who believe," including the gentiles (1:5; 4:11; cf. 4:18). God's righteousness for everyone who believes creates a new kind of community that is defined no longer by ethnic ties but by faith in Jesus Christ. With the transition to the first-person plural (4:23–24) that dominates chapters 5–8, Paul addresses predominantly gentile readers, indicating that they now belong to the people of God, composed of those "who believe that God raised Jesus our Lord from the dead" (4:24).

Although Paul speaks in the third person as he describes the dismal state of humanity in 1:18–3:20, he is also speaking of the community's own story—the starting point of their transformation. The description of humanity enslaved to the passions (1:24–26) and failing to keep the commandments (1:32; 2:17–24) corresponds to the community's own past, for Paul describes their former behavior as "enslaved to sin" (6:6; cf. 6:17) and under the control of the "sinful passions" (7:5). He concludes that "all have sinned and fall short of the glory of God" (3:23), anticipating the later statement that their common hope is to share in God's glory (5:2). Thus 1:18–3:20 describes the *adikia* (1:18) of humanity that exists apart from God and is in need of transformation. Those who "fall short of the glory of God" need to be restored to the glory that they lack.[8]

The portrayal of unredeemed humanity in 1:18–3:20 elaborates on what is implicit in all of Paul's letters. As the frequent theme of "once . . . now" indicates, the community shares the memory of slavery and rescue. The "now" of their experience (5:9, 11; 6:21–7:6) corresponds to the "now" of God's eschatological revelation (3:21, 26). The "once . . . now" dimension of their existence marks not only their conversion but also their entry into the eschatological people of God. The depiction of the old humanity enslaved to sin (3:9–18; 5:12–21) was their story (cf. 6:17–19, 22; 7:5–6). Now they belong to the new humanity as a result of their baptism into Christ (5:12–6:11), which marks the decisive moment when believers leave the old aeon and enter into "newness of life" (6:4).

Conversion as the entry into the new aeon is a common theme in Paul's letters. The description of the Philippians' conversion (Phil. 1:6) as the event when God "began a good work" (*ho enarxamenos*) is probably an echo of

---

8. Gorman, "Romans," 22.

Deutero-Isaiah, according to which God is the beginning and the end (Isa. 41:4; 44:6; 48:12, 13), and he will soon "do a new thing" for Israel that is analogous to the primordial act of creation (Isa. 42:5, 8–9).[9] Similarly, at their conversion the Galatians were rescued "from the present evil age" (Gal. 1:4), received the Spirit (3:2–3; 5:16–25) promised by the prophets, and now live in the new creation (6:15) announced by Deutero-Isaiah (Isa. 65:17; 66:22).

In the defense of his ministry in 2 Corinthians, Paul develops these themes at some length. In response to the Corinthians' request for letters of recommendation (3:1), he responds, "You yourselves are our letter, written on [your] hearts,[10] . . . and you show that you are a letter of Christ, prepared by us, written not with ink, but with the Spirit of the living God, not on tablets of stone but on tablets of human hearts" (3:2–3). Paul is the minister of the new covenant (3:6) announced by Jeremiah (31:31–34). In the statement that the Corinthians are a letter of Christ (2 Cor. 3:2–3) he contrasts the church's identity as a letter from Christ with Israel's reception of the covenant "written on stone tablets," echoing Ezekiel's description of the renewed people of God gathered from among the peoples (Ezek. 11:17). The prophet announced that God would remove Israel's heart of stone and give them a heart of flesh (Ezek. 11:19) and a new spirit (36:26–27). Thus the church, composed primarily of gentiles, is the eschatological people of God anticipated by the prophets.

Paul elaborates on this new existence later in the defense of his ministry, as he moves from his own story (2 Cor. 5:16) to the story of the entire community (5:17).[11] In 5:16 he refers to the transformation in his own epistemology. The contrast in 5:16 between the past, when he knew (*egnōkōmen*) Christ "from a human point of view" (*kata sarka*, literally "according to the flesh"), and the present (*nyn*), when he no longer knows (cf. *oidamen, ginōskomen*) in this way, may be a reference to Paul's conversion (cf. 4:6), which marked a change in his epistemology, including his evaluation of Jesus's death on the cross (cf. 5:14–15). In the parallel statement in 5:17, Paul adds, "If anyone is in Christ, there is a new creation," extending the statement about his change in epistemology to include anyone who is "in Christ." The new creation is the new reality for believers. The connection with the epistemological statement in 5:16 suggests that the "new creation" for believers is the new epistemology

9. Thompson, *Pastoral Ministry according to Paul*, 38.
10. On the text variant "our/your hearts," see note 26 below.
11. Consistent with the entire defense, "we" in 5:16 refers to Paul himself. Note the distinction between "we" and "you" in 5:11–13. James W. Thompson, "Reading the Letters as Narrative," in *Narrative Reading, Narrative Preaching*, ed. Joel B. Green and Michael Pasquarello III (Grand Rapids: Baker Academic, 2003), 100.

according to which they no longer make judgments from the human point of view. As in Galatians 6:15, the new creation has become a reality. Both "new creation" and the statement that the "old has passed away" and "everything has become new" echo the prophetic words of Deutero-Isaiah. In Isaiah 43:18–19 he says, "Do not remember the former things, or consider the things of old. I am about to do a new thing." The former things are God's past redemptive acts—creation, exodus (Isa. 51:10–11), and the giving of the covenant. When God does a new thing, Israel will return to Zion in a new exodus (43:16–17), and God will establish a new covenant (42:6; 49:8; 54:10; 55:3; 61:8). Paul's phrase "new creation" is a paraphrase of the promise of "the new heavens and the new earth" (Isa. 66:22). Both the new covenant and new creation have become a reality (2 Cor. 3:1–18; 5:17) at the foundation of the church. The "new creation" began for the church with its founding. The church is the community of both the new covenant and the new creation. Consequently, as an anticipation of the future that God has determined, it stands in sharp contrast to the people of the old creation. As Michael Gorman has said, "Paul's experience and vision of the Church are grounded in this eschatological or apocalyptic reality: the future is present; everything must be viewed in that perspective."[12] The church is a counterculture that rejects the values of the old world and embodies an alternative existence.

TRANSFORMATION AND THE COMMUNITY OF HOPE

Entry into the eschatological people of God does not mark the end of the believers' story, as Romans 4:23–8:39 indicates. Having redefined the people of God as those who believe that God "raised Jesus our Lord from the dead" (Rom. 4:24; cf. 4:11) in 1:16–4:22, Paul makes the transition from the third-person to the first-person plural in 4:23–8:39,[13] expressing the ecclesial identity of the predominantly gentile church. He also proceeds from the saving event of the past (1:16–4:22) to the future hope (5:2, 4; 8:18, 24). Whereas all in the old humanity "fall short of the glory of God" (3:23), the community of believers boasts in the "hope of sharing the glory of God" (5:2). The past events described in 1:16–4:22 become the basis for the future hope described in chapters 5–8.

12. Michael J. Gorman, *Cruciformity: Paul's Narrative Spirituality of the Cross* (Grand Rapids: Eerdmans, 2001), 354.
13. Within this section dominated by the first-person plural, Paul illustrates the community's experience with the third person in 5:12–21, the fictive first person in 7:7–25, and the second-person plural in 6:12–14 and 8:9–11.

Since we are justified by faith, . . . we boast in our hope of sharing the glory of God. (5:1–2)

Hope does not disappoint us, because God's love has been poured into our hearts through the Holy Spirit that has been given to us. (5:5)

Much more, surely, then, now that we have been justified by his blood, will we be saved through him from the wrath of God. (5:9)

If while we were enemies, we were reconciled to God through the death of his Son, much more . . . will we be saved by his life. (5:10)

If we have been united with him in a death like his, we will certainly be united with him in a resurrection like his. (6:5)

Paul reaches the climax of this section with the memory of what God has done: "Those whom he predestined he also called; and those whom he called he also justified; and those whom he justified he also glorified" (8:30). Because of these saving acts in the past, God will bring the community to salvation (5:9–11). The church—those who believe (cf. 4:24–5:1)—lives in hope for the final redemption (8:23–24). It is thus a community of hope.

The ultimate destiny of the believing community is to "be united with him in a resurrection like his" (6:5) and "be conformed to the image of his Son, in order that he might be the firstborn within a large family" (8:29). God's eternal plan is to create a family of siblings who will ultimately bear a family likeness.[14] Christ is the image of God (2 Cor. 4:4; cf. 3:18), and believers will ultimately be conformed to the image of the Son (cf. 2 Cor. 3:18). While the old humanity "exchanged the glory of the immortal God for images resembling a mortal human being or birds or four-footed animals or reptiles" (Rom. 1:23) and "[falls] short of the glory of God" (3:23), the new humanity will share in the glory (*doxa*) of God (5:2, 5; cf. 8:18, 21).[15]

The depiction of the *telos* of the community in Romans 5–8 corresponds to Paul's description of his apostolic mission to present the gentiles as an offering to God, "sanctified by the Holy Spirit" (Rom. 15:16). His task is not only to proclaim the gospel and initiate converts into the new existence but

14. Gorman, "Romans," 27.
15. Despite the title of his book, James George Samra (*Being Conformed to Christ in Community: A Study of Maturity, Maturation and the Local Church in the Undisputed Pauline Letters*, Library of New Testament Studies 320 [Edinburgh: T&T Clark, 2006], 108) does not give adequate attention to the corporate nature of transformation. Paul considers the new humanity as the new people of God redeemed in Christ.

also to complete the task of sanctification (cf. 1 Thess. 3:13; 5:23). The *telos*, therefore, is the ultimate holiness of a community that began its journey in unrighteousness.

Paul's description of the *telos* of the church is an elaboration on his comments in earlier letters. In his first letter, he assures the community that its destiny is to be "with the Lord" (1 Thess. 4:17) and prays that they will be sanctified at the parousia (1 Thess. 3:13).[16] He further elaborates on the church's destiny in 1 Corinthians, assuring the community that "we will all be changed" into an imperishable body (1 Cor. 15:51). His claim in Philippians echoes his description of the ecclesial *telos*: "He will transform the body of our humiliation that it may be conformed to the body of his glory" (Phil. 3:21). The ultimate goal, therefore, is a community transformed into the image of Christ.

TRANSFORMATION IN THE PRESENT

The church that lives in the new aeon has not yet been "conformed to the image of the Son." Indeed, the church lives in the paradoxical situation in which "in hope we were saved" (Rom. 8:24) and "we will be saved" (5:9–10). Although part of the new age, believers still live in the midst of the creation that is subject to decay (8:19–22) in bodies that have not yet been redeemed (8:23). Both bodily temptation and suffering are still present for the community, which lives in a Janus-like situation and can either return to the slavery to sin or live in anticipation of the *telos* that God intended for them.[17] Romans 5–8 describes the present as a period between the times, a time of communal transformation.

Participation in the Destiny of Christ

Those who will ultimately be "conformed to the image of the Son" (Rom. 8:29) have shared, and continue now to share, the destiny of the crucified one. The numerous compounds with *syn* depict this transformation. Believers have been "baptized into Christ" (6:3), "buried with him" (*synetaphēmen*, 6:4), and "crucified with him" (*synestaurōthē*, 6:6). Interpreters have noted that, although Paul indicates that "we died with Christ" (6:8) and were "buried with him" (6:4), he does not say that we have been raised with him, for we will be raised with him in the future. "If we have been united [*symphytoi*, literally 'planted'] with

16. See Schmidt, *Heilig ins Eschaton*, 345–93.
17. As the god of gates and doors, beginnings and endings, Janus was represented with a double-faced head, each looking in opposite directions.

him in a death like his, we will certainly be united with him in a resurrection like his" (6:5). Paul adds, "If we have died with Christ, we believe that we will also live with him" (6:8). Indeed, according to 8:17, "we suffer with him [*sympaschomen*]" in order that we may be "glorified with him [*syndoxasthōmen*]." Paul portrays a path of transformation that will ultimately result in sharing the glory of God (5:2; cf. 3:23) and being conformed to the image of the Son, which begins with sharing in the suffering and death of the Son.[18]

Transformation as the participation in the suffering of Jesus is a familiar theme in Paul's letters. Indeed, it plays an especially important role in 2 Corinthians, Paul's most autobiographical letter, in which he claims that "all of us . . . are being transformed" (2 Cor. 3:18). Confronted by the opponents' criticisms of his ministry and their claim to be "ministers of Christ" (*diakonoi christou*, 11:23), Paul defends his ministry (*diakonia*, 3:7, 9; 4:1; 5:18; 6:3) in 2 Corinthians, using forms of *diak-* more than in all the undisputed letters combined. Although Paul's defense is a demonstration of his own transformation (cf. 2 Cor. 4:10–11), it is inseparable from his ecclesiology, for the existence of the church is the center of his defense. Thus he affirms in the *propositio* that "on the day of the Lord Jesus we are your boast [*kauchēma*] even as you are our boast" (2 Cor. 1:14).

Paul's defense begins with a blessing (2 Cor. 1:3–7) that resonates with the language and rhythm of the Old Testament and functions as the exordium, introducing the themes of the letter.[19] The description of God as "the Father of compassion and God of all comfort, who comforts us in all of our troubles" (1:4 NIV), echoes both the Psalms (69:20; 71:21; 77:2; 86:17; 119:50, 52, 76, 82) and Deutero-Isaiah (Isa. 40:1; 49:13; 51:3, 12, 18; 54:11; 61:2), which describe God as the one who comforts (LXX *ho parakalōn*) those who are in distress. These words also introduce Paul's defense of his ministry; "our affliction" here refers to Paul's suffering, introducing the topic of his affliction (*thlipsis*), a central focus of his defense (cf. 2 Cor. 2:4; 6:4; 7:4; 8:2, 13). Although Paul alternates between the first-person plural (1:3–11; 2:14–8:6, 17–24) and first-person singular (1:15–2:13; 8:8–10; 10:1–11; 11:1–13:10), he speaks autobiographically in each instance, distinguishing himself from the opponents ("many," 2:17; "some," 3:1; 10:2 [NRSV "those"], 12) and the community ("you").

18. See also Gorman, *Cruciformity*, 32; Samra, *Being Conformed to Christ in Community*, 110–11.
19. Cf. "Blessed be the God who . . ." (*eulogētos ho theos ho*) in Gen. 14:20; 1 Kings 5:21; Pss. 17:47; 65:20 LXX. The blessing replaces the usual thanksgiving (cf. Eph. 1:3–14; 1 Pet. 1:3–11). On the rhetorical function of the passage, see Gerhard Hotze, "Gemeinde als Schicksalsgemeinschaft mit Christus (2 Kor. 1, 3–11)," in *Ekklesiologie des Neuen Testaments, für Karl Kertelge*, ed. Rainer Kampling and Thomas Söding (Freiburg: Herder, 1996), 336.

Second Corinthians 1:4–7 indicates that ecclesiology is the central focus of Paul's defense. Paul distinguishes himself from "those who are in any affliction" (1:4)—the churches he established.[20] He elaborates on this claim in 1:5–7, indicating the church's participation in suffering and comfort. According to 1:5, Paul's sufferings are nothing less than the sufferings of Christ (*pathēmata tou christou*),[21] which, along with God's comfort, overflow (*perisseuei*) to him. This anticipates the later claim that he carries around the dying of Jesus (4:10) but lives by the power of God. This surplus of both suffering and comfort overflows to his churches as they share in the same sufferings that Paul endures.[22] The ecclesiastical dimension becomes evident in the added explanation in verses 6–7. Twice Paul indicates that his suffering is for their sake (*hyper hymōn*). As the frequent use of the second-person plural indicates (1:6, 13–14; 1:23–2:11), his concern for his churches lies at the center of his defense. "If we are being afflicted, it is for your consolation and salvation; if we are being consoled, it is for your consolation, which you experience when you patiently endure the same sufferings that we are also suffering" (1:6). This partnership in suffering becomes explicit in verse 7. The shared experience of suffering means that hope is firm (*bebaia*), as Paul looks beyond the present suffering to their ultimate destiny at the day of Christ (cf. 1:14). In the meantime, they are partners (*koinōnoi*) in both suffering and comfort.[23] Thus the Corinthian church experiences fellowship not only with Paul but also with Christ.[24] As a result, the members have fellowship with each other.[25]

In response to the opponents' criticisms of his weakness (cf. 2 Cor. 10:10–11), Paul introduces an alternative vision of ministry and church (2:14–7:4) that becomes the central focus of the defense. He responds to the community's request for letters of recommendation (cf. 3:1) with an ecclesiological answer, using an image for the church that he uses nowhere else. The parallel "you are our letter" (3:2 NASB) and "you are a letter of Christ" (3:3) is comparable to the terms that he uses elsewhere to describe his relationship to the churches he founded. They are the "seal of [his] apostleship" (1 Cor. 9:2), his "joy and

20. On the expectation of suffering in Paul's churches, see also Rom. 12:12; 2 Cor. 8:2; Phil. 1:27–30; 1 Thess. 1:6; 2:14; 3:3–4.

21. Compare Paul's experience of the "fellowship [*koinōnia*] of his sufferings" (Phil. 3:10).

22. The theme of abundance (*perisseuei*) plays a major role 2 Corinthians (cf. *perisseuei* in 3:9; 4:15; 8:2, 7; 9:8, 12).

23. See the discussion in Michael Wolter, "Der Apostel und seine Gemeinden als Teilhaber am Leidensgeschick Jesu Christi: Beobachtungen zur paulinischen Leidenstheologie," *New Testament Studies* 36 (1990): 550–57.

24. Hotze, "Geimeinde als Schicksalsgemeinschaft mit Christus," 349.

25. Ibid., 352.

crown" (Phil. 4:1), his "boast" (*kauchēma*, Phil. 2:16; cf. 2 Cor. 1:14), and his "glory and joy" (1 Thess. 2:20). Inasmuch as Paul maintains that his preaching ministry divides the world among "those who are being saved" and "those who are perishing" (1 Cor. 1:18; 2 Cor. 2:15), the community is among those who are being saved, unlike those unbelievers who have been blinded by the "god of this world" (2 Cor. 4:3–4). Thus its existence is the evidence of the validity of Paul's ministry.

Paul extends the metaphor of the letter, adding "written on your hearts" (3:2),[26] echoing the prophetic promise of the new covenant that God would write on the hearts of Israel (Jer. 31:33). The parallelism between the "letter written on your hearts" and the letter written on the "fleshy hearts" (3:3; NRSV "human hearts") of the community indicates the close relationship between Paul and the church that he founded. Like Moses, Paul is God's instrument in establishing the community's covenant with God (cf. 3:7–18). As founder of the church, Paul is the minister of the new covenant announced by Jeremiah (31:31).

The midrash in 2 Corinthians 3:7–18 (cf. Exod. 34:29–35) is both a defense of Paul's ministry and a description of the church as the people of the new covenant. The focal point in 3:7–11 is the comparison between the glory (*doxa, doxazō*) of the two covenants and the conclusion that Paul is the minister of the more glorious of the two. The contrast between Moses and Paul (3:12–18), God's servants in inaugurating the two covenants, is also a contrast between the past and present children of Israel (3:13–15) and the church, as Paul's transition from "we" (3:1, 4–6, 12) to "we all" (3:18; NRSV "all of us") indicates. While the sons of Israel could not look at Moses because of the glory of his face (3:7), believers now see the glory (3:18). Whereas the veil on Moses's face prevented the people of Israel from seeing the end of the glory (3:13), "we all"—the whole church—see the glory "with unveiled faces" (3:18). "We all" forms an inclusio with the description of the church as a letter of Christ. Thus the church stands in contrast not only to the "people of Israel" (3:13) but also to the rest of humanity, whom "the god of this world has blinded" in order to keep them from seeing "the light of the gospel of the glory of Christ" (4:4). Like Paul, who sees "the light of the knowledge of the glory of God in the face of Jesus Christ" (4:6), the church sees what neither Israel nor the rest of the world can see: "the glory of the Lord" (3:18).

26. The textual variant "written on our/your hearts" reflects the copyists' dilemma, inasmuch as either variant can fit the context. That Paul can speak of a letter "in our hearts" is obvious in his later claims that "our heart is open to you" (6:11) and "you are in our hearts" (7:3). However, the imagery suggests that "written on your hearts" fits the context better, for 3:1–6 is filled with echoes of the descriptions of the renewed people of God in Jeremiah and Ezekiel.

"The glory of the Lord" that "we all" see is parallel to the divine theophany in 3:7–11; the *kyrios* is Yahweh himself, and the believers see God's glory "as though reflected in a mirror" (3:18). Although the image of the mirror suggests the opaqueness of the vision elsewhere (1 Cor. 13:12), the context here suggests that believers see God's glory fully as it is reflected in a mirror.[27] The glory of God visible in the mirror is apparently Jesus Christ, who is the image of God (2 Cor. 4:4). Just as Paul, as a result of his conversion, now sees "the glory of God in the face of Jesus Christ" (4:6), the church also sees the glory of God in Jesus Christ. Jesus is the mirror, or image, of God.[28] Thus believers see the glory in the face of Jesus "as in a mirror." As a result, they are being transformed "from one degree of glory to another" (3:18),[29] unlike Israel who could not bear to see the glory.

As the midrash in 3:7–18 indicates, glory (*doxa*) is the attribute of God (3:18), which becomes manifest in divine theophanies (3:7–11; 4:6). Just as Moses shared in God's glory, the church makes continued progress in sharing the glory, as the phrase *apo doxēs eis doxan* suggests.[30] Even in the midst of affliction, the inner being of believers is being renewed daily, preparing them for "an eternal weight of glory" (4:17; cf. Phil. 3:21).

Believers ("we all"), in contrast to the rest of humanity, are being transformed "into the same image" that they now see.[31] That Jesus is the "image

27. The deponent middle *katoptrizomenoi* can mean "look at something as in a mirror," "contemplate" something," or "reflect." BDAG 535. The most suitable meaning in 2 Cor. 3:18 is "behold (an object or a person) as in a mirror." Jan Lambrecht, "Transformation," *Biblica* 64 (1983): 247.

28. Since as *doxa* and *eikōn* are sometimes synonymous (cf. 1 Cor. 11:7), Paul equates the believers' perception of the glory of God with his seeing the "image of God in the face of Jesus Christ." One may compare Philo's expression of a desire to see God (*Alleg. Interp.* 3.101; cf. Exod. 33:13): "I would not that Thou shouldst be manifested to me by means of heaven or earth or water or air or any created thing at all, nor would I find the reflection of Thy being [*katoptrisaimēn*] in aught else than in Thee who art God, for the reflections in created things are dissolved, but those in the Uncreate will continue abiding and sure and eternal" (trans. Colson and Whitaker, LCL).

29. On the concept of transformation through contemplation, see Volker Rabens, *The Holy Spirit and Ethics in Paul: Transformation and Empowering for Religious-Ethical Life*, WUNT 2/283 (Tübingen: Mohr Siebeck, 2010), 184–90.

30. Most interpreters maintain that the phrase is a reference to a continual transformation in ever-increasing glory until believers fully share the glory of God. See Thomas Schmeller, *Der zweite Brief an die Korinther (2 Kor. 1,1–7,4)*, Evangelisch-katholischer Kommentar zum Neuen Testament 8 (Neukirchen-Vluyn: Neukirchener Theologie, 2010), 228. For the view that the phrase refers to the believers' conversion until the present, see Paul Brooks Duff, "Transformed 'from Glory to Glory': Paul's Appeal to the Experience of His Readers in 2 Corinthians 3:18," *Journal of Biblical Literature* 127 (2008): 771–74.

31. Throughout the apologia in 2:14–7:4, Paul has used the first-person plural for himself. In the phrase "we all," he includes the whole community; cf. 5:14–15.

of God" (4:4) recalls the creation story and the making of humanity in God's image. The risen Christ is also the "image of the man of heaven," the new Adam (1 Cor. 15:49; cf. Col. 1:15). This corresponds to the view that the new creation has come in Christ (2 Cor. 5:17). Elsewhere Paul uses *metamorphoō* only in Romans 12:2, where it appears in the imperative. He looks forward to the time when all believers will be "conformed" (*symmorphous*, Rom. 8:29; cf. Phil. 3:21) at the end. In 2 Corinthians 3:18 he speaks in the present indicative of the transformation of the community "from glory to glory," indicating that transformation is progressive and continuous (cf. Gal. 4:19, "until Christ is formed among you").[32]

The nature of transformation is evident throughout Paul's defense, for Paul himself embodies this transformation as "the sufferings of Christ are abundant" to him (2 Cor. 1:5). In 4:10–11 he describes his task of carrying around the dying of Jesus Christ. Thus the church is being transformed as it participates in the sufferings of Jesus (cf. 1:6–7). As participation in the sufferings of Christ, this transformation "from glory to glory" is not what the opponents had envisioned but an alternative vision of transformation into the image of the suffering Christ.[33]

The nature of transformation becomes further evident in 4:7–5:10 as Paul describes his weakness in the midst of suffering, the divine power (4:7) that enables him to speak (4:13), and the hope of the resurrection (5:1–10). While transformation may include God's power in the midst of the weakness of the body (cf. 1:8–11; 4:7–12), it also includes the daily renewal of the inner person (4:16–18). The church that is being transformed in the present (3:18) will share in the resurrection with Paul (4:14).

In 2 Corinthians 5:11–6:2 Paul gives the theological defense of his ministry in order to articulate a response to the boasts of the opponents and equip the Corinthians to reciprocate his boasting on their behalf (cf. 5:11–12). He offers a summary of his defense: "If we are beside ourselves, it is for God; if we are in our right mind, it is for you" (5:13), which reiterates that his ministry is for the sake of the church (cf. 1:23; 2:4; 4:15, "everything is for your sake"). *Gar* in 5:14 introduces the supporting statement, "For the love of Christ urges us on, because we are convinced that one has died for all; therefore all have died." The love of Christ, a subjective genitive, refers to the love of Christ that was

32. Rabens, *Holy Spirit and Ethics in Paul*, 193.
33. See Michael J. Gorman, *Inhabiting the Crucified God: Kenosis, Justification, and Theosis in Paul's Narrative Soteriology* (Grand Rapids: Eerdmans, 2009), 92: "Because believers now gaze on the image of God manifested in the exalted Christ, who remains forever the crucified one, their ongoing metamorphosis into the image of God, or the image of the Son (2 Cor. 3:18), is a participation in his cruciform narrative identity and a transformation into his crucified image."

evident when "one died for all" (cf. Rom. 5:7–8), the church's foundational story (cf. 1 Cor. 15:3). Here, as elsewhere, Paul returns to the most basic creed to answer the questions that emerge in the community.[34]

The present tense (*synechei*, 2 Cor. 5:14) indicates that the love manifested in Jesus's death for others is the continuing reality of Paul's life. *Synechei* ("impel, urge on"; NRSV "controls") suggests that Paul is not his own master.[35] The phrase recalls his description of his role as captive in the victory processional (2:14; cf. NIV "captives in Christ's triumphal procession").[36] Love determines not only his travel plans (cf. 2:4) but also the life of the community (cf. 2:8; 8:7, 24) and his continuing love for them (cf. 7:3–4). Paul's interpretation of the basic creedal statement indicates why the love of Christ is a continuing reality: "therefore all died" indicates that his life for the Corinthians (5:13) is based on his identification with the one who died for others. His ministry is determined by his participation in the death of Christ (cf. 4:10–11). "All died" indicates not only that Paul's ministry is defined by participation in the death of Jesus but also that all believers share in the death of Jesus (cf. *pas* in 3:18; 5:10). Paul reiterates the same creedal statement in 5:15 and offers an additional interpretation: "He died for all, so that those who live may no longer live for themselves, but for him who died and was raised for them." The general principle applies especially to Paul, who has consistently reminded the Corinthians that his ministry is for them. He describes his life as "for you" (5:13), because he is constrained by the one who "died for all" (5:14).[37] The whole church is defined by its participation in the death of Jesus, for they no longer live for themselves (cf. 1 Cor. 10:23–11:1; Phil. 2:1–4). As in Philippians 2:1–11, Paul hopes that the foundational story will create a new kind of community that is based on selflessness.

Nevertheless, the church anticipates the end. The conflict between Paul and the Corinthians indicates that the church still waits on the ultimate outcome when all "must appear before the judgment seat of Christ" (5:10). Paul concludes this section with a reiteration of the basic creed and its consequences: "He made him to be sin who knew no sin, so that in him we might become the

---

34. Paul summarizes the creed in 1 Cor. 15:3, indicating that this creedal statement summarized what he had originally delivered to them and what they had believed (15:11). When the Corinthians face division, he elaborates on this confession in 1 Cor. 1:18–4:21, indicating that it should determine their conduct, putting an end to their partisan rivalries. See other references to the basic creed, which Paul cites with slight variation: Rom. 8:32; 15:15; 1 Cor. 8:10; Gal. 1:4; 2:20; 3:13; 1 Thess. 5:10.

35. BDAG 971.

36. Thompson, "Reading the Letters as Narrative," 97.

37. Ibid., 100.

righteousness of God" (5:21).[38] "In him" is parallel to the earlier "in Christ" (5:17). Soteriology and Christology are here connected to ecclesiology, for the church is in the process of becoming God's righteousness, just as it is being "transformed into his image" (3:18) as it shares in the destiny of Jesus. As the community dies with Jesus (5:14–15), it is involved in the process of transformation.

The People Free from Sin

Unlike the old humanity, which knows the will of God but is enslaved to sin (Rom. 3:9, 23), the church is the new humanity that is dead to sin (Rom. 6:2, 11–12). Paul reminds the Roman believers of their baptism as the occasion for the radical break in their existence from the old to the new humanity, where sin has lost its power. Paul probably shifts suddenly from his description of the community as those who believe to those who have been baptized because baptism, as an event at a specific point in time, vividly depicts the suddenness of the change from the old to the new humanity. Paul's consistent use of the singular *hamartia* for the power that "invades" (5:12 my translation) and "rules" (6:12 my translation) indicates that sin is the power that ruled the old humanity. While Paul indicates elsewhere that members of the communities will be guilty of specific offenses,[39] which he wants to be eradicated (1 Cor. 5:1–13), he speaks of sin as a force, or power, from which believers have been liberated. The church is thus the community that is free from the realm of sin (Rom. 6:11, 14).[40]

The juxtaposition of the indicative "consider yourselves dead to sin" (6:11) and the imperative "do not let sin exercise dominion in your mortal bodies" (6:12) shows that a return to the old aeon of enslavement remains a possibility (6:12–23). Thus the church is the sphere that is free from sin only as members yield themselves to righteousness. Indeed, Paul presents sin and righteousness as two opposing powers, challenging the readers to become slaves of righteousness (6:18) for sanctification (6:19), separating themselves from the surrounding culture (see chap. 2). While sanctification is an event

38. Although "we" throughout 2:14–7:4 is used for Paul himself, in contrast to "we all" (cf. 3:18; 5:10; 5:14–15), the creedal nature of 5:21 indicates that Paul is referring to the whole community.

39. Paul speaks of sexual immorality (*porneia*) in the church (1 Cor. 5:1), of "one who did the wrong" (*ho adikēsa*, 2 Cor. 7:12), of those who sin (*hamartanontes*) against a brother (1 Cor. 8:12), and of one who is "detected in some transgression" (*en tini paraptōmati*). He uses the plural "sins" (*hamartiai*) primarily in creedal formulae (1 Cor. 15:3; Gal. 1:4) and citations of Scripture (cf. Rom. 4:7).

40. Schnelle, *Apostle Paul*, 573.

associated with conversion (cf. 1 Cor. 6:11), it also continues into the present by the divine power. The *telos* of the believers is to be "sanctified by the Holy Spirit" (Rom. 15:16; cf. 1 Thess. 3:13; 5:23). This process is equivalent to the transformation of believers into the divine image.

The claim that the church is the realm free from sin raises questions about the role of the rebukes, warnings, and moral instructions consistently present in Paul's letters. Paul assumes that believers can fall again under the power of sin. While baptism opens new possibilities for the ethical life (Rom. 6:4–5), the imperatives indicate that sin is still present in the world. Existence in the new aeon does not guarantee that believers will reach the goal. This aspect of transformation is especially evident in Galatians. Here the community that has been set free "from the present evil aeon" (Gal. 1:4) has abandoned the God who called them (1:6), returned to the "weak and beggarly elemental spirits" (4:9) from which they had been liberated, and "fallen away from grace" (5:4). Thus Paul fears that he has labored over them in vain (4:11).

Paul's other letters maintain the same emphasis on the church as the community that is free from sin. The frequent distinction between "once" and "now" indicates that sin belongs to the past. Consequently, the church is not a *corpus mixtum* but a community with strict boundaries.[41] When the Corinthians permit sexual immorality in the congregation, Paul instructs the community to expel the offender (1 Cor. 5:1–13). In the first letter to the Corinthians, Paul instructs the members not to associate with immoral people (1 Cor. 5:9) within the church. In the later challenge to the Corinthians to "come out from them" and "be separate from them" (2 Cor. 6:17), Paul assumes that the church is the renewed people of God.

Paraenesis and Transformation

The meaning of transformation becomes most evident in Romans 12:1–15:13, which describes the implications of the righteousness of God that Paul has described in chapters 1–11. Having declared that God has acted to usher in the new age (cf. 3:21, 26) in which believers now participate (6:1–11), Paul urges readers not to be "conformed to this world" (*aiōna*, literally "age") but to be "transformed [*metamorphousthe*] by the renewing of your minds." As in 2 Corinthians 3:18, the passive voice indicates that God (or the Spirit) is the agent of transformation.[42] The imperative in Romans 12:2 recalls the earlier imperative of Romans 6:12–13 and the Pauline dialectic of indicative

41. Ibid., 575.
42. Beverly Gaventa, "The Maternity of Paul: An Exegetical Study of Galatians 4:19," in *The Conversation Continues*, ed. Robert Fortna (Nashville: Abingdon, 1990), 197.

and imperative. Thus while the passive voice indicates that transformation is a divine action, the imperative indicates the need for the human response.[43]

This imperative is an introduction to the extended paraenesis in 12:1–15:13. Paul introduces this section by describing ethical conduct as "spiritual worship" (*logikē latreia*) in response to the mercies of God, in contrast to the old humanity, which "worshiped and served [*elatreusan*] the creature rather than the Creator" (1:25). The echoes of 1:18–3:20 suggest that Paul is depicting a new humanity in which the unrighteousness (*adikia*) of the old humanity (cf. 1:18–3:20) is reversed. He contrasts the "debased mind" (*adokimos nous*) of the old humanity (1:28) to the renewal of the mind in the new humanity (12:2). This renewal of the mind is the basis for the "metamorphosis" of believers, who live in the new aeon. The present imperative *metamorphousthe* involves progress toward the *telos* of being "conformed [*symmorphous*] to the image of [the] Son" (8:29). As the community of the new age, the transformed church is a counterculture.

Having already described the new existence as the reversal of the prior behavior marked by slavery to the passions (1:24–26; 6:12–7:75), Paul gives instructions in 12:3–15:13 that describe the specific practices involved in the transformed existence. While he does not give an exhaustive description of the countercultural existence in 12:3–15:13, he depicts the basic characteristics of this life. Whereas the old humanity was characterized by antisocial vices (1:28–32), the transformed existence involves life in the community that is composed of "all who believe" (cf. 4:11). Transformation is not an individual endeavor but a life in the body of those who share in the destiny of Christ (cf. 6:1–11). Because this message obliterates the arrogance of those who claim to be "wiser than they are" (11:25), this body is a community of those who learn "not to think of [themselves] more highly than [they] ought to think" (12:3). Consequently, in this body every member has a function that is vital to the life of the community (12:3–8).

The countercultural existence also involves a variety of manifestations of love for others and the renunciation of the self-seeking vices characteristic of the old humanity (cf. 1:18–32). The encouragement to "let love be genuine" (12:9) and "love one another" (13:8) provides the frame for the specific manifestations of love described in 12:3–13:10. The transformed community demonstrates the kind of love that is normally found only in families (12:10), contributes to the needs of the saints (12:13), and practices hospitality (12:13) toward its members, who "live in harmony with one another" and "associate with the lowly" (12:16). The force of this instruction becomes evident when

43. Rabens, *Holy Spirit and Ethics in Paul*, 201–2.

one considers that Paul envisions a multiethnic community composed of "all who believe" (cf. 3:22). As Paul has demonstrated in Romans 9–11, this community is composed not of those who chose each other but of those whom God has chosen.

As people who come from a variety of backgrounds, the members bring cultural differences and differences of opinion on important matters (cf. 14:1). Despite these differences, Paul envisions a community in which members glorify God "with one voice" (15:6) and "welcome one another" (15:7). This community is possible only when members do not "please [themselves]" but please others (15:2–3). When members conduct themselves in this way, they follow the example of Christ, who "did not please himself" (15:3). Thus the transformed community is shaped by its memory of the one who became a servant of others (15:3, 7).[44]

As the reversal of the dismal condition of humanity without the righteousness of God (1:18–3:20), the ethical section in Romans 12:1–15:13 is not an appendix to the argument of the letter but its climax. God's plan for humanity, the restoration of a people conformed to the image of God's son (8:29), is becoming a reality in the church, the renewed people of God. While the community continues to wait for the ultimate transformation, it lives in the new age and is being transformed into the divine image.

The paraenetic sections of Pauline letters consistently depict the nature of transformation into the image of Christ. For example, in Galatians, Paul expresses his personal anguish over the transformation of his converts, depicting himself as the expectant mother in the pangs of childbirth. The phrase "until Christ is formed in you" (Gal. 4:19) is more accurately rendered "until Christ is formed among you" (see chap. 3).[45] Having already presented himself as one in whom Christ lives (Gal. 2:20), Paul expresses the desire that Christ be "formed" in the Galatian churches. The image is analogous to comments elsewhere that believers are being transformed into the image of Christ (cf. 2 Cor. 3:18). The paraenesis in Galatians 5:13–6:10 depicts the transformed church that Paul envisions—a church in which believers abandon self-seeking and hostile behavior toward each other (5:15–21, 26) and serve one another with love (5:14; cf. 5:22–25).

In Philippians, Paul expresses confidence in the opening thanksgiving that "the one who began a good work among [them] will bring it to completion"

44. See Gorman, "Romans," 31.
45. Gaventa, "Maternity of Paul," 196. "The plural pronoun requires comment. Formation does not belong to individual believers, as a personal or private possession only. Instead, formation refers to the community of those who are called to faith, what Paul elsewhere refers to as the body of Christ."

(1:6), anticipating the letter's emphasis on formation. The readers take on the mind-set of the one who emptied himself and took the form of a slave, and their ultimate goal is to be conformed to the body of the Son (3:21). Paul is a model of transformation, for he is "conformed" (*symmorphizomenos*) to the death of Jesus (3:10). Thus those who will ultimately be transformed follow the example of Paul in sharing the path of Jesus in suffering.

THE CHURCH IN THE POWER OF THE SPIRIT

The triumphant claim that "there is now no condemnation for those who are in Christ" (Rom. 8:1 NASB) reiterates Paul's earlier announcement of the righteousness of God (cf. 3:21–26) and introduces the ecclesiological implications of his message. "There is now no condemnation" recalls the earlier declaration, "Now . . . the righteousness of God has been manifest . . . for all who believe" (3:21–22 RSV). Those who are "in Christ" (8:1) are thus "those who believe" (4:24 NASB), the community that has responded to the gospel in baptism. The continuing use of the first- and second-person plural indicates the ecclesial identity of those in whom the slavery to sin (cf. 1:18–3:20; 7:7–25) has been reversed. In 8:1–17 Paul discusses the implications of the liberation of "the law of sin and of death" (8:2).

As the *gar* in 8:3 indicates, liberation occurred in the incarnation and death of Jesus "for sin" (NRSV "to deal with sin"; cf. 3:25; 5:7–8). Thus Jesus became what we are—"in the likeness of sinful flesh"—in order that "the just requirement of the law might be fulfilled in us, who walk not according to the flesh but according to the Spirit" (8:4). As a result, the church will ultimately become like the exalted Christ. Unlike the old humanity, which fails to keep the law's demands (1:18–3:20; 7:7–25) despite its knowledge of the divine will, the church is the community in which "the just requirement of the law" is fulfilled. As the language of interchange suggests,[46] liberation was not only the forgiveness of sins but the new possibility of a community that lives under the reign of righteousness. God not only commands obedience but offers the new possibility to meet God's demands.

The new possibility exists only for those who walk not according to the flesh but according to the Spirit (8:4). The metaphor of walking, a common image for ethical conduct,[47] suggests the equivalence of the "newness of life" (6:4)

---

46. The image of interchange is derived from Morna Hooker, "Interchange in Christ and Ethics," *Journal for the Study of the New Testament* 25 (1985): 15.

47. Karin Finsterbusch, *Die Thora als Lebensweisung für Heidenchristen: Studien zur Bedeutung der Thora für die paulinische Ethik* (Göttingen: Vandenhoeck & Ruprecht, 1996), 113.

and existence in the Spirit (8:4). The use of the passive voice, indicating that the "just requirement of the law might be fulfilled in us" (8:4), signals that the church does not live by its own power. The purpose clauses in 6:4 ("so that . . . we too might walk in newness of life") and 8:4 ("so that the just requirement of the law might be fulfilled in us") indicate that the new possibility of the ethical life has become a reality because of the power of God that was at work in the resurrection. Having announced earlier that "God's love has been poured into our hearts through the Holy Spirit that has been given to us" (5:5), Paul then distinguished between slavery to the flesh (7:5) and slavery "in the new life of the Spirit" (7:6) before elaborating on that theme in Romans 8. Spirit and flesh are two opposing powers (cf. *sarx* in chap. 6); the Spirit empowers the new humanity to overcome the power of sin.

As the people in whom the "just requirement [is] fulfilled" (8:4), the church experiences the reversal of the situation of the old humanity that failed to keep the Torah. This portrayal recalls the prophetic expectation that God would put his Spirit within Israel (Ezek. 11:19; 36:27) and make the people follow his statutes and ordinances (Ezek. 36:27; Jer. 31:31–34). As the eschatological people of God, they have received the Spirit promised by the prophets as the gift of the new age (Rom. 5:5; 7:6; 8:1–17).

Just as believers may choose between the opposing powers of sin and righteousness (6:12–21), they also choose between Spirit and flesh, knowing that only those who are in the Spirit can please God (8:9; cf. 7:7–25). In 8:5–8 the contrast between those who "set their minds on the things of the flesh" (8:5) and those who "set their minds on the things of the Spirit" corresponds to the distinction between the old and new humanities that Paul has described throughout the letter. Just as Paul has earlier indicated that believers must choose to remain in the new humanity (6:12–21), here he reminds them that they are debtors to live by the Spirit (8:12–13) that has been given to them.

In a series of conditional sentences (8:9–11), all of which assume that the protasis is true ("if [NRSV "since"] the Spirit of God dwells among you" [NRSV "in you," 8:9]; "if Christ is among you" [NRSV "in you," 8:10]; "if the Spirit of him who raised Jesus from the dead dwells among you" [NRSV "in you," 8:11]), Paul draws out the implications of life in the Spirit. The image of dwelling (*oikei* in 8:9, 11) echoes the Old Testament theme that God dwells in the temple.[48] As the repeated *en hymin* ("among you") indicates, the Holy Spirit is a gift for the whole community. Not only does the Spirit empower the community for moral living; the indwelling Spirit will also raise the mortal bodies of believers (8:11). Transformation through the Spirit occurs within

---

48. See chap. 2 for both the temple and Israel as the dwelling place of God.

the community and will culminate in the resurrection, when the faithful will be raised.

The consistent feature in Paul's letters is that the church lives in the power of the Spirit. According to Galatians, the powers of flesh and Spirit are both present, and Paul encourages readers to walk by the Spirit (5:16, 25), the means by which they overcome the desires of the flesh. Although flesh and Spirit—the powers of the old age and new age—are at war with each other (5:17), believers may choose to live according to the Spirit (5:16, 25). The description of the moral qualities within the community as the "fruit of the Spirit" (5:22) indicates that it is the Spirit's power that enables believers to live the moral life (5:17) and establishes the loving behavior among the members (5:22–23).[49]

Similarly, in response to the divisions and hyperindividualism of the Corinthian church, Paul elaborates on the earlier claim that the church is the dwelling place of the Spirit (1 Cor. 3:16; cf. 6:19), reminding the members that they were baptized by one Spirit into one body (12:13). While the Spirit is given to the whole community, individuals receive the gift of the Spirit "for the common good" (*sympheron*, 12:7).[50] Paul elaborates on this "common good" throughout chapters 12–14, indicating that it is the equivalent of love (chap. 13) and the building up (*oikodomeō*, 10:23; 14:1–5, 26; cf. 8:1) of the community. Thus manifestations of the Spirit are given to every member for the sake of the building up of the whole church.[51]

Ethical transformation is a gift of the Spirit. As the passive voice indicates in each instance where Paul speaks of transformation as an ongoing process (Rom. 12:2; 2 Cor. 3:18; Gal. 4:19), believers are not transformed by their own power. Paul consistently states that God or the Spirit enables communal transformation. He assures the Philippians that "the one who began a good work among you will bring it to completion" (1:6) and that it is "God who is at work in you [plural]" to will and to do (2:13).

CONCLUSION: THE CHURCH AS A COUNTERCULTURE

The claim of Irenaeus that Christ "became what we are that we might become what he is" is a suitable summary of a major aspect of Paul's ecclesiology. As the first-person plural throughout Romans 5–8 indicates, Paul envisions the

49. See Thompson, *Moral Formation*, 102–5, for "joy, peace, patience, kindness, and goodness" as elaborations on love, which heads the list.

50. See Rabens, *Holy Spirit and Ethics in Paul*, 238.

51. Contra Samra, *Being Conformed to Christ in Community*, 149–50, Paul speaks not of the edification of individuals but of the edification of the community, which is collectively God's building (1 Cor. 3:9).

transformation of the whole community as it progresses from the beginning to the end of its narrative.[52] While he acknowledges the role of the individual (cf. Rom. 8:9b, 11), participation in Christ is unimaginable apart from the community of faith.[53] Paul envisions a community that has a beginning, a middle, and an end. He does not envision a church that facilitates the maturation of the individual,[54] but envisions a community that grows into the image of Christ. As the people who already live in the new age in Israel's story, the church manifests the reversal of the condition of the old humanity that was enslaved to sin. Thus the church has seen the future and now embodies the life of the new creation, and it is presently being transformed.

Spiritual formation is corporate formation. The church is not a collection of individuals who devote themselves to spiritual formation but a community that shares the destiny of Christ together. The community does not exist to expand its power or influence but seeks to be an outpost of the future. Those who are being conformed no longer live for themselves (Rom. 14:7; 2 Cor. 5:15) but share the destiny of the crucified Lord.

Transformation consists of a moral life that is "worthy of the gospel" (Phil. 1:27) and "not conformed to this world" (Rom. 12:2). Thus the church is a cohesive moral community that places high expectations on its members. While it welcomes those who have been enslaved to sin, it assumes that sinners will participate in the narrative of transformation as members encourage one another. The church is thus a counterculture that embodies in its practice the life of the age to come, turning upside down the values of this age. This is a contrast between light and darkness (cf. Phil. 2:15). Those who are shaped by the cross abandon self-serving behavior and die with Christ to the old existence. The moral guidance of Paul's letters describes the characteristics of those who are shaped by the narrative of Christ.

---

52. See Grenz, "Ecclesiology," 262: "Rather than being merely the aggregate of its members, the church is a people imbued with a certain 'constitutive narrative,' namely the biblical narrative of God at work bringing creation to its divinely intended goal."

53. Ben C. Dunson, *Individual and Community in Paul's Letter to the Romans*, WUNT 2/332 (Tübingen: Mohr Siebeck, 2012), 165–66.

54. *Pace* Samra, *Being Conformed to Christ in Community*, 152.

❖ 5 ❖

JUSTIFICATION IS ABOUT UNIFICATION

The Death of Jesus and the People of God in Romans and Galatians

The first-person singular pronoun is a consistent feature of church music in the evangelical tradition.

> Amazing grace, how sweet the sound
> that saved a wretch like me.
> I once was lost, but now I'm found,
> Was blind but now I see.

Like countless other songs in this tradition, "Amazing Grace" tells of the individual who was lost in sin, unable to meet God's demands until Jesus paid it all at the cross. These songs echo Pauline themes of sin, grace, and justification. Indeed, Paul's legacy is the good news that we have been "justified by faith" (Rom. 5:1), not by our own works (cf. Rom. 3:20, 28; 4:2). In the cross God demonstrated righteousness for all who believe (Rom. 3:21–26). The death of Christ "while we were yet sinners" (Rom. 5:8 KJV) was the expression of God's love.

Interpreters have maintained that this narrative mirrors Paul's own experience. According to this view, Paul struggled with a guilty conscience, having attempted in vain to keep the law perfectly. The "wretched man" (Rom. 7:24) who could not do the good or keep the law was Paul himself, who lived within the context of a form of Judaism that had degenerated into a legalistic and hypocritical religion that no longer recognized the mercy of God and instead emphasized meritorious works. Paul then found the answer in the grace of God and recognized that God justifies the ungodly. Paul has often been regarded as paradigmatic for those who discovered God's grace when they could not keep God's commands. When he met Christ on the Damascus road, he experienced God's grace. Out of this experience, he became the example of the path of conversion for all subsequent generations, and the major theme of his writings is justification by faith. This view has been emphasized in Protestant theology, becoming the popular theme of revivalists and Christian song writers.

Krister Stendahl observed that the Pauline doctrine of justification by faith did not emerge as the center of Paul's theology until Augustine, who himself turned to Paul after struggling with a guilty conscience. Augustine found the solution to his own personal struggle in the grace of God.[1] Luther also discovered the grace of God as the solution to his own desire to find a merciful God. Beginning with Luther, the Reformers maintained that Paul's doctrine of the righteousness of God was the center of the gospel. This doctrine has been conceived in individualist terms. Rudolf Bultmann organized his classic *Theology of the New Testament* as "man prior to the revelation of faith" and "man under faith."[2] For numerous Protestant theologians, justification was the salvation of the individual. Günther Bornkamm and Hans Conzelmann placed justification at the center of Pauline theology and likewise interpreted it in individualistic terms.[3] For Augustine and the later Protestant tradition, the experience of Paul was a window into the human condition. The good news is the righteousness of God that rescues individuals from their lost condition.[4]

In the past generation, interpreters have challenged this understanding of Paul. Krister Stendahl observes that Paul never suggests that he suffered from a guilty conscience before his conversion. Indeed, Paul describes himself as "blameless" in keeping the law (Phil. 3:6). Stendahl maintains that the common

1. Krister Stendahl, "The Apostle Paul and the Introspective Conscience of the West," in *Paul among Jews and Gentiles and Other Essays* (Philadelphia: Fortress, 1976), 85. Stendahl also observes that the churches of the East have never focused on the plagued conscience in the way that Western churches have.

2. Rudolf Bultmann, *Theology of the New Testament* (London: SCM, 1965), 1:270–306.

3. Günther Bornkamm, *Paul*, trans. D. M. G. Stalker (New York: Harper & Row, 1969), 146–47; Hans Conzelmann, *An Outline of the Theology of the New Testament*, trans. John Bowden (New York: Harper, 1969), 205.

4. See Dunson, *Individual and Community*, 1–10.

portrayal of Paul's struggle is the result of centuries of superimposing the experiences of Augustine and Luther onto Paul's doctrine of justification. E. P. Sanders demonstrates that the common depiction of Judaism as legalistic is a Christian caricature.[5] The Jewish teachers of Paul's day maintained that God, having provided the means of atonement for those who did not keep the statutes of the law perfectly, is merciful toward those who fall short of perfect obedience. Thus although Luther found the answer to his own guilt in Paul's doctrine of the righteousness of God, Paul never describes the righteousness of God as the answer to the individual's guilty conscience.

Paul employs the verb *dikaioō* (commonly rendered "justify") and the noun *dikaiosynē* ("righteousness") primarily in the two letters in which he is engaged in polemic about membership in the people of God. In Galatians he appeals to this doctrine in the defense of the full membership of gentiles in the church. In Romans he writes to explain his work as God's minister to the gentiles (Rom. 15:16). The doctrine of justification, therefore, is neither the center of Paul's theology nor the doctrine that he uses to explain God's response to the generic human condition. Paul writes to specific circumstances, and his doctrine of justification is used in the context of polemic over the question of membership among the people of God.

Traditional interpretations of justification have treated the topic as the individual's salvation from sin, separating Paul's teaching from the church. This raises the question that I will explore in this chapter: what is the relationship between the death of Jesus and the identity of the church?

SIN AND JUSTIFICATION IN JEWISH LITERATURE

Paul's terminology of sin and justification was undoubtedly dependent on the Scriptures and subsequent Jewish tradition. Justification was the answer to Israel's dilemma. According to the exilic prophet, Israel is in captivity as the result of her own sin (Isa. 40:2; 42:24; 43:25), and the problem will be solved when God acts to vindicate the people. God's righteousness (*dikaiosynē*) is the saving deed that will rescue Israel (cf. Isa. 41:2; 42:6; 45:8, 13; 46:13);[6] it is used synonymously with salvation (*sōteria*) as the restoration of Israel and return from exile (Isa. 45:17; 46:13; 52:7, 10). If Israel's sin resulted in exile, forgiveness will mean the restoration of national identity (Isa. 43:24–25;

5. E. P. Sanders, *Paul and Palestinian Judaism: A Comparison of Patterns of Religion* (Minneapolis: Fortress, 1977), 233–37.

6. The NRSV renders *dikaiosynē* with a variety of terms: "victor" in Isa. 41:2; "deliverance" in Isa. 46:13.

50:1; 53:5–6, 10–12; 55:7). The prophet promises to the exiles that "he who vindicates [*ho dikaiōsas*] me is near" (Isa. 50:8). At that time "the righteous one . . . shall make many righteous [*dikaiōsai dikaion douleuonta pollois*]" and "bear their iniquities" (Isa. 53:11). Thus the phrase "forgiveness of sins" is not in the remission of individual sins but in the remission of the whole nation's sins. God's righteousness is the saving event for the exiled people of God when God will restore the fortunes of Israel. Since the exile was the punishment for those sins, "the only sure sign that the sins had been forgiven would be the clear and certain liberation from exile."[7] Sin, justification, and forgiveness were understood in corporate terms as the exile and restoration of Israel. As the exilic prophet indicates, Israel hoped for the time of salvation when God would act to vindicate the people.

JUSTIFICATION AND ECCLESIOLOGY IN GALATIANS

Prior to Galatians, Paul established gentile churches and addressed them in terms that suggested their identity as the people of God in continuity with ancient Israel. They were the elect, the saints, and the *ekklēsia* (see chap. 1). Thus he assumes their identity as the people of God with roots in ancient Israel. Unlike his predecessors, he did not regard gentile converts as proselytes, for he regarded them as full members of the people of God without circumcision. The Israelite story is their story. Where their full membership in the *ekklēsia* is not in question, Paul does not develop the theme of the righteousness of God. He does not refer to the righteousness of God in 1 Thessalonians, and he has only scattered references to the concept in his other letters to gentile churches (cf. 1 Cor. 1:30; cf. 6:11; 2 Cor. 5:21; Phil. 3:6).

The righteousness of God becomes a major topic in Galatians and Romans, the letters in which he defends the presence of gentiles as full members in the people of God.[8] As Galatians indicates, Paul's practice of admitting gentiles without requiring circumcision is challenged by teachers who offer an alternative ecclesiology. Although we have access only to Paul's portrayal of the events, we can draw some conclusions about the ecclesiology of the participants in the conflict. These teachers agree with Paul that Jesus is the Messiah of Israel and that gentiles are welcome to enter the community in the same way that proselytes have always entered. Thus they probably welcomed gentile

---

7. Wright, *New Testament and the People of God*, 279.
8. See Michael Theobald, "Rechtfertigung und Ekklesiologie nach Paulus: Anmerkungen zur 'Gemeinsamen Erklärung zur Rechtfertigungslehre,'" *Zeitschrift für Theologie und Kirche* 95 (1998): 108.

converts as children of Abraham, provided that they keep the law. Indeed, the opponents represent a common understanding of the terms for membership among the people of God. Isaiah 56 speaks of the time when gentiles who keep the commandments will join the outcasts among the people of God. In the Second Temple period, the commandments that were central markers of Jewish identity were circumcision, food laws, and the Sabbath. Thus the attempt by the teachers to compel the gentiles to be circumcised (Gal. 6:12) exposed a fundamental ecclesiological conflict over the terms of membership among the people of God. This became a pervasive issue in Paul's churches. The ecclesiological model for the teachers was the Jewish synagogue, where gentile proselytes were welcome.

Paul's autobiographical report in Galatians 1:10–2:21 is probably a response to the teachers' accusation that Paul has unilaterally changed the time-honored rules for membership in Israel. In Galatians 1:10–24 he appeals to his call to apostleship as the warrant for his gospel for the uncircumcised. In Galatians 2:1–14 he appeals to two incidents as precedents for the Galatians' struggle. At the Jerusalem council (Gal. 2:1–10), the situation of the gentile Titus was identical to that of the readers. Titus, unlike the readers (cf. 6:12), was not compelled (2:3) by the pillars to be circumcised. Peter, James, and John acknowledged the legitimacy of Paul's ministry among the gentiles, agreeing on a division of responsibilities: Paul would go to the gentiles, and they would go to those who were circumcised (2:9). Thus all agreed that gentiles would be full members in the people of God. They apparently assumed that Jewish believers would continue to maintain the boundary markers of circumcision, Sabbath keeping, and food laws, but accepted the gentiles as members of the people of God, probably assuming that the two groups would occupy separate locations.

The incident at Antioch (2:11–14), the second precedent for the Galatian situation, suggests that the pillars did not envision the problems that would occur when Jewish and gentile converts came together in cities such as Antioch.[9] The separation of spheres envisioned at the Jerusalem council did not work out in practice, for in Antioch the Christian mission had reached gentiles (cf. Acts 11:20), and Jews and gentiles met together for table fellowship. Although the men from James apparently accepted the gentiles apart from circumcision (cf. Gal. 2:10), they continued to insist on separation at common meals, assuming that the Jewish boundary markers precluded joint participation in meals. Table fellowship was the occasion for eating with the people of God,

9. See Martyn, *Galatians*, 221: "The formula was both a momentous recognition of the character of God's outreach to the world and a bomb waiting for a spark to ignite its fuse."

all of whom maintained the distinction between clean and unclean. Thus they insisted on maintaining separate communities.[10]

Cephas joined Paul in eating with gentiles on a regular basis,[11] thus erasing one of the boundary markers in his own practice. But when the men from James came, Cephas withdrew from table fellowship, fearing the circumcision faction.[12] As in the episode involving the circumcision of Titus, Paul regards this separation as a violation of "the truth of the gospel" (Gal. 2:14). Paul then confronts Cephas, accusing him of violating the truth of the gospel and of compelling the gentiles to "live like Jews" (2:14). That is, the truth of the gospel involves the full membership of the gentiles among the people of God. Like the opponents who compel the Galatians (6:12) and who wished to compel Titus to be circumcised (2:3), Cephas sought to compel the gentiles to live like Jews by regarding them as less than full members in the people of God. Thus Paul confronts him over a basic ecclesiological issue.

Paul's theological argument occurs in 2:15–16 as he defends the "truth of the gospel." Interpreters have correctly noted that 2:15–21 is the propositio of Galatians.[13] As the punctuation in English translations indicates, the reader is uncertain whether 2:15–21 includes Paul's response to Peter or is directed to the Galatian situation. Since the statement is an appropriate response to both the Galatian situation and the specific incident in Antioch, we may assume that it responds to both. Thus, in keeping with 2:1–10, Paul insists that gentiles not be compelled to "live like Jews." By separating himself from table fellowship with gentiles, Peter has broken the agreement made in Jerusalem, where Titus was not compelled to be circumcised, for Peter has compelled them to "live like Jews."

Paul begins by acknowledging that he and Cephas are both by nature (*physei*) Jews, not gentile sinners, and then appeals to the common ground that he and Cephas share (*eidotes*). He speaks in a chiastic fashion in Galatians 2:16 (my translation).

10. Cf. 3 Macc. 3:3–4, "The Jews, however, continued to maintain goodwill and unswerving loyalty toward the deity; for because they worshiped God and conducted themselves by his law, they kept their separateness with respect to foods." According to *Joseph and Aseneth* 7:1, "Joseph never ate with the Egyptians, for this was an abomination to him." According to *Jub.* 22:16, Isaac instructs Jacob, "Separate yourself from the gentiles, and do not eat with them."
     The food of the gentiles was considered impure (Ezek. 4:13; Hosea 9:3), either because it had been sacrificed to idols (Exod. 34:15; 1 Cor. 10:28), because it came from impure animals (Lev. 11:1–30; Deut. 14:3—21), or because it was prepared in an improper way (cf. Exod. 23:19).
11. The imperfect tense *synēsthien* indicates that Cephas had regularly eaten with the gentiles. See Franz Mußner, *Der Galaterbrief: Herders Theologische Kommentar zum Neuen Testament* (Freiburg: Herder, 1977), 138.
12. The imperfect tense "he drew back and kept himself separate" (*hypostellen kai aphorizen heauton*) suggests that Cephas only gradually separated himself.
13. Cf. Betz, *Galatians*, 181.

A A person is not justified by works of the law but by the faith of Christ

B We have believed in Christ

B' In order that we may be justified by faith in Christ

A' Because all flesh will not be justified by works of the law.

As the passage indicates, Paul works from the framework of the Scriptures, but his recent experience demonstrates to him that those who will be vindicated are those who believe in Christ. That is, the redefinition of justification has profound results for his ecclesiology. Justification is not a private experience but the event that determines the nature of the community.[14] The idea that faith in Christ is the basis for ultimate justification reshapes Paul's understanding of the people of God. Justification apart from the boundary markers of the law establishes a new kind of community. Those who are justified cannot live in isolation from others whom God has justified, for they all come together in the table fellowship of both Jews and Greeks. Justification redefines the church and opens membership to all who believe in Christ. If God justifies apart from the boundary markers, the church is a new humanity that does not recognize the distinctions between Jews and Greeks. Whatever Peter's motivation was in leaving the table fellowship with gentiles, he denied the truth of the gospel. "Every attempt at segregation and every motive of segregation is branded by Paul as a denial and rejection of justification through Jesus Christ."[15]

Paul announces the general principle (no one is justified by the works of the law) and maintains that he and Cephas have conformed to that principle, having believed in Christ. They agree that God's ultimate standard for justification is no longer one's faithfulness in keeping the law but belief in Christ. The "works of the law" in question are the boundary markers of Jewish identity that are under debate in Antioch and Galatia. As Paul develops this principle, those who have faith are the children of Abraham (3:7, 9, 26, 29). That is, the result of this principle is that gentiles are full members in the people of God. The principle of justification by faith abolishes the barriers between Jew and gentile and creates a community without distinctions. As Paul indicates in Galatians 3:26, all—not only Jews—are children of God through faith. In the parallel verse that follows, he says, "As many of you as were baptized into Christ have clothed yourselves with Christ" (3:27). In the

14. Contra Frank Thielman, "The Group and the Individual in Salvation: The Witness of Paul," in *After Imperialism: Christian Identity in China and the Global Evangelical Movement*, Studies in Chinese Christianity, ed. Richard R. Cook and David W. Pao (Eugene, OR: Pickwick, 2011), 140–41.

15. Markus Barth, "Jews and Gentiles: The Social Character of Justification in Paul," *Journal of Ecumenical Studies* 5 (1968): 250.

climactic statement, he declares, "There is no longer Jew or Greek, there is no longer slave or free, there is no longer male and female; for all of you are one in Christ Jesus" (3:28). The principle of justification by faith creates a community that has no ethnic or social barriers.[16]

As Paul's condemnation of Cephas indicates, the principle of justification by faith was neither the answer to the individual's quest for a merciful God nor an abstraction. It was the answer to a concrete problem in the life of the church. Paul appeals to this theological principle to answer questions about segregation at the table. He expects justification by faith to be implemented in practice in the encounter of Jews and gentiles. As he argues in the midrash in 3:6–29, the principle of justification by faith results in a community in which the old marks of identity are submerged in the people of God.

Paul extends this principle to the encounter of rich and poor in the Lord's Supper at Corinth. While the communal expectations assumed the appropriateness of separate tables for the rich and poor, Paul appeals to the foundational story to urge his readers to transcend common understandings of community and cultural expectations in order to eat at the same table (see chap. 3).

EXTENDING THE CONVERSATION: THE EPISTLE TO THE ROMANS

Paul elaborates on the righteousness of God in his letter to the Romans, as he once more faces the major challenge to his ministry: the inclusion of the gentiles in the people of God. Romans is, at least in part, Paul's final account of his theology of mission,[17] as Paul indicates near the end of the letter: "On some points I have written you rather boldly, by way of reminder, because of the grace given me by God to be a minister of Christ Jesus to the gentiles . . . so that the offering of the gentiles may be acceptable, sanctified by the Holy Spirit" (15:15–16). The letter comes at a critical juncture of his life's work, for he now plans to go to Jerusalem with a collection from gentile churches, an act of solidarity between Jews and gentiles. He is not certain that this major project will be acceptable to the believers in Jerusalem, and he prays for deliverance from those who do not believe in Jesus (15:30–31). Thus he writes to explain his work among the gentiles to the Roman audience. Because Paul had changed the time-honored terms for admission of gentiles, the crisis he faced in Galatia has probably been repeated elsewhere.

16. Nils Alstrup Dahl, "The Doctrine of Justification: Its Social Function and Implications," in *Studies in Paul: Theology for the Early Christian Mission* (Minneapolis: Augsburg, 1977), 108.
17. Krister Stendahl, *Final Account: Paul's Letter to the Romans* (Minneapolis: Fortress, 1995), ix.

Although Paul never speaks explicitly about a crisis in Rome, his repetition of the themes from Galatians suggests that he either knows of or anticipates similar problems in Rome. The existence of multiple house churches in Rome (cf. 16:5, 10, 11, 15) in different parts of the city and the demographic diversity reflected in chapter 16 inevitably created the potential for division among Paul's churches.[18] Paul's exhortation near the end of Romans for the strong and the weak to glorify God "with one voice" (15:6) indicates the importance of the unity of the church for his mission.

Although interpreters debate the extent to which Paul knows the Roman situation, we have no doubt that Paul speaks to an ecclesiological issue that confronts his churches everywhere.[19] Thus ethnic issues dominate the argument of the book. Paul is a debtor "to Greeks and to barbarians" (1:14), and his gospel is for the Jew and the Greek (1:16; cf. 2:10–11). Because there is no distinction between Jew and Greek (2:10–11), God has called both (9:24) in the gospel, which raises the inevitable issue of whether and on what terms the ethnic groups can live together in community.

The relationship between Paul's defense of his ministry to the gentiles and the doctrine of the righteousness of God becomes evident in the propositio of Romans. Paul explains his indebtedness to Greeks and barbarians (1:14) by declaring that his gospel is the "power of God for salvation to everyone who has faith, to the Jew first and also to the Greek" (1:16). The word pas ("all, every") is a thread that runs throughout the letter. This declaration anticipates the argument that admission to the people of God is not limited to those who are circumcised, and it addresses the potential tensions between the strong and the weak.[20] It also anticipates Paul's caution against boasting by either those who have the law (3:27–30) or the gentiles who have been grafted into

18. On the location of the house churches in Rome, see Peter Lampe, *Die stadtrömischen Christen in den ersten beiden Jahrhunderten* (Tübingen: Mohr Siebeck, 2nd ed., 1989), 10–52. On the demographics reflected in Rom. 16, see Francis Watson, *Paul, Judaism, and the Gentiles: A Sociological Approach*, Society for New Testament Studies Monograph Series 56 (Cambridge: Cambridge University Press, 1986), 97–102; Lampe, *Die stadtrömische Christen*, 124–53.

19. The common explanation of the Roman situation as the result of the expulsion of the Jews from Rome and their subsequent return, first suggested by Wolfgang Wiefel ("The Jewish Community in Ancient Rome and the Origins of Roman Christianity," in *The Romans Debate*, rev. ed., ed. Karl P. Donfried [Peabody, MA: Hendrickson, 1991], 89–96) and widely accepted in Romans scholarship, remains hypothetical because of the absence of any reference to it in Romans. Nevertheless, as the argument of Romans indicates, Wiefel is correct that Paul is addressing the relationship of Jews and gentiles throughout the letter.

20. Interpreters debate whether 1:16–17 describes an individualistic or a corporate salvation. See the survey of the debate in Gary W. Burnett, *Paul and the Salvation of the Individual*, Biblical Interpretation Series 57 (Leiden: Brill, 2001), 131–47. Both the historical circumstances of the writing of the letter and the letter's major theme indicates that Paul's primary concern is not the individual's salvation but membership in the united church.

Israel (11:18). For "all have sinned and fall short of the glory of God" (3:23; cf. 1:18–3:20), and "everyone who calls on the name of the Lord shall be saved" (10:13). Thus Paul lays the foundation for a united and multiethnic church.[21]

Paul elaborates on his gospel in 1:17, declaring that "in [the gospel] the righteousness of God is revealed." He repeats the proposition in 3:21: "The righteousness of God has been disclosed, and is attested by the law and the prophets." As the verb *apokalyptetai* ("is revealed") indicates, the apocalyptic moment of vindication promised by the prophets has become a reality in the Christ event. What Israel expected for the end of time has already become a reality. This justification is inseparable from God's grace (*charis*, 3:24), redemption (*apolutrosis*, 3:24), and atoning sacrifice (*hilastērion*, 3:25). This vindication is not, however, restricted to Israel but extends to "all who believe" (3:22; cf. 1:16).

God's righteousness is the solution not only for Israel's plight but for the universal human situation. Sandwiched between the two announcements of the righteousness of God is the description of the wrath of God that is also "revealed" (*apokalyptetai*, 1:18). While the description of human sinfulness in 1:18–3:20 only obliquely identifies the offenses as those of Jews and gentiles, the reader would have recognized that the wrath of God "revealed from heaven against all ungodliness" includes both Jews and Greeks. Paul summarizes this description of humanity in 3:10: "There is no one who is righteous." Both Jews and Greeks are under God's judgment. Whereas no one is righteous, God's righteousness is for "all who believe" (3:22).

As in Galatians, Paul appeals to the story of Abraham to redefine the people of God. While in traditional Jewish interpretation Abraham was the father of Israel, Paul's focus in Romans 4 is on Abraham as the father of all who believe (4:11). "Abraham believed God, and it was reckoned to him as righteousness" (4:3) before he was circumcised (4: 9–11). Hence he embodied the principle of believing in the one who justifies the ungodly (4:5). Indeed, *pas* is the continuing thread in the midrash on Abraham. Because his faith was "reckoned as righteousness" before his circumcision, he is the father of Jews and gentiles. His seed includes not only those who have been circumcised (4:16), for he is "the father of all" (4:16) and "the father of many nations" (4:18).

Although the church (*ekklēsia*) is not mentioned in Romans until chapter 16, the doctrine of the righteousness of God in 1:16–4:22 has major ecclesiological implications. If the righteousness that the prophets announced for Israel extends to all, the church now includes both Jew and Greek. As the story of Abraham (4:1–22) indicates, the church is thus a multiethnic community rooted in ancient Israel. The righteousness of God is not God's answer to the

---

21. Theobald, "Rechtfertigung und Ekklesiologie nach Paulus," 107.

individual's search for a gracious God but a redefinition of the boundaries of the people of God to include all who believe. Indeed, the transition from the third-person to the first-person plural in 4:23–24 reflects the ecclesiology of the righteousness of God: God's righteousness is reckoned "to us who believe in him who raised Jesus our Lord from the dead."

Collective Identity in 5:1–8:39

As the transitional statement in 4:24 indicates, "we" are the ones who believe that God raised Jesus from the dead.[22] Having spoken in the third person to lay out the principle of justification by faith and redefine the people of God in 1:16b–4:22, Paul speaks primarily in the first-person plural in 5:1–8:39, including his readers in his elaboration of the implications of the righteousness of God. "We" refers to a predominantly gentile church—those who have believed Paul's message (4:24)—in contrast to the majority of ethnic Israel who have not believed (9:1–5; 10:16–21; 11:1–26). Throughout chapters 5–8, the inclusive "we" and "you" (plural) indicate the collective identity of the hearers and distinguish them from others. Whereas Paul spoke only in past tenses to describe the saving event as a present reality, he employs past, present, and future tenses in 4:23–8:39 to elaborate on the full implications of the righteousness of God for the church.

Interpreters have observed the inclusio that provides the frame for chapters 5–8, indicating that the revelation of God's righteousness in the past is not the end of God's saving acts. The church lives between the revelation of God's righteousness (1:17; 3:21) and the ultimate glory prepared by God.

"hope of sharing the glory of God" (5:2)	"the glory about to be revealed" (8:18)
	"in hope we were saved. Now, hope that is seen is not hope" (8:24)
"sufferings" (5:3)	"hardship" (8:35)
	"sufferings of this present time" (8:18)
"endurance" (5:3–4)	"we wait for it with patience" (8:25)
"God's love" (5:5)	"Who shall separate us from the love of God?" (8:35)
	"[Nothing] is able to separate us from the love of Christ" (8:39)
"God's love has been poured into our hearts through the Holy Spirit" (5:5)	"Have the first fruits of the Spirit" (8:23)
	"The Spirit helps us in our weakness" (8:26)

22. Klaiber, *Rechtfertigung und Gemeinde*, 55.

Paul's readers undoubtedly recognize that, despite the claims of chapters 1–4 that God's eschatological vindication has come, the world has not changed and the manifestations of the old aeon still exist. The power of sin is still present (6:1–7:25), and the world still waits in futility (8:19–23) for the ultimate revelation of the children of God (8:19). The believing community also lives in the midst of sufferings (5:3; 8:18). Paul's use of the diatribe (6:1; 7:1, 7) may suggest that he now answers real or potential questions raised by chapters 1–4. That is, if God has acted to justify the people, why do we still see the signs of the old aeon? What is the destiny of the church? How can we believe in the ultimate glory? Paul's answer indicates the ecclesiological implications of justification by faith.

According to 5:1–11, the church looks not only to the past but also to the future. This section is a bridge from the declaration of God's righteousness for all who believe in 1:16–4:22 to the themes that he develops in chapters 5–8. The aorist "having been justified by faith" (*dikaiōthentes oun ek pisteōs*, 5:1; NRSV "since we are justified by faith") summarizes chapter 4, pointing to God's saving event in the past. In 5:6–8 Paul elaborates on the past event, reiterating that, because of God's love, "Christ died for the ungodly" (5:8; cf. 3:21–26). In 5:9–11 Paul draws the logical conclusion that justification in the past (5:9, "having been justified") is the guarantee that "we will be saved" (5:9–10). In the present, the church ("we") suffers as it lives in hope for future glory (5:3–4). We live between God's saving act in the past and the ultimate salvation in the future. Having redefined the people of God in chapters 1–4, Paul now describes its destiny in the present and future. "We" who have been justified will be glorified. In 5:12–8:39 Paul argues the case.

As in chapter 4, Paul builds his case by appealing to an ancestor to establish a general principle (5:12–21). He again speaks in the third person to show that prior to Abraham, the father of all who believe, the first man brought sin, and death passed to all people (5:12, 18–21) through his disobedience. Assuming that the deed of one determines the destiny of the many, Paul declares that by the "act of righteousness" (*dikaiōma*, 5:18) and the obedience of one man "the many will be made righteous" (*dikaioi*, 5:19). Thus God justifies the many through the saving death of Jesus. Like the deed of the first man, the effects of Jesus's death are universal.

In 6:1–11 the narrative of humanity becomes the experience of the church, as the first-person plural indicates. The argument that the destiny of one determines that of the many (5:12–21), stated in the third person, sets the stage for Paul's application of this principle to the church ("we") in 6:1–11: "We . . . died to sin" (6:2), the invading power brought by the first man. "All of us . . . were baptized into Christ" (6:3), "buried with him by baptism into death" (6:4) and "united with him in a death like his" (6:5). "Our old self was crucified with him" (6:6) as "we have died with Christ" (6:8). As a result, "whoever has died is freed from sin" (6:7). That is, we who have been buried with Christ in baptism share in his destiny. As in the story of the first man, the destiny of one is the destiny of the many. Paul's use of the multiple compounds with *syn-* (6:4, 5, 6; cf. *syn* in 6:8) indicates the total identification of the believer's destiny with that of Christ. Those who have died have been "justified [NRSV "freed"] from sin" (6:7). Thus the community that has been "justified by faith" (5:1) has also been "baptized into his death" (6:3–4). In being dead to sin, the community has left the old aeon, where sin once ruled (5:12–21), and entered the new aeon, where sin no longer rules (6:11).

Paul's consistent use of "we" and the plural "you" (cf. 6:12–23) indicates the corporate nature of justification. The compounds with *syn-* and the use of the plural reflect the communal participation in the death of Jesus. As Paul will show later in expressing his grief over Israel (9:1–5), not all humanity has believed the message or participated in the death of Jesus. Thus the use of "we" demarcates the church from those who have not entered the new age. The collective identity of the community is suggested at the climax of chapters 5–8 in Paul's use of the parallel phrases "those who love God" (8:28) and those whom he "foreknew" (8:29) and "predestined" (8:29, 30). These were the ones that God "called" and "justified" (8:30). As in his appeal to the Abraham story, Paul describes the church in terms borrowed from Israel's experience. We are children, heirs, and joint heirs with Christ (8:17), the elect (8:33). The church is the new humanity as it shares the destiny of its founder.

The church lives in the expectation of the final triumph of God. "Those who love God" (8:28) are the ones who believe in Christ. They are the ones whom God foreknew and foreordained to be conformed to the image of the Son (8:29). Hence nothing will separate us from the love of God in Christ Jesus our Lord.

The first-person plural plays a decisive role in the lyrical ending of Romans 8. The community asks, "If God is for us, who is against us?" (8:31) and "What will separate us from the love of Christ?" (8:35). Paul concludes that nothing shall "separate us from the love of God in Christ Jesus our Lord" (8:39).

Ecclesiology in Romans 9–16

The prospect of gentile believers conformed to the image of Christ evokes from Paul the grand style that expresses his amazement in 8:18–39. However, he descends suddenly from the pathos of celebration (8:18–39) for the triumph of the gentile church to the pathos of grief (9:1–5) over Paul's own people, his "kindred according to the flesh" (9:3) who have not believed his message. They have not submitted themselves to the righteousness of God (10:3) or obeyed the gospel (10:16), although they have heard (10:18) and known (10:19) God's word. The presence of only a remnant (11:5) among believers raises the basic question that Paul answers in Romans 9–11: Has the word of God failed (cf. 9:6)? This situation calls into question Paul's claim for the righteousness of God (1:16–17; 3:21–26) for all. Consequently, Paul asks, "Is there injustice on God's part?" (9:14), and then develops his answer in three parts. In 9:6–29 he offers a preliminary answer: God's word has not failed (9:6a), for God has always elected people based not on their works (cf. 9:12, 16) but on God's sovereign choice. This principle extends to the present time, for God has now called both Jews and gentiles (9:24). The claim that God called "us"—both Jews and gentiles—reflects the composition of the church and indicates that God's righteousness for "everyone who has faith/all who believe" (1:16–17; 3:21–22) has become at least a partial reality. As Paul explains later, in this new situation "there is no distinction between Jew and Greek" (10:12). Thus God's intention is a community without ethnic distinctions (cf. 10:13).

Applying words once addressed to the northern tribes (Hosea 2:25), Paul mentions that God has called a "no people" (NRSV "not my people") to be his people (Rom. 9:25–26). The "no people" are now the gentiles who have become God's people. Recalling the words from Isaiah (Isa. 10:22; 28:22), Paul describes Jewish Christians of his own day as the remnant (Rom. 9:27–29) that remains. Thus in the present situation the community at Rome is composed of a majority of gentiles and a minority of Jewish Christians. The presence of the Jewish remnant in the church ensures that the community is not exclusively gentile.[23]

In 9:30–10:21 Paul interprets the present situation, explaining why a majority in the community are gentiles. The majority of Jews did not pursue the righteousness by faith (9:30) and did not recognize that Christ is the *telos* of the law for all who believe (10:4). However, Paul insists that salvation is available to everyone who confesses that Jesus is Lord (10:9–10), for there is no distinction between Jew and Greek (10:12). He supports this claim by citing two Scriptures to demonstrate the universality of the message, adding "everyone" (*pas*) to the citation from Isaiah 28:16 ("anyone ["everyone"] who believes in him will never be put to shame" NIV) and adapting the citation from Joel 2:32 ("everyone who calls on the name of the Lord shall be saved"). With the emphasis on "everyone" (cf. 1:16, 18; 2:9–10; 3:22–23), he insists that the message of salvation has been offered to all. Citing the words of Psalm 18:5 LXX (Rom. 10:18), he claims that the message has gone out to the end

---

23. Pablo T. Gadenz, *Called from the Jews and from the Gentiles: Pauline Ecclesiology in Romans 9–11*, WUNT 2/267 (Tübingen: Mohr Siebeck, 2009), 327.

of the earth. Thus if only a remnant of Israel believes that Jesus is Lord, it is not because they have not heard (10:18) or understood (10:19) the message. Recalling ancient words spoken to Israel, Paul interprets the present situation (10:19–21) and anticipates the final stage in the argument (11:1–32). God will make Israel "jealous of those who are not a nation" (Deut. 32:21 LXX)—the gentiles. Adapting the words of Isaiah 65:1–2, Paul contrasts Israel with the gentiles. Of the gentiles God declares, "I have been found by those who did not seek me" (Rom. 11:20; Isa. 65:1 LXX), but of the Jews he adds, "I held out my hands to a disobedient and contrary people." Thus the current problem for Paul is not the injustice of God but the disobedience of Israel. The fact that the message went to all indicates that the plan of God is a church that includes all ethnic groups.

In chapter 11 Paul argues that the present situation is not permanent. The question "Has God rejected his people?" (11:1) corresponds to the earlier questions about whether God's word has failed (9:6) or whether God is unjust (9:14). Paul gives the definitive answer in 11:2: "God has not rejected his people whom he foreknew." He supports his claim in the remainder of chapter 11, contrasting the current situation (11:1–10; cf. 11:5, "the present time") with the future events (11:11–32). At the present there is a remnant (cf. 9:27) who have entered the community in the same way that gentiles do—by grace (11:6) and election (11:7), not by works. These Jewish Christians are a minority in the church. Paul supports the claim that the "rest were hardened" (11:7) by applying ancient words for disobedient Israel (11:8; cf. Deut. 29:3; Isa. 29:10; 6:9–10; 11:9; cf. Ps. 68:23–24 LXX) to the current situation. Thus the presence in the church of a Jewish minority is a sign that God has not rejected his people.

The question "Have they stumbled so as to fall?" (11:12) corresponds to the earlier questions about the justice of God (9:6, 14; 11:1) and introduces the second stage in Paul's answer, as he turns toward Israel's future. Here, as he addresses the gentile readers (11:13), Paul argues that the current situation is not final. With the extended metaphor of the olive tree, he reminds gentile readers of their indebtedness to Israel. When he says, "If the root is holy, then the branches also are holy," he reminds gentile readers of God's relationship to Israel, for the root that is holy is the people of God, the descendants of Abraham (4:1–25; 9:6–13), and the branches that are holy are all Israel. The branches that have been cut off ("some," 11:17) are those who have not believed the message, while others are faithful (cf. 11:1–10). Gentile believers are the wild olive branches that are grafted in (11:17, 19) through faith (11:20). The sovereign God who has elected the gentiles, grafting them into the olive tree, can both cut them (the gentiles) off and restore the branches (Israel) that have been cut off. That is, if God has always acted according to his sovereign choice (cf. 9:6–29), he can continue to do so. Because God will continue to save those who have faith, he will save unbelieving Israel if they do not remain in unbelief (11:23–24). This argument continues the theme that there is no distinction between Jews and Greeks, for all will be saved by faith.

Paul concludes the argument with the affirmation that the current situation is not permanent, for the hardening (cf. 11:7) has come only on part of Israel until the full number of gentiles come in. Then "all Israel will be saved" (11:26), and the current situation will be reversed. The promise that all Israel will be saved is the answer to the question about the justice of God (9:14). God's word has not failed (cf. 9:6), and God has not rejected his people. "All Israel" are those for whom Paul is in anguish (9:1–5)—those whom he describes in 9:30–10:21. They will ultimately meet the conditions for entry into the people of God (cf. 10:9–13) when they come to believe (11:23). Paul does not refer to every individual Israelite but refers to Israel as a whole, both the remnant and "the rest" (11:1–10).[24] Nor does Paul indicate how this event will occur. He apparently envisions that his mission will provoke the unbelieving Jews to jealousy, resulting in the salvation of all Israel. The ultimate outcome of the plan of God in which Paul is the servant is that God will "be merciful to all" (11:32). God's righteousness for all who believe will become a reality when God has mercy on all. Paul anticipates that a united humanity will ultimately be saved.

This panoramic view of the purposes of God is not an abstraction but has a decisive significance for life in the Roman church. Romans 9–11 has a paraenetic purpose, as Paul speaks directly to gentiles in 11:13–36. He writes to warn against gentile arrogance (11:18), reminding them of the "goodness and severity of God" (11:22 KJV) and declaring that the God who once chose to graft them into the wild olive tree can also restore Israel. The gentile church has become part of the people of God. The paraenetic purpose is evident in Paul's warnings. He warns gentiles not to boast (11:18), be proud (*hypsēla phronei*, 11:20), or "claim to be wiser than you are" (*hina mē ēte par heautois phronimoi*, 11:25). The righteousness of God demands a church that transcends ethnic distinctions.

This paraenetic focus provides the introduction to the final argument of the letter, the paraenesis in 12:1–15:13. This unit forms a fitting conclusion to the letter, for it describes the life in the new aeon (12:1–2), which sharply contrasts the state of humanity described at the beginning of the letter (1:18–3:20). Jews and gentiles live together in the new humanity. Because all have entered the community as a result of God's sovereign choice (9:6–13, 24), believers should

24. Ibid., 276.

not think more highly of themselves than they ought to think (12:3; cf. 11:18, 25), for they cannot claim works of their own (cf. 9:12). The image of the body and its members (12:4–8) offers an appropriate basis for the prohibition of arrogance. In contrast to the use of this image in 1 Corinthians 12:12–27, here it refers to a multiethnic church. God's election of both Jews and gentiles has resulted in the formation of a body composed of many members.[25] Christian existence is lived only within a body with its different functions. In a body composed of all whom God has called, "we, who are many, are one body in Christ, and individually members one of another" (12:5). Here there is no room for arrogance, for individual existence in Christ is impossible without membership in the body.

The ethical vision described in 12:9–13:13 presupposes a cohesive community that shares a moral life founded on love. The community lives "in harmony" and is not arrogant (12:16), and the members are not wise among themselves (12:16). At the center of the community's existence is love, as the inclusio of 12:9 and 13:8 indicates. This is love toward those whom God has chosen. The ethical advice draws from the Torah but does not contain the markers of Jewish identity. The advice for life in community takes on special force as the conclusion to Romans, for it is a portrayal of life under the righteousness of God. "All who believe" include gentiles and Jews who live together in a community.

In 14:1–15:13 Paul addresses the challenges of living as one body in contexts where different cultures come together in one community. Having encouraged the predominantly gentile readers neither to boast (11:18) nor to think too highly of themselves (12:3) but to "live in harmony with one another" (*to auto eis allēlous phronountes*, 12:16), he now acknowledges that the harmony of the church does not preclude different opinions (14:1), which inevitably result in a community open to all who believe. Despite the differences of opinion, Paul reiterates the advice he had given earlier (12:16), concluding this section with the prayer that they "live in harmony" (*to auto phronein*, 15:5) and glorify God "with one voice" (15:6). Indeed, these words, along with the summation in 15:7–13, mark the appropriate conclusion to the argument of the entire letter. If the gospel is for Greeks and barbarians, Jews and gentiles, the wise and the foolish (1:14), members of the community do not live in isolation but come together in worship.

Unlike the paraenesis in chapters 12–13, which takes up a variety of topics, 14:1–15:13 is a sustained paraenesis addressed to one specific problem, in which Paul explains what love entails (14:15). The address in 14:1 suggests

25. Theobald, "Rechtfertigung und Ekklesiologie nach Paulus," 111.

that Paul assumes the existence of two groups in Rome who live in isolation from each other. Paul is probably addressing two house churches, attempting to give them a single ecclesial identity. In contrast to the earlier argument, he does not use ethnic categories to describe the two groups but uses the categories of strong and weak, which he used earlier in 1 Corinthians 8:1–11:1 to address the issue of meat offered to idols. The initial imperative, "Welcome those who are weak in faith" (14:1), indicates that Paul addresses those whom he later identifies as the "strong" (15:1). He later abbreviates the phrase "weak in faith" (14:1) to "the weak" (15:1). The term "weak in faith" recalls the description of Abraham, who did not "weaken in faith" (4:19) when he waited on God's promise. Paul gives further insight into the weak in faith in 14:21–23, describing the one who is "at odds with oneself" or "wavers" (*ho diakrinomenos*; NRSV "doubts") while participating in an activity that is contrary to one's scruples.[26]

While Paul does not indicate who introduced the categories of strong and weak, he identifies himself with the strong (15:1), to whom he addresses the major part of this discussion. Recognizing that living in harmony in a community of people from different ethnic groups is no easy task, Paul argues the case in 14:1–15:13. His instructions consist of four parts (14:1–12; 14:13–23; 15:1–6; 15:7–13), each of which begins with either an imperative (14:1; 15:7) or its equivalent (14:13; 15:1), followed by a theological argument. He states the basic thesis of the argument in 14:1–3 and then elaborates on it in the remainder of the section. Paul's initial exhortation, "Welcome [*proslambanesthe*] those who are weak in faith, but not for the purpose of quarreling over opinions" (14:1), corresponds to the concluding imperative, "Welcome [*proslambanesthe*] one another" (15:7).

In the command to welcome the weak in faith (cf. "weak" in 14:2), Paul accepts the characterization of the two groups as "weak" and "strong" (15:1), using terminology that he had earlier used in 1 Corinthians in the discussion of meat offered to idols (cf. 1 Cor. 8:9–12). In this instance, however, the difference of opinion does not concern idolatry but involves one group, whose members "eat only vegetables" (Rom. 14:2) and observe special days (14:5), and another group, whose members "believe in eating anything" (14:2) and observe no special days (14:5). The more restrictive group may also abstain from wine (14:17).

Paul does not specifically identify the two groups as Jews and gentiles, but the distinction by "the weak" between what is unclean (*koinon*, 14:14) and clean (*kathara*, 14:20) suggests that the differences of opinion are rooted in

26. BDAG 231.

the Jewish Christians' maintenance of *kashrut* and the gentiles' rejection of these practices.[27] The contrast between those who "judge one day better than another" and those who "judge all days to be alike" (14:5) also suggests differences between gentile and Jewish Christians over one of the markers of Jewish identity. The fact that Paul concludes the discussion by describing Christ as the servant of the circumcised (15:7) so that the gentiles would glorify God (15:9) also suggests that Paul confronts the problems that emerge when gentiles and Jewish Christians come together. Thus the reference to differences of opinion between those who eat anything and those who eat only vegetables (14:2) is an oblique way of describing the opinions held by gentile and Jewish Christians, as is the description of those who observe days and those who do not (14:5).

Interpreters have noted that the description does not actually fit Jewish concerns, inasmuch as Jewish law prohibited neither the eating of meat nor the drinking of wine (cf. 14:21), and they have cited numerous examples of Jews in the Diaspora who refused both food and wine for fear of consuming unclean food.[28] However, it is most likely that Paul is giving only a generalized description of Jewish views of both *kashrut* and the Sabbath, as his reference to those who "eat anything" (surely an exaggeration) suggests. The fact that Paul is oblique in identifying gentiles and Jewish Christians may reflect the fact that the differences between these two groups were not entirely along ethnic lines. Some gentiles may also have insisted on keeping the law, and some Jews, such as Aquila and Prisca (cf. 16:3–4), may not have observed Jewish dietary regulations or the Sabbath. As the incident at Antioch indicates, these controversies probably emerged in numerous places. This challenge may be exacerbated by the existence of multiple house churches in Rome and their differing understandings of the law.

What Paul calls "quarreling over opinions" (14:1) is an explosive issue and a test as to whether a gospel "to the Jew first and also to the Greek" could result in a unified church. For the Jewish Christians, this was a question of Jewish identity. The eating of clean food and the observation of the Sabbath were essential boundary markers that Jewish Christians saw no reason to abandon. While different practices were possible in separate house churches, one common practice would be necessary for community meetings. Jewish Christians would be wary of the food provided at the homes of the gentile

27. See John M. G. Barclay, "'Do We Undermine the Law?': A Study of Romans 14:1–15:6," in *Paul and the Mosaic Law* (Tübingen: Mohr Siebeck, 1996), 290.

28. See Gary S. Shogren, "'Is the Kingdom of God about Eating and Drinking or Isn't It?' (Rom. 14:17)," *Novum Testamentum* 42 (2000): 248–51, for numerous examples of Jews who refused to eat the food of gentiles.

majority.[29] Those who abandoned these markers of identity would sever contact with the Jewish synagogue.

Although Paul later instructs members to "welcome one another" (15:7), he addresses the strong in 14:1 and then directs most of the instructions to them.[30] They are probably the gentile majority whom Paul has addressed throughout the letter (especially chaps. 9–11). *Proslambanō* means "to receive into one's home or circle of acquaintances (cf. Acts 18:26; 28:2; Philem. 17)."[31] Paul gives the instructions to the strong, who probably control the meetings. The full context indicates that Paul is instructing gentiles and Jews to come together for table fellowship and worship and to recognize each other as full members of the community. Paul elaborates on the word when he insists that those who "eat everything" not despise the other and that those who observe Jewish food laws not judge those who do not (Rom. 14:3, 10). The instruction to the strong not to "despise" the weak recalls the earlier instruction for the gentiles not to boast of their status (11:18). The temptation of the strong is to show disdain toward the weak in faith, and the temptation of the weak in faith is to judge the other. To welcome the weak is to invite them into the respective house churches and share table fellowship without quarreling over different opinions and practices. The even-handed advice Paul gives to the strong and the weak (14:3, 10) indicates that he permits a diversity of practices within the church on these issues and the legitimacy of each. Although he takes the position of the strong (14:14), he accepts the continuing practice of Jewish food laws.

The thesis statement in 14:1–3 contains a theological warrant that Paul consistently maintains throughout this section. The strong and the weak welcome each other because "God has welcomed [*proselabeto*] them" (14:3). This command anticipates the later instruction to the strong and the weak to "welcome one another" because Christ welcomed them (*proselabeto*, 15:7). In 14:4–12 Paul gives the additional warrant: everyone is a servant (*oiketēs*, 14:4), and Christ is the master (*kyrios*). Indeed, Christ died and lived again so that he might be *kyrios* of all. Consequently, no servant is his own master (14:7), and all answer to the same *kyrios* (14:12). By placing the strong and weak on the same level, Paul undermines the arrogance of the strong—the gentile majority. Having established earlier that God's righteousness is for everyone who believes (Rom. 1:16; 3:22), he insists that "each of us" will stand before

29. Carl N. Toney, *Paul's Inclusive Ethic: Resolving Community Conflicts and Promoting Mission in Romans 14–15* (Tübingen: Mohr Siebeck, 2008), 66.
30. Ibid., 94. Toney observes that Paul consistently addresses the strong (14:1, 3, 13, 15, 16, 19, 20, 22; 15:1, 5–6, 7, 13) but only sporadically addresses the weak (14:3, 13; 15:5–6, 7, 13).
31. BDAG 883.

the judgment seat of God and give an account (14:11–12). Because the two groups stand equally before God, they should welcome one another.

Although the second section begins with "let us therefore no longer pass judgment on one another" (14:13), Paul directs the advice to the strong. He now argues that the burden for maintaining unity lies with the strong. Restating the argument that he made earlier to the Corinthians, who faced the issues involving food offered to idols, Paul instructs the readers not to put a stumbling block (*proskomma*), or hindrance (*skandalon*), in the way of the one who insists on Jewish food laws (14:13, 20). That is, while gentile Christians do not regularly observe Jewish food laws at home or in meetings, they should observe these laws in the presence of Jewish believers as the price for maintaining unity. Although Paul agrees with the strong that nothing is common or unclean (14:14), he insists that ignoring Jewish food laws in the presence of Jewish Christians would bring the latter into a serious dilemma posed by their uncertainty and temptation to violate their convictions (14:22–23). In the common meals the strong are to observe Jewish food laws, because "the kingdom of God is not food and drink but righteousness and peace and joy in the Holy Spirit" (14:17).[32] As Paul told the Corinthians under different conditions, the task of the believer is not to please oneself (Rom. 15:1–3) but to pursue what makes for edification of one another (14:19). The righteousness for everyone who has faith finds concrete expression in a community that transcends cultural barriers without obliterating cultural differences.

Paul also places a burden on the Jewish believers. While he asks gentiles to accommodate those who observe food laws, he challenges the latters' fundamental beliefs by stating his opinion that nothing is common or unclean. He asks them to recognize that gentile Christians are full members in the people of God without submitting to the Torah. For Gentiles the law, especially circumcision, the Sabbath, and food laws—the badges of Jewish identity—is purely optional.[33] He also challenges a fundamental tenet of the Jewish tradition, the call for separation from others. Jewish tradition mandated not only the avoidance of unclean food but also the avoidance of those who did not maintain the distinctions between clean and unclean. This advice would ultimately sever the law-keeping believers from the synagogue.[34]

Paul gives the additional theological warrant (15:1–6) that the strong should not please themselves because "Christ did not please himself" (15:3). He concludes the argument with the exhortation to "welcome one another," arguing

32. Barclay, "'Do We Undermine the Law?,'" 304.
33. Watson, *Paul, Judaism, and the Gentiles*, 97. See also Horrell, "'No Longer Jew or Greek,'" 340.
34. Barclay, "'Do We Undermine the Law?,'" 306.

that "Christ has become a servant of the circumcised . . . in order that the Gentiles may glorify God" (15:8–9). The divine welcome that Paul describes is the revelation of God's righteousness at the Christ event (cf. 3:21–26), which is now the basis for Christian community.

If the issue in Romans 14:1–15:13 is the tension between law-observant Jewish Christians and nonobservant gentiles, the passage becomes an appropriate conclusion to Paul's insistence on the righteousness of God for all who believe, for it demonstrates the practical consequences and the challenges that accompany the message of the righteousness of God when "all" come together in the church.[35]

We may observe the impact of Paul's instruction. He does not permit gentile and Jewish believers to separate into exclusive homogeneous churches, and he places a special burden on the strong, the only ones who can accommodate others without violating their consciences. Common meals and worship are so important that he challenges all the believers to recognize that the unity of the community is more important than "food and drink" (14:17); no one should make eating and drinking a central issue.[36] Paul protects the rights of the Jewish Christians to maintain food laws and cultural identity, and he assumes their cultural legitimacy by insisting that gentiles observe Jewish food laws in their presence. At the same time, he insists that the Jewish Christians recognize the legitimacy of believers who do not observe the food laws and that they associate regularly with those who are not bound by the regulations of the law. Despite the differences in opinion and practice, Paul insists that believers come together for common meals, glorify God with one voice in worship (15:6), and also "greet one another with a holy kiss" (16:16).[37]

Tolerance, Multiculturalism, and Boundaries

The body of Romans begins with the announcement that the gospel "is the power of God for salvation to everyone who has faith" (Rom. 1:16) and concludes with the prayer that "together you may with one voice glorify the God and Father of our Lord Jesus" (15:6), followed by the final instruction to "welcome one another" (15:7). Throughout the letter Paul argues for the revelation of the righteousness of God (1:17; 3:21)—God's impartial justice for Jews and Greeks (2:11–12). Jews and Greeks come together as one community and "live in harmony" (*to auto phronein*, literally "think the same

---

35. Theobald, "Rechtfertigung und Ekklesiologie nach Paulus," 110.
36. Shogren, "Kingdom of God," 240.
37. Barclay, "'Do We Undermine the Law?,'" 306.

thing," 15:5; cf. 12:16; 2 Cor. 13:11; Phil. 2:2).[38] Paul faces the unprecedented challenge of establishing a harmonious community not only among ethnic groups but also among people from different social levels. Justification by faith, therefore, is not a private matter but the foundation for a united church.

As Romans 14:1–15:13 indicates, Paul sees no contradiction between different opinions (14:1) and a community of those who "think the same thing." The unity of the church is not uniformity, inasmuch as cultural identities are not obliterated for the sake of unity. Paul's acknowledgment that Jews may continue to maintain the badges of their cultural identity is a reminder that other badges of cultural identity have a place in the church. However, believers in Christ share a common identity that transcends that of differing cultures.[39] The common identity challenges believers to "pursue what makes for peace" and make concessions to others for the sake of the unity of the church.

When Paul acknowledges that believers receive each other despite differences of opinions, he is not suggesting a general tolerance of all views or practices, for he specifically describes the issues where believers are not in agreement. Nevertheless, the fact that we all stand before the Lord of all is a reminder of the ultimate truth that unites. Paul consistently reminds the readers of the common story that transcends their differences: God welcomed the other (14:3); "Christ died and lived again" (14:9), "did not please himself" (15:3), and "welcomed" (15:7) all believers. This shared story unites believers of different traditions and challenges them to come together for worship and service.

CONCLUSION: JUSTIFICATION AND THE UNITED CHURCH

Galatians and Romans are responses to the critical question that confronted Paul's ministry: what will be the shape of the church? Paul faced opponents whose understanding of the church was shaped by the models they knew. Some insisted that gentiles become Jews in order to be incorporated into the people of God, while others advocated two separate churches, living in isolation from each other. The doctrine of justification by faith was Paul's answer. The implication of this message was that existing models were inadequate. Those who accept this teaching will come together in worship and overcome cultural

38. BDAG 1065.
39. On Paul and multiculturalism, see John M. G. Barclay, "'Neither Jew nor Greek': Multiculturalism and the New Perspective on Paul," in *Ethnicity and the Bible*, ed. Mark G. Brett (Leiden: Brill, 1996), 212: "As Romans 14–15 indicates, Paul's protection of the rights of law-observant Christians to keep Sabbath and food laws in fact subtly undermines their social and cultural integrity, since they are forced to acknowledge the equal validity of *non-observance* even while being allowed (with some condescension) to observe."

and sociological barriers. While others advocated homogeneous churches, Paul insisted that different ethnic groups both accept their differences and glorify God with one voice (Rom. 15:6). The church is not a balkanized collection of interest groups, but a community in which ethnic identities are subordinated to shared existence in Christ.

The instruction to "welcome one another" (15:7), despite differences of opinion, presents a continuing challenge for the churches to cross the lines created by doctrinal differences and acknowledge those whom God has welcomed. Paul's hope that believers in the different house churches of Rome glorify God with one voice is a reminder that the unity of the church does not require uniformity. Paul's doctrine of justification is the basis for this united church.

6

"MISSIONAL" MAY NOT MEAN WHAT YOU THINK

Evangelism and Social Action according to Paul

The term "mission(s)" entered the English vocabulary in modern times. The Jesuits introduced the Latin *missio*, a rendering of the Greek *apostel-* ("send"), to describe the spreading of the Christian faith into distant lands.[1] Those who first used the term envisioned a world divided between Christendom and the non-Christian societies. Churches within Christendom sent missionaries to convert indigenous people, establish churches, and build schools. In the nineteenth century, churches discovered the "Great Commission" as the permanent mandate for missionary activity.[2] Since the latter part of the twentieth century, cultural changes have resulted in a challenge to the old paradigms of missions. Many have regarded the original idea of Christianizing other cultures as a form of cultural imperialism but have

1. Michael Goheen, "Bible and Mission: Missiology and Biblical Scholarship in Dialogue," in *Christian Mission: Old Testament Foundations and New Testament Developments*, ed. Stanley E. Porter and Cynthia Long Westfall (Eugene, OR: Pickwick, 2010), 211.
2. See Bosch, *Transforming Mission*, 340. According to Bosch, the Great Commission played a minor role in the Reformation. William Carey "put it on the map" in a tract written in 1792 entitled *An Enquiry into the Obligations of Christians to Use Means for the Conversion of the Heathen*.

maintained a lively interest in acts of compassion and social change as the church's mission, while others continue the task of evangelizing and planting churches. The recognition that Christendom no longer exists has also changed the paradigm, for the West has become a post-Christian culture. Thus mission no longer involves the encounter between the Christian and non-Christian worlds. While scarcely anyone would deny the importance of mission for the life of the church, the question remains: What is the mission of the church after Christendom? I use the term "mission" in its original sense of "sending" for a task, assuming that the term refers to the *telos* of the church's existence. Mission involves God's engagement with the world, and the church as God's instrument.[3] It includes, but is not limited to, the proclamation of Jesus Christ and the invitation to receive him. As Lesslie Newbigin asked, "What would be involved in a missionary encounter between the gospel and this whole way of perceiving, thinking and living that we call 'modern' Western culture?"[4]

As I observed in the opening chapter, advocates of the missional church have recognized the need for the church to reconsider its approach to mission in the post-Christian world. As a challenge to the traditional understanding of the church as the place where the word is preached and the sacraments are administered, the missional church regards mission not as one program among many but as the core of the church's identity. Mission is no longer regarded as the sending of evangelists to increase the numbers of the church. Rather, mission is participation in the *missio Dei*,[5] the sending of the church into the world. God's concern for the whole world is the scope of mission; thus it does not take place exclusively through the church, although the church may participate in it.[6]

In our search for biblical insights and models of mission, the voice that is almost entirely missing is that of Paul, the apostle to the nations. Thus, as the term *apostolos* indicates, Paul defines himself as one who was sent by God. As the one who was sent to preach (1 Cor. 1:17), he was a paradigm of mission. Living in a pre-Christian world, he provides insights for those who live in a post-Christian world.

---

3. See Bosch, *Transforming Mission*, 7–10.

4. Lesslie Newbigin, *Foolishness to the Greeks: The Gospel and Western Culture* (Grand Rapids: Eerdmans, 1986), 1.

5. See Bosch, *Transforming Mission*, 389, who maintains that Karl Barth, when he read a paper at the Brandenburg Missionary Conference in 1932, became one of the first theologians to articulate mission as the activity of God himself. In the classical articulation of the *missio Dei*, God the Father sends the Son, and God the Father and the Son send the Spirit. The church is the instrument of God's mission.

6. Ibid., 391.

THE MISSION OF PAUL

When Paul began his ministry sometime in the early thirties of the Christian era, the Christian movement was unknown to the larger populace, for it was only one of the sects within Judaism. Within one hundred years, the movement was so numerous that Pliny wrote to Trajan to find out what to do with this group, and Tacitus described it as an infectious disease.[7] The growth of this movement is evidence of a missionary spirit, motivated by the exclusive claims of its adherents that routinely disturbed the peace of ancient communities by making converts and demanding their rejection of other religions. Christianity moved from Judea in all directions. By the beginning of the second century, we know of its presence in Egypt, Syria, and the westernmost part of the Roman Empire.

We know little of the evangelists and missionaries who spread this movement to directions other than the West.[8] Paul the apostle stands as the one who was intent on spreading this message throughout the upper Mediterranean world. Paul was what later Christians would call a "missionary." He traveled to declare his message, never settling in one place for an extended period. He exhibited an interest that became characteristic of this movement: the desire to convert others. With his intense missionary activity and exclusive claim for his message, he is unprecedented in both Judaism and Hellenism.[9]

Paul explains his missionary work most clearly near the end of Romans, a letter that was written, at least in part, to explain his missionary career and introduce himself to the Christians of Rome as he prepared for his first visit to the capital of the empire (Rom. 15:14–21). He explains that he has completed his work in the East and now plans to visit Rome on his way to Spain (15:24), thus completing the circle of the upper half of the Mediterranean world. He desires to go west because he has run out of room, having already "fully proclaimed the good news of Christ" (*peplērōkenai to euangelion tou christou*) in a circle from Jerusalem to Illyricum (15:19). His ambition is to

7. See Wright, *New Testament and the People of God*, 341–54. Pliny, *Letters* 10.96–97; Tacitus, *Ann.* 15.44.

8. See Martin Hengel, "The Origins of the Christian Mission," in *Between Jesus and Paul: Studies in the Earliest History of Christianity* (Philadelphia: Fortress, 1983), 48–64, for the earliest Christian mission.

9. Wolfgang Reinbold, *Propaganda und Mission im ältesten Christentum: Eine Untersuchung zu den Modalitäten der Ausbreitung der frühen Kirche*, Forschung zur Religion und Literatur des Alten und Neuen Testaments 188 (Göttingen: Vandenhoeck & Ruprecht, 2000), 211. On Jewish missionary activity, see John P. Dickson, *Mission-Commitment in Ancient Judaism and in the Pauline Communities: The Shape, Extent and Background of Early Christian Mission* (Tübingen: Mohr Siebeck, 2003), 11–50.

preach where Christ has not been named (15:20), in each instance planting churches, which he then nurtures through letters and visits. Although others within the Christian movement were involved in missionary activity (cf. Gal. 2:7–8), we have only Paul's reflections on his missionary task.

As Paul's frequent references to his own mission indicate, God has called him to a special task that is clearly distinguishable from the mission of others. He "received grace and apostleship to bring about the obedience of faith among all the Gentiles" (Rom. 1:5). Christ sent him not to baptize but to preach (*euangelizesthai*, 1 Cor. 1:17), because necessity (*anankē*) was laid upon him (1 Cor. 9:16). Hence Paul says, "Woe to me if I do not proclaim the gospel [*euangelisōmai*]!" (1 Cor. 9:16). God revealed his Son to Paul in order that he might preach Christ among the nations (Gal. 1:15–16). In these passages, Paul indicates that he has a special calling from God for proclamation.

His description of his calling resonates with the language drawn from the prophets. Like the prophets, Paul has been "called" (Rom. 1:1; 1 Cor. 1:1; Gal. 1:15; cf. Isa. 49:1) and "sent" (1 Cor. 1:17; cf. Rom. 10:15) by God (or Christ); hence he is an *apostolos* "neither by human commission nor from human authorities" (Gal. 1:1).[10] Like Jeremiah (Jer. 1:5) and the servant of Isaiah 49:1, he was called "from [his] mother's womb." His claim that "necessity" has been laid upon him (1 Cor. 9:16) recalls Jeremiah's compulsion to speak for God (cf. Jer. 20:9). Like Jeremiah, he has been given authority to build and not to tear down (2 Cor. 10:8; cf. Jer. 24:6). Like Moses, he is not "sufficient" to speak (2 Cor. 2:16; Exod. 4:10) but has been commissioned by God to be a minister of the new covenant announced by Jeremiah (2 Cor. 3:6). Thus he belongs to the prophetic tradition of those who were called and sent to speak for God.[11]

Paul's mission is to preach the gospel (*euangelisasthai*). Whenever he describes the purpose of his mission, the *euangel-* terminology "appears almost without exception."[12] Indeed, of the words for proclamation, the root *euangel-* is the dominant one.[13] *Euangelion* is the common term for the content of Paul's message (Rom. 1:1, 16; 1 Cor. 15:1; 2 Cor. 4:3; Gal. 1:6–9; 2:2, 5, 14; 1 Thess. 1:5; 2:2, 4), while the verb *euangelizomai* refers to the activity of

10. On the divine sending of the prophets, see Isa. 6:8, "Then I heard the voice of the Lord saying, 'Whom shall I send [*tina apostellō*], and who will go for us?' And I said to him, 'Here am I, send me!'" Cf. Jer. 1:7; 14:14; 23:21; 27:15. Cf. Karl Olav Sandnes, "Paul, One of the Prophets?," in *A Contribution to the Apostle's Self-Understanding* (Tübingen: Mohr Siebeck, 1991), 62–68.

11. See the discussion by Sandnes, "Paul, One of the Prophets?," 77–153.

12. Dickson, *Mission-Commitment in Ancient Judaism*, 88.

13. See ibid., 87. *Laleō/lalia* appears sixty times. *Didaskō/didachē* occurs fifty-five times. *Kēryssō/kērygma* occurs twenty-seven times.

proclaiming. The term *euangel-* "takes us to the heart of Paul's self-identity as a "missionary."[14]

Although the verb *euangelizomai* and the noun *euangelion* were known to all Greek speakers, Paul's usage is derived from the reading of Deutero-Isaiah. The prophet announces to the despairing exiles, "Get you up to a high mountain, O Zion, herald of good tidings [*euangelizomenos*]" (Isa. 40:9). The prophet announces the captives' return from exile, exclaiming, "How beautiful upon the mountains are the feet of the messenger who announces [*euangelizomenou*] peace, who brings good news [*euangelizomenos*]" (52:7). Multitudes will come and announce (*euangeliountai*, 60:6) the salvation (LXX *sōteria*; NRSV "praise") of the Lord. The prophet proclaims, "The Spirit of the Lord God is upon me . . . he has sent me to bring good news [*euangelisasthai*] to the oppressed, to bind up the brokenhearted, to proclaim liberty to the captives, and release to the prisoners" (61:1).

The good news to the captives was the return from exile and the rebuilding of Zion after two generations in captivity. The prophet explains this good news with the forensic metaphor of the judge who exercises judgment in righteousness (*dikaiosynē*, Isa. 42:6; 51:5, 7) and justifies (*dikaioi*, 42:21; 43:26; 50:8) Israel by redeeming the people from their sins. To the captives who have experienced the silence of God in captivity, wondering if God had divorced them (50:1), the prophet offers comfort (40:1; 61:2), indicating that Israel has "served her term" and paid the penalty for her sin (40:2). God has redeemed Israel from slavery (43:1, 14). The rise of Cyrus and the Persian Empire in the East signals the downfall of the Babylonian captors (41:2). This event is nothing else than the righteousness (*dikaiosynē*) of the God who judges the peoples, vindicating the oppressed and punishing the oppressors. The God who once called Israel in righteousness (*dikaiosynē*) and covenant faithfulness (42:6) is about to do a new thing (42:9). The prophet claims, "He who vindicates [*dikaiōsas*] me is near" (50:8). Equating salvation and righteousness, God says through the prophet, "My salvation will be forever, and my deliverance will never be ended" (51:6).

Paul understands his proclamation of the good news to be nothing less than what the prophet announced centuries before him. Through the death and resurrection of Christ, God has rescued humankind from its transgressions (Rom. 4:25; 2 Cor. 5:19). The forensic metaphor employed by the prophet for God's saving deeds becomes a favorite image for Paul as he interprets the meaning of the death and resurrection of Christ. Paul declares that in the gospel "the righteousness of God is revealed" (Rom. 1:17). Indeed,

14. Ibid., 91.

he insists that the righteousness of God has already been made manifest in the coming of Christ (Rom. 3:21; cf. 8:30). Those who have been united with Christ have been justified by faith (Rom. 5:1; 6:7). Nevertheless, God's righteousness remains a future reality, for we continue to await the righteousness of God (Gal. 5:5). Thus Paul claims that the prophetic hope for the righteousness of God has become a reality through Jesus Christ. The good news announced by the prophet is the righteousness of God in Jesus Christ.[15]

Paul places his role within the prophetic narrative of Deutero-Isaiah. He is the herald who has been called to announce the good news (Isa. 52:7; 61:1) that God reigns. Like the ancient prophet, he meets resistance from Israel (Isa. 52:5; Rom. 2:24) as he expresses grief (Rom. 9:1–5) over the fact that Israel has not believed (Rom. 10:16; cf. Isa. 53:1). The good news is not limited to Israel, however, for it goes out "to the end of the world" (Rom. 10:18). Deutero-Isaiah incorporates the ancient tradition of the pilgrimage of the nations to Zion (cf. Isa. 2:2–4; 11:10; 25:6–10),[16] declaring that salvation includes the entire world. Israel is a "light to the nations" (42:6), and the task of the servant is to be "a light to the nations" (49:6). God not only calls Israel but says through the prophet, "Turn to me and be saved, all the ends of the earth" (45:22). He envisions a time when the foreigners, the outcasts of Israel, and even the eunuchs will be gathered into the people of God (56:6–8). Nations will come to the light of Israel (60:3). Paul concludes the argument of Romans with the words of Deutero-Isaiah, "Those who have never been told of him shall see, and those who have never heard of him shall understand" (Rom. 15:21; cf. Isa. 52:15). He anticipates the time when "every knee shall bow to me, and every tongue shall give praise to God" (Rom. 14:11; cf. Phil. 2:9–11; cf. Isa. 45:23). Thus he understands himself as the prophet to the nations whose special role is to offer the sacrifice of the gentiles to God (Rom. 15:16). He is a "debtor" to the Greeks and barbarians (Rom. 1:14).

Paul adopts the servant's role, not only in the task of evangelism but also in the continued formation of his churches, hoping to present them to God at the eschaton. When he challenges the Corinthians "not to accept the grace of God in vain" (2 Cor. 6:2), he echoes the words of the servant: "I have labored in vain" (Isa. 49:4). Indeed, a common theme in Paul is the concern that his labor not be in vain (cf. Gal. 4:11; Phil. 2:16).

---

15. Roy E. Ciampa, "Paul's Theology of the Gospel," in *Paul as Missionary: Identity, Activity, Theology, and Practice*, ed. Trevor J. Burke and Brian S. Rosner, Library of New Testament Studies 420 (Edinburgh: T&T Clark, 2011), 181.

16. Seyoon Kim, "Paul as an Eschatological Herald," in *Paul as Missionary* (London: T&T Clark, 2011), 13.

The mission of God, as the prophetic tradition indicates, is the restoration of Israel and the incorporation of the nations in a covenant relationship with God. Humanity will bow down before God (Isa. 45:23). Foreigners and all who had been excluded will be accepted among the people of God (56:4–8) when they keep the commandments. God's servant is the instrument of God's mission who offers comfort to dispirited Israel (40:1), announces the good news (52:7), and challenges Israel to respond to God's offer of forgiveness (44:22).

THE MISSION OF THE CHURCHES TO THE WORLD

Paul's understanding of his mission raises two important and related questions. First, inasmuch as he has established only a few house churches in the major cities, what does he mean in claiming to have "fully proclaimed the good news" from Jerusalem to Illyricum? Second, what was the mission of his churches? Interpreters have assumed that Paul intended for the message to spread throughout the empire from the strategic areas where he planted churches. That is, he established churches in strategic locations—the major cities of the eastern Mediterranean—assuming that the gospel would spread from Corinth to all Achaia, from Ephesus to the rest of Asia, and from Philippi and Thessalonica to all Macedonia.[17] Adolf Harnack maintained that Paul's missionary strategy was designed so that the gospel would spread from the population centers into the surrounding regions.[18] Michael Green argues, "Evangelism was the prerogative and the duty of every Church member. We have seen apostles and wandering prophets, nobles and paupers, intellectuals and fishermen all taking part enthusiastically in the primary task committed by Christ to his Church."[19] Roger Gehring maintains, "From both Acts and the Pauline epistles it is clear that Paul practiced 'cell planting' missional outreach in these centers." He adds, "Paul believed that his main objective was to establish small cells, that is, bases of operations in these cities, and to develop missional outreach for these support bases. From these bases outward, the city itself and then the surrounding area were to be reached with the gospel. . . . These churches were trained by Paul to take the responsibility for their own community life and the missional outreach in their city and to the surrounding area."[20] The amazing growth of Christianity suggests that the movement spread to the hinterlands

17. Brian K. Peterson, "Being the Church in Philippi," *Horizons in Biblical Theology* 30 (2008): 164.

18. Adolf Harnack, *The Mission and Expansion of Christianity in the First Three Centuries* (New York: Harper, 1962), 77–79.

19. Michael Green, *Evangelism in the Early Church* (Grand Rapids: Eerdmans, 1970), 274.

20. Gehring, *House Church and Mission*, 179–80.

from the major cities. Indeed, although it would appear to be self-evident that Paul the missionary would urge his congregations to participate in his mission, the letters give little indication that he exhorts his readers to engage in missionary outreach. Although the letters contain exhortations on a variety of topics, in none of them does Paul urge his readers to engage in missions and evangelism or to effect social change in the larger society.

One is struck by the intramural character of Paul's instructions. Although he engages in extended catechesis and urges his converts to "lead a life worthy of God" (1 Thess. 2:12), he never instructs the converts to engage in evangelism or plan mission programs. The weight of his instructions involves the building up of the community and his desire that the communities be blameless at the coming of Christ (cf. 1 Cor. 1:8; Phil. 2:16). He does not encourage readers to send missionaries or to engage in local evangelism. When one considers the importance of missionary outreach for Paul, the absence of exhortations for his congregations to share in his mission is astonishing. Inasmuch as the letters contain only a small portion of Paul's total instruction, the possibility remains that his oral instructions contained exhortations for missionary outreach. However, since the letters present our only record of Paul's instruction, the question of the involvement of Paul's churches in missions and evangelism remains open.

Paul offers at least a partial answer to the question of the mission of his churches in the final summation in Romans 15. He hopes that the Romans will provide financial support for his trip to Spain (15:24), and he asks them to pray for his mission (15:30). Paul's other churches have already participated in his mission by providing financial support and by praying on his behalf (cf. 2 Cor. 11:7–11; Phil. 1:5; 4:15; 1 Thess. 5:25). Indeed, Paul assumes in the other letters that they will assist him in his evangelistic mission. He hopes to spend the winter with the Corinthians, who can then send him on his way (1 Cor. 16:6; cf. 2 Cor. 1:16). The churches send coworkers to assist Paul in his mission. W.-H. Ollrog has analyzed the role of Paul's coworkers in his mission, indicating that the apostle was joined by three categories of assistants: the inner circle, composed of Barnabas, Silvanus, and especially Timothy; "independent coworkers," such as Aquila and Prisca and Titus; and representatives of local churches.[21] Ollrog maintains that the churches became involved in Paul's mission through their representatives.[22] These include Epaphroditus (Phil. 2:19–30), Epaphras (Col. 1:7; 4:12; Philem. 23), Aristarchus (Col. 4:10; Philem. 24), and Jason (Rom.

---

21. Wolf-Henning Ollrog, *Paulus und seine Mitarbeiter: Untersuchung zu Theorie und Praxis der paulinischen Mission* (Neukirchen-Vluyn: Neukirchener Verlag, 1979), 92–95.
22. Ibid., 234–35.

16:21). When Paul reassures the Corinthians about the integrity of the collection, he mentions the unnamed brothers who are "messengers of the churches" (2 Cor. 8:23).[23] Thus Paul regards his mission as a function of the church, and he expects them to be partners in his evangelistic work.[24]

However, the epistles leave no record of organized evangelistic activity in their local communities. Indeed, most occurrences of *euangel-* appear in relation to the activities of Paul and his coworkers. While he assumes that others are involved in the preaching ministry (Rom. 10:15; Phil. 1:15–18) and appoints coworkers for the preaching task (cf. 2 Cor. 1:19), he does not explicitly instruct the churches to be participants in evangelism or missionary activity. The *euangelion* comes to them (1 Thess. 1:5), and they receive it (1 Thess. 1:6). In some instances, they may turn from it (Gal. 1:6). Paul expects the churches to live according to the truth of the gospel (Gal. 2:5, 14) and live "in a manner worthy" of it (Phil. 1:27), but he does not instruct them to share in the preaching of the gospel.[25] His mission is clearly distinguishable from the mission of his churches.[26]

Despite the absence of explicit commands for churches to evangelize or send missionaries, some interpreters maintain that the epistles offer evidence for Paul's expectation of evangelistic activity. For example, some scholars argue that Paul's injunctions to imitate him (1 Cor. 4:16; 11:1; Phil. 3:17; cf. 1 Thess. 1:6) are a mandate for their missionary activity. Peter O'Brien argues that "the apostle's earnest desire of saving men and women was an essential element in the servant pattern he adopted."[27] Similarly, Robert Plummer argues that Paul's call for imitation includes both his way of life and his ministry of proclamation.[28]

Interpreters commonly appeal to 1 Thessalonians 1:5–8 as the most compelling indication of Paul's expectation that his churches will imitate his ministry of proclamation. The Thessalonians became "imitators" (*mimētai*) of Paul and of the Lord (1:6) and, in turn, became a model (*typos*) for the churches in Macedonia and Achaia (1:7). Paul adds that "the word . . . sounded forth . . . in Macedonia and Achaia" (1:8). According to James Ware, the "word of God

---

23. See Eckhard Schnabel, *Early Christian Mission*, vol. 2, *Paul and the Early Church* (Downers Grove, IL: InterVarsity, 2004), 1441.

24. Ollrog, *Paulus und seine Mitarbeiter*, 234–35.

25. Dickson, *Mission-Commitment in Ancient Judaism*, 94–95.

26. Banks, *Paul's Idea of Community*, 161–70.

27. Peter O'Brien, *Gospel and Mission in the Writings of Paul: An Exegetical and Theological Analysis* (Grand Rapids: Baker, 1995), 137.

28. Robert L. Plummer, *Paul's Understanding of the Church's Mission: Did the Apostle Paul Expect the Early Christian Communities to Evangelize?* Paternoster Biblical Monographs (Waynesboro, GA: Paternoster, 2006), 85, 90.

resounded" when the Thessalonians continued Paul's work of proclamation.[29] The Thessalonians "had not only received the apostle's message, but were also active in communicating it to others."[30] According to J. Lambrecht, "The apostles and those who receive the word are so empowered that they become as it were automatically witnesses and examples in their turn. One thinks of a chain reaction: from God to the apostles; the apostles are in their turn imitated; and finally those who imitate them themselves become examples."[31]

The context of Paul's statement in 1:5–8 provides a more nuanced portrait of Paul's expectation for his churches. This statement is a part of the extended thanksgiving in 1 Thessalonians (1:2–10). Paul first expresses gratitude (1:2–5) for the Thessalonians' reception of the gospel and moral progress—their work of faith, labor of love, and steadfastness of hope. In 1:6–10 he elaborates on the Thessalonians' moral progress from his preaching to their reception of his message. The participial phrase "receiving the word in much affliction" (1:6) indicates the manner in which the Thessalonians were imitators of Paul.[32] He himself had first preached to the Thessalonians "in spite of great opposition" (2:2), after being shamefully treated in Philippi. Now the Thessalonians imitated Paul by sharing with him in the hostility of the populace. They have imitated not only Paul and the Lord (1:6) but also the churches of Judea by their endurance in the context of affliction (2:14).

The result (*hōste*, 1:7) of their imitation of Paul and the Lord was that they in turn became an example (*typos*) for believers in Macedonia and Achaia. The reference to believers (*pisteuousin*) reflects the sharp division between believers and nonbelievers—insiders and outsiders—that permeates Paul's letters. In 1:8 Paul explains the manner in which the Thessalonians became an example in two parallel statements introduced by *gar*[33] and arranged in chiastic fashion:

29. James Ware, "The Thessalonians as a Missionary Congregation: 1 Thessalonians 1:5–8," *Zeitschrift für die neutestamentliche Wissenschaft und die Kunde der älteren Kirche* 83 (1992): 127. For the view that 1 Thess. 1:6–8 describes the evangelistic activity of the Thessalonians, see also David M. Stanley, "'Become Imitators of Me': The Pauline Conception of Apostolic Tradition," *Bib* 40 (1959): 866–67; Andrew D. Clarke, "'Be Imitators of Me': Paul's Model of Leadership," *TynBul* 49 (1998): 336–38; Marshall, "Who Were the Evangelists?," in *The Mission of the Church to Jews and Gentiles*, ed. Adna Jostein, WUNT 127 (Tübingen: Mohr Siebeck, 2000), 259.

30. Ware, "Thessalonians as a Missionary Congregation," 127.

31. J. Lambrecht, "A Call to Witness by All: Evangelisation in 1 Thessalonians," in *Teologie in Konteks. Opgedra an A. B. du Toit*, ed. J. H. Roberts, W. S. Vorster, J. N. Vorster, et al. (Pretoria: Orion, 1991), 324.

32. Cf. the NRSV, "In spite of persecution you received the word with joy inspired by the Holy Spirit." On the Thessalonians' continued afflictions (*thlipseis*), see 3:1–4.

33. *Gar* in 1:8 indicates the manner in which the Thessalonians became an example. See Dickson, *Mission-Commitment in Ancient Judaism*, 96.

For the word of the Lord has sounded forth [*exēchētai*] from you . . .
your faith in God has become known [*exelēlythen*].

Gar in 1:8 indicates that the report of the resounding of the word in Macedonia and Achaia—the locale of the believers in 1:7—is among the believers.[34] The repetition of "Macedonia and Achaia" in verse 8 suggests that it is parallel to "the believers in Macedonia and Achaia" in verse 7. Thus the context suggests that the impact of the word of the Lord was made on believers rather than unbelievers. Macedonia and Achaia is parallel to "every place" (1:8), a phrase that is used elsewhere for "those who call on the Lord in every place" (cf. 1 Cor. 1:2). The statement is similar to Paul's later expression of gratitude that the Romans' faith "is proclaimed throughout the world" (Rom. 1:8). In this hyperbole, Paul is probably speaking of the reputation of the Roman church among the churches he had established.

The parallel verbs, with their similar sounds,[35] suggest the impact of the Thessalonians' faith: the word has sounded forth (*exēchētai*), and their faith in God has gone out (*exelēlythen*). Both verbs indicate the dynamism of God's word, which first came to the Thessalonians "in power" (1:5) and is still at work among them (2:13). The verb "sounded forth" (*exēchētai*), a hapax legomenon in the New Testament, connotes sounds that resound with great volume and can be heard at a great distance.[36] The word (*logos*) that they received was the gospel that came with power (1:5). Paul anticipates the later comment that the *logos* of God is "at work in [them]" (2:13). Thus, the *logos* has continuing power to work in the believers' lives. The same power at work in Paul's preaching was also at work among the Thessalonians. Paul's comment probably means that their faith is widely known among the churches of the Pauline mission.[37] Thus the word has resounded among believers who hear reports of the power of God's word among the Thessalonians. Paul is not congratulating the Thessalonians over their evangelistic preaching but is expressing gratitude for the power of God in their lives.

Further evidence that Paul is describing the impact of the Thessalonians' conversion on believers is evident in 1:9–10. Once more the introductory *gar*

---

34. Paul Bowers, "Church and Mission in Paul," *Journal for the Study of the New Testament* 44 (1991): 98.

35. Both verbs are in the third-person singular perfect tense and have the prefix *ex*-. See Dickson, *Mission-Commitment in Ancient Judaism*, 100.

36. Ibid. Philo uses the term for the "thunderous voice of God" at Mount Sinai. See *Decalogue* 33; 46. Philo also uses the term for the heavenly trumpet (*Spec. Laws* 2.189). Other ancient writers use the word for a clap of thunder (Philo, *Abraham* 160; cf. Sir. 40:13). It is used for the noises of charging armies in Egypt (*Moses* 1.169). I am indebted to Dickson for these references.

37. Bowers, "Church and Mission in Paul," 99.

indicates that Paul is giving further support for the earlier claim that the word of God has sounded forth in Macedonia and Achaia. "For the people of those regions report [literally "they are reporting about you"] . . . how you turned to God from idols to serve the living and true God" (1:9). Those giving the report are the believers mentioned in 1:7. They—the believers—are reporting the extraordinary change among the Thessalonians. Thus Paul gives thanks for the impact of the word on the lives of the Thessalonians, and he describes its influence among neighboring congregations. He does not describe the Thessalonians' work as evangelists but gives thanks for their influence on believers in distant places.

James Ware acknowledges that Paul "nowhere in his letters overtly commands his congregations to spread the gospel, or exhorts his churches to engage in missionary activity,"[38] but he says that Philippians, more than any other letter, offers abundant evidence that Paul expects his churches to spread the gospel. He notes the concentration of the language of gospel, mission, and preaching throughout the letter,[39] arguing that Philippians consistently indicates the role of the church in evangelistic activity. He maintains that Paul's thanksgiving for the Philippians' "sharing in the gospel" (Phil. 1:5) refers not only to their financial contribution to his ministry but also to their "missionizing activity."[40] This claim rests on Ware's interpretation of the larger unit in 1:3–2:18, in which he attempts to demonstrate the expectation of the church's missionary activity. Thus when Paul indicates in 1:12–15 that, despite his imprisonment, the gospel is advancing through the work of "most of the brothers and sisters" (1:14), Ware concludes that the passage "describes the spread of the gospel as a general Christian activity,"[41] not as the work of a special class of evangelists. "As such the passage is of great interest, for it is almost the sole instance in Paul's letters in which he refers to the missionizing in the sense of active verbal proclamation of Christians generally."[42]

In the paraenesis that begins in 1:27–2:4, Ware argues that the opening imperative in the letter, "Conduct yourselves" (NIV; *politeuesthe*, 1:27), accents Paul's interest in a missional purpose for the life and conduct of the church. Paul's encouragement not to be "intimidated by your opponents" (1:28) is evidence that "Paul envisions the mission of the Philippians through conduct and suffering (1:27), as complemented by an active mission of verbal proclamation

38. James P. Ware, *Paul and the Mission of the Church: Philippians in Ancient Jewish Context* (Grand Rapids: Baker Academic, 2011), 5.
39. Ibid., 165–66.
40. Ibid., 170.
41. Ibid., 181.
42. Ibid., 183.

(1:28)."[43] Ware concludes that "in Philippians 2 Paul's emphatic exhortation to boldly spread the gospel, despite personal risk and suffering, reveals that he understood active verbal mission as an essential aspect of Christian identity."[44]

The cornerstone of Ware's argument is probably his interpretation of Philippians 2:12–18, a paraenesis that develops the implications of the hymn to Christ in 2:6–11. Ware maintains that the call to "work [*katergazesthe*] out your salvation" is a call for continued missionary activity.[45] The role of the community as "stars in the world" (2:15) identifies the community with Israel's role in the Old Testament. In his interpretation of 2:16, Ware disputes the NRSV rendering, "It is by your holding fast the word of life [*logon zōēs epechontes*] that I can boast on the day of Christ that I did not run in vain," arguing that *epechontes* means "extend" rather than "hold fast." Thus he understands 2:16 as an exhortation to spread the gospel.[46]

Ware notes that since Paul nowhere else commands his churches to evangelize, the interpretation of *epechontes* as "extend" in Philippians 2:16 is critical for his interpretation. In his extended word study of *epech-*, he disputes the interpretation by Bauer and demonstrates that the word *could* be rendered as "extend" or "spread" in some contexts, while in other instances it means "hold fast." These parallels are taken from instances widely dissimilar from the usage in Philippians 2:16. In none of the parallels does the word refer to the dissemination of a message. Indeed, Paul elsewhere employs a variety of terms for the dissemination of the word of God.[47] If Paul had wished to encourage the Philippians to spread the word of God through evangelism, he had available far more unambiguous terms. Ware gives more weight to this interpretation than it can bear.

Both the context of Philippians 2:16 and general Pauline usage offer the most compelling case for the NRSV rendering, "holding fast to the word of life," and for challenging Ware's claim that Paul urges the Philippians to engage in evangelistic activity. Within the immediate context, Paul is describing the ethical formation of a community that is "blameless and innocent," shining like stars in the world (2:14–15). Paul's "boast at the day of Christ" that he did not "run in vain" echoes the servant's lament in Isaiah 49:4, "I have labored in vain." For Paul, that phrase refers to those who have been faithful to the

43. Ibid., 220.
44. Ibid., 122.
45. Ibid., 248–49.
46. See also O'Brien, *Gospel and Mission*, and the discussion in Dickson, *Mission-Commitment in Ancient Judaism*, 108–11.
47. Phil. 1:14, "to speak [*lalein*] the word"; cf. 1 Thess. 2:1, "to declare [*lalēsai*] the gospel"; cf. 1 Thess. 2:9, "to preach [*kēryxai*] the gospel."

gospel (Gal. 4:11). His "boast at the day of Christ" will be a sanctified and faithful people (cf. Rom. 15:15–17; 2 Cor. 1:14; 1 Thess. 2:19).[48] Thus Paul's boast is the ethical formation of churches that "hold fast" the word of life.

Contrary to Ware's claim, Paul never encourages his readers in Philippians to evangelize. The Philippians' participation in the gospel (Phil. 1:5) is their participation in the collection (cf. 4:10–20), not their evangelistic activity. Paul's exhortation to "conduct yourselves [*politeuesthe*] in a manner worthy of the gospel" (1:27 NIV) is a challenge for an ethical life that corresponds to the gospel. Indeed, he depicts the ethical life in 1:27b–2:18 as a life in harmony with others. When he urges the Philippians not to be intimidated by adversaries, he says nothing about their work as evangelists. The exhortation to "work out your salvation" (2:12) is no indication that the Philippians' task is evangelism. Rather, it is the life of self-emptying exhibited by Jesus. Ware regularly inserts references to proclaiming and spreading the gospel in 1:1–2:18, where Paul gives no indication that proclamation is in view.

While Paul's anticipation of the day when every knee will bow and every tongue will confess that Jesus Christ is Lord (2:11) may suggest his desire for evangelism by his churches, he never mentions this task. As a paraenetic letter, Philippians offers numerous exhortations that describe the life that is "worthy of the gospel." Paul gives no unambiguous indications of the evangelistic work of his churches.

THE CHURCH AND THE WORLD IN PAUL

An Evangelistic Witness

The absence of exhortations to evangelize in Paul's letters does not preclude an expectation that the churches would be engaged in a mission to the surrounding world. Thus Paul's expectations are evident not in exhortations to evangelize but in his understanding of the church's identity and relationship to the world. By incorporating gentiles into Israel's story, Paul insists that his converts are separate from the world. His frequent description of the church as the "holy ones" reflects their identity as people who are set apart from the world. Consequently, Paul insists on a sharp dichotomy between the church and the world, distinguishing between the saints and the world (1 Cor. 6:1–2; cf. 5:10), believers and unbelievers (1 Cor. 6:6; 7:12, 14–15; 10:27; 14:22–23), insiders and outsiders (cf. Col. 4:5; 1 Thess. 4:12), and believers and "the rest"

48. See Thompson, *Pastoral Ministry according to Paul*, 22–23; Dickson, *Mission-Commitment in Ancient Judaism*, 111.

(1 Thess. 4:13; 5:6). His understanding of mission is predicated on the fact that the church is separated from the world.

The Corinthian correspondence offers an important window into Paul's understanding of the church's mission to the world. In both letters he announces that his personal mission is to evangelize (1 Cor. 1:17; 2 Cor. 4:1–6; 5:19–6:2) a world that remains unreconciled to God (cf. 2 Cor. 5:18–20). Response to his message demarcates those who are saved and those who are perishing (1 Cor. 1:18; cf. 2 Cor. 2:15). As a consequence, Paul challenges his readers to separate from the world. Outsiders are the unbelievers (1 Cor. 6:6; 7:12; 14:22–23; 10:27; 2 Cor. 4:4; 6:14–15) and the unrighteous (1 Cor. 6:1, 9).

In his first letter to the Corinthians, Paul urges the community not to have anything to do with immoral people (1 Cor. 5:9), which he then clarifies by indicating that his exhortation applies only to fellow believers who do not observe the boundaries between the church and the world (5:1–13). He enjoins radical separation between the saints and the world, a separation that extends to law courts, matters of sexuality and marriage, and interaction with pagan cults (cf. 10:21). Probably appealing to standard catechesis, he urges the Corinthians, "Come out from among them, and be separate from them" (2 Cor. 6:17). If his communities have been incorporated into Israel, they will also be separate from the world around them.

Despite this call for separation, Paul acknowledges that believers will interact with the world, for otherwise they would have to leave the world (1 Cor. 5:10). He describes the circumstances in which believers interact with unbelievers, indicating that these interactions are opportunities for evangelism. Believers who are married to unbelievers (7:2–16) face the complication of the status of the children (7:14). Widows face decisions about marrying unbelievers (7:39). Believers also receive invitations to unbelievers' banquets (10:27). Unbelievers attend the worship services (14:24). These relationships and circumstances involving believers and nonbelievers offer a window for understanding the mission of the church.

Mixed Marriages and Family Relationships

What was the role of the church? The problem of boundaries becomes a particular issue in Paul's discussion of marriage between believers and nonbelievers (1 Cor. 7:12–16). Here he acknowledges that boundaries are not ironclad. Where mixed marriages already exist, he does not suggest that believers separate from their spouses (7:10–11). Although he insists that believers either remain unmarried or marry "only in the Lord" (7:29), he counsels those who have unbelieving spouses to remain married (7:12), offering two reasons. In the first place, the unbelieving spouse "is sanctified" and the children "are holy" (7:14 NASB). The believer is not polluted by the unbeliever; instead, holiness extends outward. In the second place, Paul offers the motivation that the unbelieving spouse might be saved (7:16). The advice recalls Paul's division of the world into the categories of the saved and the perishing (1 Cor. 1:18; cf. 2 Cor. 2:15), indicating that the unbelieving spouse is among those who are perishing.

Paul's questions to spouses, "Wife, for all you know, you might save your husband?" and "Husband, for all you know, you might save your wife?" (7:16), indicate that believers share his concern that outsiders be saved. This situation resembles that of 1 Peter, in which the author suggests that wives may "win" their unbelieving husbands without a word (1 Pet. 3:1). Paul is suggesting that appropriate behavior by the spouse may result in conversion. The interaction of believers with unbelievers provides an opportunity to evangelize the unbeliever. The passage probably offers an insight into how evangelism took place in the Pauline churches. Evangelism was the result not of organized programs but of the spread of the gospel within family and other networks.[49] If conversion occurred among spouses, it also occurred within other networks.

The questions to spouses belong to the wider context of the relationship between insiders and outsiders in 5:1–11:1. In responding to the Corinthians' insistence on their right to eat meat offered to idols (8:1–13), Paul offers his own life as an example of the renunciation of rights (9:1–18). In 9:19–23 he describes his efforts to "win" (*kerdainein*) both Jews and Greeks. He concludes, "I have become all things to all people, that I might by all means save some" (9:22), thus equating the winning of others with their salvation.

In 10:23–11:1 Paul describes another opportunity for interaction between insiders and outsiders and elaborates on his work as a model for evangelism. In this instance, Paul assumes that believers will accept invitations to pagan banquets and that food offered to idols will be served. He introduces the advice on this situation with the repetition of the phrase "all things are lawful" (cf. 6:12), adding, "but not all things are beneficial" (10:23 ESV). In contrast to the earlier part of the discussion (8:1–13), Paul is concerned not with the weaker brother but with the outsider who says, "This has been offered as a sacrifice [*hierothyton*]" (10:28). He instructs the believer to consider the conscience of the unbeliever, abstaining from the food as an act of concern for the other. He repeats the earlier claim that he does not seek his own advantage but tries to please everyone in all his activities, concluding with the exhortation "Be imitators of me, as I am of Christ" (11:1). The church that imitates Paul will

---

49. See Sandnes, *New Family*, 93–111; Reinbold, *Propaganda und Mission im ältesten Christentum*, 299–310.

"give no offense to Jews or to Greeks or to the church of God" (10:32). This instruction recalls Paul's own attempt to identify with Jews and Greeks in order to save them (9:19–23). Paul does not give direct instructions to engage in evangelistic activity, but he envisions a community that gives no offense to outsiders (Col. 4:5; cf. 1 Thess. 4:12). This could result in the winning of others.[50]

EVANGELISM AND THE CHRISTIAN ASSEMBLY

A second window for understanding the mission of the church appears near the conclusion of the discussion of the spiritual gifts in the church's corporate worship in 1 Corinthians 12–14. In these chapters Paul responds to the dominant place that glossolalia has taken in the Corinthian community, demonstrating that all the gifts are necessary for the functioning of the body (12:1–31). He corrects the Corinthians' apparent competition over gifts by demonstrating that love within the community is the greatest of the gifts (chap. 13) before responding concretely to the problems posed by the prominence of glossolalia in the worship service (chap. 14). As 14:1 indicates, the gift that corresponds most to love is prophecy, for it benefits the whole community. According to 14:3, "those who prophesy speak to other people for their upbuilding [oikodomē] and encouragement [paraklēsis] and consolation [paramythia]." Paul introduces the extended section on corporate worship with the criterion for the assembly: "so that the church may be built up" (14:5, literally "so that the church may receive edification [oikodomē]"). Edification then becomes the major theme of the chapter (cf. 14:3, 5, 12, 17, 26). Consistent with his earlier description of the church as God's building under construction (3:10–17), Paul describes worship as the occasion for the construction project to take place as an expression of the love that "builds up" (8:1).

Edification involves intelligible communication, as Paul indicates in 14:6–19. Glossolalia fails to build up the church because it does not communicate to the participants. Thus one may give thanks in a tongue, "but the other is not built up" (14:17). What matters is that one may teach others (14:19) within the church. However, as Paul indicates in 14:20–25, an unbeliever (apistos) or outsider (idiōtēs) may also enter (14:23) the assembly, for it is no esoteric group that insulates itself from the outside world to discuss unintelligible subjects.[51] Just as outsiders frequently attended synagogue services,[52] they also visited the

---

50. Dickson, *Mission-Commitment in Ancient Judaism*, 256–57.

51. Walter Rebell, "Gemeinde als Missionsfaktor im Urchristentum: 1 Kor 14:24f. als Schlüsselsituation," *Theologische Zeitschrift* 44 (1988): 127.

52. See Philo, *Moses* 2.41–44, for the multitude of gentiles attracted to Jewish festivals. Josephus, *J.W.* 7.45, speaks of the great crowds that flock to Jewish ceremonies. See Dickson, *Mission-Commitment in Ancient Judaism*, 293.

Christian assembly. Paul does not clarify the difference between the unbeliever (*apistos*) and the outsider (*idiōtēs*). The fact that he connects them with "or" (*ē*) suggests that there is little distinction. Paul has spoken consistently in 1 Corinthians about the relationship between believers and unbelievers (cf. *apistoi* in 6:6; 7:12, 14–15; 10:27; 2 Cor. 4:4; 6:14–15), calling for boundaries (1 Cor. 6:6) but recognizing the necessary interaction between them. The unbeliever could be the unbelieving spouse (7:12–16), one who invites the believer to the banquet (cf. 10:27), or one who comes to the assembly out of curiosity. Paul assumes the openness of the community's worship to the outside world.[53]

Paul presents two alternative responses from the outsider who enters the service. Glossolalia will elicit a negative response. Paul cites the words from Isaiah 28:11–12, according to which God will speak to the people "by people of strange tongues and by the lips of foreigners" (1 Cor. 14:21). From the prophet's conclusion, "They will not listen to me," Paul concludes that "they" refers to the outsider who does not understand glossolalia. The inference drawn from the citation (*hōste*, 14:23) is that tongues are a "sign" (*sēmeion*) for unbelievers. As the ensuing argument indicates, the sign functions in a negative way, for unbelievers will conclude that those who are speaking in tongues are out of their minds (*mainesthe*, 14:23).[54] Worship should be intelligible not only to believers (14:6–19) but to unbelievers as well.

The desired response to all prophecy is that the outsider "is reproved [*elenchetai*] by all and called to account [*anakrinetai*] by all" (14:24). The repetition of "all" indicates that the outsiders are moved, not by the evangelistic sermon, but by the role of the entire community in calling them to repentance.[55] Prophecy not only encourages and builds up the community (14:3) but also confronts outsiders with the truth about their own lives.[56] As a result of the

---

53. The *idiōtēs* (NRSV "outsider") is anyone who has no training and is commonly contrasted to experts and professionals, i.e., the lay person in contrast to the physician, the common soldier in contrast to the officer. In this sense Paul calls himself an *idiōtēs* in speech (2 Cor. 11:6). See Spicq, "*idiōtēs*," *TLNT* 2:213. Cf. also Reinbold, *Propaganda und Mission im ältesten Christentum*, 195–96, who argues that the *idiōtēs* is a regular visitor who has been invited to the assembly by Paul or a family member. Thus Paul distinguishes the *idiōtēs* from the stranger who comes into the assembly.

54. See BDAG 610. Cf. Acts 12:15, "They said to her, 'You are out of your mind.'" In Acts 26:24–25 Festus says, "You are out of your mind, Paul! Too much learning has made you insane!" *Mainesthai* has two basic meanings in Classical Greek: "to be furious, enraged" and "to be raving mad." In the LXX and New Testament, it appears with the latter meaning. See Spicq, "*mainomai*," *TLNT* 2.430.

55. Reinbold, *Propaganda und Mission im ältesten Christentum*, 197.

56. Both *elenchein* and *anakrinein* are used as forensic terms for a judicial hearing. *Elenchein* is used elsewhere in the New Testament to mean "point out someone's faults" (cf. Matt. 18:15) or "bring a person to the point of recognizing wrongdoing." Cf. John 8:46, "Which of you convicts

examination, "the secrets of the unbeliever's heart are disclosed" (14:25; cf. Rom. 2:16) to themselves as they recognize their previous blindness (cf. 2 Cor. 4:4) and distance from God.

The culmination of the unbeliever's response is the declaration "God is really among you" (1 Cor. 14:25). The outsider recognizes the hand of God at work in the admonitions of the church. The expression is derived from Isaiah 45:14, the familiar image of the nations coming to Zion. In this instance, the wealth of Egypt and the merchandise of Ethiopia and the Sabeans will belong to Israel. The nations will bow down and say, "God is with you alone, and there is no other."

The allusion is further evidence that Paul sees the events of his ministry as a realization of the hopes announced in Deutero-Isaiah. He envisions the turn of the nations to God. As outsiders see the harmony of the believers in worship, they will fulfill the prophet's expectation of the coming of the nations to Zion. Paul anticipates that the outsiders, upon seeing the worship, may conclude that God is present in the group. Evangelism would take place under these circumstances.

The assembly offered one of the most important means for evangelism.[57] However, Paul's description of public worship indicates that the purpose of worship is not to attract the outsider but to build up the church. When the outsider enters the assembly, the members are engaged in a practice that contributes to the lasting benefit of the community. Prophecy speaks a word of God that encourages and comforts the participants. However, worship is not insensitive to the outsider, for Paul's earlier exhortation to "give no offense to Jews or Greeks" (10:32) applies also to the assembly, in which prophecy is also directed to the outsider. Paul assumes that the whole church will be engaged in evangelism within the assembly.

Evangelism and Christian Morality

Philippians offers an additional window to the practice of evangelism in the early church. In the midst of Paul's imprisonment, he expresses his concern for the advance of the gospel (1:12). At the conclusion of the Philippian hymn, he looks forward to the day when every knee shall bow and every tongue confess that Jesus Christ is Lord (Phil. 2:10–11; cf. Rom 14:11), alluding to Isaiah 45:23 (LXX). The story of Christ becomes the basis for the conduct of the believers, who "work out [their] own salvation" (Phil. 2:12) by living in conformity

---

me of sin?" Cf. also James 2:9, "You commit sin and are convicted by the law as transgressors." See BDAG 315. *Anakrinein* is used for an examination "with a view to finding fault" (BDAG 66).

57. Reinbold, *Propaganda und Mission im ältesten Christentum*, 195.

with the story of Christ. Those who live out the story will be "in full accord and of one mind" (2:2; cf. 1:27–30; 4:2). By living in harmony with each other (2:14), they will be "blameless and innocent, children of God without blemish in the midst of a crooked and perverse generation, in which [they] shine like stars in the world" (2:15). He alludes to the statement in Daniel 12:3 that "those who are wise shall shine like the brightness of the sky," assuming that the prophetic expectation of the righteous, who are shining lights, will lead others to the truth. The images of light and darkness indicate the separation of the church from the world and the impact of the church on the "crooked and perverse generation." Christian unity will influence the hostile outside world. When believers are blameless, Paul will not have run in vain (2:16). Like the servant of Isaiah 49:4, Paul hopes that his community will be a light to the nations. Evangelism likely occurred when Christian communities provided a model of a common life that was unknown in the ancient world outside the circle of the physical family.

While Paul does not directly command his communities to evangelize, he assumes that the power of the gospel will change the lives of the converts and attract outsiders into the faith. He draws sharp boundaries between the church and the world in order that the church may, by its moral life, make an impact on the world. He insists that the Thessalonians, for example, live the ethical life not only because it is the will of God (1 Thess. 4:3) but also so that outsiders may witness their proper behavior (4:12).[58] As believers love each other more and more (4:10), mind their own affairs, and work with their own hands (4:11), they will make a positive impact on unbelievers.

While his churches have no planned evangelistic programs, Paul assumes that they will grow as husbands and wives convert their spouses, parents introduce children into the faith, and members introduce relatives and friends to the assembly. The openness of the assembly to outsiders provided an opportunity for evangelism, and the moral conduct of the believers attracted outsiders to accept the gospel.

Paul's consistent appeal to Deutero-Isaiah indicates that he expects his churches to take on the role of Israel. As in the prophet's portrayal of Israel, Paul expects his churches to be the light that will attract outsiders toward

---

58. The importance of the ethical life as a means of making an impression on outsiders is a continuing theme in the disputed letters. The readers of Colossians are instructed to conduct themselves "wisely toward outsiders" (Col. 4:5). The Pastoral Epistles consistently express a concern for the impact of behavior on outsiders. Young widows who behave in an inappropriate way give the adversaries the occasion for reviling believers (1 Tim. 5:14). Young women, young men, and slaves who conduct themselves in an exemplary way prevent the word from being discredited (Titus 2:5, 8), and slaves who behave ethically "adorn" the gospel (Titus 2:10 KJV).

the community. As in ancient Israel, the community does not go out to the nations but lives such an attractive life that the nations will be drawn to it. Thus Paul does not send his churches to evangelize but assumes that evangelism will occur in households and cities as the populace sees the power of the word of God to transform lives. When he declares to the Corinthians that they are a "letter of Christ" (2 Cor. 3:3), "known and read by all" (3:2), he likely refers to the impact of the transformed community on the larger populace.

A Social Ethic in Paul?

Unlike ancient moralists, Paul never refers to the virtue of *philanthrōpia*, the love of humanity.[59] Consistent with his strong demarcation between the church and the world, he encourages his communities to love one another (cf. Rom. 12:9–12; 1 Thess. 4:9–12). Indeed, love is the primary ethical value that Paul inculcates in his churches. However, he envisions the practice of love primarily within the circle of the house church. He cites in two instances (Rom. 13:9; Gal. 5:14) the command to "love your neighbor as yourself" (Lev. 19:18) as a warrant for the practice of believers. The neighbor is not, however, every needy person, as elsewhere (Luke 10:29, 36), but the equivalent of "one another." In Galatians 5:13–15 Paul encourages believers to "serve one another through love" (5:13 HCSB) and warns against devouring one another (5:15). The scriptural warrant is Leviticus 19:18. Hence the neighbor is the fellow believer. Similarly, in Romans Paul describes the transformed existence of those who belong to the new age (Rom. 12:1–2) as existence within the local community, the body (12:3–8). This existence is characterized by love (12:9), which Paul illustrates with instructions for "brotherly love" (KJV; *philadelphia*, 12:10), hospitality to fellow believers, sharing of resources with the saints (12:14), and harmony with each other (12:16).

In Romans 13:8–14 Paul encourages love for one another (13:8), once more citing the love command as scriptural warrant. Here also the neighbor is the fellow believer. In 14:1–15:13 he illustrates the meaning of love (cf. 14:15), encouraging believers to consider the one who is "weak in faith" (14:1). Like the ancient families, Paul's communities took care of even the weaker members.

The frequency of "one another" in Paul's writings indicates the insularity of his communities and their familial responsibility for each other. Consequently, his few references to communal evangelism correspond to the paucity

---

59. See Thompson, *Moral Formation*, 109.

of references to a mission of good deeds to outsiders. His communities assume the role of family to each other, protecting one another's honor and taking care of those in need.

Although his primary focus is the mutual care within the community, Paul erects no boundaries to care for outsiders. In 1 Thessalonians he prays that God will increase the community's "love for one another and for all" (1 Thess. 3:12)—the only reference in the Pauline literature to love for those who are outside the community.[60] Gerhard Lohfink has observed that the objects of love are members of the community and that Paul, when he adds "for all" to his instructions, normally employs other words to encourage his churches to care for those outside the community.[61] He instructs the Galatians to "work for the good of all, especially for those of the family of faith" (Gal. 6:10). Similarly, he instructs the Thessalonians not to return evil for evil but to pursue the good "to one another and to all" (1 Thess. 5:15). In each of these passages, Paul places the priority on the community's practice of love toward one another. However, the church is not the exclusive recipient of good works. The church looks beyond the local community to care for outsiders.

Romans 12:1–15:13 offers an additional insight into Paul's churches and their engagement with the world. Although Paul addresses a community that is "not conformed to this world" (12:2 KJV) and speaks primarily of love within the community, as I have noted above, he also assumes their interaction with others. Sandwiched between his instructions for mutual love within the community (12:9–16; 13:8–10) are the instructions for relationships with outsiders. He does not mention love in this section but encourages the readers to "bless those who persecute you" (12:14), and urges them not to return evil for evil but to "take thought for what is noble in the sight of all" (12:17) and "live peaceably with all" (12:18) as much as is possible. This concern for all humankind is evident in the instructions involving believers and the ruling authorities (13:1–7). Paul's instruction to "be subject to the governing authorities" (13:1) presupposes that the latter, unlike the believers, belong to "the present age" (cf. Rom. 12:2). Thus Paul clearly demarcates between the community and public institutions. Nevertheless, while believers belong to the new age, they recognize the legitimacy of the institutions of the present age. They recognize that the authorities are ministers for the good (13:4). Believers love one another, and they also conduct themselves with an interest in the public good.

60. Lohfink, *Jesus and Community*, 111.
61. Ibid., 110.

Conclusion: Paul and the Mission of the Church

As I argued in chapter 4, the mission of God, according to Paul, is a transformed humanity. The fact that Paul gave his churches extensive instruction through oral catechesis, visits, and letters leaves no doubt that he had a clear vision for the mission of his churches. Paul's ultimate goal for his churches was that they be transformed into the image of the crucified Lord. The shape of his letters, with their strong emphasis on behavior, indicates Paul's focus on the moral formation of his churches. He expects his churches to be God's colony (Phil. 3:20), living a life that is "worthy of the gospel" (Phil. 1:27).[62] He envisions a community in which members place the interests of others ahead of their own and build an edifice that lasts until the end (1 Cor. 3:10–17). This new humanity will abandon ancient hostilities and be the place where there is no longer "Jew or Greek." A community that is sanctified at the end is the goal for Paul's churches. While Paul expected their love for one another to spill over into the larger community,[63] his primary focus was on the love of members for one another. Inasmuch as Paul assumed that communities would grow, he envisioned that new members would enter because of the attractiveness of the Christian communities.

Just as Israel was a light to the nations without engaging in organized missions, Paul assumed that Christian communities were lights in the world of darkness. Brian K. Peterson has correctly noted that, for Paul, "the church's primary task was to Be the people of the new creation, to live out this life that obliterates old ethnic divisions, that treats slaves as brothers and sisters, that loves 'all,' not just members of the same class or club, and that lives out humility instead of the expected Roman competition for status."[64] Inasmuch as Paul's churches were minorities within the larger society, a mission to change the structures of society would not have been possible. Paul assumes the institution of slavery and does not challenge it (cf. 1 Cor. 7:21; Philemon). He also assumes the governmental structures of his time (Rom. 13:1–7), even if he offers a critique of those who crucified "the Lord of glory" (1 Cor. 2:6–8) and instructs believers to avoid their courts (6:1–11). His churches formed their own "commonwealth" (Phil. 3:20 RSV) within the larger political structures of the Roman Empire. They were too powerless to challenge the structures of society directly. "We must remind ourselves that, in Paul's time, the fledgling Christian movement was peripheral to society, a totally negligible entity as

---

62. Luke Timothy Johnson, "Paul's Ecclesiology," in *The Cambridge Companion to St. Paul*, ed. James D. G. Dunn (Cambridge: Cambridge University Press, 2003), 203.

63. Peterson, "Being the Church in Philippi," 170.

64. Peterson, "Being the Church in Philippi," 175. Cf. Bosch, *Transforming Mission*, 168.

far as size was concerned, and its survival—humanly speaking—in jeopardy. These factors explain, at least to some extent, the absence of any trenchant critique of unjust societal structures (such as slavery) in Paul, as well as his basically positive attitude toward the Roman Empire (cf. Rom. 13)."[65]

Although Paul's churches did not challenge the institutions of that day, they probably set in motion impulses that increased as the movement became larger. The growth of the movement suggests that the evangelism among family members and neighbors that occurred among the Corinthians increased. The regular concern to "work for the good of all" (Gal. 6:10) likely motivated the believers to establish institutions for caring for outsiders. Even the existence of the church in an often hostile environment was a challenge to society, for a community in which there was neither Greek nor barbarian was a challenge to the tribalism of antiquity. Thus while Paul spoke only indirectly to his churches about evangelism or engagement with the surrounding society, he implicitly set the stage for the church's subsequent mission.

The contemporary church, like the Pauline churches, lives as a minority community within the larger society. The first stage in the fulfillment of its mission is an identity that demarcates it from other communities by its participation in the story of Christ. Like the Pauline model, this church has both sharp boundaries that separate it from the dominant culture and doors that permit the church to have an impact on the larger society. The community is not only sent into the world; it is also a light that attracts the world to it as others observe the power of the gospel to change lives.

65. Bosch, *Transforming Mission*, 175.

7

THE UNIVERSAL CHURCH
IS THE LOCAL CHURCH

Koinōnia according to Paul

The ecclesiastical life that I have described in the previous chapters was local. Paul writes to concrete circumstances to encourage local communities and address their problems. He nowhere mentions administrative institutions that coordinate or have authority over the activities of the local community. The body of Christ in Romans (12:3–8) and 1 Corinthians (12:12–27) is the local community that assembles. Similarly, the local community is God's vineyard (1 Cor. 3:9), building (3:9), and temple (3:16). Believers have been called into *koinōnia* with Jesus Christ (1 Cor. 1:9) and now have *koinōnia* with each other at the eucharistic table (10:16–17). The ethical exhortations focus primarily on the local community. Paul's encouragement for believers to love one another (Rom. 13:8; 1 Thess. 4:9; cf. Rom. 12:9; 13:10; 14:15; 1 Cor. 13; 2 Cor. 2:4; Gal. 5:13, 22; Phil. 1:9–11), build one another up (1 Thess. 5:11), and be of the same mind (Rom. 12:16; 2 Cor. 13:11; Phil. 2:2; 4:2) can be put into practice only in a concrete place.[1] Thus the local church is paramount in Paul's mind.

1. Ulrich Luz, "Ortsgemeinde und Gemeinschaft im Neuen Testament," *Evangelische Theologie* 70 (2010): 406.

As the "minister of Christ Jesus to the Gentiles" (Rom. 15:16), Paul also brings a universal dimension to his churches, which becomes most apparent as he plans to visit Rome at the turning point of his career. Having preached from Jerusalem to Illyricum (Rom. 15:19), he now plans to visit Rome and even Spain (15:24) as part of his ministry of offering to God an "offering of the Gentiles" (15:16). This universal horizon was probably shaped by Deutero-Isaiah's vision of a message that would go to the "ends of the earth" (Isa. 49:6). Alluding to Deutero-Isaiah, Paul looks forward to the time when every knee will bow and every tongue confess that Jesus Christ is Lord (Rom. 14:11; Phil. 2:11; cf. Isa. 45:23). The claim that "our citizenship is in heaven" (Phil. 3:20) lifts the horizon of his readers beyond the local church. Thus he envisions a universal scope to his gospel and hopes to establish churches throughout the upper half of the Mediterranean.[2]

In the disputed Pauline letters, Colossians and Ephesians, the many communities comprise the universal church, "which is his body" (Eph. 1:23; cf. Col. 1:24), the "fullness" of the cosmic Lord who fills all things (Eph. 1:23). From the fourth century on, Christians have confessed, "We believe in one holy catholic and apostolic Church." To what extent did Paul in the undisputed letters establish "one holy catholic and apostolic Church" that connected the churches to each other? The extent to which Paul speaks of a church united by connections between communities remains a mystery, for he establishes no administrative structures that bind the churches together.[3] James D. G. Dunn maintains that Paul "does not seem to have thought of 'the church' as something worldwide or universal—the Church."[4] According to E. A. Judge,

> The theory and practice of interrelations between the churches, currently of great interest, is in fact quite obscure in the New Testament. We know much more about the organization of the apostolic missions and the relations of the apostles with the churches than about the churches themselves as a group. Indeed, several of the most basic formulae of modern study of the churches, such as the distinction between the visible and invisible churches, between local churches and the church universal, and even the very idea of the New Testament

2. Du Toit, "Paulus Oecumenicus," 123.
3. E. A. Judge, "Contemporary Political Models for the Interrelations of the New Testament Churches," in *The First Christians in the Roman World: Augustan and New Testament Essays*, WUNT 2/229 (Tübingen: Mohr Siebeck, 2008): 596.
4. Dunn, *Theology of Paul the Apostle*, 540. See also Josef Ernst, "Von der Ortsgemeinde zur Grosskirche: Dargestellt an den Kirchenmodellen des Philipper- und Epheserbriefes," in *Kirche im Werden: Studien zum Thema Amt und Gemeinde im Neuen Testament—in Zusammenarbeit mit dem Collegium Biblicum München*, ed. Josef Hainz (Munich: Schöningh, 1976), 123–27.

"Church" as an entity, seem to lay perilously heavy foundations upon ground that is hardly able to support them.[5]

Paul does not know the modern distinction between "congregation" and "church" (German *Gemeinde* and *Kirche*), for both words render the Greek *ekklēsia*. In most instances, *ekklēsia* signifies the local congregation. In the letter openings in 1 and 2 Corinthians, *ekklēsia* appears with the preposition "in" (*en*) to locate the congregation in Corinth (1 Cor. 1:2; 2 Cor. 1:1). Paul addresses 1 Thessalonians to the "church of the Thessalonians in God the Father and the Lord Jesus Christ" (1 Thess. 1:1; cf. 2 Thess. 1:1), and he addresses Galatians to the *ekklēsiai* ("churches") of Galatia (Gal. 1:2). He speaks also of the *ekklēsia* in Cenchreae (Rom. 16:1) and the *ekklēsia* in the house of Aquila and Prisca in Rome (Rom. 16:5) and Ephesus (1 Cor. 16:19), as well as the *ekklēsia* in Philemon's house (Philem. 2; cf. Nympha's house in Col. 4:15). When he speaks of "the whole church," he refers to the local church that assembles (cf. Rom. 16:23; 1 Cor. 14:23).[6]

The plural *ekklēsiai* is used to designate congregations within a greater geographical area (a province): the churches in Asia (1 Cor. 16:19), Galatia (1 Cor. 16:1; Gal. 1:2), Macedonia (2 Cor. 8:1), and Judea (Gal. 1:22; 1 Thess. 2:14).[7] In 1 Thessalonians Paul speaks of the churches in two provinces, Macedonia and Achaia (1 Thess. 1:7–8), as a single entity. He also speaks of the ethnic identity of churches, referring to the "churches of the Gentiles" (Rom. 16:4). At the end of Romans, having preached from Jerusalem to Illyricum (15:19), he speaks of "all the churches of Christ" (16:16). These churches are probably those within Paul's sphere of missions.[8] Paul never describes the local community as a part of the whole church. The *ekklēsia* is the concrete community that assembles together.[9]

Paul uses "the saints" as a synonym for *ekklēsia*. In 1 Corinthians he writes not only to the *ekklēsia* but also "to those who are sanctified in Christ Jesus, called to be saints" (1:2). In Philippians and Romans he does not mention the *ekklēsia* in the salutation but writes to those who are "called to be saints" (Rom. 1:7; Phil. 1:1; cf. 2 Cor. 1:1; Eph. 1:1; Col. 1:2). When he speaks of the whole community, he refers to "the saints" or "all the saints" (1 Cor. 16:15; 2 Cor. 13:12; Phil. 4:22). Except for one instance when he speaks of "every

5. Judge, "Contemporary Political Models," 586.
6. Reidar Hvalvik, "'The Churches of the Saints': Paul's Concern for Unity in His References to the Christian Communities," *Tidsskrift for Teologi og Kirke* 78, nos. 3–4 (2007): 228.
7. Ibid.
8. Ibid., 235.
9. Josef Hainz, *Ekklesia: Strukturen paulinischer Gemeinde-Theologie und Gemeinde-Ordnung*, Biblische Untersuchungen 9 (Regensburg: Pustet, 1972), 251.

saint" (Phil. 4:21), he speaks in the plural to describe the saints as the community at a specific place.

PATTERNS FROM THE EMPIRE AND FROM THE SYNAGOGUE

Paul's universal horizon was undoubtedly shaped within the context of the Roman Empire. His mission "from Jerusalem to Illyricum" and then to Spain corresponds to Greek and Roman understanding of the world as the area around the Mediterranean Sea. For Greeks and Romans, the world encompassed the area from the Pillars of Hercules in the west (which was called the end of the earth), the Euphrates River in the east, the Black Sea in the north, and the African desert in the south.[10] Paul inherited a Roman view of the world as an organism with interdependent parts. This world was divided into provinces and smaller administrative units, which existed together in concord. Paul's geographic points of reference coincide with the ancient nomenclature for the provinces. According to the prominent view, the Roman Empire was a commonwealth of nations that brought races and social classes together. The Romans were even familiar with the concept of a universal body composed of many members and guided by the caesar, the head of the body.[11] Paul envisions his own sphere of work as the lands in the west, leaving the other spheres to others.

The synagogue provided a significant model for the unity of Paul's churches. Although united by no administrative structures, the synagogues provided a variety of means for uniting the scattered communities. The annual temple tax, in which every Jewish male participated (based on Exod. 30:11–16), united the communities in their relationship to Jerusalem.[12] Pilgrimages from the Diaspora to Jerusalem united the visitors not only with Jerusalem but also with those whom they met along the way.[13] This interaction among Jewish communities afforded opportunities for merchants in distant lands. Lodging places assisted Jewish travelers, providing a model for the churches as they separated from the synagogues.[14]

10. Ksenija Magda, *Paul's Territoriality and Mission Strategy: Searching for the Geographical Awareness behind Romans*, WUNT 2/266 (Tübingen: Mohr Siebeck, 2009), 84.

11. E. A. Judge, "Contemporary Political Models for the Interrelations of the New Testament Churches," 587–95.

12. The evidence suggests that Jewish communities scrupulously maintained this practice (cf. Philo, *Spec. Laws* 1.76–78; cf. *Embassy*. 157, 291, 312–13). Convoys brought revenues from the eastern Diaspora (*Embassy* 216; Josephus, *Ant*. 18.312–13).

13. John Barclay, *Jews in the Mediterranean Diaspora: From Alexander to Trajan (323 BCE– 117 BCE)* (Edinburgh: T&T Clark, 1996), 417–18.

14. Ibid., 216.

THE UNITY OF THE CHURCHES IN THE PAULINE MISSION

That Paul thought of the church in universal terms is most evident in his use of the terms *ekklēsia* and *hagioi* ("saints"). Although he employs both terms for the local community, the language is from Israel and expresses Paul's understanding of the continuity of the church with Israel as the people of God. Paul probably inherited both terms from the earliest Jerusalem church, which identified itself as the eschatological people of God and described itself as the *ekklēsia* and the *hagioi*.[15] Like other Jewish groups, especially the Qumran community, the Jerusalem believers regarded themselves as the elect and holy people, those who have been faithful to the call of God. They are the holy people described in Leviticus 19:2 and the eschatological people of God.[16] Thus the terms *ekklēsia* and *hagioi* expressed both the continuity of the community with Israel and the claim to embody the faithful remnant.[17]

Both *ekklēsia* and *hagioi* indicate that the local community belongs to a larger network. The familiar designations "the church of God in/at _____" indicate that the local church is both a full representation of the people of God and a local manifestation of something larger. Moreover, Paul's use of *ekklēsia* without a local designation reflects his understanding of the church as more than a local phenomenon. When he says, "I persecuted the church of God" (Gal. 1:13 NIV; cf. Phil. 3:6), he undoubtedly refers to the multiple house churches. Of special importance is his statement at the end of his discussion of the church as the body of Christ in 1 Corinthians 12: "God has appointed in the church first apostles, second prophets, third teachers" (v. 28). Not all these ministries are in the local church. Indeed, as Paul indicates in 1 Corinthians 15:5–8, "apostles" is a restricted group. Thus he looks beyond the local assembly in recognition of the worldwide church.[18]

The description of the saints is particularly suited to describe the universal nature of Christianity, for Paul uses the term only in the plural. In 1 Corinthians 6:1, for example, he criticizes the Corinthians for taking legal cases before the unrighteous instead of before the saints within the local community.

15. Bohlen, *Sanctorum Communio*, 76, 81.

16. See ibid., 46–51. In Second Temple Judaism, *hagioi* is a term for both heavenly beings and the faithful Israelites. According to Tobit 12:15, Raphael is a holy angel who bears the prayers of the saints into the presence of the glory of the sanctuary (*tou hagiou*). In *1 En.* the "saints" are the righteous and elect (38:4). In *T. Levi* 18:11, the saints will be given food from the tree of life in the end time (cf. *T. Dan* 5:11). In *Pss. Sol* 17 the eschatological king will gather a holy people. In the eschatological literature, the saints are the holy ones and elect who are victorious at judgment. They are not the equivalent of ethnic Israel.

17. Bohlen, *Sanctorum Communio*, 76–77.

18. See J. Roloff, "ἐκκλησία," *EDNT* 2:413.

He adds, "Do you not know that the saints will judge the world?" (6:2). Here Paul appeals to the Jewish literature and the concept that the righteous will participate in the judgment (cf. Dan. 7:22; Wis. 3:8; *1 En.* 38:5; 48:9; 95:3, 7; 96:1).[19] In Romans 8:26–27 he assures the readers that the Spirit intercedes for the saints. Here, as the first-person plural indicates, the community ("we") belongs to the worldwide group of those for whom the Spirit intercedes.

Paul gives numerous signals that the local churches maintain relationships with other communities. The fact that he speaks frequently of churches within political units indicates that he groups communities geographically. Paul describes his missionary strategy in terms of Roman provinces.[20] He describes his mission to the Roman province of Illyricum (Rom. 15:19) and writes a single letter to the "churches of Galatia" (Gal. 1:2; cf. 1 Cor. 16:1), indicating both the grouping of churches in administrative districts and their connections to each other. When he speaks of the "churches of Asia" (1 Cor. 16:19), he could have had in mind Ephesus, Troas, Laodicea, Hierapolis, and possibly others.[21] Similarly, he groups together "the churches of Macedonia" (2 Cor. 8:1), which probably included Philippi and Thessalonica. These churches were involved in a common cause.

The relationship between churches is evident in 1 Thessalonians, Paul's first letter. Here he groups together the larger administrative unit, "Macedonia and Achaia." In the opening thanksgiving, he expresses gratitude that the Thessalonians have become "an example to all the believers in Macedonia and in Achaia" (1:7), adding that from them the word had gone out "in Macedonia and Achaia" and "in every place" (1:8). He describes how the people were reporting the good example of the Thessalonians—how they turned "from idols, to serve a living and true God" (1:9) In the paraenetic instructions, Paul encourages the Thessalonians not only to "love one another" but also to love "all of God's family throughout Macedonia" (4:10 NIV). "All of Macedonia" would have involved other communities of faith.

Both the salutations of Paul's letters and the final greetings indicate the close relationships among Paul's churches. He addresses 1 Corinthians to "the church of God that is in Corinth . . . together with all those who in every place call on the name of our Lord Jesus Christ" (1:2).[22] He addresses 2 Corinthians to "the church of God that is in Corinth, including all the saints throughout Achaia" (1:1). The reference to the church in a specific place indicates the universality of the church, for the local church is a manifestation of the whole

---

19. Bohlen, *Sanctorum Communio*, 106.
20. Magda, *Paul's Territoriality*, 6.
21. Schrage, *Der Erste Brief an die Korinther*, 4:466.
22. "Every place" probably refers to every meeting place. See Ferguson, *Church of Christ*, 234.

church. The church, therefore, is neither the local community nor the merger of local congregations, but the eschatological community founded by Christ.[23] This extended address reminds the readers that they are part of an extended community.[24]

The opening salutation in 1 Corinthians forms an inclusio with the customary greeting at the end of the letter, a familiar item in Paul's letters. Here he adds, "The churches of Asia send greetings" (1 Cor. 16:19), and "All the brothers and sisters send greetings" (16:20). In Philippians 4:21–22 he says, "The brothers and sisters" and "all the saints greet you." In Romans 16:16 he even extends this to "all of the churches of Christ greet you." The greetings have the rhetorical effect of connecting churches with each other.

Hospitality among believers of various churches also provided a link between church members from various regions. Along with other Christian writers, Paul instructs the churches to practice hospitality (Rom. 12:13; Heb. 13:21; 1 Pet. 4:9). This practice was essential for providing a place for worship and for accommodating Christian travelers, including Paul and his coworkers. Paul expected his churches to provide a guest room (Philem. 22), a place to spend the winter (1 Cor. 16:6–7), and provisions for travel. He expected the same thing for Phoebe (Rom. 16:1–2) and Timothy (1 Cor. 16:11; cf. 2 Cor. 7:15).[25]

As Paul addresses the problems of a particular community, he gives multiple indications of their connections to other communities. For example, when Timothy comes, he will explain Paul's ways—what he teaches in all the churches (1 Cor. 4:17). Paul has established traditions that he expects the Corinthians to follow (11:2). When he gives advice on the proper attire for men and women, he concludes, "We have no such custom, nor do the churches of God" (11:16). Similarly, in his instructions about the participation of women, he says, "as in all the churches of the saints" (14:33).[26]

One may assume that Paul gave traditions that were common in all the churches. The Lord's Supper tradition was a part of Paul's original catechesis (1 Cor. 11:23–26) and was probably given to all the communities. The references to previous catechesis probably indicate that Paul had a common catechesis he gave to all the churches (cf. 1 Thess. 4:1–12).

---

23. Schrage, *Der Erste Brief an die Korinther*, 1:103.
24. Ibid., 1:105.
25. Michael B. Thompson, "The Holy Internet: Communication between Churches in the First Christian Generation," in *The Gospels for All Christians: Rethinking the Gospel Audiences*, ed. Richard Bauckham (Grand Rapids: Eerdmans, 1998), 55–56.
26. The NASB places "as in all the churches of the saints" (14:33) in the preceding paragraph as a reference to the orderly exercise of prophecy.

Paul also provides moral instruction for the Corinthians that was applicable to all his churches (1 Cor. 7:17). The frequent "Do you not know . . . ?" suggests that the Corinthians had received extensive teaching on the conduct that was expected of them (1 Cor. 3:16; 5:6; 6:2–3, 9, 15–16, 19).

When Paul confronts the Corinthians who claim there is no resurrection from the dead, he responds with a tradition known to them, the basic kerygma. His indication that he received the kerygma from those who were before him (1 Cor. 15:3) suggests that the basic Christian message was shared by all. He and the pillars in Jerusalem were bound together by one gospel.

JEWISH AND GENTILE CHURCHES

Paul does not intend the solidarity of his churches with each other to extend only to the churches that he established. He reminds the Thessalonians that, just as they had served as examples to the churches in Macedonia and Achaia (1 Thess. 1:7–8), they themselves had followed the example of the churches of Judea (2:14) in suffering. The maintenance of this solidarity was nevertheless the major challenge of Paul's ministry, as his commitment to the collection for the Jerusalem Christians indicates. Four of Paul's letters, written over a period of several years, refer to the collection of funds from gentile churches to the Jerusalem church (Gal. 2:10; 1 Cor. 16:1–2; 2 Cor. 8–9; Rom. 15:25–27). Inasmuch as the project lasted several years, it must have involved more than disaster relief from affluent to poor churches. Despite turmoil in the Corinthian church over an extended period, Paul continued to insist on the Corinthians' participation in this work.

Jewish and Gentile Christianity (Gal. 2:1–14)

The challenge of maintaining solidarity between Jewish and gentile churches becomes apparent first in Galatia, where Paul had established a church composed of gentiles, following his customary practice of initiating them into the faith without insisting on circumcision. This practice inevitably created a negative reaction among those who insisted on maintaining traditional initiation of gentile proselytes through circumcision. Thus opposing teachers compelled the Galatians to be circumcised (Gal. 6:12), insisting that the practice was the badge of identity for all children of Abraham (cf. 3:1–29). Many of the Galatians were apparently eager to comply (1:6–9; 3:2–5; 5:2–5) in order to be incorporated into Israel. The opponents agreed with Paul that Jesus was the Messiah of Israel and welcomed gentile converts, probably recalling the promise of Deutero-Isaiah of the time when the foreigners who keep the commandments will come into the people of God (Isa. 56:3–6). For them, the unity of Jews and gentiles in one church would require that the converts take on the traditional Jewish badges of identity. For Paul, however, this view was nothing less than "a different gospel" (Gal. 1:6); anyone who proclaimed it was under an anathema (1:9).

In Galatians 2:1–10 Paul addresses the Galatian situation by recalling the decisive moment when the issue confronting the readers had been addressed and resolved in Jerusalem. He reports this incident within the context of autobiographical reflections (1:10–2:21) that demonstrate that his gospel came by revelation (1:16) and that he has worked independently of Jerusalem (cf. 1:17). As evidence of his independent status, he indicates that he went to Jerusalem three years after his call and remained there only fifteen days (1:18), and went again to Jerusalem a second time "by revelation" fourteen years after the first visit (2:1). Although he reports neither the specific circumstances that led to the Jerusalem meeting nor the place from which he "went up" to the city, the most likely background to the visit was the kind of crisis reported in Acts 15:1. The mission to the gentiles in Antioch had evoked a reaction from some of the Judeans over the terms of admission to the community.

Although the thread that runs through Paul's autobiography in Galatians 1:10–2:10 is his independence from Jerusalem, he leaves no doubt about the importance of this city for resolving the critical questions facing the church. His missionary labor had begun in Jerusalem (Rom. 15:19), the city where the followers of Jesus had first preached the good news and from which the movement had spread. Here the eyewitnesses to Jesus continued as the "acknowledged leaders" (Gal. 2:2). Paul and Barnabas come as representatives of the church at Antioch, while the acknowledged leaders represent the churches of Judea. By bringing along Titus, probably one of the converts from the Antiochian mission,[27] Paul presents a test case for his gospel and the future of the church. If Titus is not accepted, the church at Antioch and other gentile churches will abandon their connection to Jerusalem and Jewish Christianity or abandon the practice of admitting uncircumcised gentiles. Titus's acceptance will signify the acknowledgment by Jewish Christianity of the legitimacy of Paul's churches and the unity of Jewish and gentile believers.

Paul describes the Jerusalem conference as a drama in three acts. In Galatians 2:1–2 he describes the initial stage as consisting of a public meeting followed by a private one with the leaders. In recalling that he had "laid before them"—apparently in a public meeting—the gospel that he preached, he chooses a term (*anatithēmi*) that means (in the middle voice) "to present for

---

27. Martyn, *Galatians*, 189.

consideration," with the connotation of "asking for an opinion."[28] Consistent with his insistence on his independence from Jerusalem, he does not ask for permission from Jerusalem but consults with its representatives, undoubtedly hoping for their acceptance of Titus. In presenting his gospel privately to the acknowledged leaders, or "the influential men" (*hoi dokountes*),[29] Paul apparently recognizes their special role and needs their blessing.[30] However, he speaks with some ambivalence about them, describing them four times as *hoi dokountes* (literally "those who seem") and including at the end the names of Cephas, James, and John, describing them as "pillars" (2:9). Nevertheless, the private meeting suggests their special importance to Paul, even if he does not ask their permission for the gentile mission. Thus Paul went to Jerusalem for the sake of the unity of the church, knowing that the opponents' message would divide Jewish and gentile Christians.[31] A meeting in Jerusalem should bring a resolution and maintain this unity, indicating to everyone that Paul and the pillars were in basic agreement. Paul chooses not to turn the communities of his mission into an independent movement, but seeks unity with Jewish Christianity.

The importance for Paul of the three eyewitnesses of Jesus is evident in his comment in 2:2, "in order to make sure that I was not running, or had not run, in vain." Paul is not suggesting that rejection by the pillars would invalidate his mission, but that it would undermine his vision of a united church composed of Jewish and gentile believers. The gentile church of Antioch would be faced with two options: either to abandon admission without circumcision for the sake of unity or to sever their relations with Jerusalem. The success of Paul's mission was to be found not only in the extension of gentile churches but in the unity of these churches with their roots in Jerusalem.[32]

The second act of the drama (2:3–5) involved Titus and those "false believers" who insisted that he be circumcised. Paul continues the emphasis on his independence, rejecting a unity based on the circumcision of his gentile convert and claiming that submission to the demands of the "false believers" would be a denial of the truth of the gospel (2:5).

The resolution of the issue occurs in the final scene of the drama (2:6–10), which involves Paul and the acknowledged leaders, whose names he finally

28. BDAG 74.
29. BDAG 255.
30. Stephan Joubert, *Paul as Benefactor: Reciprocity, Strategy and Theological Reflection in Paul's Collection*, WUNT 2/124 (Tübingen: Mohr Siebeck, 2000), 84.
31. Josef Hainz, *Koinōnia: "Kirche" als Gemeinschaft bei Paulus*, Biblische Untersuchungen 16 (Regensburg: Pustet, 1982), 126.
32. Martyn, *Galatians*, 193.

mentions (2:9). Despite Paul's ambivalence about their status (2:6), their response as the leaders of Jewish Christianity is critical for Paul.[33] They "contributed" (*prosanethento*) nothing to what Paul had "laid before" (cf. 2:2, *anethemēn*) them. On the contrary (*tounantion*, 2:7), upon seeing (*idontes*) that Paul and Peter were equally entrusted to gentiles and Jews and recognizing (*gnontes*) the grace given to Paul, the three pillars extended "the right hand of fellowship" (2:9). Paul won a victory in Jerusalem that would have lasting effects. By adding nothing, the Jerusalem pillars accepted Paul's gospel. As a result, the truth of the gospel was sustained (2:5). The "false believers" (2:4), whose position is identical to that of the opponents in Galatia, were now marginalized, while Paul and the pillars were unified in the recognition of the legitimacy of their respective missions. The unity of the church rests on adherence to the one gospel for all and the separation from those who preach another gospel.

The nature of this unity is evident in the terms of the agreement. The pillars recognize that both Peter and Paul are entrusted with the gospel (2:7) and that God has been at work in their respective missionary activities (2:8). They are equally apostles, but to different spheres: Peter to the circumcised and Paul to the uncircumcised. Peter's work among the circumcised will include those who continue to maintain the badges of Jewish identity, while Paul will continue admitting gentiles without requiring that they keep the full law. The churches will not have uniformity of practice but will have unity in recognizing the one gospel.

By insisting that James, Cephas, and John demonstrated their recognition of his work by extending "the right hand of fellowship" (*dexias edōkan . . . koinōnias*, 2:9) to him and Barnabas, Paul is probably suggesting to the Galatian readers that it was the Jerusalem pillars who took the initiative in extending fellowship, the sign of an agreement between parties who have been in conflict.[34] *Koinōnia*, a term that Paul normally uses with a modifier in the genitive case to describe participation or partnership in something (cf. 1 Cor. 1:9; 10:16; 2 Cor. 8:4; 9:13; 13:13; Phil. 1:5; 2:1; 3:10; Philem. 6),[35] is

33. Joubert (*Paul as Benefactor*, 85) observes, "The argument in Galatians 2:1–10 is like a pendulum, swinging between Paul's independence from Jerusalem, on the one hand, and the acknowledgement of their superior position, on the other."

34. See Josef Hainz, "Gemeinschaft (κοινωνία) zwischen Paulus und Jerusalem (Gal. 2:9f)," in *Neues Testament und Kirche: Gesammelte Aufsätze* (Regensburg: Pustet, 2006), 128; Joachim Gnilka, "Die Kollekte der paulinischen Gemeinden für Jerusalem als Ausdruck ekklesialer Gemeinschaft," in *Ekklesiologie des Neuen Testaments, für Karl Kertelge*, ed. Rainer Kampling and Thomas Söding (Freiburg: Herder, 1996), 303. Cf. 2 Kings 10:15; Ezra 10:19; 1 Macc. 6:58. See the numerous references in BDAG 217.

35. J. Hainz, "*Koinōnia*," *EDNT* 2:304.

here used in the absolute sense (cf. Acts 2:42; 2 Cor. 6:14). The term is rare in the LXX but is common in Greek literature for an association or community based on a common bond.[36] It was used for the marriage relationship,[37] for the bond between friends or members of a philosophical school (Diodorus Sic. 10.8.2),[38] and for the bonds that hold together the fabric of society. According to Aristotle, the fabric of society requires the *koinōnia* of the *polis*, which demands of its citizens interdependence and solidarity, placing the Athenians under common obligation to assist one another.[39] *Koinōnia* manifests itself in being "of one mind," the sharing of goods (cf. Acts 2:42; cf. Phil. 1:5; 4:15),[40] equality, and mutual obligation. As with ancient friendship, the intimacy of *koinōnia* involved boundaries between those with whom one lived in harmony and those who did not share common bonds (cf. Sir. 13:1, 17; 2 Cor. 6:14). Thus when the "pillars" extended the right hand of fellowship, they committed themselves to practice on a massive scale what Luke describes as the ideal practice of the Jerusalem church: the formation of a community of mutual recognition and obligation with Paul and his churches (cf. Gal. 2:9–10). Despite the differences in their respective tasks, Paul and the pillars agreed to live in *koinōnia*, recognizing that the bond that they shared was the one gospel.[41] The unity of the church consisted of their mutual recognition of each other within the diversity of their practices.[42]

The two *hina* clauses in Galatians 2:9–10 indicate the nature of the *koinōnia* as determined by the pillars: "*that* we should go to the Gentiles and they to the circumcised" and "*that* we remember the poor." The pillars proposed those conditions, and Paul was eager to comply. All parties agreed to the division of spheres of influence. They would conduct missionary activities in full recognition of the legitimacy of the other, free from rancor or competition. Although the churches under the influence of Peter would continue to practice circumcision, the churches under Paul's leadership would continue to offer admission of the uncircumcised into the community. The churches of the Pauline mission would not be an independent form of Christianity in the Greco-Roman world; they would be united with the believers of Judea.

---

36. Julien M. Ogereau, "The Jerusalem Collection as *Koinōnia*: Paul's Global Politics of Socio-economic Equality and Solidarity," *New Testament Studies* 58 (2012): 372.

37. BDAG 552.

38. BDAG 552.

39. Ogereau, "Jerusalem Collection as *Koinōnia*," 372.

40. Luke Timothy Johnson, "Making Connections: The Material Expression of Friendship in the New Testament," *Interpretation* 58 (2004):166.

41. Hainz, *Koinōnia*, 131.

42. See ibid., 133.

The request that Paul and his coworkers "remember the poor" (2:10) is inseparable from the *koinōnia* between Paul and the pillars, for *koinōnia* was commonly expressed in the sharing of resources (cf. Rom. 12:13; 15:27; Gal. 6:6). However, Paul speaks obliquely in describing the nature of the request and what he was eager to do.[43] Although "remember" is nowhere attested as a term for financial support,[44] it most likely includes taking care of the needs of the poor.[45] The request indicates neither the identity of the poor nor whether a continuing activity is envisioned.[46] Nor do these cryptic words offer a reason for the request from the Jerusalem pillars.[47] Within the context of the *koinōnia* of Jewish and gentile churches, remembering the poor probably refers to the financial assistance from gentile churches for the Jerusalem church.[48] Paul will later speak of the collection for "the poor among the saints of Jerusalem" (Rom. 15:26). One such instance is mentioned in Acts 11:27–30. Financial assistance was also common in Judaism, as Diaspora synagogues provided financial assistance to Jerusalem.[49] Like the handshake, the remembrance of

43. Joubert (*Paul as Benefactor*, 74, 90–107) argues that the agreement is to be understood within the framework of ancient concepts of the exchange of benefits. He maintains that the Jerusalem leaders were the benefactors and that Paul followed the social convention of reciprocity.

44. See BDAG 655; Gnilka, "Die Kollekte," 302.

45. According to Exod. 30:16, the gifts to the tabernacle are a "reminder" to the people of their ransom by the Lord. Burkhard Beckheuer, *Paulus und Jerusalem: Kollekte und Mission im theologischen Denken des Heidenapostels* (Berlin: Peter Lang, 1996), 81, suggests that the request to remember the poor resonates with the language of Deutero- and Trito-Isaiah, according to which the exiles are the poor (Isa. 61:1–4; cf. 41:17).

46. *Mnēmoneuōmen* ("we should remember") is in the present tense.

47. Some suggest that it implies the permanent primacy of Jerusalem. Cf. Gnilka, "Die Kollekte," 307.

48. Steven J. Friesen ("Paul and Economics: The Jerusalem Collection as an Alternative to Patronage," in *Paul Unbound: Other Perspectives on the Apostle*, ed. Mark D. Given [Peabody, MA: Hendrickson, 2010], 51) and Bruce W. Longenecker (*Remember the Poor: Paul, Poverty, and the Greco-Roman World* [Grand Rapids: Eerdmans, 2010], 182) argue that the request to remember the poor was not directed toward Jerusalem but was the call for a voluntary distribution among Jews and gentiles in their own communities. The context, however, suggests a reciprocity between the Jerusalem church and the churches of the Pauline mission.

49. See John M. G. Barclay, "Money and Meetings: Group Formation among Diaspora Jews and Early Christians," in *Vereine, Synagogen und Gemeinden im kaiserzeitlichen Kleinasien*, ed. Andreas Gutsfeld and Dietrich-Alex Koch, Studien und Texte zu Antike und Christentum 25 (Tübingen: Mohr Siebeck, 2006), 118. Diaspora Jews paid a special kind of "membership fee"—the half-shekel temple tax, payable in Jewish law by all males over the age of twenty (Exod. 30:11–16). According to Barclay, "A large range of evidence from the Diaspora (papyri, ostraca, Roman decrees, and notices in Cicero, Josephus, and Philo) indicates that this tax was taken with utmost seriousness by Diaspora Jews, who made the collections of the money, gathered it at regional collection points and made elaborate arrangements to ensure its safe transportation to Jerusalem. The delivery to Jerusalem annually reinforced the international links of Diaspora Jews with one another, and with the Jerusalem temple." See Philo, *Spec. Laws* 1.77; Josephus, *Ant.* 14.110–13; Cicero, *Flac.* 66–69. See also Barclay, *Jews in the Mediterranean Diaspora*, 414–24.

the poor was to be a demonstration of the *koinōnia* of the Jewish and gentile churches. Paul's eagerness (Gal. 2:10) is a desire to maintain the unity of the church: the *koinōnia* at Jerusalem should have profound significance for both Jewish and gentile churches; if the pillars enter into *koinōnia*, the churches will also recognize *koinōnia* with each other.

The incident at Antioch (Gal. 2:11–14) indicates that the agreement in Jerusalem had not worked out the challenges that would occur when the spheres of influence were not kept intact. Thus in Antioch, a Diaspora city that maintained close ties with Jerusalem, events forced Paul and the pillars to determine the extent of their *koinōnia*. For Paul, *koinōnia* was no abstraction, for it was expressed in a visible way through regular table fellowship, a practice that Peter and Barnabas had also accepted. *Koinōnia* was associated with the communal meal (cf. Acts 2:42; 1 Cor. 10:16–17). For Jews to eat with gentiles was a major break from the past, as Luke's portrayal of Cornelius (Acts 10:41; 11:3) indicates. To separate, as Cephas did (Gal. 2:12), was to maintain the traditional separation from those who ate unclean foods (cf. 2 Cor. 6:17; Isa. 52:11) and one of the marks of Jewish identity. Paul, however, rejected the separation between members of Jewish and gentile churches, describing the practice as a denial of the "truth of the gospel" (Gal. 2:14). Jewish and gentile churches expressed *koinōnia* not only at a distance but at the common table.

Uniting the Churches in the Collection (1 Cor. 16:1–4)

Although Paul engages in a major effort involving numerous churches to raise funds for Jerusalem, he nowhere else mentions the agreement with the pillars of the Jerusalem church. Indeed, the connection between the oblique words of request in Galatians 2:9–10 and the collection mentioned in the Corinthian letters and Romans is a matter of debate.[50] Nevertheless, the collection for Jerusalem has a major role in Paul's work. The duration of time involved indicates that Paul has more in mind than disaster relief for Jerusalem.

Paul next mentions the collection at the end of 1 Corinthians, introducing the topic with the familiar *peri de* (cf. 7:1, 25; 8:1; 12:1), which apparently refers to the contents of a letter sent by the Corinthians to Paul (cf. 7:1). Paul's brief reference to the collection suggests that he has discussed the topic previously with the Corinthians.[51] He speaks in authoritative terms, recalling that

50. David J. Downs, *The Offering of the Gentiles: Paul's Collection for Jerusalem in Its Chronological, Cultural, and Cultic Contexts*, WUNT 2/248 (Tübingen: Mohr Siebeck, 2008), 33–40, argues that Paul fulfills the pillars' request in the disaster-relief collection mentioned in Acts 11:27–30 and insists that the collection mentioned in 1 and 2 Corinthians and Romans is a new venture that Paul determined to fulfill after the Antioch incident.

51. Schrage, *Der Erste Brief an die Korinther*, 4:424.

he "commanded" (*dietaxa*) the Galatians (1 Cor. 16:1, NRSV "directions I gave"), and now he speaks in the imperative to the Corinthians, telling them to do likewise (*houtōs kai hymeis poiēsate*, 16:1),[52] thus linking the Corinthians with the churches of Galatia, as he earlier linked the Macedonians and Achaians (cf. 1 Thess. 1:6–10). Paul offers no theological motivation, because he apparently assumes the Corinthians' acceptance of the project. His task now is to provide more details about the procedure for the collection. The joint enterprise of the Corinthians and the Galatians is the "collection" (*logeia*, used in the singular in 16:1 and the plural in 16:2), a term used nowhere else by Paul. The choice of the word indicates its significance, for it was commonly used for a collection for sacred purposes.[53] In describing the recipients as "the saints" (16:1), Paul apparently employs the term in the special sense of the Jerusalem church (cf. 16:3; cf. Rom. 16:25–26, 31; 2 Cor. 8:4; 9:1, 12), not as a reference to all believers.[54] Paul refers to the poor neither here nor in 2 Corinthians 8–9. In Romans the recipients are "the poor among the saints at Jerusalem" (cf. Rom. 15:25–26). The imperative is not only for the church as a whole, for Paul instructs "each" to participate in the collection and to "save whatever extra [they] earn" (1 Cor. 16:2).[55]

The significance of the collection is evident in the fact that Paul has already commanded the churches of Galatia[56] and now commands the Corinthians to take part. The collection thus binds together the churches of Galatia and the church in Corinth with the believers in Jerusalem. The appointment of gentile brothers accredited by letters to take the collection, which Paul now describes as "this grace" (NRSV "your gift," 16:3),[57] indicates his intention of sending a delegation of gentiles from both Galatia and Corinth to bring the collection

52. "You should follow the directions I gave to the churches of Galatia" (NRSV). Elsewhere Paul mentions his commands only in 1 Cor. 7:17. More frequently he indicates that he is not making a command but is offering an opinion (cf. 1 Cor. 7:6, 25; 2 Cor. 8:10) or making a request (Philem. 8). In 2 Cor. 8:10 Paul states that he is offering his opinion; he does not command but makes his request with *hina* (2 Cor. 8:7, literally "in order that you may excel in this undertaking").

53. BDAG 597.

54. Bohlen, *Sanctorum Communio*, 79. Gnilka, "Die Kollekte," 310, points out that in the extended discussion in 2 Cor. 8–9, Paul never mentions Jerusalem.

55. On the collection, see Schrage, *Der Erste Brief an die Korinther*, 4.428–29. The collection "on the first day of the week" is not a collection during the worship service. The church had no treasury into which one could deposit funds. Paul expects members to lay aside funds privately at a regular time.

56. He does not indicate when he commanded the Galatians. The epistle itself does not mention the request or the Galatians' participation.

57. Numerous scholars have observed that Paul does not speak directly of money but uses theologically based circumlocutions when he speaks of the collection. As Paul has indicated frequently in 1 Corinthians, *charis* is the divine gift from God in Jesus Christ (cf. 1:4; 3:10; 15:10) and the expression of gratitude to God (15:57; cf. 2 Cor. 2:14). *Charis* becomes the dominant

to Jerusalem. This gesture is a further indication of the significance of the collection for Paul in uniting gentile churches with each other and with the Jerusalem church. The personal contact between the Galatian and Corinthian representatives with the Jerusalem church will demonstrate the solidarity of the Jewish and gentile churches.[58] Indeed, Paul will accompany them only if it seems advisable (16:4).

The Collection a Year Later (2 Cor. 8–9)

The fact that Paul has not completed the collection a year later (cf. 2 Cor. 8:10), but devotes a lengthy exhortation to the topic in 2 Corinthians 8–9, indicates that the collection not only is disaster relief; it also plays an important role in Paul's strategic vision (cf. 2 Cor. 9:12). Turbulent events in Corinth have interrupted the collection, apparently resulting in the Corinthians' resistance to Paul's request. Good news from Titus (cf. 2 Cor. 7:5–16) now provides the occasion for Paul's resumption of the topic.[59] The tense situation in Corinth may be the reason that Paul does not merely repeat the command but provides a masterpiece of rhetorical persuasion in which he avoids the imperative. Paul introduces the new topic with the familiar words "We want you to know" (*gnōrizomen* in 8:1; cf. 1 Cor. 12:3; 15:1; Gal. 1:11) without directly mentioning the collection but mentioning the "grace [*charis*] of God that has been granted to the churches of Macedonia," which apparently include the Thessalonians, Philippians, and others. Several churches are united with each other at the regional level for a project that extends beyond their province, and now Paul uses them as an example in his attempt to involve the Corinthians in this project.

The *charis* of God is the familiar Pauline term for the divine gift of salvation through the cross of Christ (cf. Rom. 3:24; 5:2, 15, 17, 20; Gal. 1:6) and the divine initiative that called Paul into service (Rom. 1:5; 15:15; 1 Cor. 3:10; 15:10; Gal. 1:15). God's *charis* is the major topic of 2 Corinthians (cf. 8:4, 6–7, 9; 9:8, 14–15). Indeed, the grace of God given to the Macedonians (8:1) forms an inclusio with "the surpassing grace of God that he has given to you" (9:14). While the term is used in chapters 8–9 for the collection, it encompasses more

---

word for the collection in 2 Cor. 8–9. See James R. Harrison, *Paul's Language of Grace in Its Graeco-Roman Context*, WUNT 2/172 (Tübingen: Mohr Siebeck, 2003), 294.

58. Beckheuer, *Paulus und Jerusalem*, 101.

59. Although Paul introduces the subject of the collection for the first time in 8:1, numerous links with chap. 7 indicate that the reconciliation described in 7:5–16 prepares the way for the discussion of the collection in chap. 8. The two chapters are linked by the repetition of key terms and topics: "earnestness/zeal" (*spoudē*) in 7:11 and 8:7, 8; "boasting" in 7:14 and 8:24; and the role of Titus in 7:5–16 and 8:23.

than the collection, for Paul reminds the Corinthians of "the grace [NRSV "generous act"] of the Lord Jesus Christ, that though he was rich, for your sakes he became poor" (8:9). The collection is thus one dimension of God's grace,[60] as Paul's terminology indicates. Just as Paul and the Corinthians found strength in the midst of suffering (*thlipsis*, 1:4, 8; 2:4; 4:17), the grace of God among the Macedonians is present in their joy and poverty that overflowed into the wealth of their generosity. The principle of strength out of weakness, enunciated in the first seven chapters, is a reality among the Macedonians. In going beyond their *dynamis* (literally "power"; NRSV "means," 8:3), they experience abundance. Thus in giving out of poverty and affliction, they embodied the principle that God's power is present in weakness (cf. 1:3–7; 4:7–9; 12:9; 13:4), giving an abundance from meager resources.[61]

Paul employs the Macedonians as a model for the Corinthians in the concluding argument in 9:7–15. Just as the poverty of the Macedonians overflowed (*eperisseusen*) into generosity (8:2), Paul promises the Corinthians that God is able (*dynatei*, "has the power") to provide every blessing in abundance (*pasan charin perisseusai*, literally "to make every grace overflow") to them in order that they may "share abundantly" (*perisseuēte*) in every good work (9:8). The Macedonians are the examples of the generosity (*haplotēs*, 8:2) that Paul now requests from the Corinthians (cf. *haplotēs* in 8:11, 13). Moreover, Paul strengthens the case with the inclusio of "the grace of God among the churches of Macedonia" (8:1) and the "grace of God that he has given you" (9:14). Thus chapters 8–9 are not, as several interpreters have argued,[62] separate speeches on the collection but a carefully crafted argument culminating in the promise to the Corinthians of the benefits of their participation in the collection.

The connection between the Macedonian example (8:1–6) and the final appeal to the Corinthians is especially evident in the three terms that Paul uses for the collection. The Macedonians have asked for the "grace [*charis*] and the fellowship [*koinōnia*] of the ministry [*diakonia*] to the saints" (8:4 my translation).[63] Paul employs all three terms at the conclusion of the argument (cf. *charis* in 9:8, 14–15; *koinōnia* in 9:13; *diakonia* in 9:12–13). His language for the collection is filled with theological significance, which most English translations obscure. *Charis* is more than the NRSV "privilege," for it

60. Byung-mo Kim, *Die paulinische Kollekte* (Tübingen: Francke, 2002), 16.
61. Note the frequent use of forms of *perisseuein* in 2 Corinthians to describe the divine abundance (1:5; 3:9; 4:15; 8:7; 9:8, 12).
62. See Hans Dieter Betz, *2 Corinthians 8 and 9*, Hermeneia (Philadelphia: Fortress, 1985), 27–36.
63. NRSV "the privilege of sharing in this ministry to the saints."

is inseparable from both "the grace [NRSV "generous act"] of our Lord Jesus Christ" (8:9) and the collection. *Charis* originates with God and is present in the collection. *Koinōnia*, a term used elsewhere for participation, or partnership, in Christ and in the Spirit (cf. 1 Cor. 1:9; 2 Cor. 13:14), here refers to the unity of believers beyond the local community. Thus *charis* and *koinōnia*, when used for the collection, have great theological significance. They are connected here by *kai*, indicating that they are two equivalent concepts that are related to each other.[64] The *charis* from God creates the *koinōnia* among believers. The phrase "fellowship of the ministry to the saints" is a genitive of apposition identifying the nature of the fellowship.[65] It finds expression in *diakonia*, a term used throughout this section for the collection. Thus *charis*, *koinōnia*, and *diakonia* all express the dynamism in Paul's understanding: unity in the financial collection is not only a local phenomenon but a demonstration of the Macedonians' unity "with the saints"—the believers in Jerusalem.

In the conclusion to the discussion of the collection, Paul now promises that the Corinthians' participation in the collection will also demonstrate the dynamism of God's grace and bring the churches together. The three terms for the collection are used once more as Paul employs the image of the harvest to show the power of God. As in 1 Corinthians 16:2, he encourages "each" (2 Cor. 9:7) to give, knowing that God is able to multiply every grace (9:8–10). The ministry (*diakonia*) of this service (*leitourgia*) not only supplies the needs of the saints but provides even greater benefits. Through the "testing of this ministry" (*diakonia*), the recipients in Jerusalem will glorify God because of the gentile communities' subjection to the gospel and the generosity of their fellowship (*koinōnia*; NRSV "generosity of your sharing with them," 9:13). Moreover, the fellowship apparently extends beyond Jerusalem, as Paul's statement "with them and with all others" (9:13) suggests. Paul probably understands the saints in Jerusalem to be representatives of the larger community of Jewish Christians.

A further result of the collection is that "they [will] long for" the recipients because of this overwhelming grace (9:14). Paul envisions the collection as the means of bringing gentile churches together with the Jerusalem church as he wishes to maintain a connection with them.[66] Furthermore, he is optimistic about the prospects of a united church.

In 8:13–14 Paul develops the argument for the unity of the churches with the assurance that the collection is not meant to enrich the Jerusalem Christians

64. Kim, *Die paulinische Kollekte*, 13.
65. Ibid.
66. Hainz, "*Koinōnia*," *EDNT* 2:305.

at the expense of the Corinthians. He makes no demands for fixed sums but requests only that one give according to what one has rather than what one does not have. He appeals to the principle of equality (*isotēs*, 8:13–14; NRSV "fair balance"), a category found elsewhere in the New Testament only in Colossians 4:1. He introduces the term in 8:13 and then elaborates on it in the chiasm in 8:14–15.[67] Paul supports his emphasis on equality with the citation of Exodus (2 Cor. 8:15; cf. Exod. 16:18), recalling the equality in Israel when, in gathering the manna, "the one who had much did not have too much and the one who gathered had little but did not have too little." This passage both reassures the Corinthians that their participation in the collection will not impoverish them and suggests Paul's view of the church as an eschatological reality. Paul probably knows the common interpretation of Exodus 16:18 as a description of the abundance of the eschatological age (cf. *2 Bar.* 29:8; *Sib. Or.* 7:149). He applies this interpretation to the church, the community of the present age (2 Cor. 8:14).[68]

The term "equality" gives further insight into the nature of *koinōnia*, which has a rich history in Greek philosophy.[69] The word may be derived from ancient ideas of friendship. In ancient society, friends shared all things, including goods, mind-set, and love. Friendship required equality and reciprocation. One who receives help should reciprocate.[70] Paul is appealing to the strongly developed Greek sense of equality.[71] However, his explanation is unclear since he appeals to the principle of reciprocity: "In the present age your abundance is for their need." The purpose clause in 8:14b is also unclear: "so that their abundance may be for your need." Paul establishes the principle of reciprocity that was vital for the equality of friendship, but one can scarcely envision the reciprocity of the Jerusalem Christians. He probably means a reciprocity of another

---

67. See Joubert, *Paul as Benefactor*, 140, for the chiastic structure (NRSV "fair balance").

    A Equality (v. 13)

        B Your abundance and their need

        B′ Their abundance and your need

    A′ Equality

68. *En tō nyn kairō* is used consistently in Paul to describe "the present age" as the era of salvation inaugurated by the Christ event (cf. Rom. 3:26; 8:18; 11:5; cf. Rom. 13:11; 2 Cor. 6:2). The NRSV obscures the significance of the phrase in describing the "present abundance." See Joubert, *Paul as Benefactor*, 143.

69. For Aristotle, equality was a means of fostering unity and solidarity in the state (*Pol.* 2.2.1261a30f; cf. Philo, *Heir.* 162; Cicero, *Leg* 2.18.48). In the Greek states equality was a basic principle of democracy along with freedom (Aristotle, *Pol.* 4.4.1291b35). It was also essential to the Greek ideas of friendship. See Diogenes Laertius 8.33; cf. Aristotle's definition in *Pol.* 3.16.1287b33. See G. Stählin, "*isos*," TDNT 3:348–49.

70. Kim, *Die paulinische Kollekte*, 40–41.

71. Stählin, "*isos*," TDNT 3:348. Margaret E. Thrall, *II Corinthians*, International Critical Commentary (Edinburgh: T&T Clark, 2000), 2:540.

kind. One may compare the reciprocity of material and spiritual blessings in Romans 15:27. Paul is likely referring to spiritual blessings that they would receive from the Jerusalem Christians. He may have in mind the response of the Jerusalem Christians in 9:13–14. In response to the collection, the Jerusalem Christians will reciprocate with thanksgiving and spiritual fellowship.

Whereas we are uncertain about the nature of the reciprocity, we are certain that Paul envisions the mutuality of Jewish and gentile churches. Like Israel in the wilderness, the community will not live with surplus and need but will translate equality into concrete reality.

Paul further develops his call for unity in the commissioning of the brothers to take the collection to Jerusalem. One brother is "famous among all of the churches" (8:18) and has been appointed by the churches (8:19) to carry out this ministry. Together, the brothers are the "messengers of the churches" (8:23). A delegation of gentiles from the churches will demonstrate the solidarity of all of Paul's churches with each other and their desire for solidarity with the saints in Jerusalem.

As the conclusion to the presentation on the collection indicates, Paul is optimistic about the outcome. He envisions not only a spiritual equality but an equality of resources among Jewish and gentile churches. *Koinōnia* occurs not only on the spiritual level but in the concrete realities of wealth and poverty. Indeed, Paul assumes that the rich and poor churches will not live in isolation from each other, for he expects concrete acts of reciprocity that will unite the churches.

Spiritual and Financial Fellowship (Rom. 15:25–32)

The success of Paul's previous fundraising efforts is indicated by the claim that "Macedonia and Achaia have been pleased to share their resources [*koinōnian poiesthai*] with the poor among the saints at Jerusalem" (Rom. 15:26). Indeed, the fact that he writes from Corinth (cf. Rom. 16:1–2) suggests that they responded positively to his appeal. However, he is no longer optimistic about the reciprocity of the Jerusalem church that he had envisioned in 2 Corinthians 9:13–14, for he appeals to the Romans for prayer that he will be delivered from the "unbelievers" in Jerusalem and that his gift will be acceptable to the saints (Rom. 15:31). If they do not accept the gift, the vision of a universal church would come to nothing.

Paul's report to the Romans, appearing near the end of the epistle, has a strategic place in the peroration of the letter.[72] He explains in 15:14–22 that

---

72. The peroratio of Romans extends from 15:14 to 16:17. Here Paul summarizes the argument and declares the implications for his readers.

the body of the letter has served as an exposition of his role as "minister [*lei-tourgos*] of Christ Jesus to the Gentiles" (15:16). He indicates that he writes at a critical moment in this ministry to bring obedience to the gentiles (15:18), having preached "from Jerusalem and as far around as Illyricum" (15:19), not building on anyone else's foundation, in accordance with the words of Deutero-Isaiah that "those who have never heard of him shall understand" (Rom. 15:21; cf. Isa. 52:15). He now writes in anticipation of a visit to Rome (Rom. 15:22–24), hoping they will support his mission to Spain (15:24) as he continues effecting the obedience of the gentiles.

In 15:25–27 Paul interrupts the description of his trip to Spain (cf. 15:22–24, 28–29) to mention the task that interrupts his plans. Paul's relationship to Jerusalem is so important that he delays his mission to Rome and Spain. He neither solicits a contribution from the Roman church nor waits until he has established churches in the west to bring the collection to Jerusalem. He does not say why he is going now.

Having begun his missionary work in Jerusalem (15:19), he is now returning to Jerusalem, serving the saints (*diakonōn tois hagiois*). Although he is the minister (*leitourgos*) to the nations (15:16), he remains oriented to Jerusalem. While he neither provides his Roman audience with an extended explanation nor explicitly mentions the collection of funds, his terminology resonates with previous discussions of the collection. Paul describes the purpose of the trip to Jerusalem with the phrase "ministry to the saints" (15:25).[73] While *diakonia/diakoneō* can be a comprehensive term for ministry (cf. Rom. 11:13; 12:7; 1 Cor. 12:5; 2 Cor. 3:7–9; 4:1; 5:18), he has used "ministry to the saints" as a specific term for the collection (cf. 2 Cor. 8:4; 9:1; cf. 9:12–13).

As in earlier descriptions of the collection, the recipients are "the saints" (cf. 1 Cor. 16:1), whom Paul describes in 15:26 as "the poor among the saints at Jerusalem." The saints are not all the Christians, as in Paul's normal usage, but a specific group in Jerusalem. The reference to "the poor" is reminiscent of the request from the pillars in Jerusalem to "remember the poor" (Gal. 2:10). Both the parallel between "the saints" and "the poor among the saints at Jerusalem" and the absence of references to the poor in the Corinthian correspondence suggest that the collection is for the entire Jewish Christian community in Jerusalem.[74] "The poor" is an honorific term that could be used for the people of God. Paul is bringing the collection not to the entire community of Jerusalem (cf. Josephus, *Ant.* 20.53) but to those who constitute the

73. The participle *diakonōn* corresponds to a final clause. See Bohlen, *Sanctorum Communio*, 88.
74. "Poor of the saints" is not a partitive genitive; rather, it is epexegetic. See Beckheuer, *Paulus und Jerusalem*, 256.

eschatological people of God—the saints. Thus the collection, while designed to bind together Jewish and non-Jewish believers across huge geographical distances, also solidified the distinction between the believers and other Jews in Judea.[75]

Paul does not provide a full explanation for the necessity of this gift to the Roman church, but he offers a partial explanation in 15:26–27. He focuses on the initiative of the churches, twice introducing the participation of the churches with "have been/were pleased" (*eudokēsan*). Among the provinces from Jerusalem to Illyricum (15:19), he mentions only Macedonia and Achaia (15:26) as participants. He indicates that participation was voluntary, for they were "pleased to share their resources" (*koinōnian tina poiēsthai*, literally "make some fellowship") with Jerusalem believers.[76] Paul mentions the financial partnership (*koinōnia*) of churches with his ministry elsewhere (cf. Phil. 1:5; 4:15) but here recalls the partnership of Macedonian and Achaian churches for Jerusalem. He employs the term that he has used elsewhere for the collection (2 Cor. 8:4; 9:13). The *koinōnia* recalls the "right hand of fellowship" in Galatians 2:9 and suggests that the identity in Christ is manifest in the sharing of resources. As in the Corinthian correspondence, Paul indicates that *koinōnia* is not limited to the spiritual sphere but is manifest in the sharing of resources.

In 15:27 he offers further theological rationale, indicating the inseparability of the spiritual (*pneumatika*) and material (*sarkika*) dimensions of *koinōnia*. Just as Paul is a debtor to all gentiles (Greeks and barbarians, 1:14), the gentile churches are debtors to Jerusalem. They "make *koinōnia*" (15:26) in material blessings because the Jewish Christians have shared (*ekoinōnēsan*) spiritual blessings. Paul assumes the same association of physical and spiritual resources that he had articulated in 2 Corinthians. In this instance, however, he does not insist on financial equality, but only on a "fellowship" that is both material and spiritual.

From the time when the Jerusalem church extended the right hand of fellowship to Paul (Gal. 2:9), the collection for the poor supported those who were needy in Jerusalem. However, it pointed beyond the relief for impoverished believers, "demonstrating Paul's desire for the unity of the church across ethnic and geographic boundaries."[77] Paul desired to establish *koinōnia* between the gentile churches and the Jewish churches, although the churches maintained different practices.

75. Barclay, "Money and Meetings," 121–22.
76. Joubert, *Paul the Benefactor*, 130.
77. Hainz, *Koinōnia*, 161.

Conclusion: *Koinōnia* among the Churches Yesterday and Today

Although Paul gives no indication that he envisions a universal church that was administratively connected, he envisions *koinōnia* within the local church and among the churches at the regional and international level. The dialectic between the local and universal church provides a significant model for today. The local congregation remains the locus of Christian participation in the body of Christ. In the local congregation, believers are being transformed together into the image of Christ. They rejoice with those who rejoice and weep with those who weep (cf. Rom. 12:15), put love into practice through acts of mercy, and encourage each other. The local church provides a place to belong in a society in which individuals are commonly uprooted from their primary relationships. The local congregation is also a place for the care of the most vulnerable in the society—the aged, the lonely, those with special needs. The local congregation is small enough to recognize the special needs of its members but large enough to do for individuals what they cannot do for themselves. It is not a corporation interested only in numbers but a family in which siblings care for each other. Nor is it a theater for entertaining attendees; rather, it is a body in which all participate. Although churches often fall short of their essential task, many communities continue to provide this place to belong.

This dialectic between the local and the universal church precludes the insular focus of the local congregation that is concerned only for its own welfare. Paul's model of cooperation among churches in the region and in distant places is a reminder that the competition between the churches and the struggle for market share in metropolitan areas undermines the united witness of the churches. The competition among churches that results in appealing to consumer tastes is consistent with the spirit of capitalism, but not with the ecclesial vision that Paul offers. Paul's ecclesiology involves the cooperative work of churches in the city, the region, and the world.

The ecclesial vision of Paul challenges the churches to engage in ecumenical cooperation in the context of the diversity of cultures. The "right hand of fellowship" (Gal. 2:9) that the Jerusalem pillars extended to Paul was an indication that the unity of the church does not require uniformity. The involvement of gentile churches in the collection for the believers in Jerusalem was a major ecumenical task signifying the unity of churches that maintained differences in practice. The *koinōnia* of the more affluent gentile churches with the less affluent Jewish believers is also an important model for today. As Christianity expands into developing countries and especially into the southern hemisphere, the churches face the opportunity again for genuine reciprocity. Despite differences in practices, the churches recognize a common faith. As in the Pauline churches, the growth of Christianity today is the opportunity not for the paternalism of Western churches but for the contributions of all to the unity of the church.

The dialectic of the local and the worldwide church provides an important model for the contemporary church. Believers who meet in house churches or in large assemblies recognize that they participate in worship with believers throughout the world. Because of the mobility of our society, believers from other cultures often come into our communities, making the local church a reflection of the universal church.

8

DISCOVERING
THE REAL MEGACHURCH

Cosmic Church and House Church
in the Disputed Letters

A new stage of ecclesiological reflection is evident in the disputed letters of Paul as the Pauline communities face new challenges.[1] In Colossians and Ephesians, old issues have been settled, as the place of the gentiles in the church is assumed rather than defended (cf. Eph. 2:1–21; Col. 1:27). These letters address communities that struggle with their place in a world populated by threatening cosmic powers (cf. Eph. 1:21–22; 3:10; 6:10–12; Col. 1:16–17; 2:8). Although the letters provide little detail about the occasion for their writing,[2]

1. Throughout this chapter I speak of Colossians, Ephesians, and the Pastoral Epistles as the "disputed letters" and of the author as Paul, although most scholars reject the Pauline authorship of some or all of these letters. I have chosen to refer to the author as Paul because the letters, at a minimum, maintain the Pauline legacy. Where Paul's voice ends and that of his disciples begins is uncertain. Cf. Frank J. Matera, *God's Saving Grace: A Pauline Theology* (Grand Rapids: Eerdmans, 2012), 13, who maintains that Paul is the author of Colossians but says, "I am not quite as confident, however, that he is the author of Ephesians and the Pastorals. However, if I were to learn that he was, I would not be surprised."

2. Ephesians gives no explicit occasion for the writing. Colossians contains warnings about heretical teachings (2:8, 16, 20–22) but little definite profile of the heresy. The references suggest that the false teaching is more potential than real. See Morna Hooker, "Were There False

the focus on the principalities and powers and the emphasis on the church suggest that both letters are intended to reassure readers who face a crisis of confidence caused by the dissonance between their confession and the reality of powers in their world.[3] The readers of both letters live as minorities in their communities, having abandoned the worldview and way of life of the majority culture (Eph. 2:1–10; 4:17–19; 5:8; Col. 1:21–22; 3:5–9; 4:5).

The Pastoral Epistles address a different challenge. Their concern is not to identify the place of Christ and the church in the cosmos but to establish the continuity between Paul and the church that lives in his absence. As the polemic of all three Pastoral Epistles indicates, the church faces threats from those who "have suffered shipwreck in the faith" (1 Tim. 1:19) and whose teaching is like gangrene that infects the whole community (2 Tim. 2:17). The church can maintain continuity with the past and protect itself against this disease only when it holds to "sound" teaching (1 Tim. 1:10; 6:3; 2 Tim. 1:13; 4:3; Titus 1:9, 13; 2:8). Paul's delegates, Timothy and Titus, and the church leaders in each community act in Paul's absence and preserve what they have learned from earlier teachers (cf. 2 Tim. 2:2). Thus, although the focus both in Ephesians and Colossians and in the Pastoral Epistles is the church, these writings represent two different directions in ecclesiological reflection as the Pauline churches enter the next generation.[4] Colossians and Ephesians articulate the place of the church within the cosmos, while the Pastoral Epistles attempt to consolidate the legacy of Paul.

The Cosmic Church: Ephesians and Colossians

Continuity with the Undisputed Letters: The Church and Israel

Although Ephesians and Colossians reflect a new stage in the Pauline correspondence, they maintain considerable continuity with the undisputed letters. Both letters assume the incorporation of gentile converts (cf. Eph. 2:11–21;

Teachers in Colossae?," in *Christ and the Spirit in the New Testament*, ed. Barnabas Lindars and Stephen S. Smalley in honour of Charles Francis Digby Moule (Cambridge: Cambridge University Press), 1973; repr. in *From Adam to Christ: Essays on Paul* (Cambridge: Cambridge University Press, 1990), 315–31. See also Nicole Frank, *Der Kolosserbrief im Kontext des paulinischen Erbes: Eine intertextuelle Studie zur Auslegung und Fortschreibung der Paulustradition*, WUNT 2/271 (Tübingen: Mohr Siebeck, 2009), 216–17, for the view that the fictive nature of Colossians precludes the exact identification of a heresy.

3. See Michael Dübbers, *Christologie und Existenz im Kolosserbrief: Exegetische und semantische Untersuchungen zur Intention des Kolosserbriefes*, WUNT 2/191 (Tübingen: Mohr Siebeck, 2005), 306–10.

4. Roloff, *Die Kirche im Neuen Testament*, 223.

Col. 2:7) in Israel's narrative (Eph. 2:14–18). Like the earlier letters, they are addressed to the saints (Eph. 1:1; Col. 1:2; cf. Eph. 1:18; 4:12; 5:3; 6:18; Col. 1:12), who are also the *ekklēsia* (cf. Eph. 1:22; Col. 1:18), the chosen (Eph. 1:4; Col. 3:12), and the called (Eph. 1:1; 4:1, 4; Col. 3:15). All of these designations reflect the continuity of these churches with Israel.[5]

The familiar "once . . . now" that Paul frequently uses to describe the communal narrative of his readers also appears in Ephesians and Colossians to describe the readers' incorporation into Israel's story (cf. Eph. 2:1–22; cf. 4:17–18; Col. 1:21–22; 3:7–18). Thus they have been incorporated into Israel as "saints" (*hagioi*, Eph. 1:18; 2:19; 3:18; 4:12; 5:3; Col. 1:2–3) and the elect (Col. 3:12). Ephesians is considerably more specific: the community was once alienated from the "commonwealth of Israel" (2:12). Colossians speaks of a new circumcision (2:11–12), recalling Paul's description of the new community that is the true circumcision (Phil. 3:2; cf. Rom. 2:25–29). The two letters share the conviction that the readers' ethical lives will result in their being "blameless" before Christ (Eph. 5:27; Col. 1:22). In the present they are being transformed as they live in hope. The readers are, in fact, the culmination of Israel's story, having received the mystery that was hidden but is now revealed (Eph. 1:9; 3:3, 9; 5:32; Col. 1:26–27). This mystery is the revelation to the nations at the end of the ages (cf. Eph. 3:9–10; Col. 1:26–27). This perspective continues Paul's claim that the revelation in Christ is a mystery that has been revealed (cf. 1 Cor. 2:1, 7–17).

Although the cosmological interest emerges as the primary issue in Colossians and Ephesians, the eschatological hope that connects the church with Israel is present in both letters. Paul maintains hope for the "inheritance" (*klēronomia*, Eph. 1:14, 18; 5:5; Col. 3:24; cf. Rom. 4:13–14; 8:17; Gal. 3:29; 4:1, 7), a term that is derived from Israel's hope to inherit the land (Gen. 15:7; cf. 12:1; 15:18; 17:8). Similarly, both letters mention the hope that has now become a reality for the community. According to Colossians, the mystery that had been hidden is "Christ among you [NRSV "in you"], the hope of glory" (1:27). Ephesians echoes the earlier Pauline correspondence in describing the pagans as "having no hope" (2:12; cf. 1 Thess. 4:13) and affirming the hope (cf. Eph. 1:18; 4:4) that believers will inherit the kingdom of God (5:5; cf. 1 Cor. 6:9; Gal. 5:21). Thus both letters presuppose a communal narrative that began with their alienation from Christ and will end when their hope becomes a reality.

Both letters contain echoes of Israel's Scripture. The paraeneses in both Colossians and Ephesians allude to the Old Testament and the Jewish paraenetic

5. Contra Roloff (ibid., 225), who maintains that the church as the people of God is absent in Colossians.

tradition. Indeed, as Lars Hartmann has argued, the Decalogue provides an important background to the moral instructions in Colossians 3:5–17, an insight that also applies to Ephesians.[6] The sexual vices mentioned are expansions of the seventh commandment (Exod. 20:14) and the coveting of a neighbor's wife (20:17b). Thus they continue the Pauline understanding of the church as the people of God.

Like the undisputed letters, Colossians and Ephesians focus on the moral formation of the readers, as the structure of both letters indicates.[7] Paul challenges the readers to conduct themselves worthily of the Lord (Col. 1:10) and of their calling (Eph. 4:1). Indeed, the propositio in each letter is the encouragement for the readers to conduct themselves appropriately in light of their new identity in Christ.[8] A major portion of the letters is devoted to the specific conduct that is consistent with their new status in Christ.[9] The new dimension is the recognition that these communities do not live in isolation but participate in a universal and cosmic reality. This fact shapes the ecclesiology of both letters.

New Developments in Colossians and Ephesians

Colossians

The paraenetic concern of Colossians is evident from the beginning of the letter. Paul's expression of gratitude for the Colossians' faith and love (1:4) is reminiscent of the opening thanksgiving in the earlier letters (cf. 1 Thess. 1:3; Philem. 5). Paul gives thanks that the gospel is "bearing fruit" (*karpophoroumenon*) throughout the world and among the readers (1:6), and he offers the petition that they will "lead lives worthy of the Lord" as they "bear fruit in every good work" (1:10). This image of bearing fruit, commonly used for

6. Lars Hartman, "Code and Context: A Few Reflections on the Paraenesis of Colossians 3:18–4:1," in *Tradition and Interpretation of the New Testament*, ed. G. F. Hawthorne and Otto Betz (Grand Rapids: Eerdmans, 1987), 237–44.

7. See Matthew E. Gordley, *The Colossian Hymn in Context: An Exegesis in Light of Jewish and Greco-Roman Hymnic and Epistolary Conventions* (Tübingen: Mohr Siebeck, 2007), 231–69, for the view that Colossians is a paraenetic philosophical letter.

8. The propositio of Col. is 2:6–7, "As you therefore have received Christ Jesus the Lord, continue to live your lives in him, rooted and built up in him and established in the faith, just as you were taught, abounding in thanksgiving." The propositio of Eph. is 4:1, "I . . . beg you to lead a life worthy of the calling to which you have been called." See Thompson, *Moral Formation*, 185.

9. The division of Colossians and Ephesians into theological and ethical sections has long been noted. However, the concern for moral formation is constant in the letters. In Colossians the opening thanksgiving expresses gratitude for both the readers' and the worldwide moral progress.

ethical conduct,[10] indicates the letter's focus on the moral formation of the community. Paul emphasizes this concern in the propositio (2:6–7), in which he encourages the readers to "continue to live [their] lives in him" (*en autō peripateite*, literally "walk in him").

The new development in Colossians is the cosmological framework for the exhortation to "walk in him" (2:6). To all appearances, the communities are powerless, for they live among the "elemental spirits" (*stoicheia*) of the universe (2:8); angelic beings (2:18); and "thrones" (*thronoi*), "dominions" (*kyriotētes*), "rulers" (*archai*), and "powers" (*exousiai*) (1:16; cf. 2:14). Thus, as in the undisputed Pauline letters, moral formation requires empowerment (1:11),[11] which Ephesians and Colossians describe in cosmic terms. Paul prays that the church will be empowered (1:11), and he gives thanks that God has "rescued us from the power [*exousia*] of darkness and transferred us into the kingdom of his beloved Son" (1:13). In contrast to the undisputed Pauline letters, where entrance into the kingdom of God is a future event, here the church already inhabits the heavenly kingdom. It is not powerless among cosmic forces but has been rescued from them. This event is the equivalent of the occasion when those who had been alienated were reconciled in one body (1:21–22). Thus the founding of the church was the event in which the readers were rescued from the power of darkness, delivered into the kingdom, and reconciled in one body.

The significance of the Colossian hymn (1:15–20) becomes evident when one recognizes that it lies between the declaration that God has "rescued us" and "transferred us into the kingdom of his Son" (1:13) and the reminder that believers have been "reconciled in his fleshly body" (1:22). Thus the hymn is not only a declaration about the cosmic lordship of Christ; it also describes, as a consequence of the saving events, the place of the church amid the threatening powers and provides the foundation for the exhortations that follow.[12] After declaring the reign of Jesus Christ over the threatening "thrones or dominions or rulers or powers" and stating that Christ holds together all things (1:15–17), Paul adds, "He is the head of the body, the church" (1:18), in a place where one might have expected him to say, "He is the head of the body, the universe,"

---

10. "Bearing fruit" (1:6, 10) is a common term for the ethical life (cf. Rom. 7:4, 5; Gal. 5:22; Phil. 1:11). Paul prays that the Colossians will "bear fruit in every good work" (1:10). The propositio of the letter is the encouragement to "continue to walk in him" (2:6, NRSV "live your lives in him"). The remainder of the letter indicates both the vices and the virtues. Ephesians distinguishes between past conduct (2:1–10) and the new conduct in Christ (4:1–6:9).

11. Literally "in all power being empowered" (*en pasē dynamei dynamoumenoi*). Cf. Rom. 1:16–17; 8:1–17; 1 Thess. 1:5; 2:13.

12. Gordley, *Colossian Hymn in Context*, 263.

in keeping with ancient cosmology.[13] Instead, he introduces the subject of the place of the church in the cosmos, using imagery that he will maintain in the instructions to the community. The church participates in a reality above these powers. It is not the local congregation, as in the undisputed letters, but one universal church. Paul reiterates the identification of the body with the church (ekklēsia) when he describes his ministry "for the sake of his body, that is, the church" (1:24), which is composed of the many house churches where the gospel is bearing fruit (1:10) and the churches that came into being as a result of the preaching of the good news to "every creature under heaven" (1:23). He also depicts a church that is above the powers. Indeed, the church is the place where the cosmic lordship of Christ is a reality for the readers.[14] This illuminates the claim that the church has been delivered from darkness into the kingdom (1:13).

While Paul's identification of the body of Christ with the church (1:18, 25) maintains the image of the body present in the undisputed letters (Rom. 12:3–8; 1 Cor. 12:12–26), the body is no longer the local congregation but both the worldwide and the cosmic reality. Whereas the image in the earlier letters communicates the interdependence of all the members, in Colossians it depicts the relationship of the local community to the cosmic reality. Indeed, the description of the exalted Christ as the head (kephalē) of the church (1:18) further develops this image beyond the earlier usage. Referring to the cosmic Christ in 2:9–10, Paul says, "In him the whole fullness of the deity dwells bodily, and you have come to fullness in him, who is the head of every ruler and authority." He elaborates in 2:19, speaking of the church's identity in the head, "from whom the whole body, nourished and held together by its ligaments and sinews, grows with a growth that is from God." In conformity with ancient understandings of neurology, Paul envisions the head as the source of life, power, and growth for the body.[15]

The claim that Christ is the head (kephalē) of the body is also a new development in the concept of the body of Christ in Pauline literature. The extended image in 1 Corinthians 12:12–26 refers to the members of the local church

13. Numerous ancient sources depict the cosmos as a body ruled by the head. In an Orphic Fragment (frg. 168), Zeus is depicted as head of the cosmos, which he permeates with divine power. Plato (*Tim.* 31b; 32a; 39e; 47c–48b) depicts the cosmos as a living body that is directed by a divine soul. In *QE* 2.117, Philo says that "the head of all things is the eternal Logos of the eternal God, under which, as if it were his feet or other limbs, is placed the whole world." See Clinton E. Arnold, "Jesus Christ: 'Head' of the Church (Colossians and Ephesians)," in *Jesus of Nazareth: Lord and Christ; Essays on the Historical Jesus and New Testament Christology*, ed. Joel B. Green and Max Turner (Grand Rapids: Eerdmans, 1994), 347–48.

14. Roloff, *Die Kirche im Neuen Testament*, 227.

15. See Arnold, "Jesus Christ," 350–58.

as parts of the body but does not mention the head. This image is explained further in Colossians 2:9–10, as Paul indicates the significance of Christ as head of the body. The triumph of Christ over the powers means that believers no longer need to be concerned with the "elemental spirits of the universe" but need only focus on Christ (2:8), for in him is the fullness of the deity (2:9). The church has come "to fullness in him, who is the head of every ruler and authority" (2:10). Thus the head is the source of life and power. Because of the place of the church in the cosmos, cosmic forces no longer threaten it. It is being filled from the head, which nourishes and holds together the joints and ligaments for growth (2:19).

This imagery also suggests the new developments of the claim of the earlier letters that believers are "in Christ" or "in him." Whereas "in Christ" maintains a local dimension in the undisputed letters, it has a cosmological dimension in Colossians, for the community is now "in Christ," and the exalted Christ is in the community (1:27, literally "Christ among you"). As in Romans 6:1–4, members have been buried with Christ (Col. 2:12). However, in Colossians the believers in Christ have been "raised with him" (2:12) and "made alive" (2:13), something Paul does not say in Romans. Thus the community shares in the heavenly existence of the exalted Lord, who has defeated the cosmic rulers and authorities (2:15). As a result of this cosmic status, the church is now triumphant.

The consequence of this new situation is that the church is empowered to live the ethical life. The reassurance of the cosmic lordship of Christ serves as the reaffirmation that no earthly power can prevent them from conducting themselves "worthy of the Lord" (1:10). Believers can live ethical lives (2:6) because they are "rooted [*errizōmenoi*] and built up [*epoikodomoumenoi*] in him" (2:7). In continuity with 1 Corinthians, Paul supplements the images from plant life and construction (1 Cor. 3:5–17) with the image from physiology (Col. 2:19) to describe the identity of the community. Believers have been raised with Christ (2:12), and they are now "in him" who empowers the church. Now believers may seek the things that are above, where Christ is (3:1), and put to death "whatever . . . is earthly" (3:5). Indeed, the entire ethical life is rooted in the cosmic Lord.

This new existence in the cosmic Lord is the source of the new humanity. The heavenly church no longer recognizes the boundaries among the peoples. Colossians goes beyond the baptismal declaration of a community that recognizes no distinctions between Jew or Greek, slave or free, male and female (cf. Gal. 3:28). In this new humanity "there is no longer Greek and Jew, circumcised and uncircumcised, barbarian, Scythian, slave and free; but Christ is all and in all!" (Col. 3:11).

While the church is universal and cosmic, it is also local. The universal church is composed of house churches. The paraenesis indicates the local nature of the new existence. Paul expects the moral cohesion of a community that puts to death the vices of the old existence and puts on the qualities that build the community. The believers will bear with one another (3:13) and teach and admonish one another with psalms, hymns, and spiritual songs (3:16). The local church is composed of slaves and masters, husbands and wives, parents and children (3:18–4:1). Paul mentions the church in Nympha's house (4:15) and "the church of the Laodiceans" (4:16). Thus the many local churches throughout the world participate in the one cosmic and universal church.[16]

EPHESIANS

Ephesians is probably a circular letter to house churches in Asia Minor. While the letter offers no direct evidence of its setting, the celebration of the church—often in poetic terms—suggests that the readers, like the recipients of Colossians, are struggling to find their place in a world in which they are powerless among both the majority culture and the cosmic realities of ancient life—the principalities and powers. The letter's focus on the unity of the worldwide church may be a response to the forces that are separating Paul's churches from each other.[17] Paul's task is to reaffirm the identity of the struggling house churches by offering an alternative view of their place in the world. As the lengthy paraenesis indicates (4:1–6:9), the identity of the community (1:3–3:21) is the foundation of the community's ethos. As the letter's propositio indicates (4:1–6), the goal of Ephesians is to encourage the readers to "lead a life worthy of [their] calling." The cosmic reflections in chapters 1–3 provide the background for the exhortations.

The hymnic blessing (1:3–14) and petition (1:15–23) function as the exordium of the letter, establishing the nature of the community's calling and its place in God's eternal plan. Although Paul does not mention the *ekklēsia* until 1:22–23, the blessing with which he opens the letter is an overwhelming statement of collective identity. Here the repeated first-person plural reflects the ecclesiology (1:3–5). God "has blessed *us* in Christ with every spiritual blessing in the heavenly places" (1:3). Maintaining the theme of election that is common in the undisputed letters, Paul adds that God "chose *us* . . . before

16. Roloff, *Die Kirche im Neuen Testament*, 231; Frank, *Der Kolosserbrief im Kontext des paulinischen Erbes*, 365.

17. See Michael Gese, *Das Vermächtnis des Apostels: Die Rezeption der paulinischen Theologie im Epheserbrief*, WUNT 2/99 (Tübingen: Mohr Siebeck, 1997), 252. See also Christine Gerber, "Die alte Braut und Christus Leib: zum ekklesiologischen Entwurf des Epheserbriefs," *New Testament Studies* 59 (2013): 198–99.

the foundation of the world" (1:4), "destined [*proorisas*] *us* for adoption" (1:5), "freely bestowed [his grace] on *us*" (1:6), and "made known to *us* the mystery of his will" (1:9), "to gather up all things" in Christ "as a plan for the fullness of time" (1:10). While the community lives in apparent insignificance within the larger culture, Paul points them beyond the realities of daily life to the "heavenly places" from which they receive blessings (1:3), introducing the heavenly existence of the community that will be a dominant theme throughout the letter (cf. 2:6). Only the church has access to the mystery of the divine plan. Although it is marginalized in society, it stands at the culmination of the plan of God.

The repeated "in whom" indicates the relationship of Christ to the church. As in the undisputed letters, ecclesiology emerges from Christology. "In whom" (or "in him") maintains the primary local meaning: the identity of the church is "in" the one who has gathered "all things in him" (1:10). "In him" the church has redemption (1:7), and "in Christ" we have an inheritance (1:11). "In him" the community was marked with the Holy Spirit (1:13). The assurance that the church is "in him" anticipates the later claim that the church is the body of Christ.[18]

The church has been called to live out its destiny. God has called the church to be "holy and blameless before him" (1:4). This goal is consistent with the repeated claim in the undisputed letters that the church is being formed and will ultimately be sanctified (Rom. 15:16; 1 Thess. 3:13; 5:23) and "blameless" (1 Cor. 1:8; Phil. 2:15–16); it anticipates the claim in Ephesians that the *telos* of the church is to be "holy and without blemish" (5:27). The threefold claim that the church lives for the praise of his glory (1:6, 12, 14) also anticipates that the church has a destiny not yet fulfilled, for it is still incomplete and growing (cf. 4:13–16) but will ultimately be blameless (cf. 5:27).

In the extended petition in 1:15–23, Paul prays that the community will know its place in God's plan—its hope (1:18), the inheritance among the saints (1:18), and the power at work among them (1:19). Indeed, the focal point of the petition is the desire that the community know the power in those who believe. The same power that raised Christ from the dead and set him at the right hand of the Father and above the cosmic powers lives among believers (1:19–21). By this power God placed all things—the entire cosmos—under Christ's feet. In two parallel phrases Paul indicates the place of the church in the cosmic victory: God placed all things under Christ's feet and made him head (*kephalē*) over all things for the church (1:22).[19] This statement recapitulates

18. Gese, *Das Vermächtnis des Apostels*, 210.
19. See Gerber, "Die alte Braut und Christi Leib," 205, for the transition in metaphors from the cosmos under the feet of the exalted Lord to the image of Christ as head of the body.

the earlier claim that it was God's plan to "gather up [anakephalaiōsasthai] all things" in Christ (1:10). The exalted Christ is thus *head* of the cosmos, and all things are *at his feet*. The statement that he is "head over all things for the church" anticipates the later claims that Christ is the head of the church, his body. As the head of the body, he fills all things (1:19–23). The church is not powerless but is being filled by the one who is head over all things. As in Colossians, the church is a cosmic reality. As it exists on earth, it is being filled from above. Paul has developed that image earlier (Col. 2:10), portraying the church as the community that is being filled by the one who is seated above the principalities and powers.

THE BODY, THE TEMPLE, AND THE BUILDING

In the remainder of the letter, Paul develops the cosmic dimensions of the church and demonstrates the significance of this for the moral life. Chapters 2–3 form the *narratio* that tells the community's story, describing the contrast between "once" and "now" (or "no longer" [ouketi], 2:19) from two different perspectives. In 2:1–10 Paul describes the narrative that began when the community was under the "ruler of the power of the air" (2:2) but culminated in the loving act of God at the cross (2:4, 8–9). God not only placed Christ above the cosmic powers (1:15–23) but also "raised us up with him and seated us with him in the heavenly places" (2:6). The church participates in the universal victory and is no longer subject to the cosmic powers. Consequently, it has left behind the immoral behavior that corresponded to the cosmic powers (cf. 2:2–3).

In 2:11–23 Paul tells the community's story as the reversal from its earlier (pote, "at one time") status as outsiders—gentiles, those who are called "the uncircumcision," those who are without Christ, aliens from the commonwealth of Israel, and strangers (2:11–13)—to the current status. Believers are "no longer strangers and aliens" but "citizens with the saints" (2:19). Consistent with earlier Pauline correspondence, the dominant image for the church is that of the people of God with its sharp distinction between insiders and outsiders—the saints and "everyone else" (2:3). While the narrative focuses on the incorporation of gentiles into the people of God, it introduces new aspects to the ecclesiology of the people of God. As in 2:1–10, the reversal occurred at the cross—by the blood of Jesus (2:13) and "through the cross" (2:16). In contrast to earlier Pauline correspondence where the cross was the reconciling event between God and humankind (cf. Rom. 5:1, 9–10; 2 Cor. 5:18–19; Col. 1:21–22), the cross in Ephesians destroyed the barriers separating the peoples. The result is the creation of "one new man" (2:15 KJV) in "one body" (2:16). Thus the church is one new body created by the cross, the new humanity in which old enmities are destroyed. Paul will develop this further with the focus on the one body, claiming "there is one body and one Spirit" (4:4).

In 2:19–22 Paul describes the reversal from the believers' previous status as gentiles (2:11), people alienated from the commonwealth (*politeia*) of Israel and strangers of the covenant (2:12), declaring they are no longer strangers and aliens but fellow citizens with the saints and members of the household of God (2:19). Because of the broken wall (2:14), the gentile readers are fully a part of the people of God. In the participial phrase Paul changes the metaphor from the body to the building: the church (members of God's household) is built (*epoikodomēthentes*) on the foundation of the apostles and prophets, and it is a building (*oikodomē*, 2:21, NRSV "structure") being "built together" (*synoikodomeisthe*) into a holy temple. Thus the image moves from the members of the household to the building to the temple of God.

The metaphor of the building is reminiscent of the usage in the undisputed letters. In 1 Corinthians 3:10–17 Paul, in an extended metaphor, suggests that the church is a building under construction. He maintains this image frequently in his exhortations for members to "build up one another." In Ephesians the metaphor shifts: the foundation is now the apostles and prophets (Eph. 2:20) rather than Jesus Christ (1 Cor. 3:10), who is the cornerstone. The image of the building blends with that of the body: Christ is both the cornerstone of the building and the head of the body. The phrase "in him [*en hō*, literally "in whom"] the whole building [NRSV "structure"] is joined together [*synarmologoumenē*]" (Eph. 2:21) is parallel to the image of the body that is "joined and knit together [*synarmologoumenon*] by every ligament" (4:16). The repeated "in him/in whom" (2:21–22) fits with both images, for it suggests a local meaning. The church is "in" the exalted Lord, who is exalted above the principalities and powers. It receives redemption "in him" (1:7), and God has gathered up all things "in him" (1:10). Thus "in Christ" (1:11) the church has received an inheritance, and in him the church is being filled with the power that was at work in the resurrection.

Because of the strength that comes from existence "in him," the church will grow into a holy temple (2:21) and be built together (2:22). Here also the imagery of body and building are blended together, for the image of growth is appropriate to the body (cf. 4:16). The future tense "will grow" (NRSV "grows") and the present tense "being built" indicate that the church that sits in the heavenly places remains on earth and is still incomplete. The nature of this growth is suggested in 4:15, "We must grow up in every way into him, who is the head, into Christ." The growth of the church is the challenge of living out the consequences of God's redeeming work. The image suggests that God has created one new man and laid the foundation for a building that is still in progress. The incompleteness of the church indicates that triumphalism is out of the question. Power comes into the church that enables the church to grow up into a loving community.

In the exhortation that begins in 4:1, Paul elaborates on the image of the body of Christ in language that is reminiscent of 1 Corinthians 12 and Romans 12:3, which describe the relationship between the body and each member. According to the letter's *propositio* in 4:1–6, the task of the church is to live "worthy of the calling" and "maintain the unity of the Spirit in the bond of peace"—to maintain what God has given (2:14–18). After declaring the essential unity of the church as "one body" in 4:4–6, Paul elaborates on the task of the church in the remainder of the letter. "Each" (4:7) recalls the words in 1 Corinthians 12:7, "To each is given the manifestation of the Spirit." Paul supports this claim with the citation of Scripture (Ps. 68:18). However, in keeping with the subject of gifts to each member, Paul's citation is not "he received gifts from men," as in the LXX, but "he gave gifts to his people" (Eph. 4:8), which becomes the basis for reflection on the gifts. While interpreters have assumed that Paul has altered the citation, he has probably combined Psalm 68:18 ("receiving gifts from people") with Psalm 68:11 ("the Lord gives the command"). According to the psalm, Yahweh went to Zion and gave people the capacity to speak the good news. In Ephesians the narrative of the one who went down and ascended is the incarnation and exaltation of Christ. As the exalted one, he filled all things (Eph. 4:10). Thus the church lives by his power; he is the fullness of him who fills all in all (1:23).

The gifts are not those of 1 Corinthians but those that involve proclamation: "some would be apostles, some prophets, some evangelists, some pastors and teachers" (4:11). The ministries have a role in building the church (i.e., in *oikodomē*) as they equip the whole church for service. The ultimate goal of the church is to measure up to Christ. The church will reach this goal when believers arrive at the unity of the faith (4:13).

THE BRIDE OF CHRIST

The paraenesis of 4:17–6:10 describes the church's task of putting on the "new self" (4:24). The ethic is an ethic of love for the community, for the people are "members of one another" (4:25). Members even submit to one another (5:21) and love as Christ loved (5:1–2). The life in the new self extends also to the family, as Paul assumes a family united in faith. He assumes the relationships from the ancient family but expands the instructions to husbands and wives significantly, repeating from Colossians the instructions for wives to submit to their husbands (Eph. 5:22; cf. Col. 3:18) and the instructions for husbands to love their wives (Eph. 5:25, 28, 33; cf. Col. 3:19). The new feature in Ephesians is the ecclesiological dimension to the instructions. From this we learn not only about marriage but also about ecclesiology.

In giving the instructions to wives (5:22, 24), Paul offers a reason in 5:23: "The husband is head of the wife as Christ is the head of the church." This statement reaffirms the earlier claim that Christ is the head of the church but changes the image from the head of the body to the husband as head of the wife, introducing the metaphor of the bride of Christ.[20] As the argument has indicated, the head of the church not only exercises power but is also the source of life and power.

The weight of the instructions is to the husbands (5:25–33). That husbands should love their wives is stated three times (5:25, 28, 33). In each instance Paul gives an ecclesiological reason. In the first instance, husbands should love "as Christ loved the church and gave himself up for her" (5:25). This warrant repeats the early instruction for all to love "as Christ loved us and gave himself up for us" (5:2). That is, at the cross, Christ demonstrated his love for the church and called it into existence (cf. 2:14–18).

In the three purpose clauses that follow (5:26–27), Paul refers to the goal of the church, indicating once more that the church is not yet complete. The purpose clauses are all parallel, indicating the church's ultimate destiny. The first clause says that Christ gave himself up for the church "in order that he might make her holy by cleansing her with the washing of water by the word." Paul anticipates that the church will ultimately be holy, as in the undisputed letters (cf. Rom. 15:16; 1 Thess. 3:13; 5:23); baptism ("the washing of water") stands at the beginning of the readers' new existence. Parallel to the first clause is the second clause, the occasion when Christ presents the church to himself ("so as to present the church to himself in splendor, without a spot or wrinkle"), and the third clause, "so that she may be holy and without blemish." The language echoes Paul's declaration in the undisputed correspondence that his desire is to "present the bride to Christ" (2 Cor. 11:2). The verb "present" (*paristēmi*) is also used for the offering of a sacrifice (Rom. 12:1), and it echoes the frequent statements in the undisputed letters that Paul's ambition is a blameless church at the end. The church lives before the end, anticipating its coming "to maturity" (4:13, literally "a perfect man"). Then the church will come to "the measure of the full stature of Christ" (4:13).

---

20. See Gerber, "Die alte Braut und Christi Leib," 208–9. The feminine *ekklēsia* lies behind the personification of the church with the metaphor of the bride. This image for the church is commonplace in the Old Testament (cf. Isa. 54:5–8; 62:4–5; Ezek. 16:8–14; Josh. 2: 19–20) and is employed in the undisputed letters of Paul (2 Cor. 11:2). While Paul uses the image of the bride in Ephesians, he does not describe the church as the bride of Christ.

In the second instance, Paul repeats the call for husbands to love their wives "as they do their own bodies" (5:28), adding that the one who loves his wife loves himself. He declares that no one hates his own flesh but nourishes (*ektrephei*) and cherishes (*thalpei*) it, as Christ does the church. To "nourish" is to provide food (cf. Eph. 6:4), and *thalpei* is the term for the caring activity of the nurse (1 Thess. 2:7). The description is an image for the empowerment that the head gives to the body (cf. Eph. 4:15–16). The citation of Genesis 2:24, used elsewhere to describe the indissolubility of marriage (cf. Matt. 19:5), is used here to focus on the unity of husband and wife as "one flesh" (5:31), which Paul applies to the mystery of Christ and the church (5:32). This imagery recalls the earlier references to the "one new man" (cf. 2:15 KJV) in "one body" (2:16; cf. 4:4). In the third instance, Paul adds that each husband should love his wife "as himself" (5:33), giving reciprocal instructions to wives.

While Paul employs the images of the building and the bride to describe the church, the body remains the foundational metaphor for the church. Drawing on several traditions for the image, Paul depicts a distinctive vision of the ecclesial body. Beginning with the image in 1 Corinthians 12:12–26 (cf. Rom. 12:3–8), he portrays the relationship between the body and the members (Eph. 4:7–16). This body is no longer the local church, as in 1 Corinthians, but the organism that draws its power from the head of the cosmos (1:19–23). It is "one body" (2:16; 4:4) composed of those who once lived in enmity with each other (2:11–22). Indeed, divided human beings have now become "members of the same body" (*syssōma*) and participants in Israel's promise (3:6), as the community grows together (2:19–22; 4:15–16). These images do not fit together well, for a body composed of many members cannot also be a body composed of two hostile groups (2:11–22) that now grow into a temple.[21] Nevertheless, with the combination of images Paul depicts the vision for the church that addresses the questions confronting his communities. The body is the new humanity composed of Jews and gentiles and is both the culmination of God's election of Israel and the participant in the cosmic victory of Christ.

As in Colossians, this universal church is also local. Believers maintain the spirit of unity in the bond of peace in the local house church. Paul probably wrote to encourage the readers to maintain unity with the other house churches in the region. He envisioned that the unity between ethnic groups in the new humanity would be visible in the concrete reality of the house churches, challenging the house churches not to live in isolation from each other but to be the one body. He also envisioned the local house church to

21. Gerber, "Die alte Braut und Christi Leib," 216.

maintain a cohesive moral posture and to actually be the new person (Eph. 4:24) that God had created. Believers in the local house church will "be kind to one another" (4:32), will speak to one another in corporate worship (5:19; cf. Col. 3:16), and will submit to one another (Eph. 5:21).

The Cosmic Church as Megachurch

In both Colossians and Ephesians, Paul orients the readers to the church beyond the house church, reminding them that they participate in a universal church composed of countless other house churches. Despite appearances, the church now participates in the heavenly world above the powers that threaten humankind. Indeed, the church exists at the culmination of God's plans. Despite their marginal status, they are in fact part of a "megachurch" in a profound and expansive sense that renders banal by comparison the current use of this term for certain large and wealthy local congregations. This true megachurch is the only community that participates in the cosmic victory. Although it is apparently an insignificant minority in the cities of the Roman Empire, it worships the one who is above the powers. The cosmic victory of Christ enables the community on earth to become the new humanity that continues to grow to maturity.

The church is a demonstration of the unity of humanity.[22] The community that sits in the heavenly places can rise above nationalism and tribalism to be a demonstration of God's reconciling work. This unity is not an association of people who have already received salvation and have entered into a personal relationship with God, and it does not originate from the relationships of those who have shared convictions and interests. What establishes this unity is rather the reconciling work of Christ.[23]

Whereas the undisputed letters of Paul call for the unity of the local congregation, Ephesians and Colossians challenge the readers to recognize that the ethnic diversity of the many house churches has become transformed into the unity of one people. A plurality of churches that are isolated from each other would be an absurd thought for Ephesians.

The ecclesiology of Ephesians has been central to ecumenical discussions for a long time. Many Protestant scholars have regarded Ephesians as an example of "early Catholicism" and the decline from the ecclesiology of the undisputed letters.[24] Ernst Käsemann, for example, was critical of the

---

22. Roloff, *Die Kirche im Neuen Testament*, 224.
23. Ibid., 245.
24. See Ernst Käsemann, "Paul and Early Catholicism," in *New Testament Questions of Today* (Philadelphia: Fortress, 1969), 244; Käsemann, *Jesus Means Freedom*, trans. Frank Clarke

ecclesiological message of Ephesians, having experienced major disappointment with the established churches during the Third Reich.[25] Käsemann entered
into a lively debate with Heinrich Schlier, a fellow student of Rudolf Bultmann,
over the significance of Ephesians. Schlier was so overwhelmed by the message
of Ephesians that he converted to Roman Catholicism. This debate reflects a
continuing ecumenical challenge in the interpretation of Ephesians. Although
the vision of the "unity of the faith" in Ephesians (4:13) is an ecumenical goal,
it remains the center of controversy. Some, like Schlier, look positively on the
ecclesiology of Ephesians as a transition to the second century, while others
are wary of the ecclesiological vision of the one powerful church.

Nils Dahl, observing the high ecclesiology of Ephesians, asks, "Where do
we find the church to which this high and sublime language really applies?"[26]
Dahl adds correctly that the readers of Ephesians, like contemporary readers, had never seen this church. Indeed, both Ephesians and Colossians insist
that this church is "being built" and is "growing up" to maturity. It is not yet
"without a spot or wrinkle" but continues to be empowered to reach maturity.
Ephesians is not a claim for a unified and powerful church but an assurance
to marginalized people that they now participate in God's plan for humanity.
The church has not yet reached "the measure of the full stature of Christ" but
exists, as the letter's paraenesis (4:1–3) indicates, to maintain the unity that
God has given. Thus it is a challenge to a divided church to envision the unity
of the faith and to work toward that ideal. The vision of the unified church
in Ephesians is not a reality for the readers; it is the performative speech that
stimulates the readers to work toward that goal.[27]

THE HOUSE CHURCH: THE PASTORAL EPISTLES

Like Ephesians and Colossians, the Pastoral Epistles address problems that
threaten the existence of the church. In all three letters this issue is especially
acute because local communities must survive in Paul's absence. All three of

---

(Philadelphia: Fortress, 1969), 90: "But the church triumphant, even if it starts from the cross
and guards it as its most precious mystery, has still always stood in a tense relationship to the
crucified Lord himself. . . . Where the world is dominated by the church, . . . the church becomes
conversely a religiously transfigured world. Its real Babylonian captivity, however, consists in
making itself the focal point of salvation and the theme of the gospel." See also Nils Alstrup
Dahl, "Interpreting Ephesians: Then and Now," in *Studies in Ephesians: Introductory Questions,
Text- and Edition-Critical Issues, Interpretation of Texts and Themes*, ed. David Hellholm,
Vemund Blomkvist, and Tord Fornberg, WUNT 161 (Tübingen: Mohr Siebeck, 2000), 463.

25. See Dahl, "Interpreting Ephesians," 464.
26. Ibid., 467.
27. Gerber, "Die alte Braut und Christi Leib," 218.

these letters contain a polemic against false teachers and their toxic impact on the church. The false teachers swerve from the truth (2 Tim. 2:18), turn away from listening to the truth (2 Tim. 4:4), and are bereft of the truth (1 Tim. 6:5). Furthermore, the absence of the truth results in reprehensible behavior. Indeed, the focus of the polemic is on the impact of false teachers on morality, for false teaching leads to numerous vices (cf. 1 Tim. 6:4–6; 2 Tim. 2:16; 3:1–10; Titus 1:10–16).[28]

The Household of God and Bulwark of the Truth

The challenge of the Pastoral Epistles is to preserve the truth and the behavior that corresponds to it.[29] Although the *ekklēsia* is mentioned only three times (1 Tim. 3:5, 15; 5:16), it plays the central role as the guarantor of the truth. According to 1 Timothy 3:15, Paul writes in order that the community may know how "to behave in the household [*oikos*] of God, which is the church of the living God, the pillar and bulwark of the truth." This statement is the theological center of 1 Timothy and of the Pastoral Epistles as a whole.[30] The focus on how to behave (*anastrephesthai*) reflects the concern of all three epistles with the bad behavior of the false teachers and the good behavior expected of believers. While households routinely assume a specific behavior among family members, a particularly exemplary behavior is required of the "household of God," because it is no ordinary household—it is "the church of the living God, the pillar and bulwark of the truth."

The dominant metaphor for the church in the Pastoral Epistles is the household (*oikos*). This image is used explicitly for the church for the first time in

---

28. Despite numerous attempts to identify the heresy that threatens the churches, the letters do not provide a coherent portrayal, since Paul's purpose is not to give a full description of their teaching. Inasmuch as much of the polemic employs standard *topoi* in the debate between philosophers and Sophists, one cannot determine which parts of the polemic apply to the actual situation. See Robert J. Karris, "The Background and Significance of the Polemic of the Pastoral Epistles," *Journal of Biblical Literature* 92 (1978): 550–56; Abraham J. Malherbe, "Medical Imagery in the Pastoral Epistles," in *Texts and Testaments* (San Antonio: Trinity University Press, 1980), 19–35.

29. Numerous attempts have been made to interpret the argument of the Pastoral Epistles as a polemic against an identifiable opponent. For example, David Verner (*The Household of God: The Social World of the Pastoral Epistles* [Chico, CA: Scholars Press, 1983]) and Ulrike Wagener (*Die Ordnung des "Hauses Gottes": Der Ort von Frauen in der Ekklesiologie und Ethik der Pastoralbriefe*, WUNT 2/65 [Tübingen: Mohr Siebeck, 1994], 236) argue that these letters respond to the conflicts between office holders and women. Reggie W. Kidd (*Wealth and Beneficence in the Pastoral Epistles: A "Bourgeois" Form of Early Christianity?* [Atlanta: Scholars Press, 1990]) maintains that the focus on offices is a response to conflict between the office holders and the rich local elite. These are examples of uncontrolled mirror reading.

30. Jürgen Roloff, *Der erste Brief an Timotheus*, Evangelisch-Katholischer Kommentar zum Neuen Testament 15 (Neukirchen: Benziger Verlag, 1988), 190.

the Pastoral Epistles, but it is anticipated in the sibling relationships of the members of the Pauline churches (see chap. 1). *Oikos*, which could refer to a structure, was also the basic ancient term for "family."[31] The image corresponds to the ancient household with its established social structure and rules for living. Indeed, just as the household was the basic unit of society in antiquity, the literal household is the basic unit of the church. Both 1 Timothy and Titus assume that the church is an extended household and instruct specific members on their duties.[32] Paul draws a parallel between the large household and the local church, giving authority in the church to those who can manage their own households well. The qualification for bishop is good household management, "for if someone does not know how to manage his own household, how can he take care of God's church?" (1 Tim. 3:5). In the instructions for widows (1 Tim. 5:3–16), the church is an extended family that cares for those who have no physical families to support them (5:8), and it supports only those who have taken care of their own families (1 Tim. 5:4, 10). Indeed, the instructions to church members are actually an extension of the household codes of Colossians and Ephesians. God is the "owner of the house" (*despotēs*, 2 Tim. 2:21),[33] and the bishop is the "steward" (*oikonomos*), the manager of the house.[34] As a paterfamilias in the ancient household, the bishop becomes paterfamilias in the larger household, which is composed of husbands and wives (1 Tim. 2:1–3:15), the aged (Titus 2:2–4), young men and young women (Titus 2:4–6), children (Titus 2:4), widows (1 Tim. 5:3–16), and slaves (1 Tim. 6:1–2; Titus 2:9–10). Paul also gives instructions for the care of widows, assuming that families have the first responsibility for their care, so that "the church [is not] burdened" (1 Tim. 5:16).

The task of the *oikonomos* is to be faithful in managing what has been entrusted. The Pastoral Epistles employ the banking metaphor of a trust (cf. 1 Tim. 1:11) or a deposit (*parathēkē*, 1 Tim. 6:20; 2 Tim. 1:12, 14). Paul has been entrusted with the deposit (1 Tim. 1:11; 2 Tim. 1:12, 14), and he challenges Timothy to "guard the deposit" (1 Tim. 6:20, NRSV "what has been entrusted to you"). While Paul never states the content of the deposit in specific terms, the numerous confessional statements in the Pastoral Epistles offer indications of its content (cf. 1 Tim. 1:15; 2:5–6; 2 Tim. 1:9–10; Titus

31. BDAG 699. P. Weigandt, "*oikos*," *EDNT* 2:502.
32. First Timothy contains instructions on the roles of women (2:1–15), householders (3:1–7), widows (5:1–16), and slaves (6:1–2) and on attitudes toward the aged (5:1–2). Titus gives instructions for the householders (1:6–7), older and younger women (2:2–3), young men (2:6–8), and slaves (2:9–10).
33. The *despotēs* is one who has legal authority over another. For the term in relation to slaves in the household, see 1 Tim. 6:1–2; Titus 2:9; 1 Pet. 2:18. BDAG 220.
34. On the *oikonomos* as the manager of the household, see Luke 12:42; 16:1, 3.

2:11–14; 3:4–6). As in the undisputed letters, the confession of the incarnation and death of Jesus is the basis for the identity of the church. The hymn in 1 Timothy 3:16, which tells the story of the incarnation, resurrection, and ascension, is the "mystery of our religion"—the church's defining narrative and the truth that the church preserves. The hymn appears immediately after Paul has described the household of God as "the church of the living God, the pillar and bulwark of the truth" (3:15). That is, the community is no ordinary household, for it is the secure place that preserves the truth. This image echoes Paul's description of the community as "the temple of the living God" (2 Cor. 6:16). Although the church is a house rather than a temple, the temple imagery lies in the background in the phrase "pillar and bulwark of the truth." The image of the pillar, which supported the temple (cf. 2 Kings 7:3; Josephus, *Ant.* 8.77; Rev. 3:12), is used elsewhere for the leaders of the church (cf. Gal. 2:9) but here refers to the church as the pillar of truth. Similarly, the church is the "bulwark" (*edraiōma*) of the truth. In contrast to the earlier Pauline literature, where the church is built on the foundation of Christ (1 Cor. 3:11) or the apostles and prophets (Eph. 2:20), the church is here the foundation of the truth. It is the secure and unshakeable building because it is the repository of the truth that the heretics seek to undermine.[35] Consequently, Paul and his emissaries and the church leaders have been entrusted with the task of maintaining this truth.

Paul develops the imagery of the house and bulwark of the truth in 2 Timothy 2:19–21. After describing those who have "swerved from the truth" and upset "the faith of some" (2:18), he offers the assurance that "God's firm foundation [*stereos themelios*] stands" (2:19). The foundation is not, as in the undisputed letters, the Christ (1 Cor. 3:11; cf. Rom. 15:20) but the church itself—"those who are his" (2 Tim. 2:19), an echo of Numbers 16:5. As with the image of the church as the pillar and ground of the truth, the focus here is on the stability of a church that cannot be destroyed by the false teachers.

The context of Numbers 16:5, referenced by Paul in 2 Timothy 2:19, is Korah's rebellion against Moses, which resulted in a division between Korah's followers and the followers of Moses. The statement that "the LORD will make known who is his, and who is holy" indicates that some will be able to approach God because they are his, but others will be in rebellion against God. Consequently, at the Lord's command, Moses demands that the Israelites "turn away from the tents of these wicked men" (Num. 16:26). Paul's additional citation, "Let everyone who calls on the name of the Lord turn away from wickedness" (2 Tim. 2:19), recalls this demand. In comparing

---

35. Roloff, *Die Kirche im Neuen Testament*, 253.

the church to Israel, Paul challenges the readers to maintain the boundaries between faithful and unfaithful people.

Paul illustrates the need for boundaries in the extended metaphor of the house (2:20–21). Here he employs the image to describe the relationship between the church and its members with the image of a large house. The metaphor of utensils suggests the juxtaposition of faithful, obedient believers and the disobedient false teachers. Only those who cleanse themselves will be useful to the master. That is, the church must separate from all that is unholy. As in the undisputed letters, the church of the Pastoral Epistles is not a *corpus permixtum* but a holy community that demands separation from the members who defile it (cf. 2 Cor. 6:16–7:1). The false teachers have the opportunity to cleanse themselves (2 Tim. 2:20) and become useful to God.[36]

In Titus Paul describes the nature of the church as the heir of Israel. After giving instructions for conduct (2:1–10), he offers the motivation in 2:11–14, using confessional language. The epiphany of the Lord ("the grace of God [that] has appeared," 2:11) has taught the church to abandon "impiety and worldly passions" and "to live lives that are self-controlled, upright, and godly" (2:12). In the confessional statement of 2:14, Paul recalls that Christ "gave himself for us that he might redeem us from all iniquity and purify for himself a people of his own [*laon periousion*] who are zealous for good deeds." The language echoes Exodus 19:5 (cf. Exod. 22:23), which describes Israel as God's treasured possession out of all the peoples, and roots the church in soteriology: Christ gave himself to redeem us and to purify for himself a people. The two parallel statements—Christ redeemed us from slavery to lawlessness, and he cleansed for himself a people—identify the believers as heirs of Israel. As with Israel, those who are cleansed now maintain the covenant and separate themselves from the world around them.[37]

The role of the ministries expands on and develops those described in the earlier Pauline correspondence. In continuity with Philippians, 1 Timothy recognizes the roles of bishops and deacons (3:1–13; cf. Phil. 1:1).[38] In 2 Timothy there is the need for "faithful people who will be able to teach others" (2:2). In Titus the task of the elders is to teach sound doctrine and refute false teachers (1:9). Elders must demonstrate the traits of character that are appropriate for sound teaching. Their primary task is to teach, in keeping with the church's role

36. Ibid., 260.

37. Contra Roloff (ibid., 258), who maintains that the theme of the church as the people of God has been abandoned in the Pastoral Epistles.

38. Because *episkopos* appears in the singular in 1 Timothy, some scholars maintain a distinction between the singular "bishop" and the plural "elders" (*presbyteroi*). The words are synonymous in Titus (cf. Titus 1:5–9). Cf. also Acts 20:28.

as pillar and ground of the truth.[39] No mention is made of the role of leaders in the administration of the Eucharist. The prohibition of teaching by women (1 Tim. 2:11–13) is probably intended to consolidate teaching in an office.

The Pastoral Epistles are not an early church order or organizational chart for the church, for the primary concern of these letters is the preservation of the apostolic faith in the context of false teaching. The bishops/elders are instruments for protecting the church in Paul's absence. They teach the apostolic faith by both word and example. Whereas the heretics display reprehensible behavior as a result of their false teaching, the church leaders display the positive results of sound instruction. Other ministries are also vital for the church. Deacons (1 Tim. 3:8–12) and widows (1 Tim. 5:3–16) are not engaged in teaching but are engaged in acts of service for members of the community. They exhibit the same traits of character assumed for the bishops.

The Pastoral Epistles maintain roots with Israel as the people of God. The image of the household of God probably develops a theme from the Old Testament. This community recognizes Israel's Scripture and recognizes itself as God's chosen possession. The identity with Israel also stands behind reflections on the church and society. While these letters propose that believers live at peace with society (1 Tim. 2:2) and that leaders have a good reputation among nonbelievers (1 Tim. 3:7), they also presuppose sharp boundaries between insiders and outsiders. The church is concerned about its reputation (cf. 1 Tim. 6:1). Widows should behave in such a way as not to create slander against the church (1 Tim. 5:11–14). At the same time, believers are open to society, wanting all to be saved and to come to the knowledge of the truth (cf. 1 Tim. 2:4).[40]

The Contribution of the Pastoral Epistles

In the history of Protestant scholarship, the Pastoral Epistles are commonly regarded as a transition from the Spirit-led congregations of Paul to the institutionalized church of the second century. With the emphasis on specific offices, the Pastoral Epistles are often considered the beginnings of an ecclesiology defined by church offices and the consolidation of offices that resulted in the silencing of women's voices.[41] Thus they fit the common designation as examples of "early Catholicism." Protestants have regarded the Pastoral

39. Karl Löning, "'Säule und Fundament der Wahrheit' (1 Tim. 3:15): Zur Ekklesiologie der Pastoralbriefe," in *Ekklesiologie des Neuen Testaments, für Karl Kertelge*, ed. Rainer Kampling and Thomas Söding (Freiburg: Herder, 1996), 428.

40. Cf. Roloff, *Die Kirche im Neuen Testament*, 258.

41. Cf. ibid., 250.

Epistles as the downfall from the pure Pauline gospel of justification by faith, while Roman Catholics have regarded the Pastorals as the Spirit-guided development of the church toward maturity. Thus these letters present a challenge for ecumenical discussion.[42]

The differences between the Pastoral Epistles and the undisputed letters of Paul are undeniable. The household envisioned in the Pastoral Epistles was compatible to its own time but is alien to our own. The authority of the paterfamilias, the submission of women, and the reality of slavery in the household of God fit well into ancient society. Indeed, the restrictions on women (1 Tim. 2:9–15) and the hierarchical relationships of the household were probably an attempt to assure the ancient society that Christian faith was not dangerous to the existing order (cf. 1 Tim. 2:1–2; 5:14; Titus 2:5, 8, 10). However, what was reassuring to the ancient society is problematic in the modern climate.

Attention to these issues, however, has obscured the essential focus of the Pastoral Epistles. These letters are not a manual for church discipline. Their primary concern is the preservation of the apostolic faith. The image of the deposit (*parathēkē*), used only in the Pastoral Epistles (1 Tim. 6:20; 2 Tim. 1:12, 14), employs the banking metaphor to describe the faith and the sacred trust in preserving it. Although the content of the *parathēkē* is never given, the numerous creedal statements summarize the nature of the apostolic faith. According to the consistent polemic of the Pastoral Epistles, the apostolic faith is being threatened, and the church is the guardian of the truth (1 Tim. 3:15). While the letters do not refer frequently to the church, implicit throughout is the assumption that the church lives as guarantor of the faith and is subject to deviation from it.

Anyone who has observed the churches that are forums for nationalism, political ideology, or the gospel of success knows that the church faces an ongoing challenge to maintain its identity. As Dietrich Bonhoeffer demonstrated in his struggle against the German Christians, only those who are rooted in the Christian tradition can resist the forces of ideology that tempt the church. Because only healthy teaching will preserve the identity of the church, the Pastoral Epistles emphasize the place of teachers. The primary task of the bishop or elder is to ensure proper teaching.

42. Ibid., 267.

❖ 9 ❖

LEADERSHIP LIKE NO OTHER
FOR A COMMUNITY
LIKE NO OTHER

Authority and Ministry in the Undisputed Letters

The traditional Protestant definition of the church as the place where the word is preached and the sacraments are administered focuses on the work of those who are ordained to perform these tasks. As I argued in chapter 3, baptism and the Lord's Supper play an essential role in Pauline ecclesiology. However, Paul gives no indication that these tasks are reserved for a specific group. He employs the passive voice to describe baptism (Rom. 6:2–4; 1 Cor. 12:13; Gal. 3:27) and does not mention the agent. Indeed, in not recalling whom he baptized (cf. 1 Cor. 1:14–17), he suggests that he placed no significance on the agent of the baptism. He describes the Corinthians' practice of the Lord's Supper without indicating who presides at the meal. Nor does he indicate that someone has the exclusive responsibility for the ministry of the word (1 Cor. 14:26). Unlike the synagogue, in which the *archisynagōgos* speaks for the community (cf. Mark 5:22; Acts 13:15; 18:8, 17), the churches have no comparable leadership in the undisputed letters of Paul, who addresses his letters to the whole church rather than to the local leadership.

Local leadership structures are more evident elsewhere in the New Testament and in the second century. According to Acts, Paul appoints elders (*presbyteroi*) in every church (14:23). At the end of his career, the apostle speaks to the Ephesian elders (Acts 20:17–35), holding them responsible for continuing his work. According to 1 Timothy (3:1–15), Titus (1:5–16), Hebrews (13:17), and 1 Peter (5:1–5), local authority appears to be present and recognized by the community. The widespread consensus in the twentieth century, however, was that Pauline churches followed a path from a Spirit-led community to the institutionalized leadership of the next generation.[1] James D. G. Dunn speaks of the Pastoral Epistles under the heading "Towards Ignatius,"[2] referring to the beginnings of the monarchical bishop in the early second century. In this chapter I will examine the extent to which structures of authority are present in the Pauline churches. An additional question emerges from this study: to what extent did Paul's ecclesiology determine his understanding of leadership?

COMPETING VISIONS OF LEADERSHIP IN CORINTH

The challenge of defining the church within the context of other ancient communities is nowhere more in evidence than in the Corinthian correspondence, where questions about communal leadership become a central focus. It is a major issue in 1 Corinthians and is the dominant problem in 2 Corinthians. In both letters Paul defends his leadership against criticisms that reflect the expectations of the ancient society. The Corinthians' partisanship over leaders, expressed in the slogans "I belong to Apollos," "I belong to Paul," and so on (1 Cor. 1:12), echo political debate and suggest that the Corinthian converts understand the church as a political entity, where leaders compete for influence and people add to their own status by affiliating with them.[3] Paul's discussion of wisdom and oratory (1:18–2:5) suggests that the Corinthians have criticized him for his lack of these common qualities of the leader. His refusal of patronage (cf. 1 Cor. 4:8–9; 9:1–3) also challenged the values of those who hoped to advance their prestige.[4]

---

1. See Ulrich Brockhaus, *Charisma und Amt: Die paulinische Charismenlehre auf dem Hintergrund der frühchristlichen Gemeindefunktionen* (Wuppertal: Brockhaus, 1987), 7–46.

2. James D. G. Dunn, *Unity and Diversity in the New Testament: An Inquiry into the Character of Earliest Christianity* (Philadelphia: Westminster, 1977), 114.

3. See Mitchell, *Paul and the Rhetoric*, 68–109; L. L. Welborn, *Politics and Rhetoric in the Corinthian Epistles* (Macon, GA: Mercer University Press, 1997), 1–42; Andrew D. Clarke, *Serve the Community of the Church: Christians as Leaders and Ministers* (Grand Rapids: Eerdmans, 2000), 177.

4. Peter Marshall, *Enmity at Corinth: Social Conventions in Paul's Relations with the Corinthians*, WUNT 2/23 (Tübingen: Mohr, 1987), 165–257.

Some of these issues continue in 2 Corinthians, where Paul answers the charge that "his bodily presence is weak, and his speech of no account" (2 Cor. 10:10 ESV). The Corinthians have argued that Paul lacks the essential leadership qualities of oratorical ability (cf. 2 Cor. 11:6) and physical presence. Paul's frequent use of *peristasis* catalogs describing his sufferings in 2 Corinthians (4:7–12; 6:4–10; 11:23–33; 12:10) is an exercise of comparative boasting that was forced upon him by the Corinthians' challenge to his leadership (cf. 10:12–18; 11:18; 12:11). The consistent defense of his refusal of patronage (2 Cor. 11:7–11; cf. 12:14–15) also challenges the Corinthians' expectations about leaders. For the Corinthians, Paul lacked the Greco-Roman values of leadership.

Andrew Clarke has examined the leadership structures of a variety of ancient communities, including the civic assembly, the family, the voluntary association, and the synagogue, observing their similarities and differences. While these communities were organized for different purposes and had different structures of leadership, they held some features in common. With few exceptions, leadership emerged among the wealthy, who conferred benefits to others through patronage. A common feature was also the quest for honor and status. These expectations were evident among the Corinthians.[5] Thus Paul's challenge is to articulate a theology of leadership against the background of secular models.[6]

PAUL AS THE LEADER

Paul claims to be the undisputed authority of the churches that he established (cf. 2 Cor. 10:12–17). When his authority is in question, he opens his letters by declaring his apostolic credentials (Rom. 1:1; 1 Cor. 1:1; 2 Cor. 1:1; Gal. 1:1), indicating that he has been appointed by God for a special commission: to proclaim the good news to the nations (Rom. 1:5; 1 Cor. 9:1–18). Because the apostolic office is limited to those who have seen the Lord (1 Cor. 9:1; 15:4–9), Paul recognizes that he is one of a select number of apostles (cf. 1 Cor. 15:3–11). Although he occasionally uses the term *apostolos* for others who carry out a mission (Rom. 16:7; 2 Cor. 8:23; Phil. 2:25), he primarily uses the term for this fixed circle. Thus he says in 1 Corinthians that God has appointed in the church "apostles," which Paul places at the head of the list (12:28). He recognizes the role of the pillars and assumes that they all have

5. Clarke, *Serve the Community*, 75–77, 191. See also Andrew D. Clarke, *A Pauline Theology of Church Leadership*, Library of New Testament Studies (Edinburgh: T&T Clark, 2008), 75.
6. For the rendering of the terms *sarkikos* (1 Cor. 3:3; 2 Cor. 1:12) and *kata sarka* (1 Cor. 1:26, 29; 2 Cor. 1:17; 5:15; 10:2) as "secular," see Winter, *After Paul Left Corinth*, 32; Clarke, *Serve the Community*, 173–208.

their own sphere of responsibility (Gal. 2:1–10). Hence he conferred with those who preceded him as apostles (Gal. 1:18; 2:1–10) and even confronted Cephas, one of the pillars, for conduct that was contrary to the "truth of the gospel" (Gal. 2:11–14). Thus the ultimate authority in the church is the gospel, to which apostles are subject. Nevertheless, apostles have authority in the churches, and Paul has the authority over the churches he established.

As an apostle, he equates himself with the prophets. His claim that he has the authority to build and not to tear down (cf. 2 Cor. 10:8) is reminiscent of Jeremiah's appointment "to destroy and to overthrow, to build and to plant" (Jer. 1:10) and God's promise to "build them up, and not tear them down" (Jer. 24:6). Thus Paul commands the church to expel a member who undermines its moral cohesiveness (1 Cor. 5:2–5) and has the apostolic authority to punish a disobedient church (1 Cor. 4:14–21; 2 Cor. 13:1–10). He speaks for God, and reconciliation to him is reconciliation with God (2 Cor. 6:1–2). Because instructions are nothing less than the will of God (1 Thess. 4:3), to reject Paul's commands is to reject God (1 Thess. 4:8).

Within the larger context of the Corinthians' secular understanding of leadership, Paul offers an alternative vision in 1 Corinthians 1–4 as the basis for the instructions in the remainder of the letter. In response to their slogans "I belong to Paul" and "I belong to Apollos" (1 Cor. 3:4), he interprets his own ministry and introduces the themes that he will develop in later discussions of leadership. Although he introduced himself at the beginning of the letter as "Paul, called to be an apostle of Christ Jesus by the will of God" (1:1), he now describes himself and Apollos as *diakonoi* (3:5), introducing the term that would become the primary designation for individuals who undertook activities on behalf of the church.[7] The term commonly rendered in English as "servant," "minister," or "deacon" was used in antiquity for one who is an agent, or messenger, for the sake of another.[8] As in the ancient household, here the *diakonos* serves the master (*kyrios*, 3:5). Paul and Apollos are insignificant, for they only proclaim what they have received from the Lord (3:5). This portrayal of leadership is a direct challenge to the quest for status among the Corinthians.

Paul expands on his and Apollos's role as *diakonoi* in the extended images of the plant and the building (3:6–17),[9] which he employs to show the subor-

---

7. Cf. the term *diakonia*, applied both to Paul's activity (Rom. 11:13; 15:31; 2 Cor. 3:6; 4:1; 5:18; 6:3) and to ministries of the church (Rom. 12:7; 1 Cor. 12:5; 16:15).

8. BDAG 230. See also Karin Lehmeier, *Oikos und Oikonomia: Antike Konzepte der Haushaltsführung und der Bau der Gemeinde bei Paulus* (Marburg: Elwert Verlag, 2006), 256.

9. These images are sometimes used together in the Old Testament. See Müller, *Gottes Pflanzung—Gottes Bau—Gottes Tempel*, 70–71. See Jer. 1:10; 18:9; 24:6; 31:4, 28 (=LXX 38:4, 28); 33:7 (=LXX 40:7); 42:10 (=LXX 49:10).

dinate role of leaders. Paul and Apollos are not rivals but gardeners who are united (3:8) in a division of labor. Paul's emphasis is that God rather than human leaders gave "the growth" (3:7 KJV). This image places human leaders in perspective and undermines all boasting (cf. 3:18–23), reminding them that the plant and the building belong to God (3:9).

Paul further elaborates on the role of the *diakonoi* in the extended image of the building (*oikodomē*), which he introduces for the first time in 3:9 and to which he gives a central role in the letter (cf. 8:1, 10; 10:23; 14:3–5, 12, 17, 26). In other contexts he uses the image for service to the community (Rom. 14:19; 15:2; 1 Thess. 5:11). Here he confronts the Corinthian rivalries with parallel imagery, indicating that both the plant and the building are God's (3:10) and that the people are only construction workers. As *diakonos* Paul served as the master builder (*architektōn*) who laid the foundation, not by his own capabilities, but by the grace given to him (3:10), and "another" (*allos*, NRSV "someone else") is building on it. This statement is parallel to the earlier claim, "I planted, Apollos watered" (3:6). Paul is not referring only to himself and Apollos, however, for he extends the image to "anyone" (*tis*, 3:12) who builds on (*epoikodomei*) the foundation. Then he warns that the work of each (*hekastou*) will ultimately become manifest (4:13). Thus the members of the community are engaged in a construction project in which they either build onto the work of others to make it a permanent structure or build with materials that will not last.

The extended image of the building serves as a warning to the Corinthians who make the church a forum for exercising selfish ambition. Because the building belongs to God and is under construction, the construction worker must handle the task with care. The care of the church cannot be left to those who engage in partisan politics, for God calls believers to participate in the construction project, building onto the work that began with the laying of the foundation.

Paul regularly reinforces this view of Christian leadership, describing himself with other images that indicate that, while he is an apostle, he is also a servant. He does not preach from his own will, but he has been entrusted with a commission (1 Cor. 9:17) to preach among the nations (Gal. 2:7; 1 Thess. 2:4). As his confrontation with Peter indicates (Gal. 2:11–14), those who are entrusted with the gospel must conduct themselves in accordance with the truth of the gospel. Thus he writes to local churches with delegated authority to continue the pastoral activity that began with the community's response to his original preaching (cf. 1 Thess. 1:5–2:12).

The salutation of his letters offers an insight into the nature of his authority in the church. In both Philippians and 1 Thessalonians he does not indicate his authoritative status but addresses his listeners with the terminology drawn from family life. They are his beloved (Phil. 2:12; 1 Thess. 2:8) and his siblings (Phil. 1:12; 3:1; 1 Thess. 2:1, 9, 14, 17; 3:7; 4:10), whom he loves and longs for (Phil. 4:1). Paul employs the imagery of the family throughout his correspondence—even in writing to a community that he did not establish (cf. Rom. 1:13; 7:1, 4; 8:12; 10:1; 11:25; 12:1, 19).

The image of the family shapes Paul's understanding of his authority. He maintains a parental role throughout his correspondence. He is the expectant mother (Gal. 4:19), father of the bride (2 Cor. 11:3), nursing mother (1 Thess. 2:7), and father (1 Cor. 4:14; 1 Thess. 2:11) who is responsible for the spiritual development of his children. This role is the basis for the instructions that he gives to his children. He recalls that, after the Thessalonians' conversion, he was a "father with his children," urging (*parakalountes*), encouraging (*paramythoumenoi*), and pleading (*martyroumenoi*) with them to "lead a life worthy of God" (1 Thess. 2:11–12). Because he alone is father to the Corinthians, he admonishes (*nouthetei*) his beloved children (1 Cor. 4:14).

These verbs offer insight into the nature of Paul's exercise of parental authority. Paul prefers not to command specific behavior (Philem. 8);[10] he more frequently encourages and pleads with his congregations. The most frequent word in Paul's instructions is the verb *parakalein* (rendered "urging" in 1 Thess. 2:12) and the related noun *paraklēsis*. Paul speaks of his *paraklēsis* in the initial days of the Thessalonian church (1 Thess. 2:3) and uses the verb to describe his original catechesis (2:3, 12). He regularly introduces moral instruction with *parakalō* (Rom. 12:1; 1 Cor. 1:10; 4:16; Phil. 4:2; 1 Thess. 4:1, 10),[11] the term for a polite request (2 Cor. 8:6; 9:5; Philem. 9) but also for encouragement of the disheartened (cf. 1 Cor. 4:13) and the comforting of the bereaved (1 Thess. 4:18). Thus while Paul's *paraklēsis* is directive, it is also appeal, encouragement, admonition, consolation, invitation, and even request.[12] For Paul it is the request of a father.

As a father, Paul was actively engaged in "encouraging" (*paramythoumenoi*) and "pleading" (*martyromenoi*) with his children to adopt appropriate conduct. *Paramytheomai* and the noun *paramythia* are commonly linked with *parakalein/paraklēsis* (cf. Phil. 2:1; 1 Cor. 14:1–5). While the terms overlap in meaning, *paramythia* is a particular form of *paraklēsis*. It is used for consolation

10. He commands (*diatassei*) the Galatians and Macedonians to participate in the collection (1 Cor. 16:1–2). He also has specific instructions that he commands in all the churches (1 Cor. 7:17; cf. 11:34).
11. See Thompson, *Moral Formation*, 60.
12. Lohfink, *Jesus and Community*, 119.

and condolence (2 Macc. 15:9) in the context of distress[13] and commonly involves soothing words for those who are grieving or in distress.[14] The term is used in John's Gospel for those who came to Mary and Martha in order to console them (*hina paramythēsōntai autas*) after the death of Lazarus (John 11:19). This usage is commonplace in antiquity, as Ceslas Spicq has shown.[15] Paul responds to the distress that accompanied the Thessalonians' conversion (1 Thess. 1:6), the continuing persecution (3:3), and the grief caused by the death of some of the members (4:13) with words of consolation so that they will live in hope (cf. 4:13–18).

"Pleading" (*martyroumenoi*) can also have the connotation of "urgent persuasion"[16] or emphatic declaration. Paul uses the cognate verb (*diamartyresthai*) for the specific moral instructions (1 Thess. 4:6) and the warning for those who ignore God's commands. Paul's parental role also includes admonishing (*noutheton*) the children, as he indicates in the extended parental image in 1 Corinthians 4:14–21. In summing up the corrective instruction that he has given in 1:10–4:13, he assures the readers, "I am not writing this to make you ashamed, but to admonish (*noutheton*) you as my beloved children" (4:14). This term was central to ancient education. As a combination of the words *nous* and *tithēmi*, it meant "to put something in someone's mind"[17] or "instill sense in someone" and instructed others in what one should and should not do.[18] Its range of meanings includes "instruct," "warn," "admonish," and "reprimand."[19] The term was also central to parental instruction and included all these aspects.[20] Like a good parent, Paul admonishes his children as a demonstration of love (1 Cor. 4:14), accompanying his admonition with the example that he hopes the community will imitate (4:16). Timothy, his emissary and child, will remind them of his ways (1 Cor. 4:17). Paul will exert his parental responsibility by coming either "with a stick" or "with love in a spirit of gentleness" (1 Cor. 4:21).

13. Spicq, "*paramytheomai*," *TLNT* 3:34.

14. See Spicq, "*paramytheomai*," *TLNT* 3:31, for the numerous examples of the use of the word to denote consolation of those in grief.

15. Spicq, "*paramytheomai*," *TLNT* 3:31–34.

16. J. Beutler, "*martyreō, diamartyromai, martyromai*," *EDNT* 2:391.

17. Spicq, "*noutheteo, nouthesia*," *TLNT* 2:548.

18. Abraham J. Malherbe, "'Pastoral Care' in the Thessalonian Church," *New Testament Studies* 36 (1990): 383.

19. Spicq, "*noutheteo, nouthesia*," *TLNT* 2:548.

20. Cf. Eph. 6:4. Eli is blamed for not rebuking his sons, who had cursed God (1 Sam. 3:13); Philo, *Spec. Laws* 2.232: "Fathers have the right to admonish their children severely"; Josephus *Ant.* 4.260: parents are the first to admonish their children verbally because they have the authority of judges over their offspring. Cf. Wis. 11:10, "as a father admonishing"; *Ps. Sol.* 13:8. Texts in Spicq, "*noutheteō, nouthesia*," *TLNT* 2:550.

Paul's paternal role includes not only stern discipline but also the tenderness and devotion normally expected of parents. In the infancy of the church, he was like a nursing mother taking care of her own children (1 Thess. 2:7). To the Corinthians' dismay, he refuses to accept payment for his work because "children ought not to lay up for their parents, but parents for their children" (2 Cor. 12:14). His constant "anxiety for the churches" (2 Cor. 11:28) is the parent's concern for the welfare of the children.

The apostolic claim and the parental relationship converge in his appeal to his own life as a model for others to emulate. His autobiographical references suggest that he chooses not to use his authority but is a model of self-sacrifice (cf. 1 Cor. 9:19–23; 1 Thess. 2:7) for others to imitate. As an apostle, he could make demands (*en barei einai*) on his congregation (1 Thess. 2:7),[21] but he refuses to do so. While he has the rights to request payment and to have a wife (1 Cor. 9:3–18), he declines to use those rights. Thus while Paul has undisputed authority as apostle and father, he lives for the sake of others, and his authority is inseparable from his acts of service. He has only the authority that the Lord has given him.

He expresses gratitude that the Thessalonians imitated both him and the Lord (1 Thess. 1:6). When they received the word "in spite of persecution" (1:6), they emulated Paul, who had declared the word of the Lord "in spite of great opposition" (2:2). Indeed, Paul's autobiographical comments in 1 Thessalonians 2:1–12 serve as the model of behavior that he desires from the Thessalonians (4:1–5:22). Similarly, he instructs the Philippians to be his "co-imitators" (*symmimētai*, Phil. 3:17) and later adds, "Keep on doing the things that you have learned and received and heard and seen in me" (Phil. 4:9). In 1 Corinthians he describes his lifestyle in terms of his sufferings and manual labor (4:8–12) before challenging the readers to imitate him (4:16). He has full apostolic rights (9:1–13) but chooses to become a slave of all (9:1–23), concluding the topic with the encouragement, "Be imitators of me, as I am of Christ" (11:1).

In 2 Corinthians, Paul's most autobiographical letter, the apostle offers a comprehensive treatment of the nature of leadership in response to rivals who question his credentials. The effect of his apostolic preaching is that it divides the world into saved and lost (2 Cor. 2:15). Paul is the minister of the new covenant (3:6) promised by Jeremiah (Jer. 31:31–34). He compares himself favorably to Moses (2 Cor. 3:12) and speaks of the authority that the Lord has

---

21. *En barei einai* is literally "wield authority" or "insist on one's importance." See BDAG 167. Paul chooses the opposite demeanor: he was "gentle like a nurse tenderly caring for her own children" (1 Thess. 2:7b). See Franz Laub, "Paulus als Gemeindegründer (1 Thess.)," in Hainz, *Kirche im Werden*, 27.

given him (10:8; 13:10). Despite his authority, he has chosen to sacrifice himself for his community. His credentials are evident in his pattern of life. He carries around the dying of Jesus (4:10) for the sake of others. When the Corinthians accuse him of acting out of self-interest (cf. 1:15–22), he insists that all his decisions are for their sake (cf. 1:4; 5:14–15). His many trials commend him as a servant of Christ (6:4). The *peristasis* catalogs (4:7–11; 6:4–10; 11:23–33) demonstrate that his task is to identify with the weakness of Christ (cf. 13:4).

As a model for believers, Paul demonstrates the nature of leadership. Whereas others advocated a secular form of leadership that emphasizes oratorical ability and physical presence (cf. 2 Cor. 10:10–11), he is the example of leadership defined by the cross of Christ. With his ultimate goal of presenting a sanctified people to Christ (Rom. 15:16), he exercised authority while giving himself for the sake of others.

AUTHORITY AND MINISTRY IN PAUL'S ABSENCE

The Ministry of Coworkers

Paul expects the task of admonishing, encouraging, consoling, and building to continue in his absence. His coworkers participate in these tasks as they represent Paul among the churches. Timothy explains Paul's ways and does "the work of the Lord" just as Paul does (1 Cor. 16:10). He is a "co-worker" whom Paul sends to Thessalonica to strengthen and encourage the church in the midst of persecution (1 Thess. 3:2). Timothy is also an example to others, for he cares not for his own interests but for the welfare of others (Phil. 2:20–21). Epaphroditus risked his life for the Philippians (Phil. 2:30). Similarly, Titus shares Paul's anguish over the troubles at Corinth and his joy over their repentance (2 Cor. 7:5–16). Thus Paul does not reserve this ministerial task for himself, but assumes that his coworkers will extend his labor and join Paul in participating in the sufferings of Christ.

Mutual Ministry in the Congregation

Paul also assumes that members of the local communities will continue the work of shaping the church. The relationship between his ecclesiology and his understanding of leadership is evident in the images that he uses for the church (see chap. 1, "The Family of God"; chap. 2, "The Temple of the Holy Spirit and the Body of Christ in 1 Corinthians"). In keeping with the church's existence as God's building (1 Cor. 3:19), Paul, having laid the foundation (3:10), continually serves his churches for the sake of their edification (*oikodomē*,

2 Cor. 12:19; cf. Rom. 15:20) and expects others to build on it (1 Cor. 3:10; see "Paul as the Leader" above), hoping that the building project will ultimately be complete (3:10–17). Mutual edification becomes the criterion for ethical conduct of the members of the community. Where believers are divided by differences of opinion on matters of conduct, he encourages them, "Let us pursue what makes for peace and for mutual upbuilding" (*oikodomēs tēs eis allēlous*, Rom. 14:19). The conduct of members of the church should not be an exercise of individual rights but should be intended for the edification (Rom. 15:2; 1 Cor. 8:1; 10:23) of the whole community.

Paul maintains the focus on the community's responsibility for edification throughout 1 Corinthians. When the Corinthians claim the right to eat meat offered to idols because of their superior knowledge (cf. 1 Cor. 8:7), he introduces the discussion with the reminder that "knowledge puffs up, but love builds up" (8:1). Since self-serving behavior may result in the destruction of the weaker brother (8:11, 13), he insists that members look out for the good of the whole community rather than demand their own rights, offering himself as the example of denying oneself for the sake of others (9:1–18).

In regard to the liturgy, Paul promotes the responsibility of all for the ultimate building of the church. When the competition over spiritual gifts disrupts the assembly, Paul insists that edification of the whole community is the ultimate goal of the gathering. Consequently, he prefers prophecy to glossolalia because prophetic speech addresses other people for their upbuilding (*oikodomē*), encouragement (*paraklēsis*), and consolation (*paramythia*) (1 Cor. 14:1–3). Those who are involved in these three tasks continue the work of Paul, who first devoted himself to the *oikodomē* (2 Cor. 12:19), *paraklēsis*, and *paramythia* (1 Thess. 2:12) of his churches.

Paul introduces the discussion of public worship (1 Cor. 14:5) with the guideline for the entire service. He assumes the active participation of all the members in the service: "Each one has a hymn, a lesson, a revelation, a tongue, or an interpretation." He concludes, "Let everything be done for building up" (1 Cor. 14:26). Thus the whole church has the responsibility for edification, and their speech should be intelligible (14:6–19) and orderly (14:20–40). The call for *oikodomē* and its synonyms is a refrain throughout the chapter (14:12, 26; cf. 14:3, 19). "Edification" refers not to the building up of individuals but to the building up of the church, which exists in concrete local communities.[22] Believers engage in building up the community in their

22. Lohfink, *Jesus and Community*, 102. Lohfink cites Philipp Vielhauer: "The goal of the ways of God is not the pious individual, but the one, holy, catholic church, in the pregnant and radically eschatological sense of the New Testament; it is the church's creation and preservation, its promotion and realization, that Paul describes as *oikodomein*." Vielhauer, *Oikodome: Das*

regard for one another both in daily life and in the assembly. Paul's task of building, urging, and encouraging is thus the task of the whole church, since all have a responsibility to build a structure that can withstand every test (cf. 1 Cor. 3:10–17).

The image of the family also shapes Paul's understanding of the responsibility of members for each other. The reciprocal pronoun (*allēlōn, allēlois, allēlous*: "one another") appears with remarkable frequency in the letters of Paul.[23] This usage is drawn primarily from family life, where family members love one another (cf. Rom. 12:10; 13:8), have high regard for one another (Rom. 12:10), and have the same mind with one another (Rom. 15:5; Phil. 2:2).[24] Among these reciprocal responsibilities were the tasks in which Paul had been involved. Just as Paul had admonished his children, he assumes that members will "admonish one another" (Rom. 15:14 KJV), "encourage one another and build up each other" (1 Thess. 5:11), "admonish the idlers, encourage the fainthearted, [and] help the weak" (1 Thess. 5:14).

The image of the body provides Paul with an especially useful metaphor for delineating specific responsibilities and their interdependence within the community. In both 1 Corinthians (12:12–27) and Romans (12:3–8), the image indicates the variety of gifts that function together within the one body (Rom. 12:6; 1 Cor. 12:4). While prophecy and teaching appear in both lists (Rom. 12:6–7; 1 Cor. 12:10, 28), the lists share little else in common. Romans mentions ministry (*diakonia*), the exhorter (*ho parakalōn*), the giver (*ho metadidous*), the leader (*ho proistamenos*), and the compassionate person (*ho eleōn*) (12:6–8). When Paul lists the parts of the body in 1 Corinthians 12:14–26, he compares members with the feet, ears, and eyes, including also those parts that are considered weaker or less honorable (14:22–23), but he does not mention the head. The term "each" is important in Pauline ecclesiology within the metaphors of building (cf. 1 Cor. 3:13) and body (1 Cor. 12:7; cf. 14:26). He offers a longer list that includes the gifts of wisdom (*sophia*), knowledge (*gnōsis*), faith (*pistis*), healing, working of miracles (*dynameis*), the discernment of spirits, the various kinds of tongues, and the interpretation of tongues (1 Cor. 12:8–11). At the end of the list in 1 Corinthians, he repeats some of the list (prophecy, deeds of power, gifts of healing, various kinds of tongues, 12:28) but adds "forms of assistance" (*antilēmpseis*) and "forms of leadership" (*kybernēseis*). As Paul indicates in the developing argument, all members have a vital function in the life of the church. Even leadership is one gift among

---

Bild vom Bau in der christlichen Literatur vom Neuen Testament bis Clemens Alexandrinus (Karlsruhe: Durlach, 1940), 108.

23. Lohfink, *Jesus and Community*, 99–100.

24. See Schäfer, *Gemeinde als "Bruderschaft,"* 25. Thompson, *Moral Formation*, 57.

many. These parts are interdependent and work together "for the common good" (*to sympheron*, 12:7).

We cannot ascertain whether Paul expected uniformity within his churches, since the lists are probably not comprehensive. Nevertheless, we can still see a mutuality based on the specific responsibilities of the members. Among these ministries are tasks in which Paul was first involved.

Local Leadership

While the focus in the Pauline letters is on the reciprocal responsibilities of all the members, the apostle also assumes the emergence of leaders who are acknowledged by the entire community for the functions they perform. Because not all members have progressed equally, he assumes that some will lead on a continuing basis even though he reserves no functions for them and has no uniform titles to indicate the existence of established offices.[25] In Galatians he assumes the distinction between the one who is being taught and the one who teaches (*ho katechōn*, Gal. 6:6). Paul's use of the participle indicates that his focus is on the function rather than the title. The fact that the one who teaches receives payment indicates the communal recognition of one who exercises this function on a continuing basis.[26] Paul also identifies some as "spiritual" (*pneumatikos*) and capable of restoring one who has transgressed (Gal. 6:1).[27]

DIALECTICAL LEADERSHIP IN 1 THESSALONIANS

In 1 Thessalonians Paul offers an important window into the relationship between the ministry of the whole church and the role of leaders. Addressing the letter to the entire church (1:1), he encourages active participation of all the members. He expresses gratitude for their "work of faith and labor of love and steadfastness of hope" (1:3). Forms of *allēlōn* indicate their reciprocal responsibilities. He prays that they will have "love for one another" (3:12) and instructs them to "love one another" (4:9). The instructions to "encourage one another" (4:18; 5:11) and to "build up each other" (5:11) indicate that the whole church is involved in tasks already initiated by Paul (cf. 1 Thess.

---

25. The New Testament has no term for "office." Brockhaus (*Charisma und Amt*, 123–24) summarizes the characteristics of an office. These include (a) the element of permanency, (b) recognition by the church, (c) differentiation of the position from that of the whole church, (d) a commissioning, and (e) payment.

26. Contrary to the NRSV ("those who are taught"), "the one who is being taught" (*ho katechoumenos*, Gal. 6:6) is singular. Although this could suggest private instruction, it can also be understood as a generalizing singular. Brockhaus, *Charisma und Amt*, 102–3.

27. See the RSV for the translation "you who are spiritual." The NRSV "you who have received the Spirit" obscures Paul's assumption that some within the community have the capacity to minister to others.

2:12; 2 Cor. 12:19). This call for congregational involvement continues in the instructions in 5:15–22, to which I shall return below.

Among the instructions to the entire church is the request "Respect [*eidenai*, literally 'know'] those who labor among you, and have charge of you in the Lord and admonish you," to which Paul adds, "esteem them very highly in love because of their work" (1 Thess. 5:12–13). To "know" (5:12) and to "esteem" (*hēgeisthai*)[28] them is to recognize the legitimate functions of a group as members care for specific tasks within the community. To esteem them "highly" (*hyperekperrissou*) is to regard them "beyond all measure."[29] Paul offers similar counsel in 1 Corinthians 16:15 when he says to the community, "You know [*oidate*] . . . the household of Stephanus," the first converts of Achaia, and adds, "Put yourselves at the service [*hypotassesthe*] of such people" (16:16).[30] These verbs indicate the special regard that the community gives to local leaders.

The basis of congregational recognition is the leaders' work ("their work," 1 Thess. 5:13). Similarly, Paul expects the Corinthians to "know" those who "have devoted themselves to the service of the saints" (1 Cor. 16:15). Communal recognition, therefore, rests not on titles but on service to the community. Those who had emerged in Corinth were among the first converts in that city. The leaders in Thessalonica are probably also early converts whose work was exemplary for the whole community. Thus although the Thessalonian church is only months old, Paul recognizes that some have emerged who should be recognized by the whole community.

The plural definite article (*tous*) in 1 Thessalonians 5:12 indicates that Paul has in mind one group with multiple tasks.[31] Although he mentions no names, he is probably thinking of particular persons known to him who provide leadership.[32] The use of three participles indicates that they bear no official title but are known for their function, which they practice on a continuing basis. As the introduction to the three participles, "those who labor among you" (*kopiōntas en hymin*) may encompass the other two.[33] The verb plays

28. BDAG 201, 434.

29. BDAG 1032.

30. *Hypotassein*, literally "submit," is used in the New Testament for the submission of wives to husbands (Col. 3:18) and submission to the government (Rom. 13:1–7). It is used for mutual submission in Eph. 5:21. In 1 Cor. 16:16 it suggests "voluntary yielding in love" (BDAG 1042).

31. Holtz, *Der erste Brief an die Thessalonicher*, 241.

32. Bengt Holmberg, *Paul and Power: The Structure of Authority in the Primitive Church as Reflected in the Pauline Epistles* (Philadelphia: Fortress, 1978), 99. Cf. Brockhaus, *Charisma und Amt*, 107.

33. Holtz, *Der erste Brief an die Thessalonicher*, 242; Lührmann, "Paulus als Gemeindegründer," 33.

an important role for Paul as a description of his evangelistic and pastoral work (cf. 1 Cor. 15:10; Gal. 4:11; Phil. 2:16).[34] He uses the term for a variety of tasks, including both his work with his hands (1 Cor. 4:12) and his evangelistic and pastoral work (1 Cor. 15:10; Gal. 4:11; Phil. 2:16). He also uses it frequently for the work of others (cf. Rom. 16:12, 16) who have provided various ministries on behalf of the community, including evangelism and acts of service. Thus some continue Paul's own work in the community on behalf of the house church. This work is not limited to a select group, however, for Paul has already expressed gratitude that the entire church is involved in a labor of love (1 Thess. 1:3). The word suggests the extreme effort that the labor for Christ involves.[35] While the term designates the work of both Paul and others, it also designates some who may be described as "those who labor among you."

With the second designation, those who "have charge of you" (*proistamenoi*), the NRSV emphasizes the authority of the group that has emerged within the local community. While *proistēmi* is used frequently to designate authority, it also involves care and concern for others.[36] Paul's description of Phoebe with the related word (*prostatis*, Rom. 16:2) suggests that she has provided assistance to the church, perhaps by providing patronage.[37] In the Pastoral Epistles, both authority and care are present in the use of the word for the paterfamilias (1 Tim. 3:4) and for elders (1 Tim. 5:17). In Romans 12:8 the NRSV renders it as "leader," while the RSV renders it as "he who gives aid." Thus the word carries the connotation of "caring authority and authoritative care."[38] The word may suggest that some have emerged who have the special means to care for the needs of the community. This task probably included both teaching and nurture of the community.

Those who care for the community also "admonish" (*nouthetountas*) the members. Thus they assume the work of Paul, who had given the admonition expected of a father (cf. 1 Cor. 4:14; Eph. 6:4) or sibling. Although admonition (*nouthesia*) can mean instruction,[39] the term can also connote the reprimand (cf. Wis. 16:6), rebuke (Titus 3:10), warning (cf. Acts 20:31), and punishment

---

34. The word *kopos/kopiaō* originally referred to exhausting physical work in the field. It came to be associated with every kind of physical and moral suffering or affliction. See *TLNT* 2:322–29. Paul probably introduced the word into the Christian vocabulary as a term for missionary labor. See Brockhaus, *Charisma und Amt*, 106.

35. Holtz, *Der erste Brief an die Thessalonicher*, 242.

36. BDAG 870. *EDNT* 3:157.

37. BDAG 885.

38. Hans von Campenhausen, *Ecclesiastical Authority and Spiritual Power in the Church of the First Three Centuries* (Stanford: Stanford University Press, 1969), 65.

39. It is parallel to *didaskein* in Col. 1:28; 3:16.

(Josephus, *Ant.* 3.311) that a parent or mentor gives to a child.[40] Those who have exhausted themselves for the community in Thessalonica thus have the authority to admonish members of the community. This combination of the labor of the mentor and the authority to admonish is apparent in Paul's admonition to the Ephesians with tears (Acts 20:31), which he gives only after recalling his labor on their behalf.

Although Paul indicates in other letters that some have emerged with special recognition and work, he has no uniform nomenclature to describe the leaders in the undisputed letters. "Those who labor among you, and have charge of you in the Lord and admonish you" are analogous to the leader (*ho proistamenos*) in Romans 12:8. In 1 Corinthians 12:28 Paul mentions among the gifts "forms of assistance" (*antilēmpseis*) and "forms of leadership" (*kybernēseis*), once more juxtaposing the aspect of deeds of service and leadership.[41] The plural *kybernēseis* refers to the variety of leadership roles in the community.[42] The related word *kybernētēs* refers to the shipmaster who is responsible for the management of a ship.[43] The term was used metaphorically for people in political leadership who are responsible for human destiny.[44] While Paul neither elaborates on the relationship of the "forms of leadership" to the other gifts nor describes the task of leaders, the term contains the dimensions of care for others and authority that are present in 1 Thessalonians 5:12.

The leaders' role is probably similar to that of the "bishops and deacons," whom Paul includes in the address in Philippians 1:1 but does not mention in the rest of the letter. This reference indicates the existence of established offices in the Philippian church that are recognized by the community. While the roles of these leaders are apparently self-evident to Paul and his readers, we ascertain their functions only by the terms *episkopoi* and *diakonoi*.[45] As

---

40. See Malherbe, "'Pastoral Care' in the Thessalonian Church," 389, for the role of *nouthesia* in psychagogy. For the role of *nouthesia* in education, see Philo (*Alleg. Interp.* 3.193): "If you desire to become the slave of the wise person, then you will accept your share of reprimands and correction." Cf. *Prelim. Studies* 157: "What is good and profitable for those who need to be rebuked is admonition." Philo says of Moses: "After training the people entrusted to his rule through relatively mild directives and exhortations, then by more severe threats and admonitions, Moses called upon them to give a practical demonstration of the lessons they had learned" (*Rewards* 4; cited in Spicq, "*nouthesia, noutheteō*," *TLNT* 2:549).

41. Brockhaus, *Charisma und Amt*, 109.

42. BDAG 574.

43. BDAG 574.

44. See Plato, *Resp.* 6.488a–489a for Plato's parable of the shipmaster as an image of political leadership. The good pilot of the ship ensures the good of those in his care.

45. See Brockhaus, *Gemeinde und Amt*, 99, for the suggested functions of the *episkopoi* and *diakonoi*.

with those who receive special recognition in 1 Thessalonians, the use of the plural indicates that the leaders consist of a plurality. *Episkopos*, used here for the first time in Christian literature, was a common word in antiquity for those who assume the responsibility of leadership. It does not have the sense in Philippians that it has in later ecclesiastical literature.[46] Thus the word, like *proistamenoi* in 1 Thessalonians 5:12, probably refers to a group that is responsible for teaching and administration. Similarly, *diakonoi* does not have the later technical meaning but refers to those who serve others. This word is used elsewhere for Phoebe, the *diakonos* of Cenchreae (Rom. 16:1); Apollos (1 Cor. 3:5); and Paul (1 Cor. 3:5; 2 Cor. 3:6; 6:4; 11:23). Together, the two words *episkopoi* and *diakonoi* continue the dual focus on caring authority and authoritative care that is present in other Pauline letters.

While Paul does not employ uniform terminology, he demonstrates the specific nature of ecclesiastical leadership in the close relationship of authority and service. Like Paul himself, the leaders receive recognition when they have distinguished themselves by their service to the community. The task is not limited to a select group, however, for Paul pleads for the entire congregation to "admonish the idlers" (cf. *noutheteite tous ataktous*, 1 Thess. 5:14; cf. Rom. 15:14).[47] He knows no demarcation between the task of the leaders and the task of the whole church.[48] *Ataktoi* (NRSV "idlers") are literally "those who are out of step." In 2 Thessalonians 3:6, the phrase *ataktōs peripatein* may be rendered "behave irresponsibly." Whereas in 2 Thessalonians Paul refers to the specific irresponsible behavior as freeloading by some members, the *ataktoi* in 1 Thessalonians may undermine order in a variety of ways. They are undisciplined, apparently refusing to follow the instructions that Paul had given to the community.[49] By insisting that both a select group and the whole church admonish other believers, Paul advocates a "dialectical leadership" of tasks that the whole church is involved in, while also recognizing a group who engage in this ministry.[50]

The responsibility of the whole church is also evident in the imperatives near the end of the letter. Besides admonishing the disorderly, the community is to "encourage the fainthearted" (*paramytheisthe tous oligopsychous*, 1 Thess. 5:14). *Paramytheomai* is the word that Paul uses for his own ministry (2:12). The "fainthearted" (*oligopsychoi*) are probably those who are despondent

---

46. BDAG 379.
47. See BDAG 148. See also Malherbe, "'Pastoral Care' in the Thessalonian Church," 389.
48. Laub, "Paulus als Gemeindegründer," 34.
49. See Spicq, "*atakteō*," *TLNT* 1:225. The word was used in philosophical literature to characterize those with undisciplined, "beastlike" behavior—troublemakers, insurgents.
50. Holmberg, *Paul and Power*, 198.

or discouraged by the trials the community is facing.[51] These people can be encouraged only by a consoling and tender word (*paramythia*).[52]

Paul also encourages them to "help the weak" (*antechesthe tōn asthenōn*) and be patient with everyone (5:14). As he indicates elsewhere, converts do not mature at the same pace. In two of the letters, he recognizes the distinction between the weak and the strong. In 1 Corinthians he instructs members to show consideration to those who are weak in conscience (8:9–10). In describing the church as the body, he refers to the "less honorable parts" of the body (12:23). In Romans he identifies himself with the strong but instructs the church, "We who are strong ought to put up with the failings [*asthenēmata*, literally "weaknesses"] of the weak [*adynatoi*] and not to please ourselves" (Rom. 15:1). Weakness undoubtedly took a variety of forms. Paul uses the term for those who were physically weak or sick (cf. 1 Cor. 11:30; Gal. 4:9; 2 Cor. 10:10), for those who lacked maturity in understanding Christian freedom (1 Cor. 8:7, 9), or for those whose weaknesses of the flesh prevented them from living the virtuous life.[53] The instruction to "be patient with all" (*makrothymeite pros pantas*, 1 Thess. 5:14) challenges the whole church to exercise extreme care with others. Patience, the capacity to bear up under provocation,[54] is an expression of love (cf. 1 Cor. 13:4; Gal. 5:22). The instruction to care for all is an appropriate ending for the series, for it expands the concern from the weak and the fainthearted to the whole church.

Paul assumes the presence of prophecy in Thessalonica but challenges the church to exercise communal discernment in evaluating it. He instructs them not to "quench the Spirit" (5:19) or "despise the words of prophets" (5:20), but to "test all things," knowing that not all prophecy leads to edification (cf. 1 Cor. 14:1–5). Paul does not indicate the nature of the concerns about prophets in Thessalonica, but instructs the listeners to exercise discernment in determining the benefit of specific prophetic announcements. This is the task not of leaders but of the whole church.

The Participation of Women

With the exception of 1 Corinthians (see below), Paul makes no comment in the undisputed letters about gender roles when he instructs all members of the community to "encourage one another and build one another up" (1 Thess.

---

51. Malherbe, "'Pastoral Care' in the Thessalonian Church," 390.

52. See Isa. 57:15, literally "giving patience to the fainthearted" (*oligopsychois didous makrothymian*).

53. See Malherbe, "'Pastoral Care' in the Thessalonian Church," 390, for this theme among the moral philosophers.

54. BDAG 612.

5:11 ESV; cf. 4:18). As the baptism of entire households (cf. 1 Cor. 16:16; cf. Acts 16:15; 18:8) indicates, these churches mirror the ancient household, which includes householders, wives, slaves, and children. Thus when Paul writes to the *adelphoi*, he assumes the presence of a demographic that was unprecedented in antiquity. He insists that all are full members of the community. He recites the baptismal slogan that "we were all baptized into one body—Jews or Greeks, slaves or free" (1 Cor. 12:13), adding in Galatians, "There is no longer . . . male and female; for all of you are one in Christ" (3:28). As this slogan indicates, baptism is a marker of the unity of the church and the abandonment of old distinctions. As the instructions (1 Thess. 5:11) indicate, full membership involves participation in building up the community.[55]

Thus Paul undoubtedly includes women in all his letters when he calls for reciprocal responsibilities. Women are included when he insists that "each" builds on to the building under construction (1 Cor. 3:10) and when he describes the church as a body in which God has given "each" (Rom. 12:3) a measure of faith and a manifestation of the Spirit for the common good (1 Cor. 12:7, 11). Both men and women exercise the ministries mentioned in Romans 12:3–8 and 1 Corinthians 12:4–11. When "each one has a hymn, a lesson, a revelation, a tongue, or an interpretation" in the assembly (1 Cor. 14:26), women are not excluded.

Occasionally Paul mentions the ministries of specific women who are active in the life of the church. Euodia and Syntyche, for example, have "struggled beside" (*synēthlēsan*) Paul "in the work of the gospel" (Phil. 4:3). The image suggests that they were partners with Paul in proclaiming the gospel amid great opposition.[56] In Romans 16:1–2 Paul commends Phoebe, a deacon (*diakonos*) of the church in Cenchreae, who is apparently representing the church and bearing the letter. The word *diakonos* is the same term that Paul uses to designate himself (cf. 1 Cor. 3:5) and other servants (cf. 1 Thess. 3:2; Eph. 6:21; Col. 1:7). The phrase "deacon of the church in Cenchreae" indicates that she has a continuing and recognized function. While she is a "deacon of the church in Cenchreae," she is a *prostatis* (NRSV "benefactor") of many. As the translations indicate, the word is rendered in more than one way—as "helper" (NASB) or "patron" (ESV). Like its cognate (*proistēmi*), the word can connote responsibility for the management of the household (cf. 1 Tim.

---

55. Paul will elsewhere discuss the significance of this claim in actual practice. As the argument in Gal. 3 indicates, the issue is full membership in the community. He does not use the term "equality" but describes the unity that has replaced the separation between peoples, social classes, and the sexes.

56. See BDAG 964. See also *synathlein* in 1:27. The athletic metaphor was commonly used in Jewish martyrdom for faithful witness in the context of persecution.

3:4) or financial contributions to others (cf. Rom. 12:8, *ho proistamenos*, NRSV "the giver").

The list of greetings in Romans 16:3–16, with its inclusion of names of slaves, and of Jews and Greeks, among whom are women who play a role in Paul's churches, is an important window into the demographics of Paul's churches. Priscilla and Aquila, who are always mentioned together (Rom. 16:3–4; 1 Cor. 16:19; 2 Tim. 4:19; cf. Acts 18:2, 18, 26) as fellow workers in mission work, probably played a number of roles, including providing hospitality and teaching.[57] Paul greets another pair, "Andronicus and Junia," who are "prominent among the apostles" (Rom. 16:7). They may also be a husband and wife team.[58] Paul gives special notice of this couple because they were converts before Paul and were fellow prisoners with him later. Paul mentions several women who "labored" in the Lord. Mary (16:6), Tryphaena and Tryphosa (16:12), and Persis (16:12) worked hard in the Lord. Paul commonly uses the verb *kopiaō* for evangelistic work (cf. 1 Cor. 4:12; 15:10; 16:16; Gal. 4:11; Phil. 2:16; 1 Thess. 5:12).

This list indicates the range of activities in which women were involved. They had official functions in the church (Rom. 16:1–2), served in charitable tasks (16:2), and traveled on behalf of the community. Some served as partners with their husbands, while others apparently worked independently.

In 1 Corinthians 11–14 the issue of restrictions on the participation of women emerges. Reflections on public participation provide the frame for this section (11:2–16; 14:33b–36), which focuses on the assembly. As Paul indicates in 1 Corinthians 11:2–16, some of the women pray and prophesy in the assembly (11:5). Thus when Paul mentions prophecy in the church (cf. Rom. 12:6; 1 Cor. 12:10; 14:1, 3–6, 22, 24, 31; 1 Thess. 5:20), the activities of women may be included. Indeed, Paul assumes the participation of both men and women in prayer and prophecy but insists that their attire be appropriate for their gender. He gives an extended argument explaining why men should pray with heads uncovered, whereas women wear head coverings (1 Cor. 11:2–16).[59]

---

57. Ben Witherington III, *Women in the Earliest Churches*, Society for New Testament Studies Monograph Series 59 (Cambridge: Cambridge University Press, 1988), 114.

58. Ancient sources understood Andronicus and Junia to be a married couple. See BDAG 480. The expression *episēmoi en tois apostolois* can mean either "prominent in the eyes of the apostles" (cf. ESV) or "prominent among the apostles" (NRSV). The latter reading is the more plausible. Paul probably uses *apostolos* in the sense that it is used in 2 Cor. 8:23 and Phil. 2:25 to designate those who are active in mission work.

59. Paul gives no indication that he is reacting to a crisis in Corinth over the roles of men and women. He introduces this section (11:2) by praising the Corinthians for keeping the traditions. He is probably answering questions that emerged when people from different cultures came together for worship.

As his description of the order of creation indicates (1 Cor. 11:3), he does not assume that men and women, who are "one in Christ" (Gal. 3:28), cease to recognize distinctions in gender in their attire. Indeed, the order of creation with which he begins indicates that Paul is not strictly egalitarian.[60]

Among the undisputed letters, only in 1 Corinthians 14:33b–36 does Paul place restrictions on the participation of women. Near the conclusion of the discussion of spiritual gifts and the assembly (12:1–14:40), Paul says, "Women should be silent in the churches. For they are not permitted to speak, but should be subordinate, as the law says" (14:34). In view of the participation of men and women in prayer and prophecy (11:1–5), this instruction is problematic and has resulted in a variety of interpretations, including the suggestion that all or part of 14:33b–36 is a later interpolation, a view that is widely held in contemporary scholarship.[61] The context of these instructions is Paul's desire to avoid chaos in the assembly and ensure that the community conducts itself "decently and in order" (14:40). Paul opens the discussion by affirming the purpose of the proper meeting: "so that the church may be built up" (14:5). He encourages prophetic speech rather than glossolalia because the former builds up the community (14:4). In the remainder of the chapter he offers guidelines for orderly worship that benefits others. He expresses the concern that speakers take turns and ensures that the entire service is intelligible for both insiders and outsiders (cf. 14:13–25). In order to maintain peace, he instructs some to "be silent" (14:28, 30), adding that "God is a God not of disorder but of peace" (14:33).

This concern is the background for the instruction that "women should be silent in the churches. For they are not permitted to speak." In view of Paul's earlier reference to women who pray and prophesy and his general encouragement of prophecy, he is not likely to be demanding total silence of all women. Because *gynai* can be translated either as "women" or "wives," the most likely explanation here is that Paul addresses wives who have the opportunity to ask

60. See John H. Elliott, "The Jesus Movement Was Not Egalitarian but Family-Oriented," *Biblical Interpretation* 11 (2003): 202.

61. Schrage, *1 Korintherbrief*, 3.481, argues that 14:34–35 is among the most disputed passages in 1 Corinthians. While a growing number, including Schrage, maintain that the passage is inauthentic, scholars remain divided over the issue. Among those who regard the passage as an interpolation, the extent of the interpolated passage is also disputed. Scholars debate whether both 14:33b and 14:36 belong to the interpolation. Reasons for regarding all or part of 14:33b–36 as an interpolation include (a) the apparent contradiction to 11:2–16; (b) the textual instability of the passage (its inclusion after 14:40 in a few manuscripts); (c) stylistic features; and (d) the introduction of the topic of women's participation in a chapter focused on tongues, prophecy, and the edification of the community. For a full discussion, see Schrage, 3.482–92. In view of the overwhelming manuscript evidence of the passage, I regard it as authentic and pertinent to the topic of orderly worship in 1 Corinthians 14.

their husbands questions at home (14:35). Furthermore, prophecy was a gift only for some (cf. 1 Cor. 12:28). In view of the context in which he instructs others to be silent (14:28–29), Paul is probably addressing a similar problem. Some wives have created disorder in the church. Thus, while some women prophesy, those who do not have this gift remain silent.

CONCLUSION: LEADERSHIP SHAPED BY THE STORY

The undisputed letters of Paul give little indication of the emergence of the ecclesiastical offices that are evident in the Pastoral Epistles and the literature of the next generation. They speak instead of the task of pastoral care of the membership and the various forms of instruction—teaching (Rom. 12:7), exhortation (Rom. 12:8; 1 Cor. 14:3, 31), comfort (1 Thess. 4:18), edification (1 Thess. 5:11), and admonition (1 Thess. 5:14). These roles continue Paul's work of transforming communities. With his repeated call for the whole church to be involved in deeds of service and exhortation to one another, Paul reserves no ministry for those who hold an official position. Because the church is under construction until the end, all members are engaged in building up the body of Christ as they interact with those who have special gifts to complete the building.

Nevertheless, Paul anticipates the development of offices in his congregations, for he assumes that not all members have the same maturity. Consequently, he challenges some to care for those who have special needs, and he instructs the community to recognize their roles. Thus the teachers, exhorters, leaders (Rom. 12:7), and those who "have charge" (1 Thess. 5:12) of the community anticipate those who hold the offices of bishop (1 Tim. 3:1) or elder (1 Tim. 5:17; Titus 1:5) in continuity with the same roles. Paul assumes that others will continue to build onto the foundation that he had laid (1 Cor. 3:10–12). His consistent use of participles to describe the leaders (Rom. 12:8, literally "the one who exhorts, the one who gives, the one who leads"; 1 Thess. 5:12, literally "those laboring among you, standing over you and admonishing you") indicates that functions precede titles. Those who perform these tasks on a regular basis are acknowledged with the titles of "bishop" and "elder." The Pastoral Epistles, as I demonstrated in chapter 8, reflect this natural development when these titles portray those who have emerged as the community's teachers and overseers. This development continues into the second century.

Because this form of leadership grows out of the Christian story, it is unparalleled in other communities. Leadership in the Pauline communities was inseparable from the life of sacrifice first demonstrated by the Christ who abandoned divine prerogatives and "emptied himself" for the sake of others (Phil. 2:7). The sign of Paul's legitimacy as an apostle and servant of Christ was his participation in the sufferings of Christ (2 Cor. 4:10; cf. 6:4; 11:23). Those who continue Paul's task also deny themselves for the sake of others.

Paul's vision of ministerial leadership shaped by the church's distinctive identity has rarely been put into practice. Just as believers have superimposed their own experiences of community onto the church, they have looked to secular models to define Christian leadership. The dialectical leadership that involves the participation of all members in every aspect of community formation while they also recognize leaders who "have charge of" and "admonish" them (1 Thess. 5:12) is rare if not nonexistent. With few exceptions, two unintended consequences have resulted from the professionalization of ministry: (a) the failure to recognize that "member" is an image that suggests the indispensable participation in the body of Christ by each person; and (b) the loss of the focus on the cruciform nature of leadership. While seminaries provide the necessary skills for leadership roles, the standard academic curriculum is largely incapable of inculcating the self-denial that is inseparable from the Pauline understanding of leadership. The Pauline understanding is thus a continuing challenge for the contemporary church.

Conclusion

The Church after Christendom

Paul's letters give abundant evidence that the church has experienced an identity crisis from the beginning. In establishing communities that brought together different ethnic groups and social classes, Paul ensured a continuing struggle over the identity of the church. Confronted with the competing models of community that the converts brought with them, the churches faced numerous conflicts that threatened to destroy Paul's unprecedented attempt at community formation. Their challenge in the pre-Constantinian period has parallels to the challenges of the churches in the post-Constantinian period. Believers in Europe and North America now share with the ancient churches the challenge of living as minority communities in a society that is either indifferent or hostile to its presence. Like their ancient counterparts, they are surrounded by alternative understandings of community, as I observed in the introductory chapter. Inasmuch as a major purpose of Paul's letters is to define the church over against alternative views of community, I am convinced that Paul offers important guidance that is commonly overlooked in current discussions.

At one level the Pauline communities provided what one finds in all communities. Groups offer a place to belong, a source of personal identity, and a shared focus that holds them together. The group has its own insider vocabulary and common values that shape the outlook of the members. It also has its own narrative of the events surrounding its origins and the milestones along the way.[1] This identity creates boundaries from other groups that do not share the same values. However, while Paul's churches shared many of the characteristics

---

1. See Grenz, "Ecclesiology," 253–55.

that are common to all communities, he defined the church in a distinctive way. The church has its own narrative, practices, and *telos*, which it shares with no other community. Indeed, the people who confess the crucified Lord and participate in his destiny stand apart from other communities by living for others rather than meeting their own personal needs. As the community of the new age, it stands in sharp contrast to the communities of the present age. This identity provides a model for the contemporary church.

ECCLESIAL MODELS FOR TODAY

The Heir of Israel

Paul's insistence that the church is the heir of Israel, a common feature in all the Pauline letters, continues to give perspective to the search for identity. God calls communities rather than individuals, who live faithfully only in community. The election traditions, to which Paul frequently appeals, remind us that we enter a community with those whom we did not choose, but whom God has chosen. We do not come as consumers to choose a church according to our own tastes, for we have been chosen to enter into a covenant with God.

To live in continuity with Israel is to recognize that the believing community is a community of memory that continually repeats its founding narrative, which it reenacts through rituals. The people of God have known periods of triumph and of exile. They have been faithful at times and unfaithful at other times. Despite the moments of crisis and near annihilation, the community has survived, not because of its own strength but because of the faithfulness of God. If the church now faces decline in our own culture, it shares a history with ancestors who had to look for the remnant of those who had not bowed the knee to Baal (cf. Rom. 11:1–7). While we may appropriately devote our energies to reverse the trend, we recall that churches that decline in number may also be faithful witnesses.

The legacy of Israel is also a reminder of holiness as an essential characteristic of the church. As in ancient Israel, to be holy as God is holy (Lev. 19:2) is to maintain strong boundaries between the church and the world. Paul did not look to the world to set the agenda for the church. Nor did he ask the populace what they wished to find in a church. He recognized that only by sharply separating from the values of the world can the church serve the world and be a light to those who are in darkness (Phil. 2:15). While holiness involves separation for the surrounding community, a holy people is also a welcoming community to those who look for an alternative way of life.

The People in Christ

The church is united not only by its memory of the story of Israel but also by a shared confession. We confess that "Christ died for our sins in accordance with the scriptures" (1 Cor. 15:3) and that "Jesus is Lord" (Rom. 10:9; cf. 2 Cor. 4:5). Gentile believers have come into Israel's story, which culminates in the death and resurrection of Christ, the subject of our confession. In worship we repeat that confession in the ministry of the word and sacrament. Thus the church is not only a place to belong but also a community united by its confession of the lordship of Christ.

While the church is the heir of Israel, it has a separate identity as the people who are "in Christ." The variety of images that Paul uses for Christ—the one seed (cf. Gal. 3:16), the foundation of the building (1 Cor. 3:10), the temple (1 Cor. 3:16), the body of Christ (1 Cor. 12:12–13)—are elaborations of the phrase "in Christ." The images are reminders of the inseparability of Christ and the church. Paul knows no private relationship to Christ, for believers are incorporated into Christ with others. Unlike other communities, the church knows no boundaries between ethnic groups or social classes. Even though the presence of different social classes and ethnic groups creates the potential for conflict, the idea of the homogeneous church would be unacceptable to Paul.

In worship the church recalls its story in word, sacrament, and song. The Eucharist and baptism are occasions when the church retells the story and participates in it. While outsiders are welcome in the worship, the ministries of the word and song build up the community of faith by reaffirming the church's confession. The goal is neither the entertainment of outsiders nor the delight of the believing community but the formation of the people of God as they remember their story.

Today churches continue to remain largely homogeneous, and attempts to cross cultural boundaries frequently fail. As advocates of the church growth movement point out, people are more comfortable with those who share similar backgrounds and experiences. Indeed, most communities come together precisely because of common interests, education, and background. However, Paul challenges churches to recognize that faithfulness to the gospel requires that the church transcend the practices of other communities and bring together people of different cultures into one community.

God's Counterculture

As a people rescued from "the present evil age" (Gal. 1:4), the church is the community of the new creation (2 Cor. 5:17; Gal. 6:15). Therefore, the church has seen the future and now lives as an outpost of the new world. In bringing together different ethnic and social groups, it is a living demonstration of God's ultimate reconciling work. In baptism believers enter into "newness of life" (Rom. 6:4)—God's new world. God's counterculture is not "conformed to this world" but is "transformed" by the renewing of the mind (Rom. 12:2). Paul depicts this countercultural existence in his numerous ethical exhortations. To die with Christ is to participate in his self-denial (cf. 2 Cor. 5:14–15) and to live in a community where no members live for themselves or die for themselves (Rom. 14:7).

The Local and the Universal

Paul's dialectic of the church as both local and universal is a useful model for the contemporary church. Christian practice is fundamentally local, and each community is a full manifestation of the church. Thus the church is not a distant bureaucracy or an abstraction but a concrete reality. In Romans (12:3–7) and 1 Corinthians (12:12–27), the body of Christ is the local community, and every member is indispensable for the community's existence. The local community provides its own leadership and engages in acts of service independent of other authorities.

While the local community is the full manifestation of the church, it is not detached from the other local communities of believers. If "our commonwealth is in heaven" (Phil. 3:20 RSV), we belong to a community that is larger than the one we see regularly. Paul does not advocate a radical congregationalism that takes interest only in the welfare of the local community, for he assumes the regular cooperation among his churches in acts of service and mission. The competition between churches that accompanies radical congregationalism would have been abhorrent to him. Indeed, he envisions the cooperation among the Jewish and gentile Christian churches that maintain adherence to the Jewish boundary markers Paul has abandoned. In not requiring a uniformity of practice, Paul is thus a model for ecumenical engagement with others. When the disputed letters focus on the universal church, they emphasize what is already implicit in the undisputed letters.

This model of cooperation is especially appropriate at the present, when the expansion of Christianity has extended beyond Europe and North America. Paul's desire for *koinōnia* between the more affluent churches of the Diaspora and the impoverished churches of Jerusalem offers a model for a partnership between the churches of the developing countries and those in the traditional Christian countries. His insistence on *koinōnia* is not a form of paternalism but a form of genuine partnership in which the churches unite for a common cause.

The consciousness of the universal church liberates the local community from the narrow parochialism that identifies the people of God with one's own region or nation. The universal church can be a bridge of understanding among nations as it maintains interaction between believers around the world.

The Mission of the Church

For Paul the *missio Dei* is the transformation of a people into the image of Christ. The church is the new humanity, which is now being transformed. Paul's mission is to proclaim Christ and invite the people into this community. He writes letters and visits the churches he established to address obstacles in community formation and to encourage his converts. The converts demonstrate corporate formation as they share the destiny of Christ, deny themselves, and love others. Their mission is to grow up and to work together to complete the building that is under construction. Through this ethical behavior, they are a light to the world around them. Although they have no organized program of missions, they demonstrate a concern for evangelism as they communicate their faith to family and friends.

As the heir of Israel, the church's continuing task is to be the "children of light" (1 Thess. 5:5) who "shine like stars in the world" (Phil. 2:15). The church will fulfill this mission only when it distinguishes itself sharply from other communities and from its culture. Only when the church provides a sharp alternative to the values of its culture can it be a light shining in the darkness.

THE OUTCOME OF PAUL'S ECCLESIAL VISION

The Pauline model does not guarantee that the church will regain its prominent place in our culture or appear relevant to the majority population. Indeed, Paul never mentions the numerical growth of his congregations. In his letters he expresses disappointment over those who do not accept his message (Rom. 9:1–5; 10:16–21; 2 Cor. 3:14), and he acknowledges that his message divides the world into two groups—those who are saved and those who are perishing (1 Cor. 1:18; 2 Cor. 2:15). Despite his meager results, he refuses to alter his message, even when most do not accept it (2 Cor. 4:2–4). He continues preaching "Jesus Christ as Lord" (2 Cor. 4:5). The acceptance of his message is the result not of his own power or creativity but of the power of God at work in the church.

While Paul undoubtedly wanted the churches to grow, he gives primary attention in his letters to the transformation of communities into the image of Christ (Rom. 8:29). Legitimate growth occurs when the transformation of the believers is a light to people in darkness. If God can work through Paul's weakness, God can also empower his struggling churches to be faithful witnesses who are shaped by the story of the one who denied himself for the sake of others. Even communities of the marginalized can be a light to the larger society.

BIBLIOGRAPHY

Aasgaard, Reidar. *"My Beloved Brothers and Sisters!" Christian Siblingship in Paul.* JSNTSup 265. London: T&T Clark, 2004.

———. "'Role Ethics in Paul': The Significance of the Sibling Role for Paul's Ethical Thinking." *New Testament Studies* 48 (2002): 513–30.

Alexander, Loveday. "Paul and the Hellenistic Schools." Pages 60–83 in *Paul in His Hellenistic Context*. Edited by Troels Engberg-Pedersen. Minneapolis: Fortress, 1995.

Arnold, Clinton E. "Jesus Christ: 'Head' of the Church (Colossians and Ephesians)." Pages 346–66 in *Jesus of Nazareth: Lord and Christ; Essays on the Historical Jesus and New Testament Christology*. Edited by Joel B. Green and Max Turner. Grand Rapids: Eerdmans, 1994.

Ascough, Richard S. *Paul's Macedonian Associations: The Social Context of Philippians and 1 Thessalonians*. WUNT 2/161. Tübingen: Mohr Siebeck, 2003.

———. "The Thessalonian Christian Community as a Professional Voluntary Association." *Journal of Biblical Literature* 119 (2000): 311–28.

———. "Translocal Relationships among Voluntary Associations and Early Christianity." *Journal of Early Christian Studies* 5 (1997): 223–41.

———. "Voluntary Associations and the Formation of Pauline Christian Communities: Overcoming the Objections." Pages 149–83 in *Vereine, Synagogen und Gemeinden im kaiserzeitlichen Kleinasien*. Edited by Andreas Gutsfeld and Dietrich-Alex Koch. Studien und Texte zu Antike und Christentum 25. Tübingen: Mohr Siebeck, 2006.

———. *What Are They Saying about the Formation of Pauline Churches?* New York: Paulist Press, 1998.

Badcock, Gary D. *The House Where God Lives: Renewing the Doctrine of the Church for Today*. Grand Rapids: Eerdmans, 2009.

Balz, Horst, and Gerhard Schneider, eds. *Exegetical Dictionary of the New Testament*. 3 vols. Grand Rapids: Eerdmans, 1990–93.

Banks, Robert. *Paul's Idea of Community: The Early House Churches in Their Historical Setting.* Grand Rapids: Eerdmans, 1980.

Barclay, John M. G. "'Do We Undermine the Law?': A Study of Romans 14:1–15:6." Pages 287–308 in *Paul and the Mosaic Law.* Edited by James D. G. Dunn. Tübingen: Mohr Siebeck, 1996.

————. *Jews in the Mediterranean Diaspora: From Alexander to Trajan (323 BCE–117 BCE).* Edinburgh: T&T Clark, 1996.

————. "Money and Meetings: Group Formation among Diaspora Jews and Early Christians." Pages 113–27 in *Vereine, Synagogen und Gemeinden im kaiserzeitlichen Kleinasien.* Edited by Andreas Gutsfeld and Dietrich-Alex Koch. Studien und Texte zu Antike und Christentum 25. Tübingen: Mohr Siebeck, 2006.

————. "'Neither Jew nor Greek': Multiculturalism and the New Perspective on Paul." Pages 197–214 in *Ethnicity and the Bible.* Edited by Mark G. Brett. Leiden: Brill, 1996.

————. "Thessalonica and Corinth: Social Contrasts in Pauline Christianity." *Journal for the Study of the New Testament* 47 (1992): 49–74.

Barna, George. *Revolution.* Wheaton: Tyndale House, 2005.

Barrett, Lois. "The Church as Apostle to the World," Pages 110–40 in *Missional Church: A Vision for the Sending of the Church in North America.* Edited by Darrell L. Guder. Grand Rapids: Eerdmans, 1998.

Barth, Markus. "Jews and Gentiles: The Social Character of Justification in Paul." *Journal of Ecumenical Studies* 5 (1968): 241–67.

Barton, Bruce. *The Man Nobody Knows: A Discovery of Jesus.* Indianapolis: Bobbs-Merrill, 1925.

Bauer, Walter. *A Greek-English Lexicon of the New Testament and Other Early Christian Literature.* 3rd ed. Revised and edited by Frederick William Danker. Chicago: University of Chicago Press, 2000.

Beaton, Richard. "Reimagining the Church: Evangelical Ecclesiology." Pages 217–24 in *Evangelical Ecclesiology: Reality or Illusion?* Edited by John Stackhouse. Grand Rapids: Baker Academic, 2003.

Beckheuer, Burkhard. *Paulus und Jerusalem: Kollekte und Mission im theologischen Denken des Heidenapostels.* Berlin: Peter Lang, 1996.

Begbie, Jeremy S. "The Shape of Things to Come? Wright amidst Emerging Ecclesiologies." Pages 183–208 in *Jesus, Paul and the People of God.* Edited by Nicholas Perrin and Richard B. Hays. Downers Grove, IL: IVP Academic, 2011.

Bellah, Robert N., Richard Madsden, William Sullivan, Ann Swidler, and Stephen M. Tipton. "Individualism and the Crisis of Civic Membership." *Christian Century* 113, no. 16 (May 1986): 510–15.

Berger, Klaus. "Volksversammlung und Gemeinde Gottes: Zu den Anfängen der christlichen Verwendung von 'Ekklesia.'" *Zeitschrift für Theologie und Kirche* 73 (1976): 167–207.

Betz, Hans Dieter. *2 Corinthians 8 and 9.* Hermeneia. Philadelphia: Fortress, 1985.

————. *Galatians: A Commentary on Paul's Letter to the Churches of Galatia*. Hermeneia. Philadelphia: Fortress, 1979.

————. "Transferring a Ritual: Paul's Interpretation of Baptism in Romans 6." Pages 84–118 in *Paul in His Hellenistic Context*. Edited by Troels Engberg-Pedersen. Minneapolis: Fortress, 1995.

Beutler, J. "*martyreō, diamartyromai, martyromai.*" Pages 389–91 in vol. 2 of Balz and Schneider, *Exegetical Dictionary of the New Testament*.

Bockmuehl, Markus, and M. B. Thompson, eds. *A Vision for the Church: Studies in Early Christian Ecclesiology*. Edinburgh: T&T Clark, 1997.

Bohlen, Maren. *Sanctorum Communio: Die Christen als "Heilige" bei Paulus*. Beihefte zur Zeitschrift für die neutestamentliche Wissenschaft und die Kunde der älteren Kirche 183. Berlin: de Gruyter, 2011.

Borg, Marcus. *Jesus, a New Vision: Spirit, Culture and the Life of Discipleship*. San Francisco: HarperSanFrancisco, 1991.

Bornkamm, Günther. *Paul*. Translated by D. M. G. Stalker. New York: Harper & Row, 1969.

Bosch, David J. *Transforming Mission: Paradigm Shifts in Theology of Mission*. Maryknoll, NY: Orbis, 1999.

Bowers, Paul. "Church and Mission in Paul." *Journal for the Study of the New Testament* 44 (1991): 89–111.

Brockhaus, Ulrich. *Charisma und Amt: Die paulinische Charismenlehre auf dem Hintergrund der frühchristlichen Gemeindefunktionen*. Wuppertal: Brockhaus, 1987.

Brower, Kent E., and Andy Johnson, eds. *The Holy One of God and His Disciples: Holiness and Ecclesiology in the New Testament*. Grand Rapids: Eerdmans, 2007.

Bultmann, Rudolf. *Theology of the New Testament*. Vol. 1. London: SCM, 1965.

Burchard, Christoph. "The Importance of Joseph and Aseneth for the Study of the New Testament: A General Survey and a Fresh Look at the Lord's Supper." *New Testament Studies* 33 (1987): 102–34.

Burnett, Gary W. *Paul and the Salvation of the Individual*. Biblical Interpretation Series 57. Leiden: Brill, 2001.

Calvin, John. *Institutes of the Christian Religion*. Translated by Henry Beveridge. 2 vols. Grand Rapids: Eerdmans, 1962.

Campbell, Constantine R. *Paul and Union with Christ: An Exegetical and Theological Study*. Grand Rapids: Zondervan, 2012.

Campenhausen, Hans von. *Ecclesiastical Authority and Spiritual Power in the First Three Centuries*. Stanford: Stanford University Press, 1969.

Carter, Timothy L. "Looking at the Metaphor of Christ's Body in 1 Corinthians 12." Pages 93–115 in *Paul: Jew, Greek, and Roman*. Pauline Studies 5. Edited by Stanley E. Porter. Leiden: Brill, 2008.

Charry, Ellen T. "Sacramental Ecclesiology." Pages 201–16 in *The Community of the Word: Toward an Evangelical Ecclesiology*. Edited by Mark Husbands and Daniel J. Treier. Downers Grove, IL: IVP Academic, 2005.

Ciampa, Roy E. "Paul's Theology of the Gospel." Pages 180–91 in *Paul as Missionary: Identity, Activity, Theology, and Practice*. Edited by Trevor J. Burke and Brian S. Rosner. Library of New Testament Studies 420. Edinburgh: T&T Clark, 2011.

Clarke, Andrew D. "'Be Imitators of Me': Paul's Model of Leadership." *Tyndale Bulletin* 49 (1998): 329–60.

———. *A Pauline Theology of Church Leadership*. Library of New Testament Studies. Edinburgh: T&T Clark, 2008.

———. *Serve the Community of the Church: Christians as Leaders and Ministers*. Grand Rapids: Eerdmans, 2000.

Collins, Raymond F. "The Church of the Thessalonians." Pages 285–98 in *Studies on the First Letter to the Thessalonians*. Bibliotheca ephemeridum theologicarum lovaniensium 66. Leuven: University Press/Peeters, 1984.

———. *The Many Faces of the Church: A Study in New Testament Ecclesiology*. New York: Crossroad, 2004.

Colson, F. H., and G. H. Whitaker. *Philo, with an English Translation*. LCL. Cambridge, MA: Harvard University Press, 1962.

Conzelmann, Hans. *An Outline of the Theology of the New Testament*. Translated by John Bowden. New York: Harper, 1969.

Crossan, John Dominic. *The Historical Jesus: The Life of a Mediterranean Jewish Peasant*. San Francisco: HarperSanFrancisco, 1991.

Cummins, Stephen Anthony. "Divine Life and Corporate Christology: God, Messiah Jesus, and the Covenant Community in Paul." Pages 109–209 in *Messiah in the Old and New Testaments*. Edited by Stanley E. Porter. Grand Rapids: Eerdmans, 2007.

Dahl, Nils Alstrup. "The Doctrine of Justification: Its Social Function and Implications." Pages 95–120 in *Studies in Paul: Theology for the Early Christian Mission*. Minneapolis: Augsburg, 1977.

———. "Interpreting Ephesians: Then and Now." Pages 461–73 in *Studies in Ephesians: Introductory Questions, Text- and Edition-Critical Issues, Interpretation of Texts and Themes*. Edited by David Hellholm, Vemund Blomkvist, and Tord Fornberg. WUNT 161. Tübingen: Mohr Siebeck, 2000.

Das, A. Andrew. "1 Corinthians 11:17–34 Revisited." *Concordia Theological Quarterly* 62 (1998): 187–208.

Dickson, John P. *Mission-Commitment in Ancient Judaism and in the Pauline Communities: The Shape, Extent and Background of Early Christian Mission*. Tübingen: Mohr Siebeck, 2003.

Doerksen, Paul. "The Air Is Not Quite Fresh: Emerging Church Ecclesiology." *Direction* 39, no. 1 (2010): 3–18.

Donfried, Karl P. "The Assembly of the Thessalonians: Reflections on the Ecclesiology of the Earliest Christian Letter." Pages 390–408 in *Ekklesiologie des Neuen Testaments, für Karl Kertelge*. Edited by Rainer Kampling and Thomas Söding. Freiburg: Herder, 1996.

Dostoyevsky, Fyodor. *The Brothers Karamazov*. Translated by Constance Garnett. New York: New American Library, 1957.

Downs, David J. *The Offering of the Gentiles: Paul's Collection for Jerusalem in Its Chronological, Cultural, and Cultic Contexts*. WUNT 2/248. Tübingen: Mohr Siebeck, 2008.

Du Toit, Andrie. "Paulus Oecumenicus: Interculturality in the Shaping of Paul's Theology." *New Testament Studies* 55 (2009): 121–43.

Dübbers, Michael. *Christologie und Existenz im Kolosserbrief: Exegetische und semantische Untersuchungen zur Intention des Kolosserbriefes*. WUNT 2/191. Tübingen: Mohr Siebeck, 2005.

Duff, Paul Brooks. "Transformed 'from Glory to Glory': Paul's Appeal to the Experience of His Readers in 2 Corinthians 3:18." *Journal of Biblical Literature* 127 (2008): 759–80.

Dunn, James D. G., ed. *The Cambridge Companion to St. Paul*. Cambridge: Cambridge University Press, 2003.

———. *Jesus Remembered*. Vol. 1 of *Christianity in the Making*. Grand Rapids: Eerdmans, 2003.

———. *The Theology of Paul's Letter to the Galatians*. New Testament Theology. Cambridge: Cambridge University Press, 1993.

———. *The Theology of Paul the Apostle*. Grand Rapids: Eerdmans, 1998.

———. *Unity and Diversity in the New Testament: An Inquiry into the Character of Earliest Christianity*. Philadelphia: Westminster, 1977.

Dunson, Ben C. *Individual and Community in Paul's Letter to the Romans*. WUNT 2/332. Tübingen: Mohr Siebeck, 2012.

———. "The Individual and Community in Twentieth- and Twenty-First-Century Pauline Scholarship." *Currents in Biblical Research* 9 (2010): 63–97.

Ebel, Eva. *Die Attraktivität früher christlicher Gemeinden: Die Gemeinde von Korinth im Spiegel griechisch-römischer Vereine*. WUNT 2/178. Tübingen: Mohr Siebeck, 2004.

Eckert, Jost. "ἐκλεκτός." Pages 417–19 in vol. 1 of Balz and Schneider, *Exegetical Dictionary of the New Testament*.

Elliott, John H. "The Jesus Movement Was Not Egalitarian but Family-Oriented." *Biblical Interpretation* 11 (2003): 173–210.

———. "Jesus Was Not an Egalitarian." *Biblical Theology Bulletin* 32 (2002): 75–91.

Ernst, Josef. "Von der Ortsgemeinde zur Grosskirche: Dargestellt an den Kirchenmodellen des Philipper- und Epheserbriefes." Pages 123–42 in *Kirche im Werden: Studien zum Thema Amt und Gemeinde im Neuen Testament—in Zusammenarbeit mit dem Collegium Biblicum München*. Edited by Josef Hainz. Munich: Schöningh, 1976.

Esler, Philip Francis. "Family Imagery and Christian Identity in Galatians 5:13 to 6:10." Pages 121–49 in *Constructing Early Christian Families: Family as Social Reality and Metaphor*. Edited by Halvor Moxnes. London: Routledge, 1997.

Farmer, W. R. "Peter and Paul, and the Tradition Concerning the 'Lord's Supper' in 1 Corinthians 11:23–26." Pages 119–40 in *One Loaf, One Cup: Ecumenical Studies of 1 Corinthians 11 and Other Eucharistic Texts*. The Cambridge Conference on the Eucharist, August 1988. Edited by Otto Knoch and Ben F. Meyer. Macon, GA: Mercer University Press, 1988.

Fatum, Lone. "'Brotherhood in Christ': A Gender Hermeneutical Reading of 1 Thessalonians." Pages 183–97 in *Constructing Early Christian Families: Family as Social Reality and Metaphor*. Edited by Halvor Moxnes. London: Routledge, 1997.

Ferguson, Everett. *The Church of Christ: A Biblical Ecclesiology for Today*. Grand Rapids: Eerdmans, 1996.

Finke, Roger, and Rodney Stark. *The Churching of America, 1776–2005: Winners and Losers in Our Religious Economy*. New Brunswick, NJ: Rutgers University Press, 2005.

Finsterbusch, Karin. *Die Thora als Lebensweisung für Heidenchristen: Studien zur Bedeutung der Thora für die paulinische Ethik*. Göttingen: Vandenhoeck & Ruprecht, 1996.

Fotopoulos, John. *Food Offered to Idols in Roman Corinth: A Social Rhetorical Reconsideration of 1 Corinthians 8:1–11:1*. WUNT 2/151. Tübingen: Mohr Siebeck, 2003.

Frank, Nicole. *Der Kolosserbrief im Kontext des paulinischen Erbes: Eine intertextuelle Studie zur Auslegung und Fortschreibung der Paulustradition*. WUNT 2/271. Tübingen: Mohr Siebeck, 2009.

Franke, John R. *The Character of Theology: An Introduction to Its Nature, Task, and Purpose*. Grand Rapids: Baker Academic, 2005.

Friesen, Steven J. "Paul and Economics: The Jerusalem Collection as an Alternative to Patronage." Pages 27–54 in *Paul Unbound: Other Perspectives on the Apostle*. Edited by Mark D. Given. Peabody, MA: Hendrickson, 2010.

Funk, Robert W. *Honest to Jesus: Jesus for a New Millennium*. San Francisco: HarperSanFrancisco, 1997.

Funk, Robert W., and Roy W. Hoover. *The Five Gospels: The Search for the Authentic Words of Jesus; New Translation and Commentary*. New York: Macmillan, 1993.

Gadenz, Pablo T. *Called from the Jews and from the Gentiles: Pauline Ecclesiology in Romans 9–11*. WUNT 2/267. Tübingen: Mohr Siebeck, 2009.

Gager, John G. *Kingdom and Community: The Social World of Early Christianity*. Englewood Cliffs, NJ: Prentice-Hall, 1975.

Gaventa, Beverly. "The Maternity of Paul: An Exegetical Study of Galatians 4:19." Pages 189–201 in *The Conversation Continues*. Edited by Robert Fortna. Nashville: Abingdon, 1990.

Gehring, Roger W. *House Church and Mission: The Importance of Household Structures in Early Christianity*. Peabody, MA: Hendrickson, 2004.

Gerber, Christine. "Die alte Braut und Christus Leib: Zum ekklesiologischen Entwurf des Epheserbriefs." *New Testament Studies* 59 (2013): 192–221.

Gese, Michael. *Das Vermächtnis des Apostels: Die Rezeption der paulinischen Theologie im Epheserbrief.* WUNT 2/99. Tübingen: Mohr Siebeck, 1997.

Glad, Clarence E. *Paul and Philodemus: Adaptability in Epicurean and Early Christian Psychagogy.* Novum Testamentum Supplement Series 81. Leiden: Brill, 1995.

Gnilka, Joachim. "Die Kollekte der paulinischen Gemeinden für Jerusalem als Ausdruck ekklesialer Gemeinschaft." Pages 301–15 in *Ekklesiologie des Neuen Testaments, für Karl Kertelge.* Edited by Rainer Kampling and Thomas Söding. Freiburg: Herder, 1996.

Goheen, Michael. "Bible and Mission: Missiology and Biblical Scholarship in Dialogue." Pages 208–32 in *Christian Mission: Old Testament Foundations and New Testament Developments.* Edited by Stanley E. Porter and Cynthia Long Westfall. Eugene, OR: Pickwick, 2010.

Gordley, Matthew E. *The Colossian Hymn in Context: An Exegesis in Light of Jewish and Greco-Roman Hymnic and Epistolary Conventions.* WUNT 2/228. Tübingen: Mohr Siebeck, 2007.

Gorman, Michael J. *Cruciformity: Paul's Narrative Spirituality of the Cross.* Grand Rapids: Eerdmans, 2001.

———. "Romans: The First Christian Treatise on Theosis." *Journal of Theological Interpretation* 5 (Spring 2011): 13–34.

———. *Inhabiting the Cruciform God: Kenosis, Justification, and Theosis in Paul's Narrative Soteriology.* Grand Rapids: Eerdmans, 2009.

Green, Michael. *Evangelism in the Early Church.* Grand Rapids: Eerdmans, 1970.

Grenz, Stanley J. "Ecclesiology." Pages 252–66 in *The Cambridge Companion to Postmodern Theology.* Edited by Kevin J. Vanhoozer. Cambridge: Cambridge University Press, 2003.

———. *Renewing the Center: Evangelical Theology in a Post-Theological Era.* Grand Rapids: Baker, 2000.

Grundmann, Walter. "σύν, κτλ." Pages 766–96 in vol. 7 of Kittel and Friedrich, *Theological Dictionary of the New Testament.*

Guder, Darrell L., ed. *Missional Church: A Vision for the Sending of the Church in North America.* Grand Rapids: Eerdmans, 1998.

Hainz, Josef. *Ekklesia: Strukturen paulinischer Gemeinde-Theologie und Gemeinde-Ordnung.* Biblische Untersuchungen 9. Regensburg: Pustet, 1972.

———. "Gemeinschaft (κοινωνία) zwischen Paulus und Jerusalem (Gal. 2:9f)." Pages 125–36 in *Neues Testament und Kirche: Gesammelte Aufsätze.* Edited by Josef Hainz. Regensburg: Pustet, 2006.

———, ed. *Kirche im Werden: Studien zum Thema Amt und Gemeinde im Neuen Testament—in Zusammenarbeit mit dem Collegium Biblicum München.* Munich: Schöningh, 1976.

———. "*Koinōnia.*" Pages 303–5 in vol. 2 of Balz and Schneider, *Exegetical Dictionary of the New Testament.*

———. *Koinonia: "Kirche" als Gemeinschaft bei Paulus*. Biblische Untersuchungen 16. Regensburg: Pustet, 1982.

Harnack, Adolf. *The Mission and Expansion of Christianity in the First Three Centuries*. New York: Harper, 1962.

———. *What Is Christianity?* Edited by T. Bailey Saunders. New York: Harper & Row, 1957.

Harris, Murray J. *Prepositions and Theology in the Greek New Testament: An Essential Reference Resource for Exegesis*. Grand Rapids: Zondervan, 2012.

Harrison, James R. *Paul's Language of Grace in Its Graeco-Roman Context*. WUNT 2/172. Tübingen: Mohr Siebeck, 2003.

Hartman, Lars. "Code and Context: A Few Reflections on the Paraenesis of Colossians 3:18–4:1." Pages 237–47 in *Tradition and Interpretation of the New Testament*. Edited by G. F. Hawthorne and Otto Betz. Grand Rapids: Eerdmans, 1987.

Hauerwas, Stanley. *A Community of Character: Toward a Constructive Christian Social Ethic*. Notre Dame, IN: University of Notre Dame Press, 1981.

Heard, Gerry C. *Basic Values and Ethical Decisions: An Examination of Individualism and Community in American Society*. Malabar, FL: Krieger, 1990.

Hengel, Martin. "The Origins of the Christian Mission." Pages 48–64 in *Between Jesus and Paul: Studies in the Earliest History of Christianity*. Philadelphia: Fortress, 1983.

Hofius, Otfried. "Gemeinschaft am Tisch des Herrn: Das Zeugnis des Neuen Testaments." Pages 169–83 in *Einheit der Kirche im Neuen Testament*. Dritte europäische orthodox-westliche Exegetenkonferenz in Sankt Petersburg, 24–31. August 2005. Edited by Anatoly A. Alexeev, Christos Karakolis, and Ulrich Luz with Karl-Wilhelm Niebuhr. WUNT 2/218. Tübingen: Mohr Siebeck, 2008.

———. "The Lord's Supper and the Lord's Supper Tradition: Reflections on 1 Corinthians 11:23b–25." Pages 75–115 in *One Loaf, One Cup: Ecumenical Studies of 1 Corinthians 11 and Other Eucharistic Texts*. Edited by Otto Knoch and Ben F. Meyer. The Cambridge Conference on the Eucharist, August 1988. Macon, GA: Mercer, 1991.

Hogeterp, Albert L. A. *Paul and God's Temple: A Historical Interpretation of Cultic Imagery in the Corinthian Correspondence*. Biblical Tools and Studies 2. Leuven: Peeters, 2006.

Hollander, Harm W. "The Idea of Fellowship in 1 Corinthians 10.14–22." *New Testament Studies* 55 (2009): 256–70.

Holmberg, Bengt. *Paul and Power: The Structure of Authority in the Primitive Church as Reflected in the Pauline Epistles*. Philadelphia: Fortress, 1978.

Holtz, Traugott. *Der erste Brief an die Thessalonicher*. Evangelisch-Katholischer Kommentar zum Neuen Testament 13. 3rd ed. Neukirchen: Neukirchener Verlag, 1998.

Hooker, Morna. "Interchange in Christ and Ethics." *Journal for the Study of the New Testament* 25 (1985): 3–17.

———. "Were There False Teachers in Colossae?" Pages 315–31 in *Christ and the Spirit in the New Testament*. Edited by Barnabas Lindars and Stephen S. Smalley in Honour of Charles Francis Digby Moule. Cambridge: Cambridge University Press, 1973. Reprinted as pages 121–36 in *From Adam to Christ: Essays on Paul*. Cambridge: Cambridge University Press, 1990.

Horrell, David G. "'No Longer Jew or Greek': Paul's Corporate Christology and the Construction of Christian Community." Pages 321–44 in *Christology, Controversy, and Community: New Testament Essays in Honour of David R. Catchpole*. Edited by David G. Horrell and Christopher M. Tuckett. Leiden: Brill, 2000.

———. *The Social Ethos of the Corinthian Correspondence: Interests and Ideology from 1 Corinthians to 1 Clement*. Edinburgh: T&T Clark, 1996.

Horsley, Richard A. "1 Corinthians: A Case Study of Paul's Assembly as an Alternative Society." Pages 242–52 in *Paul and Empire: Religion and Power in Roman Imperial Society*. Edited by Richard A. Horsley. Harrisburg, PA: Trinity Press International, 1997.

———. *Jesus and the Powers: Conflict, Covenant, and the Hope of the Poor*. Minneapolis: Fortress, 2011.

Hotze, Gerhard. "Gemeinde als Schicksalsgemeinschaft mit Christus (2 Kor 1,3–11)." Pages 336–55 in *Ekklesiologie des Neuen Testaments, für Karl Kertelge*. Edited by Rainer Kampling and Thomas Söding. Freiburg: Herder, 1996.

Hunsberger, George. "Missional Vocation: Called and Sent to Represent the Reign of God." Pages 77–109 in *Missional Church: A Vision for the Sending of the Church in North America*. Edited by Darrell L. Guder. Grand Rapids: Eerdmans, 1998.

Hunter, James Davison. *To Change the World: The Irony, Tragedy, and Possibility of Christianity in the Late Modern World*. New York: Oxford University Press, 2010.

Hvalvik, Reidar. "'The Churches of the Saints': Paul's Concern for Unity in His References to the Christian Communities." *Tidsskrift for Teologi og Kirke* 78, no. 3–4 (2007): 227–47.

Jeremias, Joachim. "*Abraam*." Pages 8–9 in vol. 1 of Kittel and Friedrich, *Theological Dictionary of the New Testament*.

Jewett, Robert. *The Thessalonian Correspondence: Pauline Rhetoric and Millenarian Piety*. Philadelphia: Fortress, 1986.

Johnson, Andy. "The Sanctification of the Imagination in 1 Thessalonians." Pages 275–92 in *Holiness and Ecclesiology in the New Testament*. Edited by Kent E. Brower and Andy Johnson. Grand Rapids: Eerdmans, 2007.

Johnson, Luke Timothy. "Making Connections: The Material Expression of Friendship in the New Testament." *Interpretation* 58 (2004): 158–71.

———. "Paul's Ecclesiology." Pages 199–211 in *The Cambridge Companion to St. Paul*. Edited by James D. G. Dunn. Cambridge: Cambridge University Press, 2003.

Joubert, Stephan. *Paul as Benefactor: Reciprocity, Strategy and Theological Reflection in Paul's Collection*. WUNT 2/124. Tübingen: Mohr Siebeck, 2000.

Judge, E. A. "Contemporary Political Models for the Interrelations of the New Testament Churches." Pages 586–96 in *The First Christians in the Roman World: Augustan and New Testament Essays*. WUNT 2/229. Edited by E. A. Judge and James R. Harrison. Tübingen: Mohr Siebeck, 2008.

————. "The Early Christians as a Scholastic Community?" Pages 526–52 in *The First Christians in the Roman World.* WUNT 2/229. Edited by E. A. Judge and James R. Harrison. Tübingen: Mohr Siebeck, 2008.

Kaminsky, Joel S. *Corporate Responsibility in the Hebrew Bible.* Journal for the Study of the Old Testament: Supplement Series. Sheffield: Sheffield Academic, 1995.

Kampling, Rainer, and Thomas Söding, eds. *Ekklesiologie des Neuen Testaments, für Karl Kertelge.* Freiburg: Herder, 1996.

Karris, Robert J. "The Background and Significance of the Polemic of the Pastoral Epistles." *Journal of Biblical Literature* 92 (1978): 549–64.

Käsemann, Ernst. *Jesus Means Freedom.* Translated by Frank Clarke. Philadelphia: Fortress, 1969.

————. "Paul and Early Catholicism." Pages 236–51 in *New Testament Questions of Today.* Philadelphia: Fortress, 1969.

Kidd, Reggie W. *Wealth and Beneficence in the Pastoral Epistles: A "Bourgeois" Form of Early Christianity?* Atlanta: Scholars Press, 1990.

Kilde, Jeanne Halgren. *When Church Became Theatre: The Transformation of Evangelical Architecture and Worship in Nineteenth-Century America.* Oxford: Oxford University Press, 2002.

Kim, Byung-mo. *De paulinische Kollekte.* Tübingen: Francke, 2002.

Kim, Seyoon. "Paul as an Eschatological Herald." Pages 9–24 in *Paul as Missionary.* London: T&T Clark, 2011.

Kittel, Gerhard, and Gerhard Friedrich, eds. *Theological Dictionary of the New Testament.* Translated by G. W. Bromiley. 10 vols. Grand Rapids: Eerdmans, 1964–1976.

Klaiber, Walter. *Rechtfertigung und Gemeinde: Eine Untersuchung zum paulinischen Kirchenverständnis.* Göttingen: Vandenhoeck & Ruprecht, 1982.

Klauck, Hans-Josef. *Herrenmahl und Hellenistischer Kult: Eine religionsgeschichtliche Untersuchung zum ersten Korintherbrief.* Neutestamentliche Abhandlungen. Second Series 15. Münster: Aschendorff, 1982.

Klehn, Lars. "Die Verwendung von ἐν Χριστῷ bei Paulus: Erwägungen zu den Wandlungen in der paulinischen Theologie." *Biblische Notizen* 74 (1994): 66–79.

Knoch, Otto, and Ben F. Meyer, eds. *One Loaf, One Cup: Ecumenical Studies of 1 Corinthians 11 and Other Eucharistic Texts.* The Cambridge Conference on the Eucharist, August 1988. Macon, GA: Mercer University Press, 1988.

Kraftchik, Steven J. "Death in Us, Life in You: The Apostolic Medium." Pages 156–81 in *Pauline Theology,* vol. 2, *1 and 2 Corinthians.* Edited by David M. Hay. Minneapolis: Fortress, 1993.

Kraus, Wolfgang. *Das Volk Gottes: Zur Grundlegung der Ekklesiologie bei Paulus.* WUNT 2/85. Tübingen: Mohr Siebeck, 1996.

Kremer, J. *"Thlipsis."* Page 152 in vol. 2 of Balz and Schneider, *Exegetical Dictionary of the New Testament.*

Küng, Hans. *The Church.* New York: Sheed and Ward, 1967.

Lambrecht, Jan. "A Call to Witness by All: Evangelisation in 1 Thessalonians." Pages 321–43 in *Teologie in Konteks. Opgedra an A. B. du Toit*. Edited by J. H. Roberts, W. S. Vorster, J. N. Vorster, et al. Pretoria: Orion, 1991.

———. "Transformation in 2 Corinthians 3.18." *Biblica* 64 (1983): 243–54.

Lampe, Peter. "The Eucharist: Identifying with Christ on the Cross." *Interpretation* 48 (1994): 36–49.

———. *Die stadtrömischen Christen in den ersten beiden Jahrhunderten*. 2nd ed. Tübingen: Mohr Siebeck, 1989.

Laub, Franz. "Paulus als Gemeindegründer (1 Thess)." Pages 17–38 in *Kirche im Werden: Studien zum Thema Amt und Gemeinde im Neuen Testament—in Zusammenarbeit mit dem Collegium Biblicum München*. Edited by Josef Hainz. Munich: Schöningh, 1976.

Lee, Michelle V. *Paul, the Stoics, and the Body of Christ*. Society for New Testament Studies Monograph Series 137. Cambridge: Cambridge University Press, 2006.

Lehmeier, Karin. *Oikos und Oikonomia: Antike Konzepte der Haushaltsführung und der Bau der Gemeinde bei Paulus*. Marburg: Elwert Verlag, 2006.

Levison, John R. "The Spirit and the Temple in Paul's Letters to the Corinthians." Pages 237–47 in *Paul and His Theology*. Edited by Stanley Porter. Leiden: Brill, 2006.

Lindemann, Andreas. "Die Kirche als Leib: Beobachtungen zur 'demokratischen' Ekklesiologie bei Paulus." *Zeitschrift für Theologie und Kirche* 92 (1995): 140–65.

Lohfink, Gerhard. *Gegen die Verharmlosung Jesu: Reden über Jesus und die Kirche*. Freiburg: Herder, 2013.

———. *Jesus and Community: The Social Dimension of Christian Faith*. Philadelphia: Fortress, 1984.

Loisy, Alfred. *The Gospel and the Church*. Translated by Christopher Home. Philadelphia: Fortress, 1976.

Longenecker, Bruce W. *Remember the Poor: Paul, Poverty, and the Greco-Roman World*. Grand Rapids: Eerdmans, 2010.

Longenecker, Richard N. *Galatians*. Word Biblical Commentary. Dallas: Word, 1990.

Löning, Karl. "'Säule und Fundament der Wahrheit' (1 Tim. 3:15): Zur Ekklesiologie der Pastoralbriefe." Pages 409–30 in *Ekklesiologie des Neuen Testaments, für Karl Kertelge*. Edited by Rainer Kampling and Thomas Söding. Freiburg: Herder, 1996.

Luz, Ulrich. "Ortsgemeinde und Gemeinschaft im Neuen Testament." *Evangelische Theologie* 70 (2010): 404–15.

Mack, Burton. *A Myth of Innocence*. Philadelphia: Fortress, 1988.

Magda, Ksenija. *Paul's Territoriality and Mission Strategy: Searching for the Geographical Awareness behind Romans*. WUNT 2/266. Tübingen: Mohr Siebeck, 2009.

Malherbe, Abraham J. "God's Family at Thessalonica." Pages 117–28 in *The Social World of the First Christians: Studies in Honor of Wayne A. Meeks*. Edited by L. Michael White and L. O. Yarbrough. Minneapolis: Fortress, 1995.

———. *The Letters to the Thessalonians: A New Translation with Introduction and Commentary*. Anchor Bible 32B. New York: Doubleday, 2000.

———. "Medical Imagery in the Pastoral Epistles." Pages 19–35 in *Texts and Testaments*. Edited by W. Eugene Marsh and Stuart Dickson Currie. San Antonio: Trinity University Press, 1980.

———. "'Pastoral Care' in the Thessalonian Church." *New Testament Studies* 36 (1990): 375–91.

———. *Paul and the Thessalonians: The Philosophic Tradition of Pastoral Care*. Philadelphia: Fortress, 1987.

———. *Social Aspects of Early Christianity*. Baton Rouge: Louisiana State University Press, 1977.

Marshall, I. H. "Who Were the Evangelists?" Pages 251–63 in *The Mission of the Church to Jews and Gentiles*. Edited by Adna Jostein. WUNT 127. Tübingen: Mohr Siebeck, 2000.

Marshall, Peter. *Enmity at Corinth: Social Conventions in Paul's Relations with the Corinthians*. WUNT 2/23. Tübingen: Mohr, 1987.

Martyn, J. Louis. *Galatians: A New Translation with Introduction and Commentary*. Anchor Bible 33A. New York: Doubleday, 1997.

Matera, Frank J. *God's Saving Grace: A Pauline Theology*. Grand Rapids: Eerdmans, 2012.

McGavran, Donald. *Church Growth: Strategies That Work*. Nashville: Abingdon, 1980.

———. *Understanding Church Growth*. Rev. ed. Grand Rapids: Eerdmans, 1980.

McKnight, Scot. "Five Streams of the Emerging Church," *Christianity Today* 51, no. 2 (2007): 35–39.

McLaren, Brian. *Everything Must Change: Jesus, Global Crises, and a Revolution of Hope*. Nashville: Thomas Nelson, 2007.

———. *Generous Orthodoxy: Why I Am a Missional, Evangelical, Post/Protestant, Liberal/Conservative, Mystical/Poetic, Biblical, Charismatic/Contemplative, Fundamentalist/Calvinist, Anabaptist/Anglican, Methodist, Catholic, Green, Incarnational, Depressed-Yet-Hopeful, Emergent, Unfinished Christian*. Grand Rapids: Zondervan, 2004.

Meeks, Wayne A. *The First Urban Christians: The Social World of the Apostle Paul*. New Haven: Yale University Press, 1983.

Michel, Otto. "*oikos ktl.*" Pages 119–59 in vol. 5 of Kittel and Friedrich, *Theological Dictionary of the New Testament*.

Minear, Paul S. *Images of the Church in the New Testament*. Philadelphia: Westminster, 1960.

Mitchell, Margaret M. *Paul and the Rhetoric of Reconciliation: An Exegetical Investigation of the Language and Composition of 1 Corinthians*. Hermeneutische Untersuchungen zur Theologie 28. Tübingen: Mohr Siebeck, 1991.

Müller, Christoph Gregor. *Gottes Pflanzung—Gottes Bau—Gottes Tempel. Die metaphorische Dimension paulinischer Gemeindetheologie in 1. Kor 3,5–17*. Fuldaer Studien 5. Frankfurt am Main: Knecht, 1995.

Murphy-O'Connor, Jerome. *St. Paul's Corinth: Texts and Archaeology*. Collegeville, MN: Liturgical Press, 1990.

Mußner, Franz. *Der Galaterbrief: Herders Theologische Kommentar zum Neuen Testament.* Freiburg: Herder, 1977.

Newbigin, Lesslie. *Foolishness to the Greeks: The Gospel and Western Culture.* Grand Rapids: Eerdmans, 1986.

———. *The Open Secret: An Introduction to the Theology of Mission.* Rev. ed. Grand Rapids: Eerdmans, 1978.

Niebuhr, H. Richard. *Christ and Culture.* New York: Harper & Row, 1951.

O'Brien, Peter Thomas. *The Epistle to the Philippians: A Commentary on the Greek Text.* Grand Rapids: Eerdmans, 1991.

———. *Gospel and Mission in the Writings of Paul: An Exegetical and Theological Analysis.* Grand Rapids: Baker, 1995.

O'Donnell, Matthew Brook. "Two Opposing Views on Baptism with/by the Holy Spirit and of 1 Corinthians 12:13: Can Grammatical Investigation Bring Clarity?" Pages 311–36 in *Baptism, the New Testament and the Church.* Edited by Matthew Brook O'Donnell. Sheffield: Sheffield Academic Press, 1999.

O'Donovan, Oliver. *On the Thirty-Nine Articles: A Conversation with Tudor Christianity.* Exeter, UK: Paternoster, 1986.

Ogereau, Julien M. "The Jerusalem Collection as Koinōnia: Paul's Global Politics of Socio-economic Equality and Solidarity." *New Testament Studies* 58 (2012): 369–78.

O'Leary, Amy. "Building Congregations around Art Galleries and Cafes as Spirituality Wanes." *New York Times*, December 29, 2012. http://www.nytimes.com/2012/12/30/us/new-churches-focus-on-building-a-community-life.html.

Ollrog, Wolf-Henning. *Paulus und seine Mitarbeiter: Untersuchung zu Theorie und Praxis der paulinischen Mission.* Neukirchen-Vluyn: Neukirchener Verlag, 1979.

Perrin, Nicholas. "Jesus's Eschatology and Kingdom Ethics: Ever the Twain Shall Meet." Pages 92–114 in *Jesus, Paul and the People of God.* Downers Grove, IL: IVP Academic, 2011.

Peterson, Brian K. "Being the Church in Philippi." *Horizons in Biblical Theology* 30 (2008): 163–78.

Pew Forum. "'Nones' on the Rise." The Pew Forum on Religion and Public Life, October 9, 2012, http://www.pewforum.org/2012/10/09/nones-on-the-rise/.

Pilhofer, Peter. *Die frühen Christen und ihre Welt: Greifswalder Aufsätze 1996–2001.* WUNT 2/145. Tübingen: Mohr Siebeck, 2002.

———. "Die Ökonomische Attraktivität christlicher Gemeinden der Frühzeit." Pages 194–216 in *Die frühen Christen und ihre Welt Greifswalder Aufsätze 1996–2001.* WUNT 2/145. Tübingen: Mohr Siebeck, 2002.

———. "Περὶ δὲ τῆς φιλαδελφίας . . . (1 Thess 4:9): Ekklesiologische Überlegungen zu einem Proprium früher christlicher Gemeinden." Pages 139–53 in *Die frühen Christen und ihre Welt: Greifswalder Aufsätze 1996–2001.* WUNT 2/145. Tübingen: Mohr Siebeck, 2002.

Plummer, Robert L. *Paul's Understanding of the Church's Mission: Did the Apostle Paul Expect the Early Christian Communities to Evangelize?* Paternoster Biblical Monographs. Waynesboro, GA: Paternoster, 2006.

Pogoloff, Stephen M. *Logos and Sophia: The Rhetorical Situation of 1 Corinthians.* Society of Biblical Literature Dissertation Series 134. Atlanta: Scholars Press, 1992.

Porter, Stanley E., ed. *Paul and His Theology.* Leiden: Brill, 2006.

Porter, Stanley E., and Anthony R. Cross, eds. *Baptism, the New Testament and the Church: Historical and Contemporary Studies in Honour of R. E. O. White.* JSNTSup 171. Sheffield: Sheffield Academic Press, 1999.

Porter, Stanley E., and Cynthia Long Westfall, eds. *Christian Mission: Old Testament Foundations and New Testament Developments.* McMaster New Testament Series. Eugene, OR: Pickwick, 2010.

Powers, Daniel G. *Salvation through Participation: An Examination of the Notion of the Believers' Corporate Unity with Christ in Early Christian Soteriology.* Contributions to Biblical Exegesis and Theology 29. Leuven: Peeters, 2001.

Putnam, Robert D. *Bowling Alone: The Collapse and Revival of American Community.* New York: Simon and Schuster, 2001.

Rabens, Volker. *The Holy Spirit and Ethics in Paul: Transformation and Empowering for Religious-Ethical Life.* WUNT 2/283. Tübingen: Mohr Siebeck, 2010.

Rebell, Walter. "Gemeinde als Missionsfaktor im Urchristentum: 1 Kor 14:24f. als Schlüsselsituation." *Theologische Zeitschrift* 44 (1988): 117–34.

Reinbold, Wolfgang. *Propaganda und Mission im ältesten Christentum: Eine Untersuchung zu den Modalitäten der Ausbreitung der frühen Kirche.* Forschung zur Religion und Literatur des Alten und Neuen Testaments 188. Göttingen: Vandenhoeck & Ruprecht, 2000.

Robinson, H. Wheeler. *Corporate Personality in Ancient Israel.* Philadelphia: Fortress, 1967.

Roloff, Jürgen. *Der erste Brief an Timotheus.* Evangelisch-Katholischer Kommentar zum Neuen Testament 15. Neukirchen: Benziger Verlag, 1988.

———. *Die Kirche im Neuen Testament.* Grundrisse zum Neuen Testament. Das Neue Testament Deutsch Ergänzungsreihe 10. Göttingen: Vandenhoeck & Ruprecht, 1993.

———. ἐκκλησία. Pages 410–15 in vol. 2 of Balz and Schneider, *Exegetical Dictionary of the New Testament.*

Samra, James George. *Being Conformed to Christ in Community: A Study of Maturity, Maturation and the Local Church in the Undisputed Pauline Letters.* Library of New Testament Studies 320. Edinburgh: T&T Clark, 2006.

Sanders, E. P. *Paul and Palestinian Judaism: A Comparison of Patterns of Religion.* Minneapolis: Fortress, 1977.

Sandnes, Karl Olav. *A New Family: Conversion and Ecclesiology in the Early Church with Cross-Cultural Comparisons.* Studies in the Intercultural History of Christianity. Berlin: Peter Lang, 1994.

———. "Paul, One of the Prophets?" Pages 77–153 in *A Contribution to the Apostle's Self-Understanding*. Tübingen: Mohr Siebeck, 1991.

Schäfer, Klaus. *Gemeinde als "Bruderschaft": Ein Beitrag zum Kirchenverständnis des Paulus*. Europaische Hochschulschriften. New York: Peter Lang, 1989.

Schmeller, Thomas. *Der zweite Brief an die Korinther (2 Kor 1.1–7.4)*. Evangelisch-katholischer Kommentar zum Neuen Testament 8. Neukirchen-Vluyn: Neukirchener Theologie, 2010.

Schmidt, Eckart David. *Heilig ins Eschaton: Heiligung und Heiligkeit als eschatologische Konzeption im 1. Thessalonicherbrief*. Beihefte zur Zeitschrift für die neutestamentliche Wissenschaft 167. Berlin: de Gruyter, 2010.

Schnabel, Eckhard. *Early Christian Mission*. Vol. 2. *Paul and the Early Church*. Downers Grove, IL: InterVarsity, 2004.

Schnelle, Udo. *Apostle Paul: His Life and Theology*. Translated by M. Eugene Boring. Grand Rapids: Baker Academic, 2005.

———. *Gerechtigkeit und Christusgegenwart: Vorpaulinische und paulinische Tauftheologie*. Göttingen: Vandenhoeck & Ruprecht, 1982.

———. *Theology of the New Testament*. Grand Rapids: Baker Academic, 2009.

Schöllgen, Georg. "Was wissen wir über die Sozialstruktur der paulinischen Gemeinden?" *New Testament Studies* 34 (1988): 71–82.

Schrage, Wolfgang. *Der Erste Brief an die Korinther*. 4 vols. Evangelisch-Katholischer Kommentar zum Neuen Testament 7.1. Edited by Norbert Brox et al. Neukirchener-Vluyn: Neukirchener Verlag, 1991–2001.

Schröter, Jens. "Die Funktion des Herrenmahlsüberlieferungen im 1. Korintherbrief: Zugleich ein Beitrag zur Rolle der 'Einsetzungsworte' im frühchristlichen Mahltexten." *Zeitschrift für die Neutestamentliche Wissenschaft und die Kunde der älteren Kirche* 100 (2009): 78–100.

Schüssler Fiorenza, Elisabeth. *In Memory of Her: A Feminist Theological Reconstruction of Christian Origins*. New York: Crossroad, 1984.

Schweitzer, Albert. *The Quest of the Historical Jesus: A Critical Study of Its Progress from Reimarus to Wrede*. New York: Macmillan, 1964. Translation of *Vom Reimarus zu Wrede*, 1906.

Schweizer, Eduard. "υἱός." Pages 334–92 in vol. 8 of Kittel and Friedrich, *Theological Dictionary of the New Testament*.

Seifrid, Mark A. "In Christ." Pages 433–36 in *Dictionary of Paul and His Letters*. Edited by Gerald F. Hawthorne, Ralph P. Martin, and Daniel G. Reid. Downers Grove, IL: InterVarsity, 1993.

Shogren, Gary S. "'Is the Kingdom of God about Eating and Drinking or Isn't It?' (Rom. 14:17)." *Novum Testamentum* 42 (2000): 238–56.

Söding, Thomas. *Jesus und die Kirche: Was sagt das Neue Testament?* Freiburg: Herder, 2007.

Spicq, Ceslas. "atakteō." Pages 223–26 in vol. 1 of *Theological Lexicon of the New Testament*.

———. "*idiōtēs*." Pages 212–13 in vol. 2 of *Theological Lexicon of the New Testament*.

———. "*mainomai*." Pages 430–31 in vol. 2 of *Theological Lexicon of the New Testament*.

———. "*nouthesia, noutheteō*." Pages 548–51 in vol. 2 of *Theological Lexicon of the New Testament*.

———. "*paramytheomai*." Pages 30–35 in vol. 3 of *Theological Lexicon of the New Testament*.

———. *Theological Lexicon of the New Testament*. Translated and edited by James D. Ernest. 3 vols. Peabody, MA: Hendrickson, 1994.

Stählin, G. "*Isos*." Pages 343–55 in vol. 3 of Kittel and Friedrich, *Theological Dictionary of the New Testament*.

Stanglin, Keith D. "Barna's Revolution and the Devolution of Ecclesiology." *Stone-Campbell Journal* 11, no. 1 (2008): 59–69.

Stanley, David M. "'Become Imitators of Me': The Pauline Conception of Apostolic Tradition." *Biblica* 40 (1959): 859–77.

Stendahl, Krister. "The Apostle Paul and the Introspective Conscience of the West." Pages 78–96 in *Paul among Jews and Gentiles and Other Essays*. Philadelphia: Fortress, 1976.

———. *Final Account: Paul's Letter to the Romans*. Minneapolis: Fortress, 1995.

Stowers, Stanley K. "What Is 'Pauline Participation in Christ'?" Pages 352–71 in *Redefining First-Century Jewish and Christian Identities: Essays in Honor of Ed Parish Sanders*. Edited by Fabian E. Udoh, with Susanna Heschel, Mark Chancey, and Gregory Tatum. Christianity and Judaism in Antiquity 16. Notre Dame, IN: University of Notre Dame Press, 2008.

Stuhlmacher, Peter. *Gerechtigkeit Gottes bei Paulus*. 2nd ed. Göttingen: Vandenhoeck & Ruprecht, 1966.

Sullivan, Andrew. "Forget the Church. Follow Jesus." *Newsweek*, April 10, 2012.

Swidler, Leonard J. *Jesus Was a Feminist: What the Gospels Reveal about His Revolutionary Perspective*. Lanham, MD: Sheed and Ward, 2007.

Theissen, Gerd. *The Social Setting of Pauline Christianity: Essays on Corinth*. Philadelphia: Fortress, 1982.

Theobald, Michael. "Rechtfertigung und Ekklesiologie nach Paulus: Anmerkungen zur 'Gemeinsamen Erklärung zur Rechtfertigungslehre.'" *Zeitschrift für Theologie und Kirche* 95 (1998): 103–17.

Thielman, Frank. "The Group and the Individual in Salvation: The Witness of Paul." Pages 136–53 in *After Imperialism: Christian Identity in China and the Global Evangelical Movement*. Studies in Chinese Christianity. Edited by Richard R. Cook and David W. Pao. Eugene, OR: Pickwick, 2011.

Thompson, James W. *Moral Formation according to Paul: The Context and Coherence of Pauline Ethics*. Grand Rapids: Baker Academic, 2011.

———. *Pastoral Ministry according to Paul: A Biblical Vision*. Grand Rapids: Baker Academic, 2006.

———. "Paul and Spiritual Formation." *Christian Studies* 24 (2010): 7–19.

———. "Reading the Letters as Narrative." Pages 81–106 in *Narrative Reading, Narrative Preaching*. Edited by Joel B. Green and Michael Pasquarello III. Grand Rapids: Baker Academic, 2003.

Thompson, Michael B. "The Holy Internet: Communication between Churches in the First Christian Generation." Pages 49–70 in *The Gospels for All Christians: Rethinking the Gospel Audiences*. Edited by Richard Bauckham. Grand Rapids: Eerdmans, 1998.

Thrall, Margaret E. *II Corinthians*. International Critical Commentary. Edinburgh: T&T Clark, 2000.

Tobin, Thomas H., SJ. *Paul's Rhetoric in Its Contexts: The Argument of Romans*. Peabody, MA: Hendrickson, 2004.

Tocqueville, Alexis de. *Democracy in America*. New York: New American Library, 1956. First published in 1835.

Toney, Carl N. *Paul's Inclusive Ethic: Resolving Community Conflicts and Promoting Mission in Romans 14–15*. Tübingen: Mohr Siebeck, 2008.

Trebilco, Paul R. *Self-Designations and Group Identity in the New Testament*. Cambridge: Cambridge University Press, 2012.

———. "Why Did the Early Christians Call Themselves ἡ ἐκκλησία?" *New Testament Studies* 57 (2011): 440–60.

Umbauch, Helmut. *In Christus getauft, von der Sünde Befreit: Die Gemeinde als Sündenfreier Raum bei Paulus*. Forschungen zur Religion und Literatur des Alten und Neuen Testaments 181. Göttingen: Vandenhoeck & Ruprecht, 1999.

Van Engen, Charles, *The Growth of the True Church: An Analysis of Church Growth Theory*. Amsterdam: Rodopi, 1981.

Van Gelder, Craig, and Dwight J. Zscheile. *The Missional Church in Perspective: Mapping Trends and Shaping the Conversation*. Grand Rapids: Baker Academic, 2011.

Van Kooten, George H. "ἐκκλησία τοῦ θεοῦ: The 'Church of God' and the Civic Assemblies (ἐκκλησίαι) of the Greek Cities in the Roman Empire: A Response to Paul Trebilco and Richard A. Horsley." *New Testament Studies* 58 (2012): 522–48.

Verner, David. *The Household of God: The Social World of the Pastoral Epistles*. Chico, CA: Scholars Press, 1983.

Vielhauer, Philipp. *Oikodome: Das Bild vom Bau in der christlichen Literatur vom Neuen Testament bis Clemens Alexandrinus*. Karlsruhe: Durlach, 1940.

Wagener, Ulrike. *Die Ordnung des "Hauses Gottes": Der Ort von Frauen in der Ekklesiologie und Ethik der Pastoralbriefe*. WUNT 2/65. Tübingen: Mohr Siebeck, 1994.

Ware, James. *Paul and the Mission of the Church: Philippians in Ancient Jewish Context*. Grand Rapids: Baker Academic, 2011.

———. "The Thessalonians as a Missionary Congregation: 1 Thessalonians 1:5–8." *Zeitschrift für die neutestamentliche Wissenschaft und die Kunde der älteren Kirche* 83 (1992): 126–31.

Warner, Laceye. "Mega-Churches: A New Ecclesiology or an Ecclesial Evangelism?" *Review and Expositor* 107 (Winter 2010): 21–31.

Watson, Francis. *Paul, Judaism, and the Gentiles: A Sociological Approach*. Society for New Testament Studies Monograph Series 56. Cambridge: Cambridge University Press, 1986.

Wedderburn, A. J. M. "Some Observations on Paul's Use of the Phrases 'in Christ' and 'with Christ.'" *Journal for the Study of the New Testament* 25 (1985): 83–97.

Weigandt, P. "*Oikos*." Pages 500–503 in vol. 2 of Balz and Schneider, *Exegetical Dictionary of the New Testament*.

Welborn, L. L. *Politics and Rhetoric in the Corinthian Epistles*. Macon, GA: Mercer University Press, 1997.

Wiefel, Wolfgang. "The Jewish Community in Ancient Rome and the Origins of Roman Christianity." Pages 85–101 in *The Romans Debate*. Rev. ed. Edited by Karl P. Donfried. Peabody, MA: Hendrickson, 1991.

Wilken, Robert. "Collegia, Philosophical Schools, and Theology." Pages 268–91 in *The Catacombs and the Colosseum: The Roman Empire as the Setting of Primitive Christianity*. Edited by S. Benko and J. J. O'Rourke. Valley Forge, PA: Judson, 1971.

Willis, Wendell L. *Idol Meat at Corinth: The Pauline Argument in 1 Corinthians 8 and 10*. Society of Bibilical Literature Dissertation Series 68. Atlanta: Scholars Press, 1985. Reprint, Eugene, OR: Wipf and Stock, 2004.

Winter, Bruce W. *After Paul Left Corinth: The Influence of Secular Ethics and Social Change*. Grand Rapids: Eerdmans, 2001.

Witherington, Ben, III. *Women in the Earliest Churches*. Society for New Testament Studies Monograph Series 59. Cambridge: Cambridge University Press, 1988.

Wolter, Michael. "Der Apostel und seine Gemeinden als Teilhaber am Leidensgeschick Jesu Christi: Beobachtungen zur paulinischen Leidenstheologie." *New Testament Studies* 36 (1990): 535–57.

———. "Die ethische Identität christlicher Gemeinden in neutestamentlicher Zeit." Pages 61–90 in *Woran orientiert sich Ethik*. Edited by Wilfried Härle and Reiner Preul. Marburger Jahrbuch Theologie 13. Marburg: Elwert, 2001.

Wright, N. T. *Jesus and the Victory of God*. Minneapolis: Fortress, 1996.

———. *The New Testament and the People of God*. Minneapolis: Fortress, 1992.

———. *Paul and the Faithfulness of God*. Minneapolis: Fortress, 2013.

———. *What Saint Paul Really Said: Was Paul of Tarsus the Real Founder of Christianity?* Grand Rapids: Eerdmans, 1997.

Young, Frances M. "Understanding Romans in the Light of 2 Corinthians." *Scottish Journal of Theology* 43 (1990): 433–46.

SCRIPTURE AND ANCIENT WRITINGS INDEX

2 Corinthians

Galatians

MODERN AUTHOR INDEX

Subject Index

apocalyptic, 31, 35, 37, 39, 88n22, 97, 109, 136
associations, ancient, 19, 26, 26nn8–9, 29, 30n25, 44n77, 89, 223, 249
attractional model, 12, 16
Augsburg Confession, 6

believers, 5, 6, 8, 17, 19–21, 24–25, 27–28, 28n13, 29n43, 33–39, 39n65, 41–44, 46–49, 51–55, 55n20, 55n22, 57, 58n31, 62, 64, 71–72, 75–77, 80–86, 92–93, 95–96, 98–99, 101
boundaries, 15, 16, 20, 21, 34, 39, 43, 46, 49, 65, 71, 77, 82, 83, 84, 85, 119, 137, 158, 165, 168, 170, 172, 174, 186, 196, 218, 219, 243, 244, 245, 269
bulwark of the truth, 215, 217

capitalism, 9
Christian morality, 169
church
  as association, 11–12
  as body of Christ, 20, 23, 31, 52, 53n13, 65, 66, 68–70, 70n57, 72–73, 77, 81, 81n5, 82, 84– 87, 90, 91–93, 96, 98, 101, 120, 121n45, 124, 143, 148, 167, 171, 175, 176, 178, 179, 197, 203, 204, 204n13, 205, 205n19, 208, 209–10, 212, 229, 231, 237, 238, 241, 242, 245, 246, 266, 267
  as bride of Christ, 6, 210–11, 211n20, 212
  as children of light, 42–43
  as corporation, 9–10
  as counterculture, 16, 21, 109, 120, 124, 139
  emerging, 15–16
  as family of God, 43–46
  growth, 10, 245, 262, 268

missional, 12–15
mission of, 4, 10, 12–13, 12n51, 14, 20–21, 151–57, 159, 165, 167, 169, 173, 174, 246–47
  seeker-sensitive, 9
  as theater, 10–11
  universal, 21–22, 175–76, 178–79, 194, 197–98, 204, 206, 208, 212–13, 246–47
collection for Jerusalem, 134, 159, 182, 184n30, 186n36, 187n48, 187n49, 188–89, 189n55, 189n57, 190, 190n59, 191–97, 253, 255, 259, 263
collective identity, 24, 27, 29, 30, 34, 55, 66, 68, 69, 105, 137, 139, 206
collegium, 19
community formation, 17, 18, 20, 23, 42, 48, 242, 243, 247
community of memory, 21, 105, 244
conversion, 17, 25, 27, 33–35, 37–38, 40–41, 43, 56, 65, 94, 104, 107–8, 115, 115n30, 119, 128, 151, 161, 166, 226–27
corporate identity, 20, 23, 24, 27, 29, 66, 67, 68

dialectical leadership, 232
dikaiosynē, 129, 129n6, 155

early Catholicism, 213, 219, 259
ecclesial identity, 65–66, 86, 109, 122, 144
ekklēsia, 17–19, 23–24, 27–29, 29n16, 30n25, 30n27, 31–35, 36, 40, 42–44, 51, 54, 130, 136, 177, 179, 185n34, 201, 204, 206, 211, 215
elect, election, 28n14, 35–42, 45, 47, 51n1, 54, 77, 81, 130, 139, 140, 141, 143, 179, 179n16, 201, 206, 212, 244
Epicurus, Epicureans, 19

Praise for

WORKING STIFF

"Far from the magic we see on TV, *Working Stiff* describes forensic pathology in the real world. The book is a compelling and absorbing read."

—Kathy Reichs, author of the Temperance Brennan *Bones* series

"Haunting and illuminating . . . the stories from [Dr. Melinek's] average workdays should also transfix the reader with their demonstration that medical science can diagnose and console long after the heartbeat stops."

—*The New York Times*

"Spellbinding . . . Melinek is movingly empathetic toward the families of victims. . . . An unforgettable story."

—*Booklist* (starred review)

"*Working Stiff* is an engrossing and revealing glimpse into the making of a medical examiner with a searing insider's view into working at the New York Medical Examiner's Office during and just after 9/11. The story of how the author dealt with her father's suicide during childhood and later had to deal with suicides as part of her duties is wrenching and compelling."

—Jan Garavaglia, M.D. (Dr. G from the Discovery Fit & Health series), author of *How Not to Die*

"Fun, sentimental where appropriate, and full of smart science. Fans of CSI—the real kind—will want to read it."

—*The Washington Post*

"Melinek's enthusiasm for her calling is always apparent, and her writing is unself-consciously bouncy, absorbed and mordant (though not caustic). . . . A transfixing account of death, from the mundane to the oddly hair-raising."

—*Kirkus Reviews*

"*Working Stiff* is the grossest book you'll ever love. But it is also so much more than that: Seamlessly fusing memoir, science journalism, riveting whodunit mysteries, and light humor about a dark topic, *Working Stiff* is a relentlessly fascinating and informative book from the first page to the last. Judy Melinek . . . is an unfailingly charming and even inspiring guide to the world of medical examiners. A remarkable achievement by Mitchell and Melinek."

—Scott Stossel, editor of *The Atlantic* magazine and author of the *New York Times* bestseller *My Age of Anxiety*

"A riveting read, at once compassionate and morbidly fascinating."

—Todd Harra, coauthor of *Over Our Dead Bodies*

"*Working Stiff* is an eye-opening, gripping account of the life of a forensic pathologist working in New York City. Whether dealing with routine autopsies, surviving relatives, or the catastrophe of September 11, Dr. Judy Melinek reveals the dignity of being human in the face of death."

—Leora Tanenbaum, author of *Taking Back God*

"Fascinating case studies and a refreshing irreverence toward death and autopsies make *Working Stiff* a funny and engrossing read."

—Sandeep Jauhar, author of *Intern: A Doctor's Initiation* and *Doctored: The Disillusionment of an American Physician*

"Both chilling and heart-warming at the same time, Judy Melinek's account explains how empathy and humanity are as important